MW00561341

ALSO BY MAGGIE JACKSON

Distracted: Reclaiming Our Focus in a World of Lost Attention

*What's Happening to Home: Balancing Work, Life,
and Refuge in the Information Age*

Uncertain

THE WISDOM
AND WONDER
OF BEING
UNSURE

MAGGIE JACKSON

Prometheus Books

Guilford, Connecticut

(PB) Prometheus Books

An imprint of Globe Pequot, the trade division of The Rowman & Littlefield
Publishing Group, Inc.
4501 Forbes Blvd., Ste. 200
Lanham, MD 20706
www.rowman.com

Distributed by NATIONAL BOOK NETWORK

Copyright © 2023 by Maggie Jackson

All rights reserved. No part of this book may be reproduced in any form or by any
electronic or mechanical means, including information storage and retrieval systems,
without written permission from the publisher, except by a reviewer who may quote
passages in a review.

British Library Cataloguing in Publication Information Available

Library of Congress Cataloging-in-Publication Data

Names: Jackson, Maggie, 1960– author.
Title: Uncertain : the wisdom and wonder of being unsure / Maggie Jackson.
Description: Lanham, MD : Prometheus Books, [2023] | Includes bibliographical
    references and index. | Summary: "Featuring cutting-edge research and in-depth
    reporting, this paradigm-shifting book shows us how to skillfully confront the
    unexpected and unknown, and how to seek not-knowing in the service of curiosity,
    wisdom, and discovery"—Provided by publisher.
Identifiers: LCCN 2023008346 (print) | LCCN 2023008347 (ebook) |
    ISBN 9781633889187 (cloth) | ISBN 9781633889194 (epub)
Subjects: LCSH: Uncertainty.
Classification: LCC BF463.U5 J33 2023 (print) | LCC BF463.U5 (ebook) |
    DDC 153.4—dc23/eng/20230616
LC record available at https://lccn.loc.gov/2023008346
LC ebook record available at https://lccn.loc.gov/2023008347

∞™ The paper used in this publication meets the minimum requirements of
American National Standard for Information Sciences—Permanence of Paper for
Printed Library Materials, ANSI/NISO Z39.48-1992

For Anna, Emma, and John,
with all my heart and soul

"I know" seems to describe a state of affairs
which guarantees what is known, guarantees it as a fact.
One always forgets the expression, "I thought I knew."
—LUDWIG WITTGENSTEIN

CONTENTS

INTRODUCTION

On the night before he gave one of the most transcendent speeches of our time, Martin Luther King Jr. did not quite know what he would say. In the weeks leading up to the 1963 March on Washington, he had sought extra counsel from advisers and had closely studied their suggested drafts. On the eve of the event, his aides gathered at his invitation in a hotel lobby to press their ideas upon him. "Everyone had a stake in this speech, a predetermined angle," recalled an adviser on the address they sensed would voice their cause to the world.

That spring, news footage of police unleashing fire hoses and attack dogs on protesters had captured the world's attention and energized the faltering civil rights movement. Now its leaders were deeply divided over whether force should be met with force. Segregation was under siege, yet the way forward was far from clear. It was a hinge moment for the crusade and in the country's history. King reworked his speech long into the night and even from the dais. Then, ten minutes into its telling, he put it aside altogether and set out on his own.

In the first minutes of his remarks, King had accused the country of defaulting on the "promissory note" of equality owed to all by the Constitution. Offering a glimpse of his growing radicalism, he had vowed "whirlwinds of revolt" against prejudice and poverty. In closing, it would have been easy then to tick off the movement's wins or to set forth specific demands, historians note. Instead, he offered a distant vision of a better time, a dream that critics then and now have called "nebulous," "ethereal," and "undefined."

King rose to lead the movement with conviction and humility, often admitting to allies and skeptics alike that he did *not* know the way. Social revolutions, he once said, are not all "neat and tidy." Nor was he "the type of activist who pursued a merely finite agenda," notes author Gary Younge. That August afternoon, he asked a quarter of a million marchers and the world at large to work toward magnificent possibilities: equality, fellowship, freedom. But he shunned as weapon or reward the brittle ease of pat answers. "Go back [home] knowing somehow this situation can and will be changed," King told the protesters. *Somehow.* "That day, for a moment," wrote James Baldwin, "it almost seemed that we stood on a height and could see our inheritance; perhaps we could make the kingdom real." *Perhaps.* In the crowd, someone held a placard high for all to see: "We Demand Freedom of Mind." We cannot find the best path forward, King was saying, by assuming that we already know the way.

The revolution that he urged was left undone at his death. His legacy remains contested. Yet his words continue to provoke and inspire to a degree few could have foreseen. "Not knowing whether building [a new order] was a Sisyphean task or merely a Herculean one, he called out in the political wilderness," creating a vision "on which our modern rights are built," notes Younge. That day, argues historian Drew Hansen, he "began the long overdue process of changing America's idea of itself."

King responded to the vehement yeses and nos of the moment with the courage of a maybe—the only call to action that fully confronts the unknown. In both his soaring exhortation and its precarious creation lies a truth too urgent to ignore: the best of thinking begins and ends with the wisdom of being unsure.

⟨↓⟩

Uncertainty as strength? Indecision fueling greatness? King's feat is admittedly glorious, yet its hidden dimensions are confounding too. After all, being unsure is *not* what our species wants to be. The wrong turn that leaves you in a strange neighborhood after dark, the days spent awaiting a medical test result and the sticky choices that may follow: such experiences rattle us, and naturally so.

Humans are built for survival's sake to yearn for answers and for the predictability that offers them up. Situations that we can breeze through with just the right effort—what psychologists call a state of fluency—literally bring a smile to our faces. They are plain wonderful, all dopamine and reward. We don't want to think hard about how to exit the shadowy forest and get home. In contrast, the state that the poet Keats called "half knowledge" will always be a hard sell. It's a proven psychological finding: people tend to be more stressed if they *don't* know if an electric shock is coming than if they are pretty sure they will get one.

Now, uncertainty as a path to progress is all the harder to imagine, a seemingly antiquated way forward at best. There were deep divisions in 1963, blood on the streets, an escalating war on the horizon. But today, the furious pile-on of unknowns fueled by pandemics, disasters, tottering democracies, economic fragility, and social unrest drives laments about "these uncertain times" to fever pitch. Choosing to linger in the middle ground of the indefinite appears starkly counter to moving forward. It's dinner party dynamite just to admit that on a matter of social import, your opinion isn't set in stone. How could we find the clarity and vision so urgently needed by *not*-knowing? This book is about the unsung triumph of doing just that.

Early one morning during the fearful spring when the first wave of coronavirus struck New York, I was returning home after a walk in the park. Approaching my apartment building, I saw a neighbor a bit ahead who was about to go inside. He spotted me over his shoulder, and I could sense what he was thinking. Holding the door open for me, as we typically would do, would shatter the distance that should be kept between us. On the other hand, hurrying in first and leaving me behind would assail a moment's solidarity just when we needed it most. I knew him only by sight. He was a city guy perpetually in a rush, yet to my surprise, there he stood, musing and torn. And then, without a word, he gave the door a mighty push open, enough for him to enter and for me to follow safely in the next lingering beat. That day when so much was in question, he found a way to protect us and our humanity if only for a minute or two. It was the smallest of victories born of a remarkable feat: an uncertain mind.

This book tells the story of a kind of brilliance too often squandered, a state of mind critical to human achievement yet until recently little understood. Far from automatically miring us in cognitive paralysis, uncertainty plays an essential role in higher-order thinking, propelling people in challenging times toward good judgment, flexibility, mutual understanding, and heights of creativity. It is the portal to finding your enemy's humanity, the overlooked lynchpin of superior teamwork, and the mindset most needed in times of flux.

Rather than being a sign of deficiency or weakness, wielding the cognitive tool of not-knowing is a mark of the persuasive arguer, the most capable student, the resilient physician *and* patient, and, by multiple measures, the nimble executive. (It can even make people more romantically inviting. In the game of love, we see those who aren't sure about us as more attractive.) "So far as man stands for anything and is productive and originative at all, his entire vital function may be said to have to deal with maybes," wrote William James. "Not a victory is gained, not a deed of faithfulness or courage is done, except upon a maybe." Yet we now treat this gateway to life's richest cognitive possibilities as a secret shame.

Amidst fury, confrontation, angst, and flux, strident calls are rising for an urgent rethink of what came before. This is the moment, it is said, when we can right past wrongs and dig out from the cataclysms before us. "All kinds of narratives and shibboleths are beginning to quake," asserts historian Carol Anderson. But these fledgling hopes and stirrings of change ultimately may prove fragile, even stillborn, unless all sides first work to reenvision a culture that has transformed an innate human love of quick, sure answers into a foundational value of the time.

In an era of the algorithm and the checklist, preferred information sweeps away context and contradiction with what economists Mervyn King and John Kay call "spurious precision." In an age of ghosted lovers, online mobs, and spreading autocracy, the kind of human judgment that demands a bit of time and a second thought "begins to look quaint," warns Helga Nowotny, a leading sociologist of science. Conviction remains essential. At times, the heroic impulse will land true. But too often, our understanding is timid and shrunken beneath rising bravado and noise. It is not uncertainty that we should fear but a growing reluctance and perhaps a waning ability to seek nuance, depth, and perspective, all fruits of skillfully confronting what we do *not* know. This path does not offer the easy way out. Uncertainty unsettles us—and that is its gift.

But what do we mean when the talk turns to uncertainty? How could such a ubiquitous aspect of life be so misunderstood?

Although economists, psychologists, and risk analysts still debate the contours and boundaries of this concept, they categorize uncertainty largely into two main types: one involving life's unpredictability and another our own psychological unsureness. And most of the time, whether in scholarly circles, the day's headlines, or talk around the kitchen table, uncertainty is treated foremost as something out there, a kind of unwelcome intrusion into life. This is *aleatory* uncertainty, or what we call "*the* uncertainty," that is, the randomness of the universe. It is what we cannot know.

From there, the conversation quickly takes the "probabilistic turn." What are the odds that the markets turn bullish by spring? How likely is it that the virus will mutate again? For centuries, a complex set of statistical tools—the fuel behind the data models now in vogue—has dominated modern efforts to confront what the world throws at us. Until recently, the "taming of chance" seemed literally our best bet for trading up from ancient sacrifices to the fates to making a calculated dent in the unknown. Now, however, the science of uncertainty is expanding to encompass not just mathematical feats but also the wider, wilder territories of *our* uncertainty, the main topic of this book.

Epistemic uncertainty is the starting point of all pursuit of knowledge, scientists increasingly agree. (Even probability theories pay rising homage to people's subjectivity, i.e., how often-idiosyncratic estimates sway the tallying of likelihood.) By definition, this state of mind essentially entails recognizing that you do not know in full; your understanding is fuzzy, contradictory, or partial. This sense of incompleteness is not the blank slate associated with full ignorance. Instead, it means you have realized the limits of your knowledge and gained a glimpse of worlds beyond your own assumptions or views. Your child has the sniffles, and you begin to suspect that it may not be just a cold or allergies. Perhaps your design prototype lacks something that neither focus groups nor your team can yet articulate. What then? It might be, it could be, it's possibly this or that or another option altogether. In not-knowing, there is a golden promise of further possibilities *and* a sense of falling short.

Enter the innate drive for answers that pioneering psychologist Jerome Kagan famously called one of the foremost determinants of human behavior. The resolve to conclusively know keeps us moving forward, yet it is very much double-edged, both a strength and a weakness. In essence, we are constantly working to reduce the very cognitive capacity that most broadens our mental horizons.

Here is the dilemma posed each time we confront what's beyond our ken and why uncertainty's gifts are often elusive. Faced with a glimpse of a challenge or a question, do we rush to seize an answer, or do we slow down to wonder, to consider, and to explore? "Thought hastens toward the settled and is only too likely to force the pace," observed the philosopher John Dewey. Remarkably, even the psychology field long viewed uncertainty as simply something for humans to eradicate as fast as possible and so largely overlooked this mindset as a topic of study in itself. But no longer are researchers dismissing uncertainty as a cognitive wasteland.

Consider the executives who not long ago faced the European Union's most dramatic expansion, an embrace of Central Europe that nearly doubled the group's membership. Widely seen as enacted hastily and with little concern for its economic impact, the 2004 event was the antithesis of Brexit but nearly as controversial. Which chief executives would best adapt: those who viewed the shift as a boon or those who assumed that the vast new competitive market would hurt their company's prospects? Pro or con? In or out? The business world, in both theory and practice, often has tended to hold that in a crisis, effective leaders come down on one clear side or another. So which would it be? Two top management professors launched a study of 104 chief executives in Germany to find out. It didn't go quite as planned.

After completing an intensive first round of interviews and surveys at the time of the merger, the researchers discovered to their surprise a third group in the mix: a quarter of the executives were torn by competing possibilities. Would the shifting trade landscape offer a burgeoning customer base, an uptick in inflation, or pressure from new rivals to lower labor costs? These leaders were unsure—and they unexpectedly turned out to be the ones worth emulating. When the researchers returned a year later to see how the entire group had fared, they found that the intense ambivalence popularly equated with inertia had had the opposite effect. "We actually ran the analysis many times in different ways to make sure we weren't chasing some fluke," Klaus Weber of Northwestern University, coauthor of the study published in 2009, told me. It was no fluke.

Those who sustained a meld of positive and negative views on the crisis—who in effect saw their understanding as incomplete—considered a wider range of responses; included more diverse voices in decision making; and responded with more novel and resourceful measures, such as building a plant in a new member territory. Their ambivalence inspired a more subtle understanding of the problem and actions better calibrated to the situation. "There's a reality out there that is *not* binary," says Weber. In contrast, the executives who were most sure of the way forward or who assumed they were fully in control tended to take the path of least resistance. They stuck to the tried and true and sometimes did nothing at all.

This is not a saga of humility trumping hubris, although we can hear hints of such virtue in the tale. Instead, the study and a growing body of corresponding research across disciplines offers something more: an upending of our outdated ideas of what a wise thinker can be. When the stakes are high, those who do *not* know gain the cognitive advantage.

To understand how uncertainty can propel us forward, let us first consider the Mount Olympus of the mind, the slow-to-mature skullcap of cortical tissue draped over older regions of the brain. At the fore of the neocortex lie the frontal lobes, whose workings first came to light in studies of World War I soldiers with head injuries who could no longer master new tasks or grasp the big picture of their lives. This region is home ground of the executive you, the artful discerner that Plato compared to a charioteer steering the steeds of unruly appetite and higher instinct in pursuit of heavenly ideals. The scientific reality is less romantic, but the metaphor remains apt: the new mind is highly linked to brain systems dealing with cognitive control. And the side of ourselves that holds the reins is the one that can slow to examine the inconsistencies that our innate reactivity dashes past.

Day to day, humans spend much of their time jumping to conclusions based on cognitive shortcuts honed from what has worked in the past. To an experienced doctor, for example, a patient's chest pains instantly signal a possible heart attack. By ignoring ambiguity, intuitive thinking offers pop-up answers that serve us well in the predictable environments that scientists call "benign." Smooth and neat, what we sense from our gut typically carries a comforting "feeling of knowing." Observes the psychologist and Nobel laureate Daniel Kahneman, "A remarkable aspect of your mental life is that you are rarely stumped."

But when something goes amiss—the familiar trade bloc blows open, the algorithm wreaks havoc—we gain an astonishing chance to break from autopilot, pivot, and reassess. We have the opportunity to engage in the "conflict processing" needed to cope with error, competing choices, contradictions, and broken expectations. In essence, humans have evolved a counterweight to the drive-by reactivity that makes quick work of a situation by sticking to script.

This is when you can relinquish the safe ground of routine, take a close fresh look at what rings false or true, and grapple with new possibilities. Ever-ready gut cognition is slow to learn and resistant to change. Its speed belies its stodginess. The best of thinkers, in contrast, are willing to question and so are agile. They do not, as Aristotle once warned, measure a fluted column with a straight edge. And this wisdom can begin only with the realization that the world is imperfect, and so are you.

When trouble strikes, a mismatch emerges between old expectation and new reality, between routine and change. Recognizing this gap, we are caught short, and what follows is the key to human adaptability. For at that moment, a frisson of not-knowing ignites a "sense of unusualness" that spawns greater engagement with an issue and a widening of attentional focus. You become highly alert to what's new and better able to learn. Working memory, the capacity to hold an idea in mind and work with it, expands when we are unsure, studies suggest. The brain is directing energy to itself; this is why leading researchers consider uncertainty a good form of stress. Our uncertainty is both a signal of possible danger and the state of mind that invokes the considered thinking needed to update a now-deficient understanding of the world.

The deadline nears, an answer is demanded; this is just the time that— corner office or no—we yearn simply to act, not to decide when, how, or why. But superior thinkers do not assume that all is easily in hand. They face their ignorance and wake up to its implications, leveraging trouble into agility through the power of their uncertainty.

To see these skills in action, look no further than the famously skeptical Kahneman. His relentless questioning of long-accepted views of the mind inspired his and Amos Tversky's pioneering work revealing the limits of shortcut thought. Kahneman's defining characteristic is doubt, says a former student. "And it's very useful. Because it makes him go deeper and deeper and deeper." Uncertainty is a gadfly of the mind, jolting us from complacency—*if* we are willing to answer its call.

↩

"I am going to show you some pictures. Tell me whether each is more like a dog or a cat." With these brief instructions, a pioneering University of

California, Berkeley psychologist began giving people so-called tests of perception that were in fact extraordinary barometers of their capacity to relish the twists and turns of life.

Participants were shown a series of drawings of an animal that at first distinctly resembled a cat but then, bit by bit, with a tweak to an ear or a broadening of a muzzle, turned fully canine. The middle pictures were indeterminate, and for some, that proved unnerving. Again and again, these participants refused to surrender the safe harbor of their first answer until the sequence was nearly complete. They showed "a preference to escape into whatever seems definite," wrote the researcher Else Frenkel-Brunswik.

The famous cat–dog experiments were part of a postwar search by some of the world's leading scientists for the roots of authoritarianism and prejudice. What Frenkel-Brunswik discovered for her part was a key signature of the closed mind: intolerance of uncertainty.

Reaping the promise of not-knowing depends on a simple rubric: whether people are intent on eradicating uncertainty or are willing to stay open to it and so to a situation's subtleties and complexities. This is a decision made in the moment yet one that also emerges from an individual's personal comfort zone for uncertainty.

"Being uncertain means that I lack confidence." "There is really no such thing as a problem that can't be solved." "I should be able to organize everything in advance." These are statements drawn from the "Intolerance of Uncertainty" and "Tolerance for Ambiguity" tests, classic assessments that have been attracting new attention as tools for unlocking the upsides of not-knowing. (Ambiguity, the state of being inexact or open to multiple interpretations, is a source of uncertainty.) In essence, the tests measure the degree to which people view being unsure as a challenge or as a threat, a distinction that affects how well we learn, argue, explore, invent, and solve problems.

Those who shun the indefinite tend to see the world in shades of black and white, ignoring the gray. They are prone to jump to answers and are distressed by chaos and surprise. Their "cognitive map" is narrowed to "rigidly defined tracks," wrote Frenkel-Brunswik. In contrast, people who operate on the other side of the scale are more likely to be curious, flexible thinkers who revel in complex problems and in new experiences from living abroad to trying a new delicacy. They may even be in better charge of their minds;

evidence suggests that such thinkers have more gray matter (i.e., neural volume) in brain regions related to executive control.

In the study of the mind, a tolerance is a tendency, not a fate. We are all more or less prone to be introverted or outgoing, impulsive or reflective, and to welcome the opportunity of incertitude or not. A refusal to not-know isn't a guaranteed mark of fascism or bigotry any more than someone who dislikes parties is automatically a full-on recluse. (And while political conservatives are a little more reluctant to embrace uncertainty, the well-publicized link between these two complex concepts is weak; many liberals detest surprises, and no small number of conservatives revel in change.)

We all have a personal appetite for not-knowing, but the real news is that this leaning is malleable. Situation and context matter; under time pressure, almost everyone's eagerness to race to a conclusion deepens. At the same time, through practice and a bit of effort, we can bolster our capacity for lingering in the gray spaces where cognitive treasures abound. It is possible to move the dial.

Picture a laboratory experiment that brought together pairs of strangers with opposing political views for a brief online back-and-forth on a controversial topic such as abortion or gun control. The interactions that unfolded in the 2016 study were just the kind that so often go quickly awry. This is the moment when the cognitive mismatch that confronts us isn't a mystery virus or a trade policy shift but another person with a wholly different view, an opponent we say. The potential for "conflict processing" awaits.

At the outset, half of the pairs were coached to take on a highly competitive, point-scoring mindset. The other duos were told to cooperatively learn as much as they could from one another. In fifteen minutes, this slight difference in stance shifted the participants' approach to the world. The pairs of strangers who were gunning to outperform one another turned more absolutist, that is, lovers of sureness in learning and knowledge. They became more likely to believe that there was one unerring truth to the matter and that they held it, like a rock that they could seize and defend.

In contrast, those who had been primed to learn became more evaluative. They began to see knowing as inherently uncertain and as something best forged from multiple viewpoints. "I can absolutely see that point," said one participant. They were no less confident in their views; contrary to what we might expect, having the courage to tolerate ambiguity is associated with assertiveness. But by being open to new, challenging information, they grew willing to examine and modify their position. They treated their understanding as akin to an evolving yet durable tapestry, its strength deriving from its very suppleness and mutability. From such a vantage point, more skillful and persuasive arguments are made.

No one seminar or script can transform us into virtuosos of not-knowing. "We don't have a home-run magic bullet for this," a leading scientist of uncertainty chided when I pressed him for an antidote to our fear of the unknown. We can't "inject all this, bottle it, and put it into some easy intervention," said Paul K. J. Han, a senior physician-scientist at the National Institutes of Health. One-shot fixes are the pipe dreams of an instant-answer age, he was reminding me. Still, neither should we ignore the myriad chances that await us each day to open our minds to uncertainty and to its remarkable potential.

"If both arguers refuse to adjust their beliefs, no progress can take place," wrote the lead researchers of the 2016 study. I have read the contrasting transcripts from experiments of this kind: the raw, curt battles on one hand and the gently winding interactions on the other. But perhaps most telling are the awkward silences within each debate. When a lull arises, as they inevitably do, seekers of certainty tend to try to close down the argument in their favor, sometimes with taunts. Those who are endeavoring to learn from the back-and-forth instead often admit at that juncture that they are *not* completely sure about their position. For them, a trifling break in an exchange becomes a chance to expand their thinking with an opponent's helping hand. Such thinkers do not merely tolerate the realm of the indefinite; they actively seek its potential. For within that bewildering zone lies transformation itself.

Finding agility in the *sturm und drang*, the storm and stress, of what's unsure may always be daunting. Studies from linguistics to philosophy confirm what we suspect and brain science reveals: uncertainty is not for the faint of heart. According to psychologist Michael Smithson, the metaphors typically used to portray this state include darkness, lostness, and fuzziness as well as realms that can beckon, such as wandering, exploration, and wilderness. Being unsure is forever linked to feeling on the edge, not quite in control.

Yet a spate of not-knowing is *not* time wasted. Let go of the notion that answers are always at hand, wade into the wilderness of uncertainty, and new perspectives open to view. When we seek to deny uncertainty, life becomes a realm of "cramped and ultimately brittle experience," writes the historian of science Jerome Ravetz.

⇥

Was it a menacing smirk or an inscrutable smile? Were they the bullies or the harassed? From what little that could be seen on the film clip, the encounter on the steps of the Lincoln Memorial was strange and fraught. A throng of teen boys in blaze-red hats chanting school songs stood face-to-face with a Native man from the Omaha Nation drumming his spirituals. A video cropped to shock had its intended effects: a virtual pile-on spiraled into death threats against the youths and their families. A viral campaign to fire their principal erupted even as he threatened to expel them from school. Deplorable! Shameful! The Greek choruses of the time rose up to have their say. Within hours, lawmakers, pundits, a bishop, and scores of the video's 2.5 million viewers had treated a mystery as a certainty. A mere quarter of online posts are opened before they are shared, retweeted, or liked, studies show. Are we becoming like search engines, dispatching answers before questions are fully asked?

Soon the lens of public attention began to zoom out. There were holes in the drummer's story and a realization that provocateurs had been part of the wider crowd. There were opportunities to see the ambiguities, to pause and look again. Instead, calls for restraint were lost in a cacophony of deepening conviction. A columnist who urged uncertainty as an antidote to rising cycles of outrage was mocked by hundreds online.

When Martin Luther King stood on those steps half a century earlier, he spoke of the "fierce urgency of now." Wrongs must be undone, he argued. Yet he stressed that this work must be tempered by "dignity and discipline," by a humility in knowing. He extolled a fevered crowd to strive, to dream, and *not* to assume that being sure means being right. We have forgotten his plea.

Rights and wrongs there will be. Judgments must be made. But what deepens our plight is a rising faith in the finality of knowing. Ignoring a telling nuance or another view seems no longer the by-product merely of bustling efficiency but a goal that we deliberately seek. And in this shift from neglecting chances to not-know to asserting "I don't *ever* want to know" lies a world of difference and risk. A fifth of Democrats and an equal proportion of Republicans—tens of millions of adults—view many members of opposing political parties as not fully human. Public figures and friends alike who are deemed objectionable are "canceled" (i.e., boycotted), especially online. Inconsistencies and contradictions and the people who represent them are not merely seen as unworthy of investigation. They have no right to exist.

But we should not forget, especially amidst rising violence and calamity, that answers both right and wrong must have afterlives. The best understanding is subject to continual change and discovery, or else its foundations crumble, leaving us clinging to paper-thin stances. Unless we take up the provocation of uncertainty, we miss out on life's surprises along with chances to recognize change and opportunities to be changed and, not least, the unassuming grace of slowing down to think.

Humans share with animals a half dozen core instincts: to flee, fight, coordinate, feed, reproduce, and freeze to gather more information. Over millennia, these moments of instinctual slowing evolved into the human capacity to direct our fate by consciously working through the unknown. Unearthing an unseen connection, exploring the mystery of an opposing view, or simply realizing when a conversation has gone adrift demands what psychologist Jerome Bruner calls a "detachment of commitment." Whether it is thrust on us or is strategically sought, this discomfiting moment is not a cessation of all doing but rather a shift in tempo and cognitive gears signaling that we have begun mining the promise of the unknown. "A pause is not a time where nothing happens," says Stanford University neuroscientist Vinod Menon.

In a pioneering experiment, Menon and his research team eavesdropped on the thought patterns of eighteen people as they listened to baroque symphonies. To the scientists' astonishment, the participants' brains were most active during the morsels of silence between movements. A pause in the music brought listeners to a cognitive cliff edge. By violating their expectations of continuity, the seeming "nothingness" of the moment became a space of further possibility in thought. The tiny study made the cover of the prestigious scientific journal *Neuron* and headlines around the world.

Long ago, the Roman statesman Cicero used the word *incertus*, meaning "not-evident" or "undiscerned," as a term for uncertainty in a treatise that was part of his efforts to popularize Greek philosophy in ancient Rome. He could have been talking about the gifts of uncertainty themselves.

↑

Until a century ago, nature was assumed to be largely a realm of divine regularity, and the heavens were seen as fixed and orderly. Until a decade or two ago, the brain was thought to be modular and set in place by the time we reached adulthood; after that, intelligence and temperament were assumed to be unchanging. Until recently, humans were hailed as creatures of rationality and as predictable as the stars in the sky. The rise of early modern science and technology fueled the belief that humanity could uncover the inner mechanisms of a clockwork world and so bend nature to its will. By and large, the best thinkers were seen as detached observers, masters of logic and mathematics, and above all, as Descartes taught, slayers of the dragon of doubt.

Decision trees and moral algebra, checklists and obedience to the algorithmic: these are legacies of what the philosopher John Dewey called the *quest for certainty*, a view of the world inside and outside our heads that increasingly is being called into question as the last word in thinking. Humans are prone to race to answers, to cling to what they know, yet they also are far more cognitively capable than the ideals of classical rationality allowed. The Enlightenment, as great as its achievements were, held up a straight edge to the mysteries of the mind.

Now, we are told, the cosmos is expanding. At the smallest quantum level, space and time are indefinite, ever-shifting realms whose dynamism epitomizes life's deep impermanence. One after another, the laws of nature are being unmasked as provisional, while our understanding, as Einstein, Picasso, and Morrison taught, is relative to what we see and where we stand. Almost wherever one turns, the accepted version is under siege, from the grand schema of the heavens to what it means to know. Uncertainty rattles the chains of our assurance, like it or not.

The broken promises of the digital age taunt us; only a scant percentage of Americans believe that technology has boosted our curiosity, knowledge, or understanding. Trust in many major institutions and in one another has been pummeled in recent years. Social media and watercooler chat alike pulse with burgeoning anxiety, a state that psychologists now define as a fear of the unknown. Historian Daniel Boorstin calls this the Age of Negative Discovery, "a realm no longer of answers but only of questions."

Is a retreat into certainties old and new our best recourse? Or can we rise above days increasingly marked by clashing denials, inflexible technologies, and expectations that knowledge is effortless and moreover closely tailored to what we already like and comprehend? It's time now to shine a spotlight on a new kind of heroism: the capacity to harness the powers of uncertainty that snap judgment and classical rationality alike seek to dispel.

The product of hundreds of interviews and thousands of miles of travel, this book shows us how to skillfully confront the unknown and how to seek not-knowing in the service of wisdom, wonder, and discovery. When we stop running from uncertainty, we can tame the fear of not-knowing that keeps us at a toxic remove from a multifaceted, evolving understanding of reality and that stunts our capacity for soaring flights of imagination. We can begin to explore the contours of all that we do not understand and so adapt to what's muddy or new, from the demands of an unfolding disaster to the evidence that punctures a beloved conviction. By questioning ideals of success in thought as pat and quick, we can recognize how rarely does one tempo, a single viewpoint, or a neat template suffice. Most of all, we can discover uncertainty both as a remarkable cognitive tool—in effect, a skill—for good thinking and as a critical time and space that sets us on the fertile edge of what we do not know.

Each chapter examines a different mode of what I call *uncertainty-in-action*, from the honed unsureness that world-class experts wield mid-crisis to the guided reverie that can fuel astonishing innovation. We start by learning how to move past hubris and anxiety, forms of certainty that hobble our ability to grasp the complexity of high-stakes problems and of life itself. We next explore the mental byways of reverie and forgetting and learn why cognitive wrong turns, detours, and even errors are not the defeats that we take them to be. Even a *futile* struggle to remember a name or a fact promotes processes of knowledge synthesis and abstraction that are critical to meaning making.

In part III, we parse the social side of uncertainty, discovering unsureness as an antidote both for conformity and for hatred of the other. A dissenting opinion in a group, even if *wrong*, for example, sparks an incertitude that ultimately unearths critical information typically unshared in the race to accord. Part IV takes us to the front lines of humanity's battle for survival, both age-old and in the future. We explore the long-overlooked strengths of people raised in precarity and question the assumption that predictability is what humans above all should seek. We end with a startling look at a revolutionary new movement to tame artificial intelligence's dangerous rigidity and unstoppability by making it *uncertain*.

An unpredictable, changeable world has been with us all along. Liberating ourselves from the alluring but mistaken belief that life could be otherwise offers a new vision of human progress and of what it means to know.

⬇

By the time the world's foremost chemist entered the hunt to find the code of life, his two young rivals had been grappling with the problem for more than a year. But the chemist didn't take the pair seriously. To great fanfare, he had just revealed the structure of the alpha helix, a crucial building block of protein. In two years, he would win a Nobel Prize for the discovery. Uncovering the comparatively simple architecture of deoxyribonucleic acid, the suspected keeper of the genetic code, seemed easy for a scientist of his stature. Bold to the point of brashness, the Caltech luminary was convinced he could crack the code. "It was just a matter of time."

Half a world away in England, his rivals were persevering on a puzzle that they were, by most accounts, unqualified to solve. In world-class science, they were decided unknowns: a restless twenty-four-year-old biologist who had been rejected for graduate study at Caltech and a gregarious thirty-six-year-old physicist still working on his PhD. When they joined forces at the University of Cambridge, no one really knew what a gene was. Paradoxically, this key to survival had to be both orderly (to be replicated) and yet irregular (to seed individuality), a kind of snowflake of heredity. Protein, a cell's most active, complex molecule, had seemed the right candidate. By parsing wide-ranging work being done with viruses and X-rays, however, the young scientists sensed well before many of their peers that the answer instead lay with a less lively component of life, the DNA found in all living cells. Now the scientific world had caught up, and the endgame had begun. Could an astounding breakthrough arise from a pair of researchers whose every step was far from sure?

The pressure was on, yet the two worked as before, arguing, experimenting, moving forward and then back again. They sought out challenging evidence from rivals and colleagues and continually threw cold water on each other's closely held beliefs. Neither expected a smooth, quick path to success. (A brilliant young chemist and her colleague at King's College London made progress by studying DNA's structure on X-rays that later helped corroborate the winning solution. But her focus on a variation of the molecule only found in laboratory settings kept them a step or two behind.) "We could not at all see what the answer was," recalled the physicist turned biologist, "but we were determined to think about it long and hard, from any relevant point of view."

The challenge before them was akin to solving a three-dimensional puzzle that was invisible save for the glimpses caught on ambiguous X-rays. The molecule's proportions and makeup were roughly understood: long chains of phosphate-sugar backbones holding up pairs of nucleotide bases, the letters of the code. But no one really knew whether the chains lay on the inside or the outside of the structure. Did DNA resemble a tight flower stalk with leaf bases or a spiral staircase with nucleotide steps? And what—if anything—would it reveal of the secrets of life? The young scientists were closing in on the answer when they got the news.

After less than a week of calculating and drawing, the famous chemist told a colleague that he had found the solution. The data didn't quite fit his conclusions, but that did not deter him; his revelation of protein's alpha helix had emerged from a scientific leap of faith. The problem was that this time, he ignored any inkling that he might *not* know. Whereas he had spent years refining his hunch on the alpha helix, he now published in a month, closing his eyes to alternate possibilities and to his colleagues' critiques. "I have practically no doubt," he wrote. "The structure really is a beautiful one."

But by viewing the gene as a version of his beloved protein, he ran with a solution that the Cambridge team ruled out a year before: a triple helix in flower-stalk form. Worse, he surmised that hydrogen held together the phosphate chains, an impossibility in this chemical milieu: the center could not hold. When the challengers looked in the standard textbook of the day to check their competitor's error, they realized they were reading from the great scientist's own work. Hints of a fiasco were there all along. He had not stopped to look.

One month after learning of Linus Pauling's breathtaking mistake, James Watson and Francis Crick unveiled a code of pure poetry. It had taken two years, complete with false starts, daydreams by the fire, and a formidable capacity to withstand the allure of the easy answer. Their reward was a revelation of surpassing scientific elegance. Unzipped down the middle, the double helix's corkscrewing strands could each create a complementary copy, passing on recipes for proteins that do the work of living. In 1962, Watson, Crick, and King's College scientist Maurice Wilkins shared the Nobel Prize. (Rosalind Franklin, whose key contributions were acknowledged by Watson and Crick belatedly and minimally, died before she could be considered for the award.) Pauling missed out on one of history's greatest scientific breakthroughs, a defeat that plagued him for the rest of his life.

In later years, Crick and others asked Pauling why he had made such a fundamental error. "I don't know," he admitted. For once, he had no ready answer, and in that moment, he revealed the key to his folly and to his rivals' brilliance. Choosing the right problem fueled their success, recalled Crick. But what mattered was "making no assumptions that could not be doubted from time to time." Crick and Watson soared to victory on the wings of the uncertainty that Pauling had shunned. But the story does not end there.

After revealing DNA's structure, Crick spent more than a decade leading the quest to unveil its intricate workings. Then he led the way to gaining a foothold into the mysteries of consciousness. Throughout, he remained ever questioning—elevating guesswork to a tactic, prodding colleagues to tap new disciplines, seeing "behind the data to their meaning." Watson went on to lead the illustrious Cold Spring Harbor Laboratory and helped launch the first mapping of the human genome. But he retired in shame after asserting that some peoples were genetically less intelligent. Given numerous opportunities to reconsider, he refused to change his view. He lost the courage of a maybe.

Most of thought and life itself is the pursuit of resolution. Yet along the way, it is uncertainty that equips us to envision the unimaginable, adjust to the unexpected, value a question as deeply as an answer, and find strength in difference and in difficulty. We need not fear the indefinite. For that is where we find the better solution and the path of hope. This is uncertainty's edge.

PART I

AWAKENINGS

CHAPTER ONE

MIND UNDER FIRE

The Shadow Side of Knowing

Whoever cannot seek the unforeseen sees nothing,
for the known way is an impasse.
—HERACLITUS

The surgery is going smoothly. The patient lies anesthetized in a Toronto operating room waiting for one of Canada's top surgeons to join the team. A junior surgeon just ten weeks into the job is making the initial incision, exposing a bright-red abdominal cavern and a cancerous liver set for partial removal. Slicing into this three-pound organ, home to 13 percent of the body's blood supply, is akin to navigating a minefield. Thought by the ancient Greeks to be the seat of emotion, the liver is a nexus of life that is critical to hundreds of vital functions centered mostly on detoxifying the body. For the hand holding the scalpel, it is an organ of perilous surprise. But the senior surgeon, a cancer geneticist and one of the country's leading hepatobiliary specialists, knows the drill. He has been doing this for so many years that his mind sometimes strays mid-operation to the rest of his busy day, although his pace doesn't slacken. He takes pride in his efficiency and expects a routine resection this time. Despite the disease's advance, the sick man's chances are good.

Perched in a nearby waiting area, the senior surgeon munches a bagel and assesses the case with a colleague who will be observing the procedure. I listen in, preparing to accompany them into the operating room. I have made my way here to witness expert thinking in action and to see what

3

role uncertainty might play in the most urgent of times. Is a surgeon who hesitates in a crisis foolhardy or heroic? Are some heights of excellence best left to the resolutely sure? The surgeon's tale offers critical lessons of promise and folly in an era when the world can upend from one hour to the next. Who will we look to for wisdom in the next free fall? Who are the sages of our day? Popping a last bite of breakfast into his mouth, the senior surgeon lingers before heading off to don mask and gown and get the job done. "Most of our business deals with avoiding problems," he says. "Most surgery, and I guess most things in life, are like that."

Moments later, his scrubbed hands held high, he bursts into the surgery and saunters up to the operating field, sizing up his quarry: a cluster of hard, white tumors scarring the liver's right lobe. To excise the cancer, a kind of siege warfare must unfold, as the surgeons endeavor to isolate and remove the diseased lobe without harming the healthy left half. The crux of this work will lie in dividing three major blood vessels and a bile duct that variously connect the heart, the liver, and the intestines. Like rivers that split into two branches, these bodily supply lines each fork just inside the liver; by sealing off and then cutting one branch of the hepatic artery, portal vein, bile duct, and hepatic vein, the surgeons can keep the cancer-free half of the liver and the patient alive. But if they mistakenly cut the main trunk of any of these anatomical structures, the man may quickly bleed to death.

The trick is finding what matters amidst layers of tissue, fat, and blood so intricate and anatomically individual that even expert surgeons sometimes lose their bearings. Articles in the field warn practitioners of myriad anatomical variations that no medical textbook fully depicts. "We don't like to say, 'What the hell is that?' too often," jokes the senior surgeon. "But we do say it occasionally. It's always a bad sign." *Surgeons must be very careful*, wrote Emily Dickinson, *When they take the knife! / Underneath their fine incisions / Stirs the Culprit—Life!*

Like saboteurs on a moonless night, the surgeon and his student creep forward, excavating the liver and surrounding tissue with a cautery as the sour scent and smoke of burning flesh pervade the room. The young doctor, new and cautious, works slowly. The senior surgeon guides her, tells war stories, orders the nurses about, and grows impatient. Halfway through an operation, he usually begins watching the clock, a habit now typical in a field besieged by lean profits, overworked staff, and increasingly complex diseases. "All the pressures [in health care] are on the side of production," notes safety expert Peter Pronovost. At this hospital, any operation running overtime is tagged with a red flag; such tallies of efficiency can influence a surgeon's future allotment of cases. For a profession schooled to be relentlessly bold, the aim is clear: speed is the gold standard and doubt an unwelcome intrusion. In medicine, to deal with uncertainty is to "make it go away," says one physician-scientist, "then we're done."

"So *this* is the right artery," the senior surgeon announces. "It's big, actually," he adds, suddenly taken back. At this juncture, the pair is working at the organ's lower end to uncover a trio of close-packed vessels, including the hepatic artery that ferries oxygenated blood from the heart into the liver. Spotting a hefty bit of artery here might show that they have found their target, the vessel's expendable right branch, albeit in extra-large size. (The patient is a tall man.) Or instead, the structure's generous size could indicate they are in dangerous territory and may be about to sever the artery's main stem. The senior surgeon, mind made up, orders the trainee to seal off and cut the structure in hand. But she insists on first temporarily closing off the section of artery in question with a clamp and then feeling for a pulse in the vessel's nearby left branch to check its viability—a caution he calls "paranoid," then begrudgingly permits. Confirming his call, she makes the cut.

Yet the encounter is telling, the observing doctor later explains. A renowned scientist and surgeon in her own right, Carol-anne Moulton is my guide to the critical judgments unfolding before me. Formerly the senior surgeon's student and now his relentlessly questioning peer, she has spent more than a decade probing quandaries like these: when, amidst high-stakes predicaments, much is not as it seems. A global authority on surgical expertise whose influence extends far beyond medicine, Moulton is at the forefront of one of cognitive science's most challenging endeavors: decoding how we can wrestle a solution from the clutches of a fast-evolving problem, how we can grapple with spiraling unknowns.

That day, with a clock ticking and a life at risk, we would see the expert mind on the fly, all dexterity and decision, and witness its precarious limits. *He didn't want to spend two or three minutes clamping the artery,* Moulton tells me later. *He was happy to take that chance and divide it for the sake of efficiency and time.* Speed matters, for the longer the operation, the higher the risk of complications, especially in complex procedures. "There are times when you need to keep moving," says Moulton. Yet hasty assurance under fire, she argues, is the dangerous Siren call of our day. Calm and athletic with a strong jaw, an easy smile, and a penchant for questioning the status quo, Moulton is gaining accolades for challenging our outdated assumptions about the nature of superior performance. Her quest is helping to reveal a dramatic new understanding of how true expertise is achieved and why, more than ever, we need such prowess.

"Cut along the line," orders the older surgeon, pointing to the increasingly visible boundary between a healthy russet left lobe and the now-darkening right liver. "Go back and forth, good," he says. He is approaching the most critical point in the endeavor, the division of the crucial duct carrying digestive fluid called bile into the intestines. Would he honor the situation's complexities, recognize that danger is near? Not for the first time during the operation, Moulton interjects to urge caution. But the surgeon plows on. "Faster, faster," he says. The diseased lobe is nearly free. And that's when Moulton's warnings come home.

⤓

Quick, automatic, and assured. Know-how is synonymous with fluency, built up over time. Veteran physicians diagnose from across the room, all the more so in emergencies. Fire chiefs make 80 percent of their tactical decisions in less than a minute. A magical ease seems the epitome of professional excellence whether we are chairing a meeting or leading a battle. Experts long have been the people we trust to jump to a conclusion. Novices awkwardly lag behind. What are the roots of this facility? What makes the pros so quick and so sure? To begin to investigate the expert mind under fire, let us step back in time to August 1939, when a Belgian freighter set off for a weeks-long voyage to Argentina under the shadow of imminent war.

En route to the world Chess Olympiad were most of Europe's champions as well as a Dutch team member determined to use the royal game as a new laboratory for the study of judgment. This was a time when many in the psychology field, under the sway of behavioralism, deemed the mind's workings nearly impossible to decode. But a wave of inventive European researchers would help prove them wrong. Armed with little more than a chessboard and a notebook, budding psychologist Adriaan de Groot set up a series of onboard experiments to tease out just how experts so often select the best option in almost no time.

De Groot asked players to think out loud while pondering a mid-game move key to the outcome of a match. Masters nearly always chose the correct next play, yet in doing so, they didn't think much further ahead or test many more moves than weaker players. (Grandmasters calculate an average 6.8 turns ahead, compared with weaker players' 5.5 turns.) The best players almost immediately know what to do, and a later series of experiments gave a clue as to why. Shown a chessboard in play for only four seconds, novices recall just four pieces on average, while a master remembers four to five times as many—and a nearly perfect board on a third try.

The prowess of experts is fueled by vast stores of experiential memory "chunked" in meaningful patterns, de Groot ventured. This is what enables them so often to see the right move at a glance. To a grandmaster, twenty-six game pieces arrayed across a sixty-four-square board speedily reveal a variation of the classic Caro-Kann opening move and the starting point of victory. A novice can't see the strategy hidden in the fray. "Intuition is nothing more and nothing less than recognition," concluded Herbert Simon, a 1978 Nobel laureate in economics who was deeply influenced by de Groot.

Thinking in action typically does not begin with laboriously crunching all the possibilities before you. Who has time for endless pros and cons? Instead, we first swoop down on a good-enough answer by turning to the cognitive shortcuts that Simon dubbed heuristics. One repertoire of quick thought draws from rules of survival that emerged over tens of thousands of years, a kind of innate day-to-day expertise inherited from our ancestors. We are prone, for example, to assume that strangers are threatening; evolutionarily speaking, it's far better to err on the side of being wary of new potential friends than to place fatal trust in a possible aggressor. A second class of heuristics draws on a no less influential realm of learning: our own stock of cognitive shortcuts, accrued over time. This is the gift of knowledge that de Groot helped uncover: with practice, we perform ever more complex tasks using *less* of our brain, whether we are turning c-a-t into *cat* or sensing how to checkmate Kasparov. What is laborious at first—clamp?—becomes automatic—cut!—as the lessons of the past equip the behavior of the future.

With his simple experiments, de Groot helped inspire a vision of the mind as an information processor organized by unconscious rules, grammars, and operations. He broke open the black box of expert performance, setting the stage for a new partnering of man and machine. Just as industrial age productivity guru F. W. Taylor dissected the elements of manual work to uncover its hidden efficiencies, pioneers of the postwar cognitive revolution parsed the mind's mechanisms to decode its capabilities, using the firepower of the first computers. Cognition became seen as computation performed by a kind of machine—orderly, hierarchical, and quick. Experience could be viewed as a kind of programming. (And, in turn, the machines at our fingertips could be made "smart.") This understanding of the brain still neatly underscores our idea of skill. Experts instantly sense the winning tactic, we presume. They sail through the operation while talking about last weekend's ninth hole. Proud masters of our devices, we text while driving, tweet while conversing. We are godly machines, ascending to Olympian ease.

Or are we? De Groot's pioneering work showed that much of our know-how is not inborn but painstakingly accrued. He revealed the backstory to experts' day-to-day speed. But as scientists began to test the upper limits of human performance by subjecting skilled performers to ever more demanding tasks, they discovered an unexpected wrinkle to the tale. Accumulated knowledge forged into smooth automaticity, it turns out, is no guarantee of superior performance. The ancient adage *experto crede*— trust in one who has experience—warrants a modern caveat.

Consider the seen-it-all reporter or the veteran sales executive whose edge (but not their swagger) dulled long ago. Years of experience are often weakly or even negatively correlated with accuracy and skill in fields from chess to finance to sports. In one large experiment, senior auditors were worse on average than undergraduate accounting students at spotting unusual problems, such as embezzlement, in the account books. The patients of more experienced physicians suffer higher death rates after being hospitalized for heart attacks, according to a study of 4,500 doctors. Why does the godly machine falter? The scientific heirs to the amiable de Groot have a new story of expertise to tell. The mind is far more than a machine. Superior thinking under fire demands much more than push-button shortcuts. And the very know-how that makes us expert is all too often our downfall.

Recall that our survival-oriented brain relentlessly strains for speedy solutions. When we are faced with a problem, a single response often bursts into consciousness, roughly based on what has worked—what has been rewarding—in the past. Yet zoom in on this time of reckoning, and we begin to see another side to elegant know-how: a narrowing of the mind in action. What we experience first, for example, is typically seen as best, probably because almost anything top of the line is equated with success. Like newborn chicks eager to imprint, we give disproportionate weight to the initial option that comes into view, largely ignoring what follows. Exposure to early evidence before or during a trial can powerfully sway juries, studies suggest.

Or consider how easily we succumb to the *Einstellung* effect, named for the German term for "way of thinking." After people master one particular method of solving a problem, they become blind to better, quicker routes to resolving a similar challenge; perhaps this is why we are so wedded to *our* way of loading the dishwasher. When expert chess players are presented with a game in play that offers a famous five-step way to achieve the "smothered mate" checkmate, most fail to spot a three-move route also available there. Dozens of such heuristics mapped in the past half century reveal the Achilles' heel of shortcut thinking: amidst a sea of possibilities, we leap to the first, most familiar life raft that we can find and then cling there.

Survival naturally requires a culling of options and evidence at all levels of cognition. Even the most rudimentary mechanisms of perception engage in this effort at meaning making. The lowly neuron, foot soldier of the brain, does not, as was once assumed, simply funnel raw sensory data to higher-order regions that "think." Instead, these microcosms of the brain filter new information according to our goals and expectations as well as cues from the pulsing environment; our frontline cells recognize and learn, serving as the smallest building blocks of automaticity. The ceaseless interpretation of information up and down the food chain of cognition—one of science's greatest recent discoveries—keeps us from being helplessly overwhelmed by our complex surroundings. We quickly seem to know what's afoot and what to do. Yet this ruthless selectivity both equips and limits our thinking. Friend or foe? Clamp or cut? How we frame the problem sets the stage for all that follows. The sequel to de

Groot's chessmen takes us to a man with a candle and a closer look at the shadow side of know-how.

As a graduate student visiting the United States from Germany, Karl Duncker began concocting some of psychology's most powerful experiments, using simple household objects from candles to corks. A mentor later called them "productive problems—with beautiful solutions." Fascinated by the uncharted terrain beyond routine fluency, Duncker's tests of ingenuity were designed to expose the "mediating phases" of problem solving, the uncertain paths he sensed we must take to illumination when faced with a thorny challenge. Such problems can't be solved at a snap, he asserted. Tapping one's memory for past solutions has "a certain heuristic value" but "little to do with thinking." In probing further into the workings of the mind under fire than almost anyone had yet dared to go, however, he soon discovered just how confidently unthinking we are.

In Duncker's best-known experiment, participants are asked to attach a candle to a wall given only three matches and a box of tacks. Many attempt to tack the candle straight to the wall or glue it there with melted wax—messy efforts at best. Overall, three in five people completely miss seeing the tack box as a *platform* for the candle—and the key to the solution. ("When the crucial object was afterwards pointed out," he wrote, "it was as if 'the scales had fallen from their eyes.'") By immediately associating or "fixating" an object with its common use—in this instance, the box with containment—we blind ourselves to its full promise, marveled Duncker. We lose sight of "essential aspects" of the situation, he wrote in his life opus *On Problem-Solving*.

His findings explain why the British Admiralty initially turned down the Wright brothers' invention as lacking "any practical use" for a navy and why until the 1980s hospitals treated donated blood as primarily a source of red blood cells for transfusions and simply threw out the layer of blood containing stem cells, a practice that likely slowed the field's recognition of such master cells' value. Efficiency in problem solving has "a costly side effect," psychologists argue. In an all-out drive for an answer, people typically spring into action based on what first comes to mind and thus too often wind up seeing the world through the lens of what they already know. What follows is a "cognitive entrenchment" that deepens with experience. Tweak the rules of the game that someone has spent years mastering, and they are prone to perform at a loss.

Yet is such myopia inevitable? Seventy-five years after Duncker's original experiments, researcher Tamsin German tested children on a kid-friendly version of the candle problem: helping a stuffed bear reach a toy lion on a high shelf, using an array of toys in a box. Twice as many seven-year-olds solved the problem if the container, which made a handy stepstool, stood alongside the toys, just as nearly all adults crack the candle problem given the hint of a box placed beside the tacks. But intriguingly, five-year-olds show almost equal deftness however the tools are arranged. As yet immune to fixedness, kindergartners essentially ask, "What can an object do?" while adults and even second graders stay close to the shores of what they know, thinking, "What was it made to do?"

Because younger children don't need to get out of the way of their own assumptions, they solve the tougher tools-in-the-box problem twice as fast as their older peers. Their innate willingness to be *unsure* makes the problem easier. They show us up yet show us the way. Could we too learn to make a first conclusion not an end but a starting point of judgment? Can we recapture the promise of the not-knowing mind? At a point of trouble as simple as a candle problem or as grievous as a disaster, we bypass the messy edges and hidden layers of a predicament in a rush to find shelter in our consummate know-how. And here's the added rub: the more trying the moment, the faster people shut down their minds.

Recall that how quickly someone leaps to conclusions in part depends on how well she tolerates uncertainty. Such a disposition is in psychological terms a "trait," a kind of set point in the mind. But a baseline attitude toward the unknown is also malleable, that is, strongly "situational." In particular, stress, fatigue, information overload, time pressure, or feeling that we must give an opinion—much of life as we know it today—sharply boosts the *need for closure*, that is, the yearning for certainty, for "an answer, any answer," according to Arie Kruglanski, founder of a burgeoning field of research into this mindset.

In one of his studies, people were shown seven minutes of images either from the September 11 attacks or from a hip high-tech workplace. Those shown the cataclysm later scored far higher than people who viewed the placid scenes on a scale that measures people's intolerance for last-minute changes of plans, questions with many possible answers, or simply not knowing for a time. "They were craving certainty," Kruglanski told me.

This penchant, which he sees as intensifying among Americans in recent years, was on stark display during the early pandemic, with runs on cash, guns, and puppies and premature demands for abandoning safety measures. Kruglanski and his colleagues call the need for closure a "gatekeeper of our minds." When besieged, we tend to raise our mental drawbridges and shut out new information just when it is needed most.

The catch-22 is clear. We yearn for clarity when we know least about our predicament. Under duress, we fall into *carryover mode*, barreling on with the well-honed assumptions that form the bedrock of competence in more predictable times. Moreover, once we head down the road of a snap judgment, we become loath to turn back. In Kruglanski's terms, we seize, then freeze, growing more confident in our cursory judgments. Ready-fire sureness saves us from paralysis time and again. But when routine falls short—a box is not just a box—carryover mode cannot save the day. Just when we urgently need to raise our sights, we hunker down with a good-enough answer, guarding at all costs the underbelly of our ignorance. And most alarmingly, the more expert we are, the more deeply we fall into this trap. That is a revelation that stirred a physician with a poet's heart to greatness two centuries ago.

↵

In 1817, a London surgeon laid down his scalpel for the last time. Just twenty-one years old, he had already spent a third of his life acquiring a trade that was barely emerging from the barbershop and battlefield. Decades before the first use of anesthesia, surgery took place as rapidly as possible in amphitheaters ringing with the shouts of students and the screams of patients. In the operating rooms of the era, there was no stepping back from the fray. Change to the profession came too late for the sensitive young John Keats, who would become a poet on a par with Shakespeare. He had shown promise in his studies yet had spent the previous year assisting an infamous surgeon known even in a time of rip-and-tear procedures as "rash in the extreme." For Keats, the brutality soon became frighteningly routine. In March, he quit the profession, published his first book of poetry, and made a discovery contrary to the medicine of his era and, far too often, to the rhythms of our own.

His breakthrough began with a visit to the new British Museum gallery built for the famous sculptures, known as the Elgin Marbles, taken from the Parthenon temple in Athens. Wending his way through galleries cluttered with fossils, stuffed fauna, gems, and artwork, Keats at last entered the soaring skylit space housing remnants of the frieze from the Temple of Athena atop the Acropolis. At the time, some in the arts and literary worlds glorified the sculptures as matchless, while others saw only worthless fragments. Even then, the artwork had become a lightning rod in an ongoing debate over the treatment of antiquity in modern society. A rising literary critic as well as a poet, Keats felt pressure to take sides.

In two sonnets inspired by the visit, he first professes inadequacy for the task of speaking "definitively on these mighty things; Forgive me that I have not Eagle's wings—that what I want I know not where to seek." But then, as the poems progress, he realizes that he need not choose between single-minded worship or derision. His lines begin to celebrate life's contradictions and ambiguities, from "Grecian grandeur" marked by time's "rude wasting" to the "dim-conceived glories" of an inspired mind, as biographer Nicholas Roe notes. Coming full circle, Keats realizes that only by *not* knowing something can he start to grasp it well.

In a letter to his brothers later that year, Keats elaborates on the famous doctrine that fuels his ironic, questioning poetry and offers us in turn a potent antidote to the closed-mindedness of our day. Keats describes a fellow poet so eager for certitude that he is incapable of being content even briefly with not-knowing. Another friend, a literary critic, rests his very identity on "making up his Mind about every thing," he later writes. By contrast, Keats asserts, life's complexities demand an intense unassumingness that he calls *negative capability*, a capacity to dwell in "uncertainties, Mysteries, doubts" without impatiently leaping to conclusions. This stance is central to great achievement, he writes. Keats died at age twenty-five of tuberculosis after self-diagnosing the disease that had stumped his doctors. In life as in art, he knew how to give possibility a chance.

↪

"Here's the last big thing that needs to be divided," Moulton whispers to me as the surgeon exposes his final target: the crucial bile duct nestling in the organ's recesses. The cancerous half liver is nearing removal, the five-hour operation approaching completion. The senior surgeon keeps urging the junior doctor to hasten. He makes a move; a stapler bites down on flesh. *It was a critical moment,* Moulton explains later, *and he divided it like it was all routine.* And then he halts, saying "hold it." The small talk ceases as sweat darkens his cap and a ringing phone goes unanswered. "Don't cut," he orders. Stumbling on an unexpected glimpse of bile duct, he suspects that a minute earlier, he may have done the unthinkable and severed the duct's main stem. In medicine, such incidents are called "never events," errors that shouldn't ever be made. Has he ridden blindly into danger, mistaking the irreplaceable for the expendable?

This time, it was just a frighteningly close call. Failing to clean off enough of the surrounding tissue, he was working a few millimeters off target and sliced through an innocuous blood vessel, mistaking it for his true mark. "That wasn't the bile duct, that thing before," he murmurs, swiftly recovering his pace. "*This* is the bile duct actually, yeah, the mistake we made was, we were too far into the right side."

Over a lunch of chowder and chili in the cafeteria, he and Moulton unsparingly probe the incident.

"I clearly cleaned off the wrong structure," he admits.

"That could have been a landmine," she accuses. "You didn't check it."

"I didn't feel comfortable, I have to admit that," he says.

He had barreled into the crux of the operation, assuming success was a given. He had clung to his certainty, the badge of the old-school expert.

Agile and wiry with a lined face, a ready candor, and large, expressive hands, the senior surgeon credits Moulton with vastly improving his judgment in the operating room. She looks to him to learn how to pick up her pace when possible. They each in their own way deeply feel their fallibility. Still, he remains something of a holdout, believing or just hoping that from behind the shield of his know-how, he can keep trouble at bay. Shifting uneasily in the lunchroom, he admits a "sense of shame" while repeatedly defending his commitment to the fluency that he believes is his due. "You take pride in being quick," she says. "Yes," he concurs, "a lot of people do, I think." She looks down, pensive. "That's the system we make," she says.

As they debate, the junior surgeon works on in the operating room sewing up the sick man's torso. His wedge of dying, cancer-riddled flesh, still warm to the touch, glistens on a nearby tray. In coming weeks, his remaining liver likely will regenerate, the only human organ capable of doing so. *No harm done—this time*, says Moulton.

Two centuries after Keats put down his scalpel, Carol-anne Moulton is endeavoring to bring negative capability—the gift of uncertainty—into a world mired in antiquated ideas of expertise. The daughter of a Salvation Army minister whose humility remains her inspiration, Moulton traces the genesis of her quest to the final months of her lengthy training. As a junior hepatobiliary surgeon, she repeatedly was called in to help fix horrific injuries caused by the severing of the common bile duct, usually in the waning phase of a long operation. "It's something we fear," says Moulton. "I would often wonder, what's going on in the head of the surgeon when this is happening? . . . I started thinking about what uncertainty means." Using the power of fieldwork to explore the "how" and the "why" of expert decision making, not just the outcome, she began to unlock the story behind those moments gone wrong.

After spending hundreds of hours coaxing her peers to talk of their unspoken fears and assumptions and watching them work wrist-deep in flesh and blood, Moulton realized that true expertise begins in the unsettling transition from automaticity to a readiness to work with the unknown. Superior judgment starts with the shifting of cognitive gears from an ancient system designed to shut down deliberation in a crisis to one that seeds intentional, flexible thought. Here is the time for what Moulton calls "slowing down when you should" so that "you can actually be in charge of the moment." The challenge is, will we welcome the discord of not-knowing into the ease of our fluency?

The surgeon confronting trouble is often caught by surprise. Like a chess grandmaster blind to anything but a familiar strategy, she fails to notice signs that normalcy is crumbling and drifts into trouble. "So many surgeons talk about how it's the bread-and-butter cases where things go wrong," says Moulton.

She recounts a tight spot in a surgery of her own. To staunch blood flow from the newly exposed inner face of the liver, the surgeon must cauterize small vessels or permanently seal off larger ones with a tiny titanium clip and then the knife. Cauterize or clip and cut—she calls the shots unthinkingly and sometimes fails to double-check whether a clip has fully encircled a vein. (Situations that are clear, repetitive, or even faintly familiar boost our gullibility and lower our guard.) Ignoring the throbbing sense that something is amiss, Moulton takes a chance and makes the cut, triggering a bleed that puts the patient's life at risk. Routine is shattered. The expert is left scrambling. It's tempting then to continue to cling to a repertoire of mental shortcuts and quick sure conclusions. In a crisis, says Moulton, "many experts aren't problem solving. They think they *have* the answer."

Consider the case of a group of young anesthesiologists in training called into an emergency appendectomy on a woman whose oxygen levels were declining perilously. As the patient spiraled down, Dr. P. returned ten times in twenty-five minutes to his first wrong diagnosis of bronchospasm, a common constricting of the airways during surgery. His colleague Dr. V., meanwhile, sprinted through eight potential diagnoses, including the correct one (an obstructed breathing tube), yet he also could not halt the crisis. He latched onto one plausible conjecture after another, remaining on the surface of each. The two were taking part in a renowned 2003 Harvard simulation, one of the first studies to capture physicians' thinking in action in the operating room. Eighty-five percent of doctors in the experiment failed to slow down long enough to fully test their hasty conclusions. Their leaps of judgment paradoxically kept them running in place, a modus operandi all too common today.

"It's hard to switch tracks when the train is going a million miles an hour," says Cameron Kyle-Sidell, a New York critical care physician who early in the COVID-19 pandemic fought to warn of his field's reverence for honed know-how. At first, doctors believed that the sickest coronavirus patients' respiratory problems were caused by an infection that typically leads to acute respiratory distress. After all, most met the prime criteria for the syndrome: critically low levels of oxygen in the blood. Anticipating that such compromised lungs would "crash" and fearing that less invasive breathing supports would leak the virus by air, doctors placed up to 90 percent of patients in intensive care units onto ventilators, the mechanical breathing machines that are the standard treatment for worst-case respiratory failure. "For a while that was the only question, that was the only care: when to intubate them," Kyle-Sidell told me.

As the pandemic hit its stride, however, Kyle-Sidell and a few other frontline physicians in global hot spots questioned the rush to ventilate.

Many of the sick had low oxygen levels, but their lungs were "compliant," that is, expanding and contracting well. And many fared poorly on the machines, whose use can damage both lungs and brains. "The patterns I was seeing didn't make sense," says Kyle-Sidell. Yet his urgings and those of others to reconsider standard protocols at first met with resistance from experts slow to question their know-how.

In time, studies showed that while a significant minority of acute COVID-19 patients needed full mechanical ventilation, many healed with the help of less aggressive breathing supports. In July 2020, about a fifth of intensive care patients with COVID-19 in Britain were put on a ventilator in their first 24 hours in such units, down from about 70 percent in March, according to an independent research institute. Meanwhile, death rates for such patients fell nearly in half to 25 percent during this period, a reduction attributed in part to a greater tendency to delay or forgo invasive ventilation as well as other factors, such as the use of steroids. The situation was dire, the variables many and complex, yet that is the moment when it is most crucial to think beyond the tried and true. "When you move away from a paradigm," says Kyle-Sidell, "you can walk into the unknown."

↑

Awakening to a crisis, we cannot merely ask, "What's going on here?" and then jump. Even when time is short, we must inhabit the question, interrogating the possibilities at hand. The checklist, the protocol, the gut response should serve as cognitive waystations, nothing more. The elite few anesthesiologists who saved the Harvard patient considered an average of five potential diagnoses and then probed each possibility nearly four ways, double the depth of consideration shown by hastier colleagues. In particular, they engaged in "negative testing," the double-checking of issues that seem resolved, the unknowns masquerading as knowns that often hold the solution's key. (Is the tube that seems to be suctioning in fact blocked? Could low oxygen *not* be the death sentence it once seemed?) Under fire, it's not enough to expand your cognitive horizons, a step often seen as a one-stop cure for poor decision making. Instead, we must widen *and* deepen our frame of understanding, asking "What's missing?" *and* "What's wrong?" In this way, we give possibility a fighting chance.

Call it the power of "take two." The most crucial time for solving a muddy problem often is in the first few minutes after it surfaces, as the pioneering neuroscientist Michael Posner has shown. An initial take, or mental representation, of a problem is neat, plausible, reassuringly familiar, and often off target. Creating a full picture of the situation demands that you hold in mind and gradually refine hidden and even conflicting possibilities into nuanced understanding, a process that de Groot called "progressive deepening."

In the thick of a predicament, virtuoso thinkers consider at least one other diagnosis of the situation and then importantly take two or more steps to weigh and assess each possibility. (Generate *too* many alternative hypotheses, and the crucial testing stage will be diluted or cut short.) There is a kind of optimism in this work, notes management consultant Roger Martin. Superior experts are "forever testing what they think they know" in their search for the best approach to the situation. They keep asking questions—and question their conclusions. "Their resting state is not certainty." That is how they avert the perils of carryover mode and how you can too.

Imagine you are a seasoned high-tech executive tapped to fix your firm's biggest problem: the company will go bankrupt unless it can salvage a new product that has been languishing in development for a year. The word from the top is that you must whip into shape the global task force in charge of the fiasco. Quick, decisive leadership is what's needed, orders the CEO, and you, with your long industry experience, think you know just what to do. But despite the high stakes, you step back and *take two*—another well-considered look. While mistakes have been made all around, you consider another option: is the lead team really to blame? Then you investigate this alternative by closely observing the task force's dynamics and by tapping an array of internal experts. And contrary to what top leaders assumed, you discover that it is *they* who have helped stymy progress by micromanaging the task force. Instead, the firm's leaders need to step back and allow the task force, along with the firm's designers, to do the work needed to save the product, an improvement in the manufacture of semiconductors.

In this true story, a daring executive saved his company by working to uncover a critical problem's inner poetry, not just its surface facets. Again and again, "he was not ready to take action until a picture emerged that rang true," writes leadership researcher Joyce Osland in her case study of the event. The climax of the seven-month effort came as the task force prepared to choose the best of several solutions. Many members argued for the option they saw as a silver bullet. The executive—call him Tom—instead urged them to combine two of the strongest final designs. When initial testing seemed to support the single option, Tom again did a *take two*, asking for an eleventh-hour multilevel analysis that revealed the data had been misread and that in fact a combined solution was best.

In the end, the task force completed a product design once seen as impossible, then brought it up to manufacturing specifications in nine days instead of the typical three months. Strategic business decisions are four times more likely to succeed if managers fully investigate the roots of a problem and multiple possible solutions, yet studies show that they seriously consider only one option four-fifths of the time. "If you hadn't made that decision" to take a second look at the data, one colleague told Tom, "we would all be unemployed."

Why do so many trip up after scaling the heights of learning? In almost any domain, "routine experts" deftly practice what they know well; they seem near invincible day to day, especially when only compared to novices, as scientists at first were prone to do. Relying on what the psychologist Anders Ericsson calls "creeping intuition bias," they are quick and impressive until faced with a novel or muddy challenge. And that's when they begin to fail. Outside the "comfort zone of their achievement," they confront the unknown with a skill set forged in the dull heat of routine.

In contrast, "adaptive experts" become under duress what we least expect them to be: unsure. They welcome the space of uncertainty as a launchpad for assessing a challenging situation. In the operating room, good surgeons confronting trouble may call a halt to the procedure, fall silent, or deepen their focus, Moulton's research shows. What looks like hesitation is in fact a controlled effort to reconcile new with old knowledge, to flesh out early impressions, and to reveal not needless complications but the crucial complexity that is *already* there. In domains from medicine to physics and beyond, experts spend far more time than novices diagnosing a new or murky problem, studies show. In one recent experiment, the best chess players opted for a first gut response three-quarters of the time when the problem

on the board was simple. But when confronted with tricky game predicaments, they chose the first move that came to mind only about one-fifth of
the time. "You're in a different mode because you're uncertain," Moulton
tells me. "You're creating a space to think about holding your options open,
gathering the information."

Stepping out from routine know-how, we face a trompe l'oeil landscape
of unknowns. Are we willing to think them through? Both true expertise
and the work of thinking in action—emerging from automaticity, seeking
that crucial second take, and the problem's hidden dimensions—barely correlate with intelligence. We may have knowledge or smarts yet fail to give
ourselves fully to the messy problem before us. Adaptive experts, in contrast,
are prepared to take charge at any time by stilling the knowing mind and admitting the promise of uncertainty. They are curious, skeptical, and alert even
amidst routine. This is the remarkable cognitive skill set that offers a new future for expertise at a time when its very existence is increasingly questioned.

↓

Experts have long bestowed ready answers to the masses eagerly waiting
below. We depend on them to cure ills, expose risks, and teach us about
a complex world. But there have been creeping cracks in the public's awe.
Swaggering technocrats helped send *Challenger* and *Columbia* astronauts to
their deaths in the sky, failed to save the disadvantaged from Katrina's wrath,
and poisoned the children of Flint. Bombastic financiers unleashed a global
financial crisis. The most single-minded pundits, studies show, are those
least able to astutely look ahead. Applause for pandemic frontline doctors
and nurses was sincere and swift, yet underlying questions about the place
of expertise in medicine and in society linger. Why are the vulnerable left
behind again and again? If bias and error taint even those who have mastered the corpus, in whose knowledge can we trust? One-third to two-fifths
of Americans say doctors are rarely if ever transparent about conflicts of
interest or their mistakes, and confidence in the profession is deeply divided
by race and by political party. Has the prowess once seen as an emblem of
progress become passé?

Further stoking the wariness, instant access to answers—and to misinformation too—allows people to reject the credentialed pronounce-
ment in lieu of their own. After a bit of online searching, I can spurn a

doctor's recommendation, underscoring my disavowal with a two-star review. Traditional gatekeepers of knowledge—the librarian, scientist, or
engineer—may be sidestepped with a click, a temptation strengthened by
dogmatic discourse. By the time scientific findings are made public, for example, they are often shorn by researchers and the media of the caveats and
limitations that serve as clues to their validity, studies show. "People have
had enough of experts," asserted a British cabinet minister. "Look at the
mess we're in, with all these experts that we have," argued a president famous
for accepting no authority but his own. Are we all our own sages now?

Populist rhetoric and political ego aside, it is critical to question past
ideals and outdated hierarchies of expertise. The notion that superior skill
is synonymous with fluency; that heuristics—from gut assumptions to
ready-fire algorithms—suffice; and that discomfiting uncertainty is the
province of novices: these are telltale marks of the routine experts whose
overreliance on shortcut know-how has led us astray. For too long, we have
placed false idols on the altar of expertise.

Going forward, we must not mistake the bravado of those sated with
limited knowledge—routine experts or overconfident novices alike—for
the courage of those who ceaselessly expand the limits of their understanding. For that is the foundation stance of superior adaptive performers:
they continually work at the outer edge of their knowledge and capability.
(The term *expert* derives from the Latin verb *experīrī*, "to try.") In quiet
times and rough, the best thinkers look ahead for subtle signs of impending
problems and deficiencies in their own thought. They operate in the bor-
derland that routine experts shun, where hope of ease gives way not just
to an expectation of trouble but to a willingness to continually take on
ever-greater challenges. Great surgeons sign up for the most complex cases.
The most proficient artisans, says wood-carver David Esterly, inhabit "a
world permeated by error." By seeking to extend—not just apply—their
knowledge, they ward off the "arrested development" of routine expertise.
This is the wisdom that should count.

Now many in medicine are beginning to see a culture that values not-
knowing as integral to nurturing a new generation of experts who can
thrive in a volatile era. Doctors who fear uncertainty tend to overprescribe
antibiotics, shy from treating underserved patients, and may fall prey to the
anxiety and depression that have risen to alarming levels in the field. Their

yearning for neat answers and rising angst when quick fixes are not at hand fuel some of health care's worst ills. It's crucial to address our "unhealthy reaction to uncertainty," writes physician-scientist Arabella Simpkin in a *British Medical Journal* commentary. Some frontline visionaries are joining Moulton in doing just that.

Not long ago, faculty at a family medicine residency program in Maine noticed that their charges were increasingly uneasy treating outpatients whose ongoing care often involves more complexity and ambiguity than the acute ills seen by specialists or hospitalists. The care that cardiologists dispense, for example, is one-third less complex per hour than that of family doctors, who in one morning might see an anorexic teen, an elder with late-stage cancer, and a thirty-year-old chronic diabetic. "This is what the residents chose to do with their lives, why are they unhappy?" senior doctors at Central Maine Medical Center asked themselves.

It took a while to pinpoint the problem: a fear of the uncertainty that is endemic in the trainees' chosen profession. In a sense, the residents already were striving to be routine experts who view the world through the lens of what they know well. "I was hoping every patient would be right out of my textbook," Nupur Nagrare, a 2017 graduate of the program, told me. Said one leader of the Center, "We set them up for that."

To the trainees' initial dismay, their professors began stressing that uncertainty was a welcome constant in their work, not a shameful flaw. In essence, the faculty were provoking the residents to see multiple facets of a question while equipping them with the openness to contend with them. The aim was "to make things muddier and messier, to make sure they didn't get comfortable with what they perceived as the obvious," whether they were learning to interview a patient or better diagnose a disease, says psychologist Deborah Taylor, cocreator of the program. For example, a practitioner who treats a patient's diabetes while failing to discover her depression may neglect the best course of care. "We reframed the learning in a way to allow people to be open to not-knowing, not to resist it but to seek it," said program director Bethany Picker, a physician. That's when "we saw the lightbulbs going on."

In one year, the subtle but radical teachings had a dramatic result: a significant and lasting drop in residents' tendency to see ambiguity as threatening, a 2018 pilot study shows. Before experiencing the new rotation, for example, the young doctors on average heartily concurred that "an expert who doesn't come up with a definite answer probably doesn't know too much." Afterward and even six months later, they tended to strongly disagree. The lessons shifted their professional identity and even the culture of work.

"It was reiterated to us that it's okay to say, 'I need to look this up' or 'I don't know the answer right now,' which is a very hard thing to do by the way," recalled Nagrare, who practices medicine in upstate New York. The training changed her practice and her life. "If you're open to ambiguity, you don't have tunnel vision, and things are not so set in stone," she told me. "You're a little more malleable, in your relationships, in your practice, or your expectations of yourself." You can push beyond the comfort zone of practiced know-how. You can test not just the problem but yourself. In turn, this stance instills confidence, even courage, she and other doctors noted. "When you value uncertainty," said Picker, "there is a confidence that builds and allows continued thinking and rethinking about next steps, as the picture changes." The crumbling of normalcy is no longer the abyss that you once feared.

Heeding the unease of uncertainty to get ahead of trouble, moving past the perceived obviousness of a first off-base answer, deeply inhabiting the question at hand, continually working at the outer edges of your knowledge, creating a culture that values not-knowing: this is how you can pursue the prowess of adaptive expertise every day, whether you are roughing out a first take on a crisis or approaching the critical phase of a routine. Practicing such skills in your lifework exposes your limitations and expands your options.

In the service of a *take two*, for example, try considering the opposite. What-if questions, especially those most contrary to our assumptions, propel us beyond the familiarity that we seek to preserve and expand our budding notion of what's going on. Perhaps you are heading the search for a new design lead, a client-facing job that demands a sociable persona. Yet you pause and ask yourself, "What if I was seeking an introvert for the position instead?" By posing a counterfactual, you become more likely to ask questions that probe for both traits and so gain a firmer grasp of a candidate, studies show. As a result, you may better understand just how extroverted the leading applicant is or find an extroverted designer who is unafraid to take time alone to reflect.

Or take another page from the adaptive expert's playbook and expand your understanding of a fast-evolving situation by breaking it down. Sometimes called "Fermi-izing," this technique was inspired by the physicist Enrico Fermi's habit of deconstructing seemingly intractable scientific mysteries to gain toeholds on what he *could* know. Asking a single overarching question about a point of trouble—is this the right branch artery?—is hardly sufficient in high-stakes situations. Instead, the superior surgeon might ask, how can I tell if I am targeting the correct anatomy, using the appropriate instrument, and fully aware of the ripple effects of taking this nonreversible step? By breaking the challenge into smaller pieces, you "flush ignorance into the open," explains political scientist Philip Tetlock. You start to hear the stories that the problem, not your first assumption, wants to tell.

↵

As I left Toronto, I thought of the moment just before the senior surgeon headed off to take up his scalpel. When he described his work and indeed life itself as an exercise in avoiding problems, Moulton immediately had countered him. *Life isn't about avoiding problems*, she said. *Most of the time, it's about solving them.*

Just two years after completing her PhD, Carol-anne Moulton gave one of her profession's most prestigious keynote speeches, where she appealed for a surgical identity valuing "thoughtfulness and uncertainty and even indecisiveness." No one before her had dissected as precisely the decisions that surgeons make amidst enormous pressures to be quick and all-knowing. She is mobbed after lectures, and her studies win international awards. She is heartened by the progress she has helped to inspire: frank talk about the costs of surety, training that broaches uncertainty as an asset.

But her profession and so many others have far to go, she asserts. "There's a world of difference between where we are now—admitting uncertainty while feeling so uncomfortable in it—and where we should be," says Moulton. "Until we are celebrating uncertainty, until we're not killing the wonderment and curiosity of what we're doing, we are *not* where we should be." Her work is far from done, yet her calls for change should speak to us all. Moulton is not importing what Keats called "uncertainties, Mysteries, doubts" into our lives; rather, she is bringing our fears about them to light. She is freeing us to realize a new vision of skill that carries with it both prowess and humility. "When you're uncertain," says Moulton, "that's when you care."

It is not too late for the truth-tellers in our midst: the analyst who heeds a whisper of doubt as a first step to fully grasping a problem, the poet alert to alluring complacency, no matter her level of experience. With competence comes the assurance to do most things right day to day. Yet knowing just what to do is tempting far beyond its usefulness, especially for those revered for their reactivity. True experts instead know when to break the inertia of knowing in order to pursue greater ends. Even at the top of their game, their understanding is lightly held. Knowledge strengthened by uncertainty is at the heart of superior performance under fire and the key to creating a new standard of expertise—questioning, open, adaptive—for a volatile time. Uncertainty is wisdom in motion.

CHAPTER TWO

"FRESH EYES"

Seeing What Matters by Taking Uncertainty's Lead

*What I like about experience is that it is such an honest thing. You may
have deceived yourself, but experience is not trying to deceive you.*
—C. S. LEWIS

When the shy mathematician arrived at the top-secret British intelligence base in September 1939, no one was working on the most crucial cipher of the new war. Deemed unbreakable, the German navy's Enigma code held the key to the sea contest that would span the entire conflict and determine victory or defeat. "Everything happening elsewhere, on land, on sea, or in the air, depended ultimately on the outcome" of the Battle of the Atlantic, Churchill later recalled. Britain needed millions of tons of commodities and materials a year to survive, to arm, and to prepare for the continent's liberation. It wielded a third of the globe's merchant shipping and the world's greatest navy. But German U-boats maneuvering under Enigma's cloak of secrecy could pose an insidious threat to the country's economy and to its maritime strength. Days after the Nazis launched their invasion of Poland on the first of September, the sinkings began.

Convoys of freighters and cargo ships tied to the pace of the slowest vessel began falling prey to U-boat "wolf packs" coordinated via encrypted radio traffic. The submarines ranged from coast to coast but especially targeted the northern mid-Atlantic, beyond the reach of military sea or air escorts. Slipping silently within the convoy, they unleashed torpedoes fore and aft, bringing down grain, oil, weapons, wood, ships, and lives into the cold sea depths. Some seamen slept fully clothed on deck, although surviving a sinking hardly guaranteed safety. Forced to keep moving to bolster chance of escape, unscathed members of the convoy, eyes averted, routinely churned past survivors struggling in waters just feet away. In one 1940 foray, U-boats sank eleven of the forty-one ships in convoy HX72 steaming from Halifax. A month later, they took down more than half of the thirty-five-member group SC7 out of Cape Breton. In October of that year, a Nazi fleet of twenty-seven operational submarines destroyed more than double their number in ships. Here was a mortal predicament: a stealth enemy on a vast, shifting battlefield and an outcome that would turn less on speed or force than on feats of mental perception. In this corner of war, the unseen would be one's downfall. It was, one historian noted, a "battle of wits."

Before the war, Germany had worked to bolster not only the ranks of their submarine fleet but also the power of the code that made its novel pack-based nautical attack strategy feasible. In the interwar era, the German military started using various forms of Enigma, a typewriter-like encryption machine originally created for businesses trading proprietary messages by telegraph. Bristling with wiring, rotors, and rings, the navy's ramped-up version of Enigma offered up to a hundred and fifty quintillion settings to transform a mere word into seeming randomness. As the war opened, the Third Reich's cryptological prowess gave it a decided edge on the high seas. Worse, the British had played straight into their hands.

"The submarine should never again be able to present us with the problem we were faced with in 1917," a British naval staff report concluded in 1937. The use of convoys late in World War I, along with the fledgling inventions of sonar and radar, had lured the navy into deeming submarines impotent. "Our goal must be under all circumstances to leave England in this belief," observed Hitler's U-boat commander, Karl Dönitz, later chief of the navy. In a further lack of foresight, the U.K. government had let cipher work fall off its strategic radar screen. As the country's military code breakers, euphemistically called the Government Code & Cypher School, evacuated to a rambling Victorian mansion outside London, its unit responsible for tracking the German navy did not include a single cryptanalyst. By the fall of 1939, the British navy was fighting in darkness, typically learning the enemy's whereabouts only when it had sunk one of His Majesty's own. Only two people at Bletchley Park were said to believe that naval Enigma could be cracked: the head of that unit, because they *had* to, and the boyish, blue-eyed mathematician Alan Turing, because the problem's intractability meant that "I could have it to myself."

At age twenty-four, Turing had solved mathematics' foremost logic conundrum, the "decision problem," which asks whether there is a mechanical, that is, an algorithmic, method for deciding whether any general mathematical assertion is provable. Paring thought to its barest mechanics, he showed that the decision problem and some similar questions could *not* be answered by such means. To do so, he went to the root of the problem and of mathematics itself, ingeniously defining computability by imagining the work of an ideal, universal calculating and processing machine. At a stroke, he set the stage for the computer revolution and helped reveal uncertainty as a revelatory form of knowledge in itself.

It was quintessential Turing: slicing through irrelevancies to reach an unexpected solution for a problem that most had dismissed as impossible. "A. M. Turing," wrote a math examiner from his boyhood, "showed an unusual aptitude for noticing the less obvious points to be discussed or avoided in certain questions." Throughout his life, Turing would prize what he called "that most important faculty which distinguishes topics of interest from others." How did he know what to look for? How could he reach heights of perception in an era of misinformation, volatility, and threat much like our own?

That year, a sultry autumn gave way to the coldest winter in nearly half a century. Towering snowdrifts buried cars and trains, stretches of the Thames River froze, and Bletchley Park's code breakers worked in coats and gloves behind blackout curtains. Day after day, Turing searched from every possible angle—guesswork, math, mechanics—for an overlooked chink in the armor of Enigma. Many of his achievements long remained shrouded in secrecy or were publicly forgotten. But decades later, the truths of his genius have emerged and can help to inspire a new understanding of how we can win a key battle of our day: astutely perceiving the world around us without ceding this critical task to the very machines that Turing brought to bear.

This is the story of how the brain constructs a reality that we too often take at face value and the ingenious ways that humans have evolved to awaken to their misreadings of the world. How do we see what matters? By following uncertainty's lead. On the trail of the discernment so urgently needed today, I headed to France to catch up with another brilliant, blue-eyed mathematician, one who is leading efforts to decode how the mind plays a remarkable game of question and answer with life.

↓

After two trains, a bite of baguette, and a taxi ride, I arrived one June morning at the gates of a high-security government research center encircled by barbed wire and wheat fields. Visitor cell phones were forbidden, yet when I wandered into an unmarked building to ask for directions, the front desk staff acted as if my appearance was a shocking breach of security. Pushing forward on foot past institutes for nanotechnology and nuclear safety, I at last found NeuroSpin, a world-renowned institute for brain imaging a few miles outside Paris. Rippling down the side of NeuroSpin's glass and metal complex was a series of enormous wave-shaped concrete vaults. Within were helium-cooled superconducting electromagnets that fueled the work of functional magnetic resonance imaging (fMRI) scanners up to eight times as strong as the average hospital's. Here was the scientific base camp of Stanislas Dehaene.

Elected in 2005 at age forty to France's elite Collège de France, Dehaene is one of his field's most influential visionaries. His theories on how we perceive the world are gaining traction, backed by a stream of discoveries using imaging, computer modeling, psychological experiments, and electrodes implanted in human brains. He made his name by mapping the brain's innate mathematical capacities—our "number sense"—and then advanced understanding of neural plasticity by helping show that learning to read demands a literal rewiring of the brain. His research-driven theory that consciousness emerges from a heightened state of neural connectivity inspires experimental work around the world.

I waited two hours in the NeuroSpin lobby before Dehaene burst in, apologizing. A compact man, he wore a straw fedora, a beige sports jacket, and a somber look. Tensions had flared in an international project to map the brain, derailing his packed schedule. He had just returned from a conference north of the Arctic Circle and soon would be leading experiments in Brazil. Would a fifteen-minute interview suffice? Not waiting for an answer, he sprinted away, leaving me to follow. For both of us, the morning had been a cavalcade of broken expectations. And that, I came to realize, was a clue to the mysteries that I was seeking. Astute awareness begins in the recesses of the mind with our response to the unexpected.

Unconscious perception was once written off as a kind of cognitive assembly work that occurred deep in the brain where photons and phonemes are converted to imagery and language. But people with brain injuries kept teasing researchers with the depth of their unwitting perceptual capacities. There were "blindsight" patients who had lost their vision yet somehow could deftly traverse a cluttered hallway. People with "spatial neglect" had lost half their sight but could draw meaning from their surroundings. One woman, for example, saw no difference between two sketched houses, one on fire, yet insisted that she would not live in the blazing dwelling. The patients' losses were severe, yet they could navigate the world. In particular, one poignant case gave the young Dehaene his first window into how the capacity for awareness unfolds. Much of his scientific work began the day that he asked Mr. N, "What is two plus two?" After a pause, came the answer: "Three."

A salesman lives by his numbers, and Mr. N could not perform a single calculation. He was forty-one in 1986, when he likely suffered a severe cerebral hemorrhage that injured large parts of his left-rear brain and left his life in tatters. Mr. N's wife soon left him, taking their two small daughters, and he lived with his aging parents. By the time Dehaene met him three years after his injury to test his severe acalculia, the effects of the lesion remained stark. Mr. N spoke slowly, could hardly use his right hand, and was largely unable to read or write. He recognized just four letters of the alphabet. He could add only by slowly counting out loud on his fingers, Dehaene wrote in a case study. Subtraction was beyond him.

Yet for all his cognitive deficits, Mr. N retained an impressive grasp on reality. When asked, he reported that January has fifteen or twenty days and that a year has about 350. A dozen eggs, he said, is about six or ten in number. His responses often were "both clearly false and yet not that far from the truth," observed Dehaene. The case of Mr. N inspired Dehaene's groundbreaking discovery of the neural roots of mathematics. But at the same time, his "strange fuzzy universe" offered an even larger clue to what makes us human. Essential to our survival is a constant striving to anticipate and appraise the world. The brain is a guessing machine. Dehaene dubbed his patient the Approximate Man.

Consider the rituals celebrated in your culture or the grammar of the language you speak. Picture making a cup of coffee or the route of your morning commute. To understand how we size up the world, we must first realize that we do not harbor floating bits of disconnected data in our heads. Much of our understanding instead takes the form of mental models, or what Dehaene calls "miniature mock-ups more or less faithful to reality," that we largely unconsciously construct. Animals survive by forming mental maps of their location; a rat's journey through a well-learned maze literally can be seen in the sequential activation of cells in the networks of its brain. Over time, model-based spatial skills evolved into humans' remarkable abilities to navigate not just a room but also a tricky procedure or an abstract idea, such as an ethical dilemma. And from there, people use their mental models as springboards to understanding a changing world.

Mental models are the foundation of *predictive processing*, the relentless future-oriented appraisal work increasingly seen by neuroscientists as playing a central role in human perception. Listen to how Nathaniel Silberschlag, who was named principal horn at the Cleveland Symphony at age twenty-one, describes how he pulls off a difficult solo. "Playing the notes—there are so many variables," he told an interviewer. "If you can't hear the note *before* you're playing it, it may not happen. In my head, while there is silence, the music has already kind of begun." Silberschlag uses his mental models of the horn, of music in general, and of that evening's score as the basis for anticipating what will be happening around him. His predictions then serve as real-time filters through which he sifts the tumult of information coming at him. (In contrast, heuristic know-how offers strategic mental shortcuts used to solve problems rather than expectations about what we are perceiving.) Our ability to anticipate in this way helps us stay a step or two ahead of life, boosting our chances of survival. As neuroscientists like to say, we see with our brain.

The guesses that people make about what's happening around them are necessary work-arounds to our species' woefully limited sensory capacities. We can see, hear, feel just a fraction of the world's light, sounds, and textures. In contrast to insects, for example, humans have no direct way to sense wetness; we apparently infer this feeling from a patchwork of thermal and tactile signals registered on the skin. Moreover, raw sensory data—images hitting the retina or air pressure registered by the ears—are highly ambiguous, as Dehaene notes. Something round could be any number of objects: a dish, a frisbee, a flower pot, or a hat. While sensory neurons calculate the likelihood of various possibilities, higher-order brain regions fill in the rest of the emerging picture with a steady stream of guesstimates and interpretations. "That round thing is on a table, next to a fork," the brain might say. "Ah! It's dinnertime."

The downside of such efficiency, however, is that much of what we think, feel, and do arises from what neuroscientists call a "carefully controlled hallucination." I recall a friend who began to feel ill a few days after spending time with an acquaintance who had COVID-19. She kept attributing her budding illness to a sunburn until tests showed otherwise. Reluctant to let go of normalcy, she let her predictive mind take the upper hand. Minor hallucinations, such as the phantom buzz of a phone or the imagined smell of smoke, are simply times when expectations triumph over the senses. Such uncanny experiences are far more common than once thought. For half of people, they occur on average at least once a month. And while they are typically related to imagined threats, they are largely harmless. We can think of them as piquant little reminders of how often we unwittingly live in the shadow of our assumptions.

Since ancient times, it has been difficult for humans to relinquish the belief that they are clear-eyed creatures who see the world as it really is. Many early Greek philosophers assumed that visual errors were rare failures of a system that neatly captured snapshots of reality. One prominent theory of the time held that vision occurred when tiny replicas of an object flew into the eye. In his seven-volume *Book of Optics*, the eleventh-century Arab polymath Ibn al-Haytham dismissed such nonsense, presciently surmising from his seminal experiments that perception unfolds as the mind unconsciously elaborates on images created in the eye. Still, his nascent understanding of vision's frequent subjugation to the brain was lost to the West for seven hundred years, even as his discoveries of the workings of the eye earned him global acclaim.

Early Buddhist thinkers went further in exploring the implications of the subjectivity that colors the smallest acts of human sensing. Dharmakīrti, a leading seventh-century Indian philosopher, foresaw that even before we sense an object, our predictions condition our concept of the phenomenon in question. Bump into a colleague whom you haven't seen in a while, for example, and your expectations based on your past relations likely will shape your reaction to her. That kind of cognitive efficiency "radically distorts our experience of the world," often creating in Dharmakīrti's view a form of ignorance (*avidyā*), the scholar John Dunne explains. We wind up treating "things that are actually different—the person I met a year ago and the person I am seeing now—as if they were the same." Buddhist thinkers long have debated how to attain "reliable cognition," yet this tradition's greatest minds are optimistic too. Thought, they teach us, is a mutable stream of cognitive events that we can shape and enhance. We can with effort and practice see the world more clearly. Now neuroscience is helping to reveal how central uncertainty is to this awakening.

↵

Consider a "very happy war," a startling phrase, perhaps treasonous in 1939. Chances are this incongruity set off a flare of activity in your brain, a kind of cortical "huh?" dubbed the N400 brain wave for the number of milliseconds it appears post-oddity. As you galloped along reading these three short words one after another, your brain probably predicted that "very happy" would be followed by "news," "celebration," or "child." Instead, the final word "war" likely came as a bit of a blow to your mental models of what constitutes contentment or conflict. In an instant, your brain signaled what scientists call a *prediction error*, a gap between what you had expected and what your senses reported was on offer at that moment.

The brain doesn't just weave story-like predictions from experiences past and present. It simultaneously runs an astonishing series of reality checks on these tales. Along with computing probabilistic interpretations of raw sensory data, frontline processing regions compare whether our first readings on the world sync with our expectations. If your guesses prove correct, "then your neurons are already firing a pattern that matches incoming sense data," explains neuroscientist Lisa Feldman Barrett. "Your brain has efficiently prepared you to act." That's the moment when Silberschlag deftly pulls off the critical opening horn solo in Brahms's Piano Concerto no. 2, making the conductor's day. But when a prediction is off even by a bit, we arguably are even further ahead in life. For it is an "oops" moment and the recognition of this shortfall that starts us down the path to updating our now-insufficient internal models. Are there times when battles sadly bring joy? What could I do to get in better sync with the rest of the orchestra? Waking up to the world first demands puncturing our own treasured realities.

All kinds of prediction errors constantly ripple across the brain, creating a living registry of the ways that we trip up in reading the world. Two decades after meeting Mr. N, Dehaene began exposing people to expressions such as "very happy war" and "very angry party" to catch this brain work in action. Reading such phrases sparks strong N400 waves in people's brains; the strength of an N400 reflects the perceived "degree of absurdity" of an incongruity, he found. But then Dehaene dug deeper, showing participants the same phrases while hiding the incongruous words—"very happy"— behind circles of flickering shapes. Although people only consciously saw "war" or "party," the subliminal phrase set off an N400 wave nearly as strong as if they knowingly had read the entire expression.

The perceptive powers of the unconscious brain are limited, fleeting, yet impressive. Both above and below our conscious awareness, the expectant mind relentlessly keeps an eye on its failings. "You have to know about your own illusions," Dehaene tells me. We are seated in his bright airy office, where stacks of books are piled two dozen high and three replicas of the brain are displayed, including one of his own. The quarter-hour limit to our conversation is long gone. He warms to the topic that never ceases to fascinate him—the potential of the human mind.

The extraordinary work of signaling prediction error even continues into the night albeit in a minor key, Dehaene discovered. When his team played a series of varying tones to people who were fast asleep, their brains still faintly registered unexpected shifts in the patterns of sound. While sleep muted the P300 brain wave that is typically related to consciously hearing new sounds, another error signal called the "mismatch negativity" fired although less dramatically than when we are awake. Dehaene could see from brain recordings what the sleepers could not tell him: at rest, the senses are removed yet not cut off from unexpected changes in the environment. A partner turning over in bed or the distant swish of a car coming down a dark road likely will not disturb us. But what is most surprising or unfamiliar can break through the fog of sleep. At the sound of the baby's cry or a thunderclap, we startle awake, the call to wrestle with a *new* reality triumphing even over our physiological need for rest.

Psychologists long considered learning to be a process of associations built on repetition. Think of Ivan Pavlov, the early twentieth-century Russian-Soviet researcher who conditioned dogs to salivate at the sound of a bell rung before their dinner appeared. Their behavior was seen as a mere linking of a stimulus to a response, the forging of a connection. Growing evidence reveals, however, that it is the unexpected, not the rote and routine, that is the starting point to expanding our knowledge. If a false fire alarm suddenly rings during your first week on the job, a gap will emerge in your budding model of office life, bringing with it the opportunity to question and explore. How safe am I in this skyscraper? Where are the exits anyway? But if the alarm starts to ring a couple of times a week, you likely will ignore that sound, and there the lesson ends—until a new change in the environment occurs. This is why babies spend most of their time exploring objects that startle them and why they gain the most knowledge from the parts of their environment that violate their expectations. As Dehaene says, "No surprise, no learning."

Unlike some patients with brain injuries, Mr. N was aware of his condition. Unable at one point in his testing sessions with Dehaene to label a series of numerals odd or even, Mr. N became so upset that Dehaene had to stop the day's work prematurely. Still, while Mr. N may have been able to register prediction errors, he could not carry his guesswork forward. He was mired in a life where "5 + 7 = 19" was implausible yet impossible to verify. He was stuck forever where we begin to engage the world.

Words are spinning/leaving a faint trail majestic trail behind their meaning scarcely a meaning, wrote Tristan Tzara, a founder of the art movement Dadaism in his 1931 epic poem "Approximate Man." In this surrealist masterpiece, Tzara tells of a man journeying through a chaotic world struggling with the mysteries of his own thoughts. *Wild fragments of knowledge . . . Oh powers I have glimpsed only in rare flashes*. When I mention the poem to Dehaene, he asks me to send him a link to it when I get home. He is surprised and delighted by the literary connection to his work. After we gulp down a lunch of pizza, crème brûlée, and espresso, he bids me good-bye and races back to his research, ever eager to know more.

↱

The model is cracked. The blooming, buzzing confusion of life has asserted itself. Where do you look now? How do you grasp a *new* reality beyond your knowledge? Even by the light of day, the critical work of perception begins in a sense when we startle awake.

As people encounter a slice of life's instability, waves of stress hormones and chemicals flood their brains. The release of powerful neurotransmitters such as norepinephrine boosts neuronal receptivity to new data, primes various brain regions to share information, and fires up cognitive circuits that flexibly control our focus. Bursts of dopamine help prioritize data from the outside world by escalating transmissions of sensory data from the parietal cortex—the center of the "relevance network"—to higher-order frontal regions. Within milliseconds, the trip wire of a prediction error triggers the realization that the current program of action must be interrupted. It is time now to evoke the cognitive systems that we evolved to highlight the information most likely to be essential in a new situation. The brain is telling itself, "Hey, there's something to be learned here," says neuroscientist Joseph Kable. "Arousal is adaptive."

Imagine that there are two players on base and a couple of outs in the inning and your team is falling behind as you get ready to bat at the company softball game. Suddenly, a towering new pitcher who looks practically semipro takes the mound. This is not the at-bat that you had pictured. Should you keep your eye on the ball or look to your baffled coach for guidance? Advances in decoding vision, the crown jewel of the senses, reveal the intricate calculations that the brain constantly and almost instantly makes to decide *attentional priority*. In particular, specialist neurons at the side of the parietal cortex track and compute which objects or locations offer the most "information gain" over time. And day to day, what's new and surprising rises to the top of that list. By highlighting what's attention-worthy in the environment, the brain constructs an ever-shifting *priority map* that inspires where we will tend to look. The mind in effect is signaling that new information is available and that it's time to try to determine what it is. With Goliath on the mound, you start keeping a close eye on the ball.

A few racing heartbeats later, you find yourself one swing away from striking out. The mystery pitcher is unleashing not-in-this-league fancy throws. Tension is rising on the field. Your perceiving brain, however, has a new trick up its sleeve: amplifying your attention according to the situation's volatility.

In a groundbreaking series of studies, Columbia University neuroscientist Jacqueline Gottlieb set up a little ball game of her own. In the experiments, two monkeys could earn sips of juice by indicating with their gaze whether a cluster of dots on a screen had just moved up or down. For minutes at a time, the dots would move in only one direction, then for a while their trajectory would vary trial after trial. When the task started to become more unpredictable, neurons in the animals' parietal cortexes began to fire intensely even *before* they looked at the dots. Their alert minds were noting the situation's uncertainty, and when that occurred, they grew more persistent and accurate. Something's to be learned here, the brain is telling itself, and it's all the more important to focus *now*. "Uncertainty is another kind of knowledge," says Gottlieb, whose findings are echoed in human behavior as well. She calls this critical work of selecting and amplifying important information *focused arousal*.

How can we begin to harness these innate capacities for wakefulness, focus, and discernment? Just being willing to expect change makes us more alert to shifts in the fabric of life, studies show. By presuming that the Monday morning meeting will be more of the same blah-blah, you may be missing subtle shifts in a rival's opinion or a critical dip in your team's mood. Clinging to the belief that a situation is stable when it is *not* "licenses you to say, 'I will ignore that new data,'" says Kable, a leader in computational studies of learning in dynamic environments. Britain's complacency about submarine weaponry between the world wars is a case in point. At the same time, it's important to recognize that rising to the occasion of topsy-turvy times is discomfiting; arousal isn't easy street. "You want to be *most* stressed by the *most* unpredictable situations," says Yale neuroscientist Robb Rutledge.

In 2016, Rutledge and his colleagues dissected the neural anatomy of skilled vigilance with an unnerving game. They showed digital photos of rocks of different sizes and hues to adults and asked them to guess one by one whether a snake would be hiding underneath. If someone guessed correctly, they won a bit of cash. But there was a catch: if a snake had been lurking there, the player would get a mild shock even if they had foretold the outcome. In this way, the scientists could tease apart the stress of the game's rising and falling levels of uncertainty from the pressure to play well.

Over time, the players began to pick up on their prediction errors and learn the ins and outs of the game. They might notice, for example, that big speckled rocks spell trouble, while small gray boulders don't "bite." Yet they still had to stay on their toes: without warning, suddenly the rules would switch, and a once-harmless stone would begin to expose a snake as often as not or more. These times of heightened uncertainty were stressful to players, as shown by their sweaty skin, dilated pupils, and higher cortisol levels. In fact, people were more stressed when they didn't know what was in store for them than when they pretty much could tell that a shock was imminent, a finding trumpeted by many a news article. "We're hardwired to hate uncertainty," ran one headline.

Another more subtle lesson emerged, however, from the hidden serpents game. Those whose stress levels were most closely calibrated to the game's fluctuating unpredictability made the most accurate predictions. In essence, the best players were marvelously in sync with the unexpected, as illustrated by their rising and falling stress. Humans as a species are highly sensitive to the vagaries of life. Error signals such as the N400 register the very degree of discrepancy between our expectations and reality. In addition, the neurotransmitter acetylcholine is released when we experience routine uncertainty, such as a glitch in the morning commute, while big-gun norepinephrine is unleashed in the face of unexpected changes, such as a surprise six-month road closure or a rule shift in a tricky game. What set apart the elite players in the snake game from the mere mediocre was that they leaned into the arousal that kept them on their toes. We can see in their sweat and in their success a willingness, even an eagerness, to step up their game during the critical moments when the world invited them to learn. Norepinephrine also is a barometer of cognitive effort, studies show. Arousal is a marker of how much we strive to open our eyes to the world.

"We are not simply *homo sapiens* but *homo docens*, the species that teaches itself," marvels Dehaene. The arousal sparked by surprise inspires the wakefulness that we need to actively interrogate our environment. What clues will help me drive home this softball pitch? What made this project fail and the last one succeed? Without perceptual systems to flag mistaken assumptions, to focus the mind on what is attention-worthy, and to stay in tune with the level of unpredictability we face *now*, humans would be dangerously out of step with a dynamic world. With expectations broken and minds startled awake, we are on our way to grasping a new reality. We are information seekers.

⬆

Yet if wakeful learning is, in Dehaene's words, the "singular talent of our species," why do we waste time pursuing information that is apparently useless, trivial, or off track? We have remarkable cognitive systems for tuning into life's surprises and for prioritizing the sweep of our focus. Why then gravitate to the informational detour, an aimless surf of the Web, a bit of trivia or gossip? In laboratory settings, for example, humans routinely give up hefty chunks of experimental earnings just to learn a squib of information that carries no immediate benefit. There are limits to this inquisitiveness and individual differences too. But overall people want the advance scoop, actually *any* scoop, even when they believe that the information won't do them a bit of good, an attitude long branded as suboptimal by economists, evolutionary theorists, and scholars of decision making.

According to the tenets of both natural selection and modern rationality, organisms and even societies should prioritize a "laser-like focus on knowledge with immediate utility," observe leading economist George Loewenstein and colleagues. By this light, only choices that reap direct, tangible benefits, that is, the most bang for the buck, are rational. Wanting a stock tip that's guaranteed to be profitable makes sense. But getting the early word on the results of a chancy gamble that we cannot control? That should be a pass. Good cognition long has been assumed to be "strictly a means to material ends," writes Loewenstein, one of the first to consider the psychology of economics. Yet is our seemingly indiscriminate hunger for information an obstacle to overcome or instead an unexpected strength of the perceiving mind? That was the riddle that the neuroscientist Ethan Bromberg-Martin began trying to crack not long ago.

To probe this fundamental question, he turned to the brain's most famous court of worth and value: the dopamine network. In some of his studies, monkeys repeatedly had opted to find out about an upcoming gain or loss in gambling games whose outcome they could not control. And at that moment, their midbrain neurons that release the neurotransmitter dopamine had fired furiously. Why? This molecule is popularly equated with pure pleasure, yet its true work is more complex. In both humans and their primate relations, dopamine circuitry continually assesses whether something is *relatively* better or worse than expected via its own systems of prediction error. If you buy a slice of cake and discover that it is sweeter than you had anticipated, a "positive reward prediction error"—read: happy surprise—will inspire you to trot back to that bakery another day. And these same neural structures process not just sweets and paychecks but also information, Bromberg-Martin's studies show. By signaling information prediction errors, dopamine neurons prioritize opportunities to get data. For the cake lover, word of a new bakery in town becomes a treat in the mind's eye too.

Information—any information—is so critical to our survival that a range of brain regions sounds a steady drumbeat favoring its pursuit. In a 2015 experiment, another two monkeys opted repeatedly for advance word on a gamble with a flick of their eyes. This time, Bromberg-Martin and colleagues tracked activity in a cluster of neurons in the orbitofrontal cortex, an area just above the eyes that is involved in learning and reward processing. Neurons in that region fired more or less actively, depending on the size of the pending reward. But some orbitofrontal cortex neurons used a separate neural code to tag as valuable the mere anticipation of new information.

Ultimately, higher-order brain regions will take into overall consideration both the worth of a reward and the value of the information we have in hand. *Is it worth leaving work a little early to get to the bakery in time?* We are born, after all, to pursue whatever furthers our survival, that is, food, money, friendship, and all else that scientists call rewards. But early on in the process of information seeking, the brain treats a nugget of new data— or simply the anticipation of one—not just as a means to an end but also as something worthy in itself. In essence, the brain seems to wield multiple neural languages for valuing information seeking *before* we can know its ultimate merit or utility. "Evolution has endowed us with a sort of innate sense that in almost every situation, we can do better if we first know more," Bromberg-Martin tells me excitedly. After all, he notes, the utility of a bit of data often is not apparent at a glance. "What can you immediately know when you enter an environment? Often very little."

This is how babies explore: strategically yet without knowing the ultimate worth of their play. And it is a capacity that remains within us all, helping us, in Loewenstein's words, to "balance the immediate benefits of satisfying tangible wants against the delayed benefits of investing in knowledge." Without this deep yearning to essentially take a chance on not-knowing, we would not pursue a liberal arts education, toil a year on a thorny problem, or create great art for little pay. It took many a monkey gamble and hundreds of hours in the lab, but Bromberg-Martin had the germ of an answer: a hunger for the seemingly useless is not a cognitive glitch but a remarkable gift.

In his enthusiasm for decoding the mysteries of perception, Bromberg-Martin speaks at an incandescent clip. He has a gee-whiz demeanor but is known as a brilliant, creative scientist whose work is influential in the field. His research unfolds on a precise molecular scale, yet he nonetheless endeavors to see the larger implications of his work. "I believe that learning about the world is not simply a passive process of parameter estimation and error-reduction, but an active delight of exploration and discovery," he writes on his website.

And that's just what his research is showing. "We're exactly the sort of creature who ought to have systems to figure out not just the value of things that we know but to value the exploration of the unknown, even if that seems useless at the moment," explains Bromberg-Martin. In essence, our innate inquisitiveness means that we do not just yearn for information in the wake of the unexpected; we are born with a capacity to *pursue* surprise itself. "Seeking information is like bringing prediction error [into play] earlier," says Bromberg-Martin. "You could think of it as seeking out prediction error."

⬇

Life's surprises invite us to pay attention, to tune into a charged situation, as stressful as that might be, and *then* to probe the world around us generously and patiently for a time. But too often, we derail these wondrous capacities to wake up to a chancy, mutable world by keeping a myopic focus on outcome. Naturally, it is essential to search for the juiciest fruit and to work hard for that raise. The pursuit of reward spurs people to do their best. Yet tunnel-vision attention to what is at stake down the line—the hoped-for trophy, the top grade, the specter of failure—can paradoxically impair ongoing performance, a wealth of research attests. By being too entranced with reward, we wind up retreating from the teachings of uncertainty.

In one experiment, people lying in brain scanners earned small or large sums by capturing a little gray circle darting about an online maze. In rounds worth just one dollar, people snagged the prey on average 75 percent of the time. But in trials offering a hefty ten dollars, they succeeded less than two-thirds of the time and more often lost ground just when they were achingly close to the target. Even more intriguingly, those who later reported wanting the money more did worse on the lucrative trials and showed high activity in brain regions related to assessing rewards. They got caught up in chasing the golden ring. The study was titled "Choking on the Money."

Some people underperform in demanding situations by succumbing to paralysis by analysis, a crippling focus on the rules of the game or on their technique. Others are prone to anxiety. But significant numbers of poor test takers, athletes who choke, and performers felled by stage fright suffer from a phenomenon that scientists call *reward-driven distraction*. Mesmerized by the stakes of the situation, people become trapped in the cage of their own expectations and tune out of the play, sometimes literally suffering blind spots in their attention as they perform, studies show. Just when they need to be on their toes and attuned to the world, they grow disengaged from the dynamic situation at hand. They refuse to not-know.

When the trophy in a lucrative, high-profile professional tennis tournament is displayed prominently near the court during the finals, for example, the favorite is far more likely to underperform, a data analysis of more than one hundred matches shows. In such situations, the better players do not lose the match more often, yet they tend to perform no better on rallies than their underdog competitors, and they win a smaller proportion of total points scored. They struggle.

What then helps to loosen the chokehold that an overfocus on outcome can have on us? Some of the most promising routes to combating this kind of performance anxiety entail back-burnering the specter of "utility" and fully tuning in to the work at hand. Today, athletes from high schoolers to professionals are trained to use brief personalized mental prompts known as "cue words" to nudge their attention from the future consequences of their play back to the twists and turns of the game. For example, a competitor might quietly tell herself mid-game to "focus on every play." A similar practice involves giving a deliberate look called the "quiet eye" to important elements in the scene in order to reorient yourself to the current moment.

Such techniques protect you from letting your expectations about an outcome eclipse the demands of the moment. But perhaps the most promising way to reawaken to the world is to make peace with the arousal that goes hand in hand with wakeful discernment.

Imagine being asked to give a five-minute talk before a trio of people clad in white coats who are evaluating you for a job. You are told to speak about your strengths and weaknesses, and have just ten minutes to prepare. As you wade in, the judges jot down notes and stare at you without so much as a hint of a smile. Then, when your shaken self is done, they sock you with a pop quiz: count backward from the number 996 in increments of seven. This is the infamous Trier test, psychology's gold standard for inducing and assessing acute stress. At stake in the unnerving experience is not prize money, a trophy, or even a real job but something equally critical: social dignity. The scenario may be fake, but your sweaty palms and the butterflies in your gut are all too real. "People don't realize how long five minutes is," says Jeremy Jamieson, a social psychologist who studies stress in body and mind. The occasion delivers one prediction error after another. Tuning out is a surefire way to flop.

In 2010, Jamieson and colleagues began developing a lifeline for Trier test takers and other daunted performers. After years of experimenting, they discovered a brief, powerful prompt: see stress not as something to fear but as the body's way of revving up for a demanding situation. People who are taught in mere minutes that arousal is a resource for both body and mind become no less stressed by a challenge, Jamieson's research shows. Instead, they become revved up, not defeated, by tricky situations.

Recall how norepinephrine can prime the brain to learn. Its release in the wake of surprise makes our hearts beat faster and our blood vessels dilate as oxygen is shuttled to major muscles and to the brain. The mind is going into *approach mode* and effectively telling itself, "We can do this!" says Jamieson. We can begin to sense the world anew. In contrast, when we fear the uncertain or the new, a different stress chemistry unfolds. Blood flow is constricted and is channeled toward the body's core and away from peripheral regions, including the brain. Threat is top of mind, and survival, not optimal performance, is the goal. Both body and mind start shutting off the world.

People who learn to reappraise stress as natural and useful are more perceptive and effective in challenging situations, a decade of research in the lab and in the wild shows. They tend to be less overwhelmed by predicaments ranging from a tough math class or a graduate school admissions exam to an impromptu speech before a stern audience. Liberated from distress yet still energized, they become more invested in the task at hand. "They actually do not worry about the evaluation," Jamieson told me.

Those taught the technique before undergoing a videotaped Trier test, for example, later are rated by independent analysts as less anxious and more engaged with the situation than those who receive no such briefing. They have a more open posture and make more eye contact with the judges. They are fully present to the moment and to its surprises; perhaps they begin to notice a subtle hint of interest, for example, by an initially stern judge. It's not uncommon for people to botch the test. Sometimes they simply fall silent after a couple of minutes. In contrast, those who see arousal as adaptive tend to ace the speech. Says Jamieson, "If it was a real job interview, they would have nailed it."

The model is broken. We are being tested. Yet if we are willing, the disquieting surprise and uncertainty that follow can provoke us to become alert and focused and to honor the occasion of *not* knowing. The neurotransmitters norepinephrine, acetylcholine, and dopamine are the brain's own messengers, signaling that the time has come to awaken and orient ourselves to exploring a new reality. Adaptive arousal (aka the approach mode) helps us to tune into the challenge before us and so avoid the myopic focus on outcome that can derail our ability to perceive. Being fully attuned to the intricacies of the moment: isn't that in a sense what adaptive stress really is? There's something to be learned here, the brain is telling itself. Open your eyes, your heart, and your mind to the unknown. The challenge is daunting, yet this is exactly where hungry minds seek to be. Who are the discerning explorers of our day? We call them curious.

Both a state of mind and a personality trait, curiosity takes myriad forms. It ebbs and flows, rising after exercise and receding in times of psychological depression, studies by David Lydon-Staley, Danielle Bassett, and Perry Zurn show. It can be social, as in gossip, or a solitary kind of wonder. Sometimes people "frisk about and rove about" in the information sphere, hardly pausing on any one topic for long, the ancient Jewish thinker Philo of Alexandria observed. At other times, this bent takes the form of a bloodhound-like search for knowledge, with each promising trail pursued in turn. In one fascinating study, the researchers asked people to browse Wikipedia for a few minutes a day for three weeks. Using network analysis, they found that while people fall in and out of what Zurn and others call "busybody" and "hunter" styles each day, they tend to loosely favor one archetype over another.

But however curiosity is expressed, highly inquisitive people tend to share one quality: a willingness to tolerate the stress of the new and unexpected, studies show. Neuroscientists have yet to fully map the neural roots of curiosity, but early studies suggest that this state of mind dovetails with some of the same brain circuitry that fuels our hunger to seek information. Curious minds operate in approach mode.

"It's not that curious people never feel anxious, never feel wary," says Paul Silvia, a pioneer in the modern study of curiosity. "They try a lot of things, and they do feel uncomfortable doing so. It does feel awkward, but that's not stopping them from doing it." Highly curious people are drawn to difficult books, unusual movies, new experiences of all kinds, and evidence that conflicts with their point of view. They refuse to let the effort and unease inherent in exploring the unknown keep them from discovering its treasures. "That's a gem of an idea," Silvia tells me.

As he speaks, I recall how the best players in the serpents game synced their sweat equity with times of peak unpredictability. I thought of the Trier test takers who saw their stress as a resource and so attuned to the challenge, even as their hearts beat faster and the judges glowered. They all eventually scored victories, but even more important, they attained a kind of wakefulness that is its own reward.

Being consistently inquisitive is linked to higher satisfaction with life and to experiencing more pleasurable and meaningful moments each day. Curious people tend to be playful, unreserved, often unconventional thinkers who handle uncertainty well, according to their friends, family, and psychological assessments. They even visually explore the world around them more broadly, a style of gaze that scientists call "curious eyes."

It may seem surprising that those who are drawn to stressful challenges tend to take such delight in living. But it is precisely the capacity to open up to *all* of life, as disquieting as that may be, that buoys the body and mind. Stress tolerance is the facet of the curious disposition that is most linked to overall well-being. Those who lack this capacity might recognize gaps in their knowledge "but are unlikely to step forward and explore," notes curiosity researcher Todd Kashdan. By treating broken expectations as chances to investigate possibilities within the dynamic *now*, curious people free themselves of the entrancement with outcome that hobbles our capacities for discernment. They trade paralyzing angst for engagement and wonder. This is how we can turn life itself into a time of active discovery.

↩

Tapping into the vitality of curiosity-driven approach mode is critical as well in our online lives, where shirking the discomfort of not-knowing is becoming increasingly easy to do. People rely on online information to make some of life's most critical decisions yet commonly stop searching after a first result appears. The crisp look and click-driven feel of the Web feeds humanity's innate craving for effortless knowing. Moreover, the results urged on us are ad driven and ranked according to their similarity with our query and our overall tastes, a process that minimizes surprise. "Web search engines are not designed for complex tasks that require exploration and learning . . . despite the fact that a quarter of Web searches are complex," concludes a report from twenty-six multidisciplinary search experts from around the world. Perhaps most alarmingly, as we turn to devices that seem omniscient, we grow confident that we too can know at a glance. "Through online search tools, the world is your information oyster," gushes Daniel Russell, senior scientist for search quality at Google, in his book *The Joy of Search*.

After even a brief online search, information seekers tend to think they know more than they actually do, according to a decade of studies. In one set of five experiments, people were asked to study weighty topics, such as autism or inflation, before taking a quiz on the subject. Half the participants were told to find an online article on the topic, while others were simply given the same information without having to search for it. People who searched online were far more overconfident going into the quiz. In one round, they predicted that, on average, they would get two-thirds of the questions right, although they scored less than 50 percent.

In contrast, people who had been given the information studied longer, absorbed more, and got about 60 percent of the questions right—about what they had expected. Rarely if ever in life are we just handed information.

Searching and seeking are the human condition. But how we do so matters. In the virtual realm, we seem to lose the ability to sense that we *don't* know, the starting point of discernment. This false confidence blossoms even when people learn *nothing* from an online search, further studies show. By assuming that we can know effortlessly, we close our eyes to our failings and so to chances to explore. We run from the work of fully attuning to the here and now, finding in hubris a retreat from the challenges of facing up to reality as potent as that of outcome-oriented fear.

Yet once again, the wisdom of the sages can be heeded. Enhancing awareness is possible if we invite the provocation of uncertainty into our interactions with the world, whether we are playing a match, giving a talk, or searching online. In an intriguing effort to repair alarmingly low levels of digital literacy and counter rampant misinformation, a growing number of educators, psychologists, software designers, and data scientists are re-envisioning online search as far more than a quick netting of information. The "Search as Learning" movement is rethinking ranking systems, testing new looks for the Web, and launching studies that for the first time reveal the habits of the most discerning online information seekers. Those who can find what matters do not shy from or even simply tolerate the provocation of surprise. They remind themselves, says literacy scholar Sarah McGrew, that "our eyes deceive us." They seek out the teaching signal of prediction error.

As a graduate student at Stanford University in 2017, McGrew tested a few dozen people on a roster of tricky online challenges, such as determining the credibility of a duplicitous site or uncovering the covert funding for a controversial lawsuit. These were no ordinary Web users but rather an impressive group of top fact-checkers, history professors at four-year universities, and undergraduates from McGrew's own highly selective school. In one task, participants read articles about child bullying posted on the website of the world-renowned American Academy of Pediatrics and on the site of a splinter group called the American College of Pediatricians, which is hostile to gay people. Both sites featured fancy logos, academic citations, prestigious-looking credentials, and official-sounding language. Which group was the wolf in sheep's clothing? McGrew challenged.

Nearly all the students and most of the scholars spent the bulk of their time reading the initial Web page they had been given. Many briefly dipped into the rest of each organization's site, but only one student and two historians navigated to the wider Web. "I can automatically trust this source just because it looks official," reported one student. Said a historian, "I am looking at some of the footnotes, and they all seem like perfectly credible sources. I can trust this site." In the end, the elite students overwhelmingly chose the fringe group as more reliable, while a remarkable 40 percent of the professional historians rated the organizations as equally valid.

In contrast, the fact-checkers almost immediately set off from the pages containing the initial articles and headed into the unknown. They looked at multiple additional websites and scanned full pages of search results before clicking on a link as they sought to cross-check the two groups' assertions and their own initial assumptions. It was a demanding process, filled with pauses, backtracking, and skepticism. With curious eyes, they were seeking the deeper learning that can come only from a willingness to seek uncertainty. After exploring widely, one fact-checker began to recognize the college's veiled language of hate. "That's the kind of thing I never would have known had I just looked [at the first article]," he said. Taking a page from the language of physical navigation, McGrew calls this form of information seeking "taking bearings." By being fully present to the moment and its possibilities, every fact-checker was able to discern the valid entity.

In 2022, Google's Daniel Russell addressed students and faculty at the University of Maryland's College of Information Studies. For all his corporate boosterism, he was clearly concerned by the poor quality of modern information seeking. "Research allows you to see outside the ordinary," said Russell, a computer scientist with a white goatee and a bit of a swagger. "But we live in a time of a great debasement of the notion of research." Calling out common failings such as accepting first results as correct, he exhorted the students who would one day be librarians or his peers to be curious, to treat search as a "rolling evaluation," and to remember that the world is not made up of black-and-white dichotomies.

At the end of the talk, however, a department head kicked off the discussion with a question that he said many in the audience had been asking over chat. "Google is increasingly providing an answer," the professor ventured a bit sheepishly. "That seems to be kind of incongruous with what you're talking about, which is being engaged online." How does that play out? he asked. At first, Russell shifted uncomfortably, crossed his arms, and punted. "Increasingly Google *is* trying to provide an answer mostly because [our data show] people are looking for short answers," he said.

Then he paused and warmed to the challenge. "But if you're doing something critical, important, or more subtle, take the time to understand a little more context. . . . Understanding nuance is never a waste of time." Step up, he was saying, and invite yourself back into the game. Because, as he constantly warns in his talks and writings, search engines "don't signal that they lack the knowledge to give an answer." *The machine does not admit that it does not know.* Instead, search engines are built to "fall back" on simply offering another set of results. "But there's an important difference between *an* answer and a set of search results—one that's worth noticing," says Russell. Unless we honor the discomfiting work of *not*-knowing, we squander the potential of a perceptive mind.

As the frigid British winter of 1940 eased into spring, a "phony war" gave way to an increasingly bloody conflict. In the fall, a U-boat had snuck into the Home Fleet anchorage in Scotland and wrecked the elderly battleship HMS *Royal Oak*, killing more than eight hundred sailors. By March, German submarines had sunk two hundred Allied ships and narrowly missed another fifty. Belgium, Holland, Denmark, Norway, and France all would be occupied by June, giving U-boats a priceless string of coastal bases. Rationing of bacon, butter, and sugar began. Churchill, who had just returned to power, later admitted that the only thing that had really frightened him during the war was the U-boat peril. It "gnawed my bowels," he wrote.

At Bletchley Park, there were successes, including a break into the simpler Luftwaffe (air force) Enigma. But these codes were minnows compared with naval Enigma. So far, Turing's team had broken only five days of naval Enigma messages dating from 1938 and discovered little more than the code's depth of encryption. "You know, the Germans don't mean you to read their stuff," Bletchley Park's director Alastair Denniston told Turing's frustrated boss Frank Birch. "And I don't suppose you ever will." Turing, nicknamed "Prof," was becoming known for his eccentricities. He belted his pants with string and wore a gas mask to curb his hay fever as he bicycled through the countryside. Given to intense bouts of concentration, he sometimes pondered the intellectual implications of a conversation for days. At age twenty-seven, he was about to prove Denniston's pessimism and Germany's assumptions of invincibility to be much mistaken.

"The cryptographer, like all discoverers, must proceed from the known to the unknown," notes Christopher Morris, a Bletchley Park code breaker. In other words, predictive guesswork is the first weapon of decryption. Does an uptick in radio traffic signal the start of an invasion, or is it just a ruse? Could a repeated symbol be an "e," the most frequent letter in both German and English? In particular, British code breakers used likely words or phrases, such as place-names or standard greetings, as entry points into coded messages. This hunt for *cribs* was aided by Enigma's main weakness: its mirror-like symmetry, which meant that no letter could be encrypted as itself. If a code breaker saw the word "rvzxiq" in a German message, for example, she could tell that the crib "convoy" was at least possible since none of its letters matched the code word. "The popular view that scientists proceed inexorably from well-established fact to well-established fact . . . is quite mistaken," Turing once wrote. "Conjectures are of great importance since they suggest useful lines of research." It was in the power of the perceptual mind that Turing began to find his way into solving naval Enigma.

He had an inheritance: technical knowledge of a prewar Polish machine that had helped decode traffic from early versions of Enigma with some success. Essentially a series of linked replica Enigma machines, the Pole's ingenious device—dubbed the "Bomba"—painstakingly searched through reams of messages for patterns of repeated letters in the internal instructions used to set up the Nazi machines each day; such clues helped shine light on Enigma's settings.

Turing, however, met the far greater challenge of his day by devising a machine that assaulted the entire logic of Enigma via the weapon of conjecture, the crib. In encrypting a message, Enigma essentially created logical chains of connections, like hidden forest paths, between a message's initial plaintext and encoded letters. Turing's "Bombe" searched through millions of chains of encryption to find those that would be revealingly consistent or inconsistent with a code breaker's crib. With the help of mathematician Gordon Welchman, Turing devised a machine that essentially exploited a crib's implications and so vastly narrowed the code breakers' search space. Building on a lifelong fascination with the potential of both human and machine thought, he harnessed the golden moments when guesses hit home—or go wrong.

No perfectly decoded messages resulted. But from clever guesswork, ten miles of wiring, and a clickety-clackety din, a stream of solid leads appeared for the code breakers to investigate. The machine was not a computer per se. Nevertheless, by harnessing logic, statistics, and the idea of a mechanical instruction or algorithm, Turing created in the Bombe a forerunner to the modern search engine. He found a way to peer into the hidden workings of the Third Reich with a device that in time would become one of our foremost windows on the world.

Yet Turing presciently knew what we may be just beginning to admit: automated machines from the Bombe on through the computer are no more omniscient than humans are. "Computing machines aren't really infallible at all," he said after the war. And if we take their data at face value, we slip into the fallacy that we can know at a glance. We fall into the trap—as Turing said philosophers and mathematicians are prone to do—of assuming that "there is no virtue in the mere working out of consequences from data." So it is fitting that our machines, like life itself, continually should surprise us, he said. *Their data, like our imperfect assumptions, are simply invitations to learn*. Said Turing, "Machines take me by surprise with great frequency."

The first Bombe broke down frequently, leaked rivulets of oil, and took days to offer up paths into Enigma. Its rocky birth was accompanied by Bletchley Park's own growing pains. To infiltrate Enigma's changing settings day after day, an entire system of intelligence had to be built up: cribs guessed or stolen, messages intercepted and interpreted, and military skeptics won over by an eclectic band of intellectuals far from the battlefront. Still, Turing's visionary work on Enigma and the innovations of his colleagues slowly helped to save convoys, shape strategy, and shift the course of the Battle of the Atlantic and so the war. (If Turing had not broken the U-boat code, the war's final stages could have been delayed by months or years at the potential cost of millions of lives, historian B. Jack Copeland argues.) The Nazi command, meanwhile, blamed their rising losses on treason, spies, improved Allied radar, one-off captures of bits of Enigma, and chance while retaining a steely belief in naval Enigma's invulnerability. Admiral Ludwig Stummel, head of German navy communications, wrote in a 1944 internal investigation that there was no "special evidence of insufficient security" in Enigma.

The victory over Enigma could have been engineered only by a mind with a remarkable hunger to perceive the world. Turing was not interested in seeking titles or even trying to make a name for himself. He was "impatient of pompousness and officialdom of any kind," wrote a Bletchley Park colleague. Instead, he was driven by the thrill of the intellectual chase, by heart-pounding investigations of hidden new realities. Awkward, nervous, and boyishly eager, Turing lived in approach mode whether he was tackling the heights of pure mathematics or building electrical circuits for a multiplier, a kind of calculator that he designed for an experimental prewar encryption machine. "I see! I see!" he would say with delight when a Bletchley Park code breaker brought him a tantalizing new revelation.

But most of all, it was his ability to question what is assumed that secures him a place on the world stage, according to biographer Andrew Hodges. Turing tackled some of the most intractable problems of our time with utter freedom of mind. He did not get caught up with failed attacks on the decision problem but instead forged his own maverick way into the question. After the war, he ingeniously drew on physics, chemistry, and his own close observations of wildflowers, pine cones, starfish, and other natural phenomena to crack open one of biology's greatest mysteries: how complex patterns and forms, such as a zebra's stripes, emerge from homogeneous embryonic cells. From this seminal work, the new field of mathematical biology and decades of scientific revelations were born.

Turing could see what was important and what was not because he did not injudiciously dismiss anything as obvious. "Processes that are learnt do not produce a hundred percent certainty of result; if they did they could not be unlearnt," wrote Turing, who died at the age of forty-one, two years after being persecuted by the government for being gay. His close friend Lyn Newman observed that Turing's bright, richly blue eyes held such "candour and comprehension . . . that one hardly dared to breathe." Writes Hodges, Turing saw the world with "strangely fresh eyes."

Prediction errors constantly ripple through the brain, tagging and assessing the gaps between what we know and what experience is endeavoring to teach us. What's most unexpected carries the shock of surprise, the mind's own signal that the time has come to pay attention to the here and now. An intricate neural chemistry of arousal then readies us to explore the contours of a new reality. For at least a time, the brain is primed to seek information generously and patiently, often before judging its ultimate worth. *Something's to be learned here*, a voice within us sounds. The racing of your heart, the quiver in your gut, the growing unease you may feel at this moment are simply signs that you can rise to the occasion, that your curious eyes can open, that with trepidation and even glee, you can head into the unknown. Turing's brilliance underscores what a new understanding of the mind attests: attuning fully to the mysteries before you is a kind of honesty.

PART II

BYWAYS OF THE MIND

CHAPTER THREE

WHY FORGETTING IS NOT A LOSS

*Not knowing is a permissive and rigorous willingness to [leave]
knowing in suspension, trusting in possibility without result.*
—ANN HAMILTON

Late one night in a world-renowned sleep laboratory, a young scientist waits impatiently. It is ghostly quiet in the lab set up in a converted wing of a Boston hospital where fluorescent lights cast an eerie glow down deserted hallways. "She's going in and out," Nam Nguyen says softly to me, his eyes on a flickering EEG monitor. "Oooh, almost ..." Through the one-way glass of the booth where he and I sit, I can just make out the restless form of a college student, her head swathed in electrodes, tossing and turning in bed in the murky dark of the room next door. Nguyen is watching for the alpha waves of her wakeful mind to ebb into the slow, rhythmic theta and bodily stillness that mark our initial descent into sleep. "She's slipping back and forth," he whispers as rapid-fire electromagnetic tracings on his screen flatten into languid squiggles and back again. "Okay, okay, so close."

Yet the dawn of Katie's elusive sleep is not Nguyen's ultimate quarry. Earlier, she had changed into her own T-shirt and Dr Pepper pajama pants, answered a battery of questions (*How well did you sleep two nights ago? How sleepy are you now?*), and sat texting as Nguyen attached electrodes to her eyelids, chin, and forehead and the bones behind her ears. Then she climbed into bed and set off with console in hand to play a video game in which she had to shoot green-eyed monsters lurking around the stone corridors of a virtual maze. Crashing and burning time and again, Katie at first failed to reach what Nguyen calls the "butter zone" of an under ten-minute escape from the maze before she warmed to eight- and then seven-minute scores. Over the next several hours, he repeatedly will awaken her just as she falls asleep to ask via two-way radio what she is thinking, seeing, and dreaming. Will a nascent memory of the game begin to form at a time long assumed to be nearly barren of cognition?

Nguyen's mentor, the eminent scientist behind the night's experiment, has spent his career pursuing the mysteries of the mind at rest. After studying biochemistry and working briefly in software, Robert Stickgold began to research sleep in an era when it just was beginning to be seen as something more than "diffuse cortical inhibition," a nightly cognitive shutdown. Hints of the mind's nocturnal activity were revealed in 1953 when a graduate student stumbled on rapid-eye movement (REM) sleep as a late-night font of dreaming. Decades later, groundbreaking research showed that learning could improve during these hours before dawn, which make up just a quarter of sleep. But for decades, most of sleep remained a scientific riddle and a research backwater, a state assumed to be hardly essential for cultivating the wisdom of the mind.

Then in the late 1990s, Stickgold and his colleagues discovered cognitive treasure in cycles of non-REM that begin early in the night and make up the lion's share of sleep. These are the night's slow hours, when giant wave-like oscillations traverse the brain, quieting and synchronizing the mind, their rhythms interspersed with frenetic "ripples" and "spindles" of activity. Early on in these cycles, we dream in fragments with snatches of the day floating before our eyes. Stickgold's epiphany came one night as he closed his eyes after a morning of rock climbing in Vermont. Suddenly, he felt as though he was scrambling back up the mountain, feeling the boulders under his hands, reliving the challenge from his bed. "I startled awake," he recalled and said to himself, "whoa, that's telling us something." He had glimpsed his mind constructing new knowledge at a time of stillness, silence, and suspense.

Stickgold famously validated sleep's essential role in memory making in 1999 with his first controlled dream incubation, using the computer game Tetris. After seven hours of play over three days, most newcomers to the puzzle game and half of experienced players drifted off to sleep dreaming of

Tetris. Intriguingly, almost all of the players' visions of the game began only on their second night in the lab. But it was his third group of participants that stunned Stickgold. As part of the experiment, five severely amnesic patients put in the same daily sessions of play. And even though they all had to be retaught the game each day, a majority saw Tetris-like puzzle pieces dancing before their eyes as they fell sleep. Rest and the hand of time had done what the day could not: inspire forgetful minds to begin digesting and preserving a new experience.

The morning after my visit to the sleep lab, I report in to Stickgold at his offices at the hospital. He is a slight man with receding white hair, a pale face, and a seemingly mischievous, scientifically unfashionable tendency to reference Freud. He listens intently as I recount Katie's eclectic cache of dream fragments, most involving her childhood. "I was remembering the time I was little," she had mumbled after midnight, "and my grandma and mom and sister were watching *Titanic* and I wasn't allowed, so I snuck out and watched from the hallway." In other dreams, she was in her family dining room, on the street outside a friend's house, in high school class-rooms, or in an auditorium just before a choir concert. I was disappointed. No monsters or mazes seemed to invade her thoughts. But Stickgold is immediately interested. "These are the kind you'd put an asterisk next to," he tells me.

Katie's shadow worlds were often cramped and dark, with a reigning mood of expectancy. More than once, she gazed down or stood in hallways, seemingly scanning for exits. These were not the disjointed musings of a homesick student but signs of the mental metamorphosis that Stickgold has studied for decades. Minutes into rest, thoughts of the day loosen and shift. A maze game prompts thoughts of getting lost in a dark cave. A virtual corridor evokes a childhood hallway. In the dark of night, the mind is weaving together past and present, weighing relevance and resonance, embarking on the critical work that Stickgold calls "memory evolution."

There is something far larger than a dream at stake when we turn down the volume of life. During sleep, rest, or a pause, parts of the mind be-yond our ken reach out to parse experience and so strengthen the troves of knowledge that equip us to face the future. Bleary-eyed and intrigued, I stood that morning at the edge of the fallow hour, the time when we un-cover the overlooked clues and unseen inferences of life. Yet this paradox of productivity is not the end of the story. Building knowledge demands both quiet time *and* cultivation. To retrieve a memory of a fact or an event, we often must struggle to search for what's fading and forgotten. Yet this discomfiting effort itself, *even if futile*, further strengthens the branching connections of our networked knowledge.

The spark of uncertainty equips the mind to tackle a crisis with expanded options and to awaken to our continual misreadings of the world. But the wisdom of not-knowing can equally occur when we make time for seemingly doing "nothing" at all. By stepping back from the onslaught of the day and relinquishing expectations of an instant answer, we can find brilliance in delay and in suspense. By letting our understanding percolate and working to catch up with its evolution, we learn firsthand that knowledge is not the bedrock that we assume but rather a living realm of vibrant change. How does lingering in the space of uncertainty rescue us from the cruel prison of shallow understanding? Why bother to tangle with the fickle work of remembering in an age of downloadable knowing? The revelations of the fallow hour begin with a boy, a tumble, and the accidental discovery of the origins of memory. His name was Henry, but in the annals of science, he will always be known as "H.M." He was neuroscience's most famous muse.

⌄

In 1933, seven-year-old Henry Molaison briefly lost consciousness after being knocked down by a bicyclist. At age ten, he started having epileptic seizures that burgeoned in severity and frequency, often leaving him in a stupor. By twenty-seven, he could no longer hold down an assembly-line job. So Hartford, Connecticut, surgeon William Scoville proposed a "frankly experimental operation," a largely untried version of the procedures used to treat severe mental illness during the short-lived heyday of psychosurgery. Lobotomies, the extraction of the frontal lobes, were undertaken to tame schizophrenia yet often made patients docile and lethargic. Scoville hoped that by excising a neighboring brain region thought to be linked to seizures, he could subdue Molaison's epilepsy but not his mind.

When Molaison woke up in the hospital on September 1, 1953, he chatted with family and staff. His major seizures would diminish from near weekly to once every two or so years. But to his doctors' shock, the operation produced a "striking and totally unexpected behavioral result:

a grave loss of recent memory," Scoville and psychologist Brenda Milner wrote in the first case study of Molaison. The patient could keep up with a conversation, get the punch line of a joke, and hold a number briefly in mind, yet he "forgot daily events nearly as fast as they occurred," wrote another memory researcher. Quiet and intelligent, he apologized again and again for forgetting people's names. Shortly after a meal, he could not recall having eaten. "Every day is alone in itself, whatever enjoyment I've had, and whatever sorrow I've had," he once told Milner. "It is like waking from a dream."

At the time, memory was believed to be a facet of perception or intelligence, not a separate capability rooted in a particular seat or mechanism of the mind. When Scoville excised H.M.'s hippocampus, he unwittingly revealed this small seahorse-shaped region deep in the brain as central to the making of memories. Yet the surprises of the case, the first scientific study of an amnesic, had only begun.

Unlike frantic amnesic movie characters whose identities are entirely erased, Molaison could remember a high school love, his teenage jobs, and how to mow a lawn or put together a jigsaw puzzle. H.M. had retained his deep past. The hippocampus therefore could not be memory's final resting place, the ultimate storehouse of experience. Nevertheless, H.M. had little to no recollection of events ranging from a few hours to nearly a dozen years before the operation. He could not recall meeting Scoville just before the surgery. He had completely forgotten that a favorite uncle had died in 1950. The black hole of his amnesia had a surprisingly long reach.

Others stripped of their hippocampi and nearby brain regions also showed this strange bifurcation. Like H.M., such patients typically could not make fresh memories or recall recent events, even though they often remembered long-held skills and knowledge. Their surgeries seem to have interrupted "some secondary process, . . . the transition to long-term storage of information," Milner and colleagues presciently surmised in 1968. What are the slow forces that turn new knowledge—a maze, a death, an operation—into ours to keep and hold? In 1991, a young scientist discovered the opening song of the fallow hour in a small animal that like all living creatures depends on memory to survive.

Picture a brain cell. Its pyramid-shaped body sprouts a branching "tree" of dendrites at one end and a long pole-shaped axon with whisker-like terminals at the other. These feathery protrusions respectively receive and send electrical and chemical signals across the junctions called synapses separating one neuron from another. Cellular communications are essentially threshold based; brain activity arises from trends in the synaptic activity of ensembles of neurons. As a result, no single neuron, however specialized, can tell the story of a long-ago madeleine dipped in tea, the boyhood fall that changed memory science, or the triumphal route through a maze by a girl or a rat. A thought is a pattern of neuronal activation. And memory is the strengthening of the ties that bind cells and make one thought more lasting than another. These were the connections that postdoc Matt Wilson was trying to capture when he left a rat's brain hooked to recording equipment after it had ended its day's work in a maze.

Wilson had just sat down at his workbench at the University of Arizona to analyze a trove of data when he heard a familiar tune: neural firing patterns that sounded like a rat navigating a maze. But what caught his attention was the fact that the animal was asleep. The hippocampal neurons called place cells that register an animal's location were retracing the rat's earlier steps. Scientists previously had recorded bursts of nocturnal activity in the same hippocampal cells yet could not discern whether these flares of thought were coherent or why they occurred when an animal was immobile. By leaving the microphone on, Wilson discovered *replay*, the mind's reliving of the day's key fragments to strengthen a nascent memory.

If replay is interrupted, rats with intact hippocampi begin to act like tiny H.M.s, unable to recall their last meal. In one study, rats were allowed to traverse an eight-armed radial maze multiple times a day, with treats planted in the same three spokes each time. The rats that slept afterward performed better than chance on the task after five days of practice. Those whose replay was silenced by electrical stimulation for an hour at night were still guessing wildly after a week. In particular, they were woefully indecisive at the first turns, just as H.M. proved to be when tested in a tabletop touch maze.

In time, the mysteries of these mental rehearsals began to be teased out in both four- and two-legged animals. Early proof in humans emerged without imaging or electrodes when a French-Swiss team filmed sleepwalkers, who sometimes act out their dreams. Trained during the day to push sequences of colored buttons, many of the sleepwalkers' motions at night echoed the task, sometimes uncannily so. The next day, all improved on the work. Scaling the mountain as he drifted off to sleep, Stickgold in essence was mentally practicing a situation that he might encounter in life again. The greater the magnitude of hippocampal reactivation during replay, the better we remember the relived task. And remarkably, replay unfolds as well in still moments of wake.

Ears now attuned to the reverberations of a nascent memory, scientists soon discovered replay in rats that were simply pausing, often at a crossroads in a new maze. Interrupt these silent rehearsals, run at seven to twenty times faster than life, and the rats' new-won understanding of the labyrinth is lost. Echoed in humans, the findings inspired scientists for the first time to consider a key player in memory making beyond active wake and sleep. A darkened room, a moment of stillness: just a few minutes of rest dramatically boosts memory for new knowledge.

In one pioneering set of experiments, scientists exposed healthy older adults and Alzheimer's patients with amnesia to two short passages of prose, followed by a ten-minute rest for some participants and a brief on-line computer game for others. Tested a week later, amnesic people who had rested recalled more than one-third of the stories, profiting slightly more from quiet time than even their healthy peers. In contrast, a majority of the patients who had played the computer game remembered little or nothing of the prose after a week despite strenuous prompting. Young and older healthy adults also benefit from a bit of rest after learning. People who pause quietly for as little as six minutes after learning new vocabulary, stories, or a virtual maze can remember roughly one-fifth more than those who turned straight to a new task, a decade of research led by Edinburgh University's Sergio Della Sala has shown. The initial experiments, done in Italy, were so stunning that he flew there to confirm the news.

Memory making seems to be opportunistic, a process springing vibrantly to life in downtime, scientists note. We might run through memories across the day either deliberately or when an experience or word prompts a bit of the past to surface in mind. Yet scientists now believe that fallow time especially seems to provide the protective quiet necessary for the brain to begin processing and stabilizing fragile traces of new experience. In both times of momentary stillness and non-REM sleep, there is a steep drop in the neurotransmitter acetylcholine associated with arousal. The hippocampus dims its communications with sensory brain regions as it erupts in the high-frequency sharp-wave electrical ripples that mark replay.

And so beyond earshot of consciousness, is the brain simply drilling fresh experience into mind, rehearsing by rote all that we seek to remember? The very word "replay" conjures visions of the easy copy-and-paste duplication so often idealized in memory. After its discovery as a center for memory processing, the hippocampus initially was seen as a mere holding pen for freshly captured snapshot-style recollections. The gradual revelation of the region's complex anatomy, however, helped to reveal its true promise. Hippocampal neurons are both highly intraconnected and deeply linked to nearly all areas of the higher-order cortex, pioneering research led by Howard Eichenbaum shows. Moreover, hippocampal synapses can strengthen more dramatically and with more persistence than many others across the brain.

In replay, the mind is not pushing playback on a recording of life but rather integrating and anchoring memories in context. That first turn in the maze may seem similar to other spaces you have seen in life. A tricky new section of the cliff may need extra attention next time. Patterns of hippocampal reactivation register the time, situation, sequence, place, and function of new information so that the replay of a fresh experience can unfold not in stark isolation but in relation to existing knowledge. Replay both stabilizes a nascent memory and enables its "elements [to] function together as a whole," note neuroscientist Ray Dolan and colleagues. En route to long-term storage, nascent memories are being tagged and cross-referenced, ready for flexible use. In this way, replay nurtures "the brain's capacity for open-ended learning."

To glimpse the deep connectivity of inner knowledge, try memorizing these groups of words—"falcon, prince, salmon" or "luck, cure, glory"—the first set by rote repetition and the second by ordering them according to their desirability. (Which do you crave most: fortune, health, or fame?) In one experiment, the simple act of linking and ordering such concepts activated the hippocampus far more than rote drill and made the words significantly more memorable. Learning these and other groupings by rote, people later recalled mostly just one or two words from a set. After "elaboration," they remembered all three words in a triplet four times as often as they did when studying by drill.

Knowledge is held within the mind's vast networks, and memories live and die in the dynamic interplay between these connections. And in sleep and rest, our minds gain needed time and space to begin weaving new experience into the memory palaces that we, like rats in a maze, navigate each day. In quiet hours, the brain is probing and ordering new information to ascertain its place in our intricate hierarchies of knowledge. This is why, as Katie's dream fragments and studies of replay show, the fallow mind turns in just minutes from mere replication to cognition that is looser and more associational yet ultimately more durable and wise.

This critical work, however, seems to require that the mind is truly left to its own devices. In Della Sala's experiments, people at rest who mentally rehearsed or even thought of the material they had to remember gained no benefit from doing so. Instead, those who simply relaxed and let their thoughts go free proved to be best at later recalling the material. Even trying to recall or imagine a life episode in detail while resting—in contrast to letting the mind drift at will—interferes with the complex memory making that begins with replay. By giving in to hidden cognitive forces beyond our control, we can liberate thought to undergo a remarkable transformation, as an independent-minded young psychologist realized long ago. In 1914, Frederic Bartlett told people a ghost story, and in the twists and turns of their recollections, he caught a tantalizing peek into the unexpected brilliance of memory's evolution.

At the outset of World War I, Bartlett was left to run Cambridge University's year-old psychology laboratory, one of the first of its kind in the world. Invalided out of the war, he at first soldiered on with his duties, testing how many nonsense syllables students could recall over time. It was a state-of-the art experiment in a field eager to shed its philosophical roots and systematically dissect cognition. By boiling a psychological stimulus down to its lowest common denominator, researchers believed that they could reveal pure mechanisms of perception, imagination, or memory. Stimulus–response, stimulus–response: this was the experimental currency of the day, the grist that would "eliminate associations," one contemporary boasted. But Bartlett thought otherwise. "Uniformity and simplicity of . . . stimuli are no guarantee whatever of uniformity and simplicity of . . .

organic response," he wrote. In other words, bring on the shifting complexities of human thought.

Eschewing reductivism, Bartlett turned his sights on the puzzle of memory with an unusual series of experiments that lasted long past the war. At the time, memories were thought to be "fixed and changeless 'traces'" that could be accessed at will, observed Bartlett. Shunning rote memorization of simple stimuli, he instead exposed people to realistic experiences—a picture of a face, a story—and then patiently waited for signs of memory's evolution to emerge. Perhaps in our fascination with accuracy, we are asking the wrong questions of memory, he dared to conjecture in writings largely forgotten for decades. Could "effort after meaning" drive the act of remembering? Memory is not a dry storehouse of the past but rather the remarkable reflection of a "ceaseless struggle to master and enjoy a world full of variety and rapid change," wrote Bartlett in his seminal book *Remembering*.

In his most famous study, he told people a brief story both strange and familiar, an American folk myth that centered on bloodshed, spirits, and war. To many of his participants, "The War of the Ghosts" sounded disjointed, contradictory, and intriguing. (Published in 1901, the tale was told to an anthropologist by one of the last living speakers of the Chinook Nation's Kathlamet dialect, a language now lost to time.) In the tale, a war party canoeing up a river invites a young man on the shore to take part in a distant battle. Wounded in the fierce fighting yet feeling no pain, the young warrior overhears one of the strangers say, "Quick, let us go home: that Indian has been hit," and he realizes his allies are ghosts. "Behold, I accompanied the ghosts," he returned to tell his people. Then, as the story goes, "when the sun rose, he fell down. Something black came out of his mouth. His face became contorted. The people jumped up and cried. He was dead."

Again and again, Bartlett asked students, university staff, and townspeople to recount the tale. (And sometimes, when they met the kindly professor by chance, they offered to tell it again long after he stopped asking.) What did the listeners omit, add, shift, and remember? Over more than a decade, patterns emerged. The plot was generally preserved, yet place-names were lost, and unfamiliar words (a canoe, an arrow) became terms closer to home (a rowboat, arms). Listeners changed details, turning "something black," for example, into the dying man's breath, Bartlett wrote. Gradually, the listeners linked the new and incomprehensible to existing knowledge stores, making a tale that was deeply resonant in 1914 one of their own.

Memory is a never-ending work of metamorphosis, Bartlett concluded. And then he chose his words carefully: lasting remembrances are not just "strung together and stored within." They *belong* to us. A new experience does not "persist as an isolated member of some passive patchwork," he marveled, but instead becomes part of an "active organisation," a "living, momentary setting" that he called a *schema*. He was revealing in essence how we build the internal edifices of knowledge, also called mental models, which serve as crucial scaffolds to reasoning, to inference, and to anticipating the future.*

Such cognitive architectures are our inner song lines, born in an ancient Dreamtime and embodying how we organize our understanding of the world. Long-ago sages depicted *Memory as a Building or a city*, writes the poet Seamus Heaney, . . . *So that the mind's eye could haunt itself . . . and learn to read Its own contents in meaningful order*. Bartlett's work is now considered among the most influential psychological research of the past century. By taking the "low road" of naturalistic science, by hunting for remembrance in context, and by taking his time, Bartlett pioneered the discovery of memory's evolution.

How then do we transform the torrents of the day into understanding? Replay opens a crucial dialogue between the hippocampus and the neocortex, keeper of our lasting schema. During replay, hippocampal neurons funnel freshly tagged memories into cortical regions across the brain; in effect, the hippocampus is starting to teach the cortex which memories to store. The two regions then engage in vibrant cross talk as they sift, sort, curate, and integrate new knowledge with old. The brain "is asking the question, what's the point of these new memories?" says Stickgold. How do they fit with our understanding of the world? What *resonates* with what we already know? If a nascent memory is consistent or familiar, hippocampal

---

*While roughly interchangeable, the terms *schema* and *mental model* have slightly different connotations. A *schema* describes a class of events or objects; one might have a schema of a typical ghost story. *Mental model* is often used to describe a concept associated with a current reality or process. Bit by bit, you build a model of a specific story that you are reading. Both terms refer to dynamic internal memory structures that form the basis of our knowledge.

activity dims, and cortical neurons in regions associated with conceptual knowledge become chemically and genetically receptive to assimilating the experience into their synaptic patterns. The congruent slides into the linkages of our schema, as when we recognize that a virtual maze is laid out like a childhood home.

Faced with novel, contradictory, or inconsistent information, however, the dialogue between hippocampus and cortex may persist for days or even years. H.M. could learn, surprised scientists discovered. His cortex could absorb bits of information that were similar to knowledge erected long ago. For example, he could recall John F. Kennedy's 1963 assassination, an event that took place a decade after his surgery, perhaps because he could recall the politician as a dashing World War II war hero and congressman. Still, green growths were few in H.M.'s mind, where the touch of a knife had stilled memory evolution, leaving half-built knowledge that crumbled into dust. Molaison could remember some trivial incidents from just before his surgery, but the shocking or inconsistent ones—a favorite uncle's death, an intimidating surgeon's preoperative handshake—were lost.

Linking, anchoring, and weaving life into the shifting palaces of our mind, we are making knowledge our own. But that is not all that occurs in the pattern work of constructing understanding. As memories are melded into mind, a remarkable process begins, this time led by the cortex: the brain's search over time for new, hidden meaning. Consider that no two events are exactly the same. On your daily walk, a barking dog might break the silence one morning, the slant of the sun will shift by the season, or a hoped-for rendezvous may change your mood. Yet beyond these distinctions lie commonalities—the familiar route, a beloved ritual—that literally emerge from overlapping patterns of synaptic activation.

Here is the triumph of memory evolution and what Bartlett called the "secret quality" of lasting remembrance: the ability to abstract, a capacity that flourishes in the fallow hour. Memories are not just enhanced and parsed when we rest or sleep; they are also compressed and honed, a process that exposes the hidden rules, telling inferences, and generalities that lurk beneath the particular.

In one landmark study, people were asked to discover how pairs of patterns were ranked. By trial and error, they gleaned a rough sense of the game's secret hierarchy. Pattern A might be better than B but worse than D. After a twelve-hour delay that involved either a night's sleep or a day's wait, they were tested. Whether or not they had slept during the interim made little difference to their ability to infer close relations such as whether B outranked D. Yet the sleepers scored nearly 25 percent better on average when tested on distant degrees of separation, such as whether B was better than E. In a separate study, people who rested for ten minutes after learning to navigate a virtual town later had a far better sense of its full layout than those who had played a simple video game after learning the task.

A concealed rule for solving a series of math problems, the secret grammar of a made-up language, an in-depth understanding of a new location—we often emerge from "doing nothing" with a deeper take on a challenge. And dreams, which arise in all stages of sleep, play a particular role in such transformations. These visions, especially the more vivid and bizarre that occur during the highly active REM state, reflect times when the sleeping brain is exploring remote, unexpected connections within knowledge. Dreams are a form of sleep-based memory processing that allows us to "understand possibilities," write Stickgold and fellow sleep researcher Antonio Zadra in *When Brains Dream*. To remember is to construct, and to learn, we must abstract, glorying in knowledge that becomes over time enduring, flexible—and imperfect.

This is why memories that are utterly complete are as tragic as those that are frighteningly deficient. For all their feats of remembering, the great savant mnemonists often had trouble teasing out the gist of life. Kim Peek, who inspired the movie *Rain Man*, was called the "Mount Everest of memory," yet he found abstract concepts largely incomprehensible. Solomon Shereshevsky, known as S, could recall word lists perfectly after a sixteen-year gap but could not make much sense of a novel. "To think is to forget differences [and] generalize, make abstractions," wrote Jorge Luis Borges in "Funes the Memorious," his story about a man with a perfect memory. "In the teeming world of Funes, there were only details." Memory is not a mere datastore but a process that entails the building and honing of understanding—sometimes for years.

↱

London, October 1838. Charles Darwin is dreaming. At age twenty-nine, he is living in rented rooms crammed with specimens from his five-year circumnavigation of the globe aboard the HMS *Beagle*. As shipboard naturalist, he had dug up rare fossils of a giant anteater and a sloth, traced Earth's tectonic shifts from Cape Verde to the heights of the Andes, discovered unknown species (the smaller the better, in his beetle-smitten view), and returned to England in 1836 with a burgeoning scientific reputation and a gnawing doubt. Perhaps chancy and brutal change, not a benevolent clockwork plan, created the intricate and varied world around him. Perhaps species are *not* fixed traces of a divine hand.

It is a subversive idea formed almost against his sensibilities. Raised in an intellectual but straitlaced household, Darwin is a gentleman scientist who is conventional in habit. Educated for the life of a country parson, he has grown up in an era in which faith and science were just beginning to clash. (It was "a sort of a shock" to Darwin when he first met someone who openly disavowed the biblical flood, his son later recalled.) Yet by the autumn of 1838, he is wrestling with notions of godless change on a scale of mammoth time, with questions that he senses might take a lifetime to probe, and with ideas that he suspects will overturn much of what he and most of his contemporaries believe.

Since his return, he has been filling a series of pocket notebooks with jottings that he calls his "mental riotings" on philosophy, nature, poetry, his observations at the zoo—"do monkeys cry?"—and evolution by natural selection. Here on pages that will help usher in the modern scientific era, Darwin writes down his first words on the transmutation of species and, in testament to his curiosity about life's mutability in all forms, his only recorded dreams. "Dreamt somebody gave me a book in French," he notes on October 30, a month after conjecturing that natural selection is evolution's prime mechanism. In the dream, he reads a page, pronouncing "each word distinctly," then awakens with a start, realizing that he had fathomed "each word separately, neglecting . . . [the] general sense" of the text. He has the rough building blocks of evolution, yet how can he make sense of it all?

In this turning-point year, Darwin works in private, wrestling with tantalizing conjectures and with evidence whose ramifications most scholars of the time are failing to fully confront. At that moment, biblical stories of a young Earth are giving way to visions of an ancient planet whose forces could sculpt islands, peaks, and continents over immense scales of time. An emerging fossil record is pointing to both a wondrous continuity and a telling disjuncture with creatures from long ago. A bag of Galápagos birds, mislabeled by Darwin as separate species, proves to be finches differing in body and beak by island; their unexpected variation within near-identical habitats hints at adaptations that no godly plan would admit. "We see nothing of these slow changes in progress," Darwin later writes, "until the hand of time has marked the long lapses of ages."

A few scientists of the day are inching toward theories of evolution. The French zoologist Étienne Geoffroy Saint-Hilaire surmises that environmental change could create new species. Darwin later will cite the Chinese physician Li Shizhen's writings on natural selection. But the British scientific circles that are beginning to embrace the young Darwin are largely dismissive of such ideas. Earth may shift and animals may differ and even disappear, yet one species can never transform into another, most still believe. Life is a sturdy, orderly tableau, not a drama of unpredictable change. It will be Darwin who will work out the theory and mechanisms of evolution most comprehensively, Darwin whose conclusions will jolt the world.

Man from monkeys? Darwin scrawls as he amasses not just specimens but also facts, the smaller and more trifling, the better. Can seeds stow away on a duck's muddy foot? He sets out to experiment. How tame is a half-feral kitten? He coaxes a friend to observe. His mind reaches in myriad directions, weaving the seemingly random and trivial into a once-unimaginable notion: "the great effect," as he calls it, produced by a "multiplication of little means." Bit by bit, the Young Collector is becoming the Great Builder as he learns to probe, to compile, to connect, and, most of all, to seek inconsistencies.

"My memory is extensive, yet hazy," he wrote in his autobiography. He cannot recall lines of poetry or dates for more than a few days. Learning by rote, an educational pillar of his day, holds no interest. Instead, all his life, Darwin asks the right questions of memory. Doggedly, he searches after meaning, wrestles with the whole and the parts, and refuses to cut short the hand of memory evolution. Early on, he disciplines himself to write down "without fail and at once" any fact, observation, or thought that opposes his results. "For I had found by experience that such thoughts were far more apt to escape from memory than favorable ones." This is what he calls his "golden rule." (Many times, he urges colleagues to be similarly open to contradictory evidence.) Solutions are hidden not just in what we do not see but also in what we do not give ourselves time to digest. This Darwin knew.

It would take him twenty years to bring his intimations to light, an effort dubbed Hamlet-like by modern historians. Ultimately, he went public with his theory a year or two earlier than planned after learning that a young, unknown naturalist had independently sketched out the theory's essentials. Darwin had a cautious side and was deeply sensitive to the implications of his revolutionary ideas. But most of all, he was determined to do the monumental work to make his conjectures convincing, argues historian John van Wyhe. "I believe there exists, & I feel within me, an instinct for truth, or knowledge or discovery," Darwin writes to a colleague. His work itself is a great effect born from a multiplication of little means, including nurturing the rhythms of suspense on the grandest scale.

For decades, evolution was the "central, undisclosed hub" of Darwin's work, writes a biographer. Yet the closer we look, the more we can see him alternating between fertile and fallow time, not just by the day but also over years. Prodigious worker though he was, his bouts of illness often meant that he did no more than a few intensive rounds of work spread across a day. But throughout his life, he also strategically took up, then stepped back from scientific topics ranging from earthworms to evolution before concluding his study of such subjects years or even decades later. More than once, he set aside his work on natural selection just as he was closing in on its truths. Repeatedly, he gained perspective on one body of facts as he waded into another. And this shade of fallow hour—the dispersal of work over time—preceded some of his greatest intellectual steps forward.

By 1838, he has been wrestling at fever pitch for two years on the question of evolution while writing up the findings from his voyage. He has a theory and a range of possible evidence, and he seems close to a conclusion when he swivels his focus for years to coral reefs, earthquakes, his *Beagle* notes, and domestic breeding. All will be threads in the tapestry that he is weaving, yet the direct assault on natural selection is becalmed. Notes Darwin biographer Janet Browne, his vast new collection of ideas needed "to be thoroughly digested."

In June 1842, five years after first taking on the question, three years after letting his theory gel, a year after ending the notebooks, Darwin sits down and pours forth the first full sketch of his ideas. The order of argument is established, the objections are anticipated, the patterns are unearthed in thirty-five pages written from memory. Soon shelved, then expanded, again shelved, and once more revised, *On the Origin of Species* at last goes to press in 1859. "I gained much by my delay in publishing," writes Darwin at the end of his life, "and lost nothing by it." One of science's most important milestones, the work is the product of the very forces that Darwin reveals to the world.

Look deep within its pages, and you will see a tree, the book's only illustration and an image crucial to Darwin's vision. Initially drawn in the notebook where he wrote his first groping words on evolution, the tree's sturdy trunk and expansive branches depict our common ancestry and evolving diversity. (Above the sketch, he writes, *I think.*) It is the Tree of Life, an ancient schema that illustrates all that he has discovered: a world of gradual and often-imperceptible change, vibrant connectivity, inescapable cycles of death and life, constant struggle, and fertile time alternating with the fallow. It is in essence a vision of not only the world's memory but also our own and a reminder moreover that our minds are *part* of this story, born of nature's transforming hand.

Darwin's forgotten masterwork—a willingness to court the risks and rewards of suspense—speaks to us across the ages of this living thing called memory. There is a workmanship to quiet time beyond stilling the body to liberate the mind. We must do more than let memory catch up to experience for a minute, a night, or a year. Cycling in and out of different facets of his work, Darwin anticipated one of the most durable findings of modern psychology. When we disperse the challenge of learning, we learn to put time on our side. Remembering means building palaces of memory and then bringing their treasures to light.

↑

You can see it in a sliver or chasm of time, the force of delay that breathes new life into memory. It works its magic in toddlers, students, people with amnesia, and fruit flies; in the memorizing of nonsense syllables; or in surgical training. Proven in hundreds of studies over a century, the "spacing effect" is catholic, elastic, and robust: almost any gap between bouts of learning helps knowledge ripen and endure. Split a first-grade reading lesson into

two-minute morsels three times daily, and children's phonics skills dramatically improve. Undergraduates who practice an obscure math problem two
times across a week score twice as high when tested a month later as those
who study the same amount all at one go. Naturally, consolidation is at play
here; moments of rest or sleep arguably are forms of spacing themselves.
But "distributed learning" offers a remarkable additional boost to memory
and a paradoxical climax to fallow time.

Consider the slight delay foisted on Kent State students who studied
Swahili–English word pairs via virtual flash cards for a series of experiments.
For some, the seventy pairs were learned in batches of seven, so the word
leaf and its counterpart *jani* might crop up again in just a minute. Others
studied thirty-five pairs at a time and so experienced a roughly six-minute
lag before they tested themselves on any one pair again. The differing gap in
time seems negligible, yet on final exams given either a half hour or a week
later, the two groups' performances sharply diverged. Even after initially
knowing a word cold, the short-lag group at times performed on the exams
as if they had not studied at all. In contrast, the long-lag group did 20 to
30 percent better on average than the others even a full week later. Why?
The additional time between encountering a word inspired the students to
pause just a second longer on average and scour their minds for an answer
that was beginning to fade. By taking an uneasy step or two into further
reaches of their memory, their grasp on the knowledge strengthened.

Why struggle to recall (or even learn) a fact or event when our devices
easily offer terabytes of data? Neatly captured and then easily accessed:
docile information is becoming the ideal. Yet crucial meaning making
takes place not only when we encode and curate memories but also in the
process that scientists call retrieval—and, most intriguingly, in its failures.
Recollection is no more a neat downloading than learning is rote replication. In remembering, the mind is haunting itself, reconstructing associations, replaying, and reconsolidating experience once again. And the more
lost in the corridors of memory we allow ourselves to be, the more understanding we can gain.

In one series of experiments, scientists slyly set people up for failure
by testing them on simple word pairs that we rarely associate with one
another, such as *whale* and *mammal*. One group was first asked to wrack
their brains for the other half of the pair *before* being given the answer,

while another set of participants initially saw the full pairing outright. Those who had tried, almost always in vain, to dredge up the associated word later proved to be up to 40 percent more adept at recalling the pairs. In their futile searching, they did not find the exact answer but instead wound up exploring related branches—large, intelligent animals?—of their knowledge. They revitalized corners of their memory architecture, strengthening context, concepts, and new future pathways back to remembering. When we struggle back through the byways of fading memory, we do far more than bring traces of past experience to life. As scientists like to say, forgetting is a friend to learning.

Failures of memory often are not cognitive defeats. Instead, they can be victories cut short or triumphs not yet ripe, memory scientists increasingly believe. Forgetting details of an event can pave the way for seeing the important parallels to a different experience. An inaccurate remembrance that floats into awareness may in fact be a gleaning of gist. For example, I repeatedly thought that Bartlett called memory a "search" rather than an "effort" after meaning. Only later did I realize that I had abstracted an essence of his theory. Scientists cannot yet fully decipher the memory work of sleep and rest. But its unfolding secrets underscore the importance of being willing to work with the mind's connectivity and with its sometimes circuitous paths to insight.

Near the end of my travels across a century of research on the spacing effect, I stumbled on a small but famous experiment: the 2005 master's thesis of surgeon-scientist Carol-anne Moulton. In one of the first studies of distributed learning in surgical education, Moulton and her team schooled thirty-eight student-surgeons in the cornerstone skill of repairing a blood vessel. Half of the students learned the technique in four weekly sessions, while the others studied for a single day; total classroom time was the same for both groups. Practicing on synthetic tissue and then turkey thighs, all the residents were taught how to plan the course of surgery with care, to use their instruments skillfully, and to respect the fragility of the body. A month later, the distributed-learning group handily surpassed the others when tested on the artificial flesh. Moulton, however, did not end the experiment there.

She then gave the young doctors a tougher challenge: fix a tear in the beating aorta of an anesthetized rat. Again, those whose learning had been dispersed outperformed the others on *all* measures of surgical prowess, including "competency," that is, their readiness to lay hand and knife on a fellow human. (Three in the one-day group tore the artery beyond repair.) And that is where I saw it, a hint of the productive unease that fallow time inspires.

My visit to Toronto long past, I called Moulton, catching her one evening as she was driving home. I drew her attention to a measure deep within the study: the surgeons' efficiency as reflected in the motion of their hands. The one-day students gained fluency steadily, making fewer unnecessary gestures as they learned. But in the dispersed-learning group, each weekly return to the classroom inspired a slight uptick in their movements before they recovered to later fully outpace their peers. "You can definitely see it," says Moulton, pulling to the side of the road to speak with me. "You can see the pattern for sure, you can definitely see a struggle."

Here again is the fallow hour's sleight of hand: a gap in time that seemingly sets us back winds up propelling us forward. "I believe in this strongly," she tells me. Across her career, she has worked to persuade her colleagues, her students, and herself to slow down at times not just to think in action but also to *not actively think*. When we set aside decisions, research, and ideas to percolate, "the thinking doesn't come from thinking harder," she tells me, "it comes from letting our thoughts sift" and then confronting them once again.

Do we welcome memory's evolution? It is natural for people to free up their minds by offloading to-do lists, the week's schedule, or other minutiae to paper and devices or by turning to external information sources to augment our knowledge stores. However, there are steep costs to perpetually skirting the alchemy of making knowledge our own.

When a device such as a tablet or a smartphone is available, people are significantly less willing to try to absorb new information themselves, studies show. The information is out there, we seem to assume, waiting to be plucked and replucked from the digital sphere. The very act of searching online brings to life brain networks related to locating information rather than those involved in probing our long-term memories. Moreover, not only do we likely spend less time adding to our memory stores in a high-tech era, but "using the internet may disrupt the natural functioning of memory by interfering with mechanisms responsible for adaptive forms of forgetting, misremembering, and reconsolidation," writes researcher Benjamin Storm. New information may become a floating data point de-contextualized from what we know. Constant device use erodes time for rest and sleep, further disrupting memory processing. In one study of 2,300 Chinese youths ages six to eighteen, higher smartphone use was linked to poorer sleep and worse memory. Tech-centric students forgot where they left things, what they had said, or what they planned to do far more often than those who used their devices less.

By engaging in fallow time, we can transform fresh experience into a dynamic architecture of vibrant detail, timeless abstraction, and new reve-lation. Then, by struggling to recollect, we can strengthen the connections, patterns, and contradictions of our growing stores of wisdom. We can see knowledge as it truly is: a living thing. One midsummer morning, I found an unexpected guide to the essential work of setting our remembering minds free within what Rebecca Solnit calls the "spaciousness of uncertainty."

⬇

Chris Gustin raises his hand to the wall of a massive pot, a year's work hanging in the balance. Standing in a dusty corner of his studio in an old Massachusetts barn, he and I are talking about how ideas evolve when he falls silent, struck by a new thought on his work in progress. One of the foremost ceramicists of his day, Gustin spends his life pursuing the hidden promise of shifting memory.

I first encountered Gustin at the opening for a gallery show of his latest work, tall and stately vessels that are painstakingly built by hand. Glazed in shades of blue, brown, white, or green, they are the very archetype of a pot and radiate the quality of presence that potters call *breath*. That night and in subsequent conversations, he spoke of the fallow time demanded by his art form and of the ultimate rewards that he has found in step-ping back, in relinquishing control, and even in forgetting. "It's the not-knowing that makes a work good," says Gustin, whose pieces are held in the Victoria and Albert Museum, the Los Angeles County Museum of Art, the Metropolitan Museum of Art, and other major collections. "It's the not-knowing what the future entails . . . that can lead you to places you never thought you'd get to, you've never even imagined, in terms of your own understanding."

All ceramics is a waiting game. Once formed, a piece must be dried to "leather-hard" strength before it may be given a first bisque firing, then glazed, then a final firing in a kiln that may take a full week to cool. "The evolution of the clay . . . cannot be forced," writes legendary potter Daniel Rhodes in his classic book *Pottery Form*. "Each fallow period must be endured."

This is particularly true in handbuilding, where each addition of clay must dry before the work can hold the weight of the next. Throwing pots on a wheel is the most direct of all crafts, notes Rhodes. A product of channeled gravitational force, such work often is quick, informal, and made all at one time. In contrast, constructing a pot by hand from sinuous coils of clay is an incremental, stop-and-start process. A bit like nest building in the wild, handwork "forces the potter to slow down, to feel more intimately the clay in his hands, and perhaps, to dream a little." The process inspires pieces that are "moving, organic in character, plastic in feel, and having a sense of becoming rather than of finality."

This is the lifework that Gustin has chosen. At age eighteen, he managed one of his family's Los Angeles ceramics factories, then struck out on his own to turn out platters and urns that at first he could not even give away. It was only when his pace of production slowed that his reputation began to soar. Early bulbous, twisting teapots that one critic called "impertinent" gave way to muscular vessels bulging with surface geometry and then to the elegant curvaceous pots, some as high as several feet tall, that I am watching take shape in his studio. At most, he can finish twelve such pots a year.

His art is an unending cycle of leave-takings and returns. And this summer, the interims between progressing on any one piece were further lengthened after he broke his hip in a fall while putting up an exhibition. Since May, he had only once touched the pot before him, part of an attempt to create a wholly new cantilevered form. A year earlier, two initial forays into this new "cloud series" had failed. *Few have the patience . . . to realize the inherent freedom* of hand coiling, writes Rhodes.

As I watch, Gustin places a short rope of damp clay along the pot's raw upper edge. A barrel-chested man with unruly red-gold hair and ice-blue eyes, he has the look of a surfer and the haunted intensity of an artist. Kneading and tamping the fresh piece into the vessel wall, he works with practiced gestures to meld something new from thousands of muddy bits.

Periodically, he takes up a small flat metal tool called a rib and scrapes down the pot's body as if brushing a horse's flank. His rhythmic motions belie a lifetime of learning as surely as the pot's smoothness will mask the history of his labors. Yet within, he is struggling to work his way back into understanding the pot he had put aside months ago. He is reconciling himself with the metamorphosis of what he knows.

"You may have one sense of reality when you are working on a piece, and you move [away] and it gets lost in memory," Gustin once told me. "And by the time you get back, . . . it's like you are seeing it for the first time. It's like 'I know you—but I don't know you.'" I ask him about this transition again, and he looks up. "Coming back is like reacquainting yourself with somebody, like trying to figure out the conversation," he says. "You were intimately engaged and then you leave, so you have to find your way back in. . . . It's about where I am now, not where I was three months ago."

Take heed of a changing world. Look and look again: the pot has dried and changed, the aorta tears and bleeds, the maze is leading you astray. But what is evolving as much or more as the evidence around us is the knowledge that we hold within. This is the promise and the challenge of the fallow hour, the double-edged work that Gustin both endures and reverently seeks: letting our minds quiet to digest and parse experience, then struggling and often stumbling to catch up with our shifted knowledge.

"It's hard to stand back, hard to let things progress and let things happen, let the natural consequences take hold," he says at one of our hours-long talks at his studio and at his nearby home perched above a winding river a few miles from the sea. "It's a big deal . . . to be able to give space between reactions. Stepping away comes from trying not to be too much in control." But the cycles of quiet, anticipation, and then reconciliation make the work come alive for him. "I need that," he says. "When you keep approaching it from a place of newness and possibility, that's a place of un-knowing. . . . In that is the risk. That's the edge."

Memory is not a quick, easy process of preserving and retrieving a frozen past but rather a part of us—linked, honed, evolving—whose acquaintance we must continually endeavor to renew. By shelving and reclaiming knowledge, we affirm that we are willing to be changed by life and to adapt to memory's evolution. Falling silent once more, Gustin seizes a scalpel-like knife and holds it to the neck of the pot. An hour after pausing and seeing the work anew, a half hour after excising a small swath, he slices away weeks of effort, casually tossing the spent earth aside.

"Okay, that makes more sense," he says, softly slapping the pot, then to me, "it's one of the ways I work: I set it up so the possibilities always can change. However I may see the piece early on, I am not locked into it." Across the morning, he destroys as much as he builds. The work "evolves only because you evolve."

Do we dare to explore the back roads of memory, seeking truth in knowledge yet seeing stumbles in remembering as sometime victories in disguise? Are we willing at times to let a bit of the past go to gain a new point of view? Can we dream a little? Failures, wrote Rhodes, are merely "searches in the byways." Katie's midnight musings, Bartlett's evolving tale, Darwin's slow-wrought genius, Gustin's reconciliations with the work that he has set aside: all should remind us of what we miss when we shortchange the messy work of memory evolution. What do we expect of the past?

CHAPTER FOUR

NOTES FROM THE MIND'S OWN SKETCHBOOK

Invention, it must be humbly admitted, does not consist in creating out of void, but out of chaos.
—MARY SHELLEY

Peering into the petri dish that May morning, the graduate student saw what he had been hoping for: the hand of death. A slimy clutch of some of the world's most drug-resistant bacteria had been decimated in hours. Amid a bustling Boston University laboratory, he had brought to life a potential new weapon in the war against ever-stronger microbes, a crisis that threatens a new dark age of medicine, when a cut or blister can easily kill. With an ingeniously low-tech solution, he had beaten back one of the most inscrutable of pathogens: the "persisters."

Most resistant bacteria thwart antibiotics by mutating, swapping genes, or banding together to emerge like sci-fi monsters strengthened by the very toxins intended to kill them. But a portion simply hunker, falling semi-dormant only to reawaken and infect an organism again and again. Popping up in all manner of bacteria, persisters are thought to drive a host of chronic and recurrent infections, from severe pneumonia and staph to tuberculosis. No medicine seemed to shake their protective sleep. No treatment troubled them until Kyle Allison and his mentor Jim Collins thought of pairing an overlooked class of antibiotics with a form of sugar to entice the bugs, Trojan-horse style, to imbibe the medicine that would eradicate them.

Allison had spent two years grappling with the problem, then months fine-tuning the treatment in a test tube solution with *E. coli*, a strain of gut-borne bacteria. Now the invention had triumphed in a natural bacteria habitat, a colony called a biofilm that adheres with the strength of steel to surfaces such as wounds, bones, or catheters. This was no preliminary result but rather a solid sign of a real-world application. Assessing the finding, Allison felt elated and relieved.

A week later, he is sitting down with Collins to reveal the scientific rarity of a shockingly clear finding. "That's brilliant," says Jim Collins, a biomedical engineer and one of his field's most innovative scientists. "This is a stunning result." They are meeting in Collins's book-lined office as I look on. The older scientist tips back his chair, listening intently as Allison relates how he worked overtime to triple replicate the biofilm experiment. An editor at a prestigious journal is eyeing the unfolding discovery. Allison is confident. "So I can collect the data on this," says Allison, a lanky twenty-five-year-old with a drawn face and a sober air. "It's a few days to get everything pushed through." Collins, however, does not answer. He seems to be somewhere far away, his gaze on a distant horizon.

Ever ambitious, Collins constantly urges his stable of young scientists to attempt seemingly impossible feats. He prodded Allison, one of his most creative protégés, into tackling the impenetrability of persisters. (*It can't be done*, the student reported after two weeks of research. *Sounds like a great project*, said Collins. *Keep up the good work*.) Now Collins, a MacArthur "genius" fellow and a Rhodes scholar, again urges Kyle to think bigger. Why not try to replicate the data in a virulent staph biofilm, not just run-of-the-mill *E. coli*? How about attempting to cure infected mice, a last hurdle before human trials? Why be sated with a step forward when you might make a leap? He turns to his student, "Are you daring enough to try?"

Collins is an architect of life and a master of the "what if." He was one of the first to begin reverse engineering and rewiring complex parts of living cells to do our bidding, work that inspired the field of synthetic biology. He splashed onto the scene in 2000 by inventing the field's foundational tool, a genetic toggle switch that turns circuits of genes into programmable information stores. From there emerged a string of stunning discoveries. He designed power probiotics refitted with biosensors and revamped genetic circuits that can sense and destroy bacteria before they blossom into infectious diseases such as cholera. His cheap, paper-based diagnostic test for detecting Ebola and other infections made headlines. Year after year, he has overturned the prevailing scientific wisdom on how antibiotics succeed or fail; in 2020, he harnessed machine learning to lead the discovery of the first new antibiotic compound in three decades, creating a medicine that kills more than thirty-five powerful bacteria.

An elected member of the National Academy of Engineering, the National Academy of Sciences, and the National Academy of Medicine as well as the American Academy of Arts and Sciences, Collins is spring-step energetic, with a boyish face and the lean build of a college 4:17 miler. Sprinting through his days, he keeps up with his sprawling lab via laser-focused, one-minute meetings and speaks so rapidly that he routinely drops words. Immensely practical, he is an aficionado of all things efficient. Yet time and again in his office, on plane rides, on long walks, and at home in the evenings, he drifts into the farthest reaches of his wandering mind, steeling himself to be, by the standards of our day, unproductive. He is an unapologetic devotee of the daydream.

A few months before my first visit to his lab, Collins instituted tech-free Friday mornings to prod his team of thirty-odd scientists to read deeply, to interact in real time, and, most of all, to daydream. If he could persuade his mathematicians, biologists, physicists, and engineers to unplug for just a few hours, perhaps their minds might take flight. No mere twenty-four-hour assignment, this was his attempt to change the very culture of the enterprise. There were snickers at the mention of daydreaming and naysayers from the beginning, with Allison most vocal in airing the collective doubts. "Jim really understands how research works," Kyle told me, "so I thought, why does he suddenly want people to be inactive?"

Teachers' bane and idle sport, alluring yet scorned, daydreaming long has seemed child's play, at best a useless folly. We are immersed in reverie of one kind or another much of our waking lives, but the topic was largely overlooked by mainstream psychology well into the twenty-first century. A summer's day, a languid hour; we may remember lying on a patch of tickly grass, watching a parade of clouds and our passing thoughts float by. Now in tuning out, many of us just feel guilty. Do we fear that, Icarus-like, we will float too high on the wings of our daydreams?

That fine spring Friday morning, the good-news meeting ended quickly. The young scientist packed up his papers and hurried back to the workbench. Collins turned to his e-mail, and my mind drifted away. Why take time to wallow in the sketchiest of thoughts? Like the fallow hour, reverie carries us away from instant action and swift judgment and into overt stillness and seeming inefficiency. Could a realm of uncertainty that we so often denigrate and even fear compensate for all that it takes away?

[↓]

For truly, we are missing persons when we daydream. This is the disconcerting wellspring of a meandering mind: going within, our wakeful attunement to the world begins to fail.

Consider reading, a common trigger for reverie and an alluring chance for scientists to study the retreat that they dub "perceptual decoupling." Up to two minutes before people catch themselves going mentally astray, they begin blinking more rapidly, their pupils dilate, and their reading pace slows. As they turn within, parts of the brain related to processing visual input, such as words on a page, quiet as regions associated with internal musings grow ascendent. With their inattention to the outside world deepening by the moment, daydreaming readers lose fluency and flexibility and then subtlety in perception and understanding.

In one series of experiments, people were settled into a cozy chair and asked to spot a range of errors sprinkled in dozens of brief, banal on-screen stories. The scientists, meanwhile, tracked the movements of their eyes as markers of their drifting minds. Over several hours, the participants had little trouble spotting low-level, lexical mistakes, such as a made-up word. However, they overlooked contradictory sentences and other semantic errors that are key to a story's overall meaning. In a separate study, people who zoned out even just once while reading the Sherlock Holmes tale *The Red-Headed League* were twice as likely as attentive readers to miss a key clue to the villain's identity.

Normally when we read, our eyes linger on less common words, such as *armadillo*, and sail over everyday words, like *the*; this "frequency effect" is crucial to understanding a text's meaning. When our minds wander, however, we skip past important words and fail to slow down at the end of phrases and sentences to integrate the meaning of what we have just read.

We lose the forest, then the entire landscape. And finally, we reawaken, startled and out of sync, to realize that we have missed the point of the story, the boss's question, or a shift in the traffic ahead. According to one analysis of U.S. police reports, daydreaming causes an estimated 60 percent of fatal crashes attributed to distraction. Studies in China and France point to similar links between daydreaming and the risk of an accident.

Off task: that is the first sin of the daydreamer and the inspiration for a centuries-long discomfort with the wandering mind. "She looks as if she were thinking of something beyond . . . her situation," Charlotte Brontë's scrappy heroine Jane Eyre observes of a classmate who is constantly musing. "I have heard of day-dreams—is she in a day-dream now? Her eyes are fixed on the floor but I am sure they do not see it."

The word *daydream* came into being in the seventeenth century yet became a common term only in Victorian times. Still, lost, and the picture of escapism, daydreamers were out of step with rising machine-age expectations of efficiency. In particular, reverie became disparaged as a feminine occupation especially practiced by those affluent enough to be removed from the working world. Center stage at London's Crystal Palace Exhibition of 1851 stood *The Daydreamer*, a billowing papier-mâché armchair carved with figures depicting "winged thoughts" and flowers symbolizing repose and consolation. Women are "dreaming always—never accomplishing," railed Florence Nightingale in 1860, the year she created the first professional nursing school.

Off task and out of touch: reverie soon was considered a royal road to mental imbalance. Freud's collaborator, Josef Breuer, linked a love of daydreaming to hysteria in his famous psychoanalysis patient, Anna O. The habitual reverie that she called her "private theater," wrote Breuer, "probably influenced her decisively in the direction of her illness." Freud branded reverie as repressed play, detached from reality, and "childish and illicit" in adulthood. Except as the fuel of literary fiction, the mind's wanderings should not hold our interest, Freud made clear. "We are repelled by them or at best feel cool towards them," he wrote in 1908 in one of his few mentions of the topic.

By 1917, questions about reverie were used to screen U.S. Army recruits for mental instability. "Does your mind wander so badly that you lose track of what you are doing?" candidate soldiers were asked as part of the first personality testing. "Does a particular useless thought keep coming into your head to bother you?" Excessive fantasy or rumination is a cause for concern, yet, at the time, reverie to almost any degree was treated as an alarming distraction from life and from the serious study of the mind. How we achieve a task is what matters, early psychologists assumed. The daydream was mental froth, except to a "sweetly reasonable man" who at the height of behavioralism found reverie worthy of investigation and even of celebration.

In 1965, Jerome Singer ushered forty-two unwitting undergraduates into his laboratory at New York's City College and prepared to snare their daydreams. The young psychology professor's maverick pursuit of the wandering mind had been more than a decade in the making. After a stint in counterintelligence during World War II, he began parsing his chosen field's forbidden fruit: the mind's interior. Literary works by Joyce, Woolf, Shakespeare, Faulkner, and modern cinema as well depict the drift of our stream of consciousness, he noted. Why did his colleagues neglect the thought fabric of our days?

Nearly alone in his quest, Singer began doing the unthinkable: asking directly about thoughts then deemed so messily private that psychologists assumed people would be reluctant to admit to them. He created the first psychological questionnaires on everyday daydreaming and cajoled his family and friends to take them. He pioneered the practice of asking people what they were thinking about during a task to learn if their minds had strayed. Singer was eager to study the world of the daydreamer because he was one of their own. He admitted freely to indulging in boyhood football fantasies and fretful daydreams about his work.

In mid-1965, miniskirts and bell-bottoms were in. The march on Selma had ended bloodily, and the first U.S. combat troops had landed in embattled Vietnam. In Singer's lab, the forty-two students were taught two simple tasks. On detecting the lower of two tones, they were to press an electric telegraph key. Catching themselves daydreaming, they were told to flip a switch. After a few practice runs, they returned to a waiting room where a news flash suddenly broke into a radio broadcast playing in the background: *surprise massive air and ground attack earlier today . . . all active military units on emergency alert status . . . local draft boards to call in for physical examinations as soon as possible all unemployed youths over 18 and all eligible college students*, an announcer said. "It was difficult to keep the subjects from calling their friends," an assistant later recalled.

The broadcast on Vietnam was fake, but its impact was telling. When the students were herded back into soundproof booths for the actual experiment, their minds took flight. Compared with a control group ignorant of the "news," those who heard the broadcast were far more likely to daydream and to miss the target tone. They later reported envisioning scenes of sinking ships and marching soldiers, of being captured on a battlefield, or of escaping to Canada to avoid the draft. They were off task yet looking ahead. They were grappling, Singer wrote, with "the powerful unfinished business" of their lives.

People's minds wander on average up to nearly half of their waking lives, recent research shows. Is time off task as futile as we imagine? The wandering mind's first modern scientific defender recognized the tensions inherent in the daydream's misfires and poor timing. Yet he also glimpsed an inventive side to maligned reverie and saw that some dreamers are willing to embrace their flights of fancy. Singer, it is said, brought the study of the wandering mind out of the Dark Ages. His candor and sensibility helped dispel our doubts, wrote one philosopher. But it wasn't until mainstream science stumbled on a monumental something in the airy nothings of the off-task moment that the daydream at last began to give up its secrets. As Singer suspected, the mental digressions that we often scorn lie at the heights of human cognition.

At the heady dawn of neuroscience, a field then as much art as science, some of its pioneers were baffled. Imaging could unveil the brain's essential patterns and so begin to decode the physiological underpinnings of thinking for the first time. By simply comparing scans of someone's brain at rest and then during a task, scientists could uncover traces of a mind at work. Yet on-task images often were frustratingly faint, while those from times when subjects were told to do nothing were unexpectedly vibrant. A state of mind deemed just static or random noise was creating some of the most dramatic effects in early neuroscience. Most scientists argued about how to make it go away. A few looked closer.

Throughout the 1990s, the pioneering neuroscientist Marcus Raichle kept a folder on his desk marked "MMPA," for "medial mystery parietal area," one of the regions at the heart of the newly discovered activity. One of the first to analyze the mind at rest, Raichle and his colleagues discovered that up to 80 percent of the brain's energy is consumed by inner events. Less than 10 percent of visual neuronal synapses are devoted to incoming sights. Moreover, the network of regions that spring to life at rest and then grow quiet when people perform a task makes up a remarkable one-fifth of the brain. Why is the lion's share of our mental energy spent on turning within? A long-overlooked 1995 study by neuroscientist Nancy Andreasen provided the next hint.

The regions that activate during rest closely sync with those that operate when people remember the past and plan their future, she noticed. In addition, some regions are involved with abstract thinking and with forging a coherent sense of self. "When the brain/mind thinks in a free and unencumbered fashion, it uses its most human and complex parts," she ventured in a landmark article.

Were these scattered research findings crucial clues or a mirage? Debate grew so heated that those arguing for further study of the intriguingly active idle brain were shouted down at psychology conferences. *No task? This is not science*, they insisted. *This is the antithesis of the psychology experiment.* Other scientists dismissed the findings as just a reflection of the constant low-level hum of intrinsic brain activity that readies an organism to perceive and to move. But a curious few pushed forward, pulling the pieces together to make a discovery that was compared to finding a new continent. They uncovered the *default mode network*, a powerhouse constellation of brain regions that are at the heart of our inner lives and our capacity for reverie.

Where does the mind go when freed? For years, the taint of seeming idleness masked the true story of the default mode system. But in time, the mysteries of this widely distributed network and its major hubs began to be revealed. Within the network, a cluster of regions called the *medial temporal* subsystem fuels autobiographical memory and predictions about our future. A *dorsal medial* subsystem that includes parts of the prefrontal cortex enables us to imagine scenarios related to ourselves and also to surmise others' states of mind. The default network's *core* hub, including midline parietal and frontal regions, is thought to integrate information from across the brain to build meaning and self-understanding.

NOTES FROM THE MIND'S OWN SKETCHBOOK   89

In default mode, the brain largely is stepping away from the here and now, even if just momentarily, to conjure visions of the future and the past and to make sense of the rushing torrents of our days. Importantly, default network regions are located far from the brain's sensorimotor areas, a topography that helps untether the mind from the demands of the outer world. The network also is situated at the end of many cognitive information processing streams, a structural configuration that seeds abstract, wide-ranging thinking. From this cognitive foundation, the mind can reminisce about days gone by, spin detailed future scenarios, vividly imagine a scene, or muse about how a friend may be feeling. The network is the wellspring of our capacity to daydream.

↩

What were you thinking about? In a spartan testing room at the University of Southern California, a neuroscientist is questioning a shy, raven-haired seventeen-year-old who has just emerged from daydreaming in a brain scanner. *Was there a time when you were really lost in thought?* asks Mary Helen Immordino-Yang, probing for traces of the girl's inner wanderings. *Could you forget where you were?* The teen looks away, her body stilled, and Immordino-Yang pauses expectantly.

Immordino-Yang and her team are midway through one of the first longitudinal studies of its kind, a quest to understand the centrality of a rich inner life for creating a meaningful future for youths from under-resourced backgrounds. Two years after their last visit, dozens of mostly Asian American and Latinx kids are returning to her Los Angeles laboratory, often taller and a bit more poised. The teens attend diverse inner-city schools in neighborhoods steeped in crime and gang warfare. Many of their parents work as janitors, gardeners, cleaners, and restaurant servers; at least one caregiver in every teen's household is an immigrant. Who did the youths seek to be in a year or a decade? the scientists ask across the years. What are they doing at school or home to make their dreams happen? Where do their daydreams take them?

I have to prepare for the SATs, the girl at last answers shyly, *so I was thinking, how am I going to divide this up?* She reveals that she feels worried but inspired, and the scientist smiles. A former teacher and now a decorated scientist, Immordino-Yang is charming and brisk, with a girlish air and a knack for working across disciplines to tackle ambitious research questions. A protégé of the intelligence researcher Howard Gardner and the neuroscientist Antonio Damasio, she made her mark dissecting the cortical underpinnings of complex social emotions such as admiration. Now she is picking up where Singer left off, leading new efforts to decode the importance of transcending the here and now to ponder *what-if* questions. She is teasing out the makings of the good daydream. I had landed on her doorstep seeking an inside look at reverie's redemption.

When our minds take flight, we typically are drawn to an unexpectedly soothing space: our futures. Imagine me perched on a concrete wall at a seaside shopping plaza, waiting to dine with Immordino-Yang on the night before I visit her laboratory. I watch a trio of boys skateboarding around a fountain and the nonchalant athleticism of Californians jogging by in the dusk. A bus driver smiles at me, but I hardly see him, as my thoughts are turned within. The timing for my trip is poor, I had learned. A crucial grant deadline looms, weighing on Immordino-Yang. I envision snatched conversations, unrequited questions, a frustrating sojourn. But recalling her passion, other scenarios began to unfold like enticing film clips: meaty interviews, my confusion lifting, a buoyant return home. By the time she appears, I feel calm. This is what scientists call the "palliative effect" of future-oriented reverie.

Nearly half of our mental wanderings take us into the uncharted tomorrow. Our thoughts turn to the future roughly every fifteen minutes. Yet launching into the unknown paradoxically seems to strengthen us. Setting out to explore the consoling side of mental time travel, German neuroscientist Tania Singer, who is no relation to Jerome, put young adults through the Trier stress test, the experiment in which people give a five-minute job talk in front of stern judges. In Singer's studies, a gentle coda was added to the day's challenges: simple cognitive tests aimed at inducing mind wandering. Those who tended to let their minds drift forward in time during the tests showed lower levels of the stress hormone cortisol both before and after the Trier speech compared with those who daydreamed about the past.

But are thoughts of the future merely rose tinted, a kind of escapist wish fulfillment? My evening's reverie and Tania Singer's further scientific investigations hint to the contrary. Even negative future-oriented daydreams— visions of an interview gone awry or a boss's critique—boost our mood while reveries set in the past, even if positive, tend to sadden us. Peering into the past, we see what's done and gone. Looking ahead, we begin to think ahead, not just to any future but to our own.

When we daydream about the future, very often we are loosely sketching out our lives. Many such musings are visual and film-like, but more often, we simply talk ourselves through our daydreams, calling on the "inner speech" that is a marker of human planning. How will we fare at the cocktail party or manage that upcoming presentation? A majority of future-focused daydreams take us no further than later that day or the next. In this type of reverie, thought is loose yet fine grained, close to the texture of our days. More rarely and with difficulty, we muse on distant realms made indistinct by the limits of imagination. Casting our minds forward a year or a decade, we dream of larger goals: health, a new love, a promotion. We trade detail for gist, losing vivid specificity while gaining a sense of the big picture.

This trade-off between granular detail (the trees) or sweeping gist (the forest) is a central dimension of abstract thinking. Any time that we step away from the present moment to remember, to empathize, or to muse, we tend to construe our thoughts through the powerful mental "lens" of proximity or distance. For example, if you imagine that you are working remotely from a distant city, you likely will see the gist of a current project more clearly; your expanded horizon strips away cluttering detail. In reverie, we work on a canvas that fittingly reflects how we evolved to view the external landscape.

Yet at the same time, mental time travel liberates us from a single viewpoint or horizon. "You're moving in and out of these layers of analysis, these nested worlds," Immordino-Yang tells me as we sample meze on a chilly restaurant patio. In her own reverie, she might muse on different ways to break a piece of news to her mother or to explain her data to others. She asks herself what kind of person she wants to be in years to come—more of a scientist or more of an educator?—and casts herself in different roles. "I'll try out ways of being in my mind," she says. Good reverie entails mentally moving from vista to vista to imagine the potential inherent in the future. The agile dreamer is both in motion and in control.

Looking more closely at the resting mind, scientists were surprised to discover in 2009 that the default network at times co-activated with the executive brain, including parts of the prefrontal cortex. Why would two realms assumed to work in opposition—one freewheeling, the other a crown of controlled reasoning—be closely linked? Scientists initially thought that the executive brain was endeavoring to wrestle the mind back to attending to the outside world. But in time, they realized that often when we turn within, we are *not* entirely off task. Rather, we are on target to undertake essential inner work.

When we attune to the outer world, a specific constellation of executive regions that are highly connected to perceptual systems becomes active. As Jacqueline Gottlieb's work on *focused arousal* shows, when we drive, walk, or lead a meeting, parts of the frontoparietal control network co-ordinate with regions linked to external attention so that we can attend to the world around us. When we slow to speculate and muse, this external-facing system falls quiet, yet the mind is hardly dormant. At this time, a second frontoparietal subsystem closely aligned with the default network, along with other executive regions, keeps thoughts inward facing as well as loosely on topic and coherent. The degree of executive activity may vary widely, from a light touch in a freely drifting mind to the heightened level of control needed to undertake a creative thought experiment. But most of the time, the daydream is not the free-for-all once imagined. When you follow a trail of thought or spin out possible endings to the unfinished business of the day, you are guiding the work of your free-form mind. "What you have to remember," says Immordino-Yang, "is that your ability to daydream depends on the skills and knowledge and disciplinary thinking that you're capable of."

A picture emerges of a skilled time traveler who does not passively submit to mental abduction but instead strategically retreats from the present to explore a better future. In 2013, Tania Singer and colleagues tested adults' willingness to delay gratification along with their daydreaming prowess. In numerous trials, participants first had to choose between taking ten euros immediately or waiting from a day to half a year for up to five times more money. (In actuality, all participants were given one-fifth of one randomly selected reward.) Next, they had to determine whether numbers on a list were odd or even while sometimes also having to recall the property of a previous digit. All the while, they were asked at random times if their minds were wandering.

Those who daydreamed *more* during the easy number-identification work and *less* during the tough memory task proved to be more willing to wait for a larger reward. They could "let go of the present" strategically, the scientists write. Now or later? Trees or forest? Game plan or life goal? Adept daydreamers control the timing and wanderings of their mind's eye in the service of their aims. In Walter Mischel's marshmallow experiments, four- to five-year-old children who distracted themselves by focusing on the yumminess of the promised treat waited nearly six minutes before giving up and downing the snack. But those who turned within and expanded their mental horizons—for example, by picturing the marshmallow as a cloud— held out roughly double that time for the promised larger reward.

My visit to Los Angeles is nearly at an end. I am about to head across the city to meet with young daydreamers who had attended a summer science program at Immordino-Yang's lab. Her mammoth study is unfinished, yet already, she is bringing to light the nature of the essential cognitive realm that she calls "transcendent thinking." Her words tumble out, her eyes alight, as she relates some of her most intriguing early findings.

At the end of a long day of experiments, she had begun testing the restraint of the teens: would they like cash in hand for the day's participation or a larger sum later? Waiting, of course, is the expected answer. Or is it? Could reverie inspire us to let go of the present and the obvious? The most promising and motivated teens in the study typically opted for the larger, later reward—but not always. One girl who came into the lab at holiday time, for example, ultimately decided after much musing that less was more if it allowed her to buy her mother the gift of an urgently needed bus pass.

The kids with the brightest futures "play with ideas," Immordino-Yang tells me excitedly. They step within to work out when today's needs might surpass those of tomorrow and vice versa. High levels of imagination correlated with self-control in the study, never the reverse. "Daydreaming is a time to make connections between ideas and memories and possible hypothetical futures and bring all those things together and play them out," she says. "It's really about mental flexibility," she stresses. A youth who can muse on life's possibilities probably is "going to be the most successful in overcoming obstacles." And that is what her research suggests.

As part of the longitudinal study, Immordino-Yang and her team told the teens true stories of inspiring young people, such as the Nobel Prize–winning activist Malala Yousafzai. Then, after being interviewed about their thoughts on these heroes and on their own lives, the teens had their brains scanned first while musing further about the stories, then while rating their emotional engagement with them, and finally while just quietly letting their minds wander.

Adolescents who displayed more abstract reflection on a story during the interview later showed more default network activity and more coordinated default-executive patterns of connectivity while musing on the same tale in the scanner. They also had more complex daydreams. And over time, those teens who showed more robust growth and connectivity of default and inner-directed executive regions tended to be more successful at school, flexible, satisfied with their social relationships, and willing to reflect on their identities.

Immordino-Yang is thrilled with the emerging findings, yet she is equally alarmed about the fate of reverie in an era when inner life is under siege. She first outlined her concerns in a 2012 academic article titled "Rest Is Not Idleness" that went viral. Contemporary lives are marked by relentless doing, interruptions, and snippets of information, conditions that can sideline the work of the default network and its essential connectivity with the executive brain, she argues. Already, high-technology use by youths seems linked to less transcendent thinking, research by Immordino-Yang and others suggests. "I worry that we're potentially growing a generation of children who aren't as capable, neurologically speaking, of daydreaming," she told a radio interviewer. "What we really need are not kids who are daydreaming all the time and staring out the window but kids who can move mindfully and thoughtfully back and forth" between the states that she calls *looking out* and *looking in*. "There's a time to attend effortfully and outwardly, and there's a time to let it all go and build meaning, letting your mind play over all the things going on in your life."

Reverie, she effectively is saying, is the child's play we cannot leave behind. And those who are awake to its potential can lead us forward in an era when inventive thinking is critically needed. Bidding Immordino-Yang good-bye, I turned to a young time traveler whose reverie is a salvation. I learned from a seventeen-year-old that both a *dream* and a *plan* are leaps of faith.

"The drapes are white, the fridge is cream colored and used, because I can't afford anything else." Alysia Burbidge is relating her vivid daydreams of having her own apartment and a better tomorrow. Soon she will be the first in her family to go to college, where she plans to study neuroscience. The previous summer, she had attended Immordino-Yang's brain science summer camp for urban teens. The future is brightening after a painful past.

She has no ties to either her father or her mother. Her maternal grandparents, Vietnamese immigrants, largely raised her. After her grandfather died, her grandmother brought Alysia up in a Los Angeles suburb built on old olive groves and fading American dreams. We meet at a noodle shop in a strip mall near her high school north of Disneyland. I am late and find her at the far end of the restaurant doing her homework, her back to a noisy television. A tentative yet articulate young woman with a warm guarded smile, she has a deep reverence for the power of a drifting mind.

"I daydream probably mostly about the future," she tells me as we sip tea and nibble on hot pho noodles.

"What feeling does daydreaming give you?" I ask.

"It makes me feel excited, excited for the future," she says.

For the past year and a half, Alysia has been working at the same McDonald's across the street from her home where her seventy-six-year-old grandmother has been employed for twenty years. Up to twenty-five hours a week, Alysia takes drive-through orders. She detests the job, but it's easy, so at work, she often lets her mind drift to her future life on a campus a $7 bus ride and a world away. At other times, in what she calls a "day-nightmare," she imagines telling off guys who taunt her with catcalls on her walk home from school. Still, even then, her thoughts carry her to a better place, which is why Alysia preserves time for reverie outside of homework or classes. Daydreams helped pierce the fog of sadness and fear that gripped her after her grandfather died. "Death was always on my mind," she says, her eyes welling with tears. Now when troubles loom, she strategically turns within.

When I first phoned Alysia to set up a meeting, I asked if she daydreamed a lot. "Yeah," she said, giggling. "When I daydream, I feel different. It makes me feel complete." Later, I ask what she had meant. "Daydreaming is kind of like a reassurance," she tells me. "It makes you take a step back from your life or that moment in time, . . . and you take in what's going on in your life right now, and you get to see the whole picture of yourself and what you want and what you're, well, dreaming of, and in that moment, you can be like, 'this is me, I'm alive, this is what I'm doing, this is what I want.' You feel a sense of completeness because daydreaming, although it's a distraction, makes you more aware." Alysia gleans from reverie a foothold on the unknown. "It makes the future seem a lot more attainable. There's a solidity to the daydream."

⬆

The daydream and the future beckon. Turning within, we sketch life's tomorrows, testing out who we seek to become. Yet there is further promise in the fertile space between order and disarray: the makings not just of self-invention but also of creativity itself. Einstein, ever the thought rebel and a devout daydreamer, noted that "imagination is more important than knowledge. For knowledge is limited. Imagination encircles the entire world." Imagine, then, changing the world through reverie. Return now to a caretaker of inner life who, like Immordino-Yang, has ambitions for the daydream.

Off task and out of touch: Jim Collins knows the sins of reverie. Guilt dogs his every retreat from the world. "It's an odd situation," he tells me. "You're going all day, rushing to get stuff done, and then you're saying, 'I'm going to do nothing and see what happens.'" He typically devotes an hour or more a day to daydreaming—both mind wandering and more directed reverie—yet each time before doing so, he asks himself, "Should I be doing something else?" Time and again, he compels the busyness to wait.

Envision Collins as a junior professor, preparing to go within. He is settling into a flight home from a conference and steeling himself to set aside his papers, data, and deadlines. As the plane takes off from Montreal, Collins gazes out the window as he did so often as a boy on long drives. With his mind literally in the clouds, he chases the future. Look closer at this idle dreamer on the verge of his first world-class discovery.

At the time, Collins was studying human biomechanics or the intricacies of how humans jump, walk, run, or simply move. Inherent in the firing of the neurons and the muscles that sense and adjust our limbs are random fluctuations, like static on the radio. This noise, long seen as interference to the real work of the body, is why we cannot stand completely still. Collins, however, saw in the phenomenon an untapped source of information. Noise could speak to us, he realized. By tracking the body's "sway patterns," he could measure a person's risk of falling, the leading cause of injury in people over age sixty-five. Could we make noise work for us as well? he began to ask himself. He had the first stirrings of a daydream.

At the conference, a physicist had pulled Collins aside and challenged him to jump off from recent discoveries showing that added "static" improves complex systems from electronic circuits to lasers. Extra noise essentially nudges faint incoming data past a tipping point of significance, a phenomenon called stochastic—randomly patterned—resonance. On the flight home, Collins sets out to find in reverie a way to harness the randomness of nature. Growing up at the height of the early space age, Collins had an engineer father who worked on guided missile systems and spent hours in his basement electronics lab. But as a boy, Collins liked to tinker with ideas. "I was more of the daydreamer," he says.

He loves to tell the story of the day in elementary school that he replicated the sun. The class had broken into teams to study the sun's impact on Earth with lights and balls. Collins, however, forgot to bring in his group's flashlight. The teacher was angry, his classmates were upset, and the nine-year-old Collins had an epiphany: he grabbed a glass jar and used it to direct real rays of sunshine onto the globe. "As I was leaving class that day, the teacher said, 'That was ingenious,'" Collins recalled. "I somehow found the inner resources to make that connection."

Would you think of crumbling a brick to line an aquarium or of using one for a pillow? Would turning a shoe into an envelope ever come to mind? If so, you probably are an original thinker with high potential for creative problem solving. One of the most famous measures of creativity, the "alternate uses test," asks a seemingly innocuous question—what can you do with a brick, a tire, or a shoe?—to uncover the capacity for divergent or unconventional thinking in both the lab and life. Our potential for skillful creative problem solving, children's future success in the arts and sciences, even the quality of a jazz performance—all are correlated with this simple measure. Yet despite the test's long popularity, no one knew just how divergent thinkers spun gold from dross. Do they remember, free-associate, or dream a little?

A landmark series of investigations by psychologist Kenneth Gilhooly teased out the inner life of idea makers. Asked to think creatively about an ordinary object such as a brick, most people at first tend to conjure familiar uses like building walls. And this is where conventional thinkers get stuck; they produce a greater number of responses that are less original overall. Unusual uses emerge only to those who seek new mental vistas en route to creating a new idea. Looking more closely at an object—ah, it's pillow shaped—or seeing it more abstractly—it's firesafe, so a mini pizza stone—begins to spark scintillating ideas. But the most promising strategy is to roam between mental categories, moving from gist to detail, whole to part, abstract to concrete, and back again. "Does the examinee tend to stay in a rut, or does he branch out readily into new channels of thought?" asked creativity researcher J. P. Guilford, who invented the test in 1950. *Switching* is a marker of people with fluid, creative intelligence who also manage their minds well.

Intriguingly, creative people's knowledge networks are different too. The schema of divergent thinkers are more flat, networked, and flexible, studies show. When asked to free-associate a word such as *chair*, less creative thinkers rigidly linger on *table*, while original minds leap toward remote allusions such as *throne*. And in this alchemy of creativity, we can see the hand of reverie. Scientists neuroimaging divergent thinking in action for the first time found stronger interplay between executive brain regions and the default mode in people with more creative minds. They glimpsed the daydreaming mind at work.

On the plane, Collins asks himself, what could he do for humanity with the "brick" of stochastic resonance? How could he add noise to the body productively, and what kind of noise should he harness? Electrical? Mechanical? Muscular? He spoke the language of noise, yet the seemingly promising path of adding noise soon turned circuitous. "Many, many times it seems like you're the person in a movie going around in circles in the woods and coming back to the same spot," he says of reverie. "It takes a few seconds to realize, 'I was just here,'" back in a familiar landscape.

But Collins has faith in the daydream and a tireless willingness to shake off discouragement and to look ahead to yet another possibility. "I don't give up," he says, his voice rising, "and that includes on daydreaming." When he is stuck, he tries to release his grip on the unworkable or the obvious and zoom back out to the gist of the question, freeing his mind once more to roam over a problem's parts and its whole. He is in control yet in dreamy motion, shifting his perspective, seeking a connection, a memory, the seed of an idea.

Thresholds, Collins wonders as the plane approaches Boston. If added noise buoys weak stimuli up and over a tipping point of significance, perhaps random static can tune up our threshold-based human perception. Every time our feet hit the floor, nerve cells in our soles and ankles work with proprioceptor neurons to keep us steady. Age or an illness, such as diabetes, dulls these feedback loops, effectively raising the bar of perception and degrading balance. *Thresholds*, Collins muses, grasping hold of a tenuous idea: a vibrating insole that would steady the old and the sick or even rock climbers and construction workers. Aiming for the seemingly impossible, he chased down the future with a discovery that would inspire a new class of medical devices and earn Collins the first of dozens of patents.

Yet this is not the trumpets-please triumphal finish to his story, Collins stresses in hours of conversation with me. Inventive reverie is unruly, he takes pains to emphasize. Each time he dives within this space, he must set aside not only the pressure to be doing but also the expectation of a quick, clear outcome. He may get the fidgets or even grow bored, yet he will sit a while longer after that. He may hit dead ends or take wrong turns for months at a time, but he will keep revisiting the problem in his daydreams. An inching pace of creation is the price of admission for the chance to make a leap toward a better tomorrow.

"I may strike out again and again, but if I can have one really good idea a year, I'm going to have a *big* impact," he says, leaning forward, his Boston accent deepening as he warms to the topic. "And if I'm going to have, say, a forty- to fifty-year career, that's a lot of good ideas. At the end, your career may be defined by a few small insights, so you have to be willing to put in those months for potentially having that one idea that will be the blockbuster."

This is his ambition for the daydream: he constantly invests in this loose disciplining of disorder in order to reap the extraordinary. When I mention to him hearing a busy undergraduate complain that she does not have time to think, Collins breaks in. "I think people *have* the time to think," he argues, "but the great, great majority choose not to. . . . You have to spend time comfortably in your head—that goes against our culture." He takes the long view of the daydream and its place in society. He is unafraid to question our assumptions that reverie is thoughtless, that good thinking is free of musing, and that busyness is an end in itself. He is unashamed of reverie, a realm made illicit by our collective scorn. This is why he set up tech-free Friday mornings in his lab and nevertheless was not surprised when it failed.

"It didn't work!" says Collins. "This is Friday morning, and look around, you'll see people on their computers." A few attempts at solitude and group brainstorming soon degenerated into absenteeism and gossip. Some were willing but were unsure how to spend the time. "It was a shock," postdoc Ahmad "Mo" Khalil tells me. "We weren't quite sure how to make something from it," says Kyle Allison, who began arriving later and later on Fridays. After two months, increasingly skeptical lab members persuaded Collins to call a halt to the endeavor. "They were not comfortable with it, they didn't see the point, they asked me to stop," says Collins. "It just went against the culture they were used to and what they had adopted." Unable to see the daydream's merit, the young scientists were reluctant to secure a place for reverie in their lives. "Idleness is looked down upon," says Khalil uncomfortably. "If you're sitting down, you're almost demonized."

So often, we scorn the still remove of mental time travel both within ourselves and in others. We have little patience with those taking a moment to muse on the future. In a series of studies based on performance reviews and videos, people tended to rate MBA students, chief executive officers, and politicians as incompetent if they paused to mull complex issues that were new to them, such as an accounting fiasco. Meanwhile, disfluencies in speech, like a pause, are equated with powerlessness and hesitation, although they typically mark transitional moments in and out of planning complex thoughts. Even the drift of our gaze as we turn within can be a sign of mental effort. The more people stare into the distance when they are asked a complex question, the more detailed, imaginative answers they tend to provide, studies by Jerome Singer and others show.

How can we start to trust in the merit of an inner life? Could we learn to pursue reverie as an intimate discipline of discovery? We can begin by musing on the daydream as a sketchbook of the mind.

⤓

There they stood invitingly: shelf upon shelf of sketchbooks clad in plain brown paper. Housed in a spartan gallery in a hip New York neighborhood, the Sketchbook Project was billed as the world's largest collection of such volumes, an archive numbering tens of thousands. One winter's day, I made a pilgrimage there, hoping to learn how to treat the space of reverie as a canvas for inventive thought.

Two Atlanta art students started the venture in 2006, envisioning a crowdsourced artwork with participation open to all. In just a few years, thousands of people around the world were signing up annually to receive a thirty-two-page blank notebook, fill it in as they chose, and return it to the project. From a wall-mounted tablet, I requested a sketchbook—one at a time was the rule—and sat down at a long mahogany table to wait as a plaintive Paul Simon song swelled in the background and tourists drifted in and out. Nearby, two young women in ponytails and parkas sat side by side, each silently perusing a book. For fifteen minutes, they flipped through the pages, seemingly lost in thought. Perhaps they too were hoping to be voyeurs of minds adrift.

Picture the sketchbook, held close to the body, scaled to the hand, and rarely shared with others in a creator's lifetime. Like the daydream, the sketchbook is a private repository of the most intimate of inventive thoughts and so may be the closest we can come to witnessing the unruly roots of genius. "It's like looking over an artist's shoulder," Miriam Stewart, a curator of Harvard University's art museums, tells me. "There's a certain 'man behind the curtain' aspect to sketchbooks."

Across their pages, laundry lists, ticket stubs, notes, mnemonics, and reading lists often jostle helter-skelter alongside the wispy *primi pensieri*, or first-thought sketches, that foreshadow creative endeavors in all media. Seemingly random jottings spill across a book's gutter or somersault into its margins and corners, suggestive in their ambiguity. Incompatible thoughts converse with one another.

Here again, we see the soul of creativity in the gently guided movement from idea to idea, spurring the mind to let go of the familiar and obvious. In one series of studies, people were given four simple, abstract sketches that vaguely hinted of landscapes or simple machines. Those who focused on or regrouped the drawings' parts produced nearly twice as many new interpretations while also avoiding the classic slowdown in novel idea generation that plagues creators over time. Like the agile daydreamer, the keeper of the sketchbook plays with ideas, making room for the detour and the wrong turn.

"Confused things rouse the mind to new inventions," wrote Leonardo da Vinci, one of the first in the West to see in the messy indeterminate a path to creative discovery. Scattered, broken up, and little known for centuries, da Vinci's notebooks were fully recognized as works of genius only in modern times. In them, he worked out his evolving ideas on flying machines, futuristic cities, his paintings and theatrical spectacles, and on the science of water, bodies, and light. The manuscripts are infused with clarity and precision, writes a biographer, yet they have an "unfinished quality. Everything he writes is provisional." Observed da Vinci of his notebooks, "The mind in an instant leaps from east to west. . . . So, reader, you need not wonder, nor laugh at me, if here we jump from one subject to another." What do *we* make of the book of our reverie?

That day in Brooklyn, I failed to find the daydream. Slim and promising, the sketchbooks came to me one by one, at times revealing mere scribbles but more often disclosing memoirs, fairy tales, graphic novels, and collages that had been painstakingly readied for show. These were not glimpses into the meandering, inventive mind. Even the staff draft their books over and over, reluctant to relinquish anything but a finished work. I found in the gallery the opposite of sketchy thought.

Reverie offers us in essence the freedom to fail, to stumble and try again, as we seek a tenuous hold on the wisp of a good idea. The inefficiencies of the daydream remind us of the fragility of nascent creativity, of the impermanence of thought, and of all that we must relinquish, all that will evade us, en route to inspiration. In reverie, we can gain the raw makings of invention if we are willing to gently guide a mind adrift.

How should we honor the daydream? Let go of the present and the familiar, voyage among new perspectives, and give others the freedom to do so. Revel in the mind's capacity to leap from east to west. For good reverie, in the end, is something of our redemption. It is a chance day after day to start anew. In Brooklyn, I was unable to hold reverie in hand. But later, I learned a tantalizing postscript: many of the sketchbooks are *not* returned.

Some people just don't finish them, Sketchbook Project founder Steven Peterman told me. Others admit they cannot bear to part with them. Perhaps the exercise of keeping a sketchbook inspires them to discover the solace of the daydream, a constant companion with teasing potential. I picture a thinker, unashamed to carry within a sketchbook of the mind, a private realm of stumblings, jottings, and *primi pensieri*. She is flipping through the teeming pages of her reverie, making room for the detour. A languid moment. A step away. It is not too late for discovery.

↵

"The very best will grab this and go," Jim Collins predicted after the tech-free experiment failed. His faith in second chances remained ever strong, his efforts to school his students in the practice of daydreaming were unrelenting. A few years later, I tracked down the daydream skeptic Kyle Allison, a rising star in his field. For his youthful discovery, Allison reaped accolades, news headlines, and a million-dollar-plus grant to open his own laboratory to further pursue the mysterious persister bacteria. His innovation to pair antibiotics with sugar would provide the foundation for a number of advances, including bolstering the effectiveness of powerful existing antibiotics, such as aminoglycosides, while lowering their toxicity to patients. He was on the fast track yet also beginning to sense tantalizing potential in the daydream. He was learning to loosen the grip of productivity on the soul of his creativity.

I find him in an empty new office at Columbia University with a fresh research idea in mind. Searching for further clues to the wily persister, he has been sorting fluorescent-tagged *E. coli* strains in a flow cytometer, a device that demands near-constant monitoring to ensure data purity. Typically, he had been trying to work in the ten-second spaces between read-outs, glancing at e-mail, drafting a reference.

But that week in the off moments, he let his mind meander over a potentially groundbreaking new technique: a double overlay of dyes that could shed light on how persister gene expressions are related to their mortality. The strategy ultimately won't work, yet it will lead to an innovative new method to isolate persisters from other bacteria for further study. "All those times you're productive, you're in a valley, digging and exploring effectively," Allison tells me. "Daydreaming allows you to leap out of that, into a different space, and occupy that area for a moment and *think* about it rather than being caught in the valley that you're in. It puts me on top of a different mountain from where I had been before."

What do we fear of reverie—that we may lose ourselves in a labyrinth of thinking or meet the stranger within of a radically new perspective? In the end, there will always be another beginning, another realm of exploration, in the uncharted territory of the meandering mind. I leave Allison eyeing another vista: a new view of the daydream's place in his life. I picture a thinker, opening the sketchbook of his reverie, ready for a leap of faith in his own mind.

PART III

THINKING AS WE

CHAPTER FIVE

OUTSIDE THE WALLS
OF OUR PERSPECTIVE

How Tolerance Sets Us Free

It is dangerous to live in a secure world.
—TEJU COLE

As Steve Deline chances upon her, Amilah* is cleaning up her post-age-stamp yard in South Los Angeles, wearing flip-flops, pink sweatpants, latex gloves, and a trapper hat, flaps down. It is noon on a blue-sky Saturday in early May. A field organizer for one of the country's most innovative LGBT outreach groups, Steve is leading three dozen activists who are spilling across the neighborhood, clipboards in hand, to canvass for transgender rights. The day's turf is a largely middle-class, Black enclave of stucco houses and buckled sidewalks. A knock at door one, silence. At Amilah's neighbor, a rebuff. We can smell fish frying as a man calls out, "I'm busy!" over a blaring television. So when Steve, tall and eager, spots Amilah dumping litter into an enormous garbage bin, he begins speaking almost before he lopes over to her.

"If you were voting," he asks, "would you be in favor or against including gay and transgender people in our nondiscrimination laws?"

"Oh, I'd be in favor," she says, a bit too eagerly in his view. Experienced hands at the Leadership Lab know to suspect the pat "antidiscrimination

---

*A pseudonym.

107

declaration." No one wants to admit prejudice. "Just to be more specific, on a zero-to-10 scale, with 10 being in favor," he presses, "where would you fit?" Over her shoulder, I can hear an angry dog hurling itself into the other side of a trembling backyard fence. "Probably about a seven," she offers. She is retreating before his eyes. "I would love to actually find out about that," he says. He is setting out once again to try to open a gated mind.

That day, LGBT rights are legally protected in California, yet the threat of a rollback is palpable to the canvassers, some gay, some gender non-conforming or transitioning, others allies. Dozens of state laws hostile to LGBT people are pending. Nearly four in ten Americans disapprove of same-sex marriage, and similar numbers believe that immigrants are hurting the country's progress. A brief era of hope in race relations has bitterly burst, with most blaming individual, not systemic, prejudice. The country, as Richard Wright wrote in *Black Boy*, "hugs the easy way of damning those whom it cannot understand." In Houston, a campaign raising the specter of pedophiles in restrooms persuaded voters to reject a city ordinance banning discrimination by a range of characteristics, including race, ethnicity, and sexual orientation. Black voters proved key to rejecting the law. Before the canvass, Lab staff tell volunteers, "This is a moment of some urgency."

Yet when Amilah begins to wobble, Steve does not flinch, argue, or, as his boss would say, "bitch-slap" her with a statistic: *two-thirds of transgender people have suffered major discrimination, you know.* It has taken the Lab seven years to get to this day, and he will not rush the encounter. He is aiming for something bigger, something more miraculous than just a vote: lowering prejudice, perhaps for good.

Not long before, a landmark study, the first of many to come, stamped the Lab's work as not just scientifically bona fide but as one of the most powerful known methods for achieving lasting reductions in prejudice. The findings "stand alone," wrote a Princeton expert on bias. "They blew me away," the young scientist who led the study told me. While only one-tenth of opponents are moved to support transgender nondiscrimination laws, the encounters typically lead to a bigger average boost in tolerance toward transgender people than Americans experienced toward gay people from 1998 to 2012. A decade's transformation in as little as ten minutes. From thirteen thousand conversations, miles of walking, and hundreds of late-night video critiques, the Lab was uncovering the makings of a way to tame bias and polarization. Headlines erupted. Scientists and activists came calling. Later that year, a gunman shot dead forty-nine people in a gay nightclub in Florida.

Standing on Amilah's lawn, I am witnessing something banal and yet so rare, something essential to the very survival of democracy. Racing past one another day to day, we cling to easy and vicious assumptions about others we see as different. Instead, the secret to tolerance may lie where we least want to look, with the help of those we shun. That is where we can find the social side of uncertainty, the remarkable acts of mutual not-knowing that can bring us together in a time of growing hate.

A script stays out of sight on Steve's clipboard as the talk moves further away from where two people stand politically and closer to how they live. Amilah shares that she was raised in a diverse neighborhood. "I just think people should be treated fairly one way or another." Her two teenage boys putter about an old car, and the neighbor who had been cooking lunch wanders out of his house to listen over the hedgerow. "Do you know anyone who's transgender?" Steve ventures.

"Oh yeah, I have a lot of friends who are, yeah, absolutely," says Amilah, adding that they have made her more sensitive to the issue.

"Is there someone you know especially well?" Steve goes onto inquire. And, if so, "what pronouns do they prefer?"

"Yes, it's a female who's trans," Amilah responds. "I think she's still going through the process. . . . We just thought she was a tomboy. To us, nothing's really changed."

Casually, Steve asks the friend's name and for permission to call the person "him." "So Che is living as a boy, was raised as a girl, got it," he says. "Did you know when he came out as trans?"

"I don't think she came out," says Amilah. "We just kind of knew and just went along with the process. But no, nothing's really changed."

"How did you feel about that, this change that was happening but no one was talking about?"

"It's her life," says Amilah. "I'm different than most people. It didn't affect me or anything."

Nothing's changed for Amilah, but all has changed for Che, Steve is hinting. He mentions a former boss whose career was sidelined after he came out as transgender, and Amilah begins to open up about the discrimination she has faced at work. Well after half an hour, neither makes a move to leave. More than 70 percent of voters finish the Lab's conversations; often, they do not want to stop. How do you build understanding with those you deeply oppose? Searching for clues in the tinderbox encounters of our time, Steve and his colleagues are beginning to find their way. Painstakingly, they are learning how to coax people outside the walls of their own perspective. But first they had to do so themselves.

⬇

Where does prejudice begin? With a glance. The instant we cast our eyes on someone, we almost immediately sort them into "people like us" or not. From that cognitive fork in the road, all else follows.

Seeing a face brings to life the brain's "fusiform face areas," a pair of matching regions, one in each hemisphere, that are critical to experiencing this aspect of our social world. Register an in-group member, and the mind instantly begins taking a rich, detailed look, with active, persistent processing, especially in the right-side fusiform region responsible for distinguishing individual examples within a category. If the person is *not* seen as one of our own, however, the fusiform face areas fall quiet.

Encountering people we see as like ourselves, we also experience their facial features holistically, another powerful springboard to probing someone's individuality. (Disrupt such "configural processing" by as simple a trick as turning a face upside down, and people rate that person as less thoughtful, empathetic, considerate, and human-like.) In contrast, a face from an out-group is not just experienced superficially but also in piecemeal fashion, with less focus on the eyes and more on features such as the nose or mouth, perhaps because these act as cues to race or group affiliation.

In these ways, other people's faces are considered, acknowledged, and remembered—or not. In one pioneering imaging study, White people showed nearly ten times better memory for countenances of their race than for Black faces. Black persons also recalled other people from their own race best of all, although perhaps due to the vigilance demanded of minority people, their memory for White faces nearly rivaled that for their own.

This is *in-group bias*, a narrowing of the mind recognized in psychological circles for a century but only recently discovered as a headwater of prejudice. We swiftly show a sweeping "cognitive disregard" not just for other races but also for almost every shade of difference, from economic class, sexual orientation (if known), and political hue to the fans across the stadium. Faces that are categorically unlike ours and especially those that are stigmatized "may not be 'faces' with the same intensity," a team of neuroscientists marveled in summing up the research. By our own doing, they begin to all look alike, as neuroscientist Roberto Caldara dramatically proved.

While their brains were monitored via electroencephalography (EEG), White Europeans and East Asians newly emigrated to Europe studied successive pairs of faces. Sometimes they saw the exact same White or Asian person twice and at other times two different people of the same heritage. Typically, when our mind sees anything twice, our neurons relax a bit the second time around; this *repetition suppression* effect helps us efficiently discriminate the familiar from the new. And so, as expected, this occurred for the second in a pair of identical in-group faces. But to the scientists' surprise, the brains of viewers looking at two *different* other-race people exhibited the same suppression effect. A unique human, guilty only of being unlike oneself, casually became to the mind's eye "just another one of them," literally unworthy of distinction, in a bare 170 milliseconds.

With one abbreviated look, we leave our understanding for the other, as scientists say, at the "category level," a process that also can occur in virtual realms via social cues that trigger mental categorization. In so doing, a person becomes an object ripe for labeling (Those people . . .), stereotyping (are lazy . . .), and discrimination (so don't deserve this job). *The only time I really saw* [black people] *was when we would go downtown in Durham on occasion late in the day*, recalled Richard Nixon of his time as a Duke University law student in the 1930s. *Pouring out of the factories like a black smoke from a furnace came the thousands of Negroes who worked there. . . . No one really seemed to think of them as individuals*. Averting our minds from another's uniqueness, we are a step away from dehumanization, the gateway to callous violence.

To survive, humans must continually categorize the world, yet there is perhaps no more volatile social moment than when we turn this capacity on one another. A line in the sand is drawn, and those on the other side become shadow figures, seen as homogeneous in kind and cruelly distanced from our gold standard of worth: ourselves.

Take any group of related objects and divide them down the middle, and we begin to assume a stark gap between the two "sides," a famous British study of prejudice revealed. In the 1963 series of experiments by Henri Tajfel, a row of eight simple lines ranging from about six to nine inches each were shown repeatedly to college students who were then asked to estimate each one's length. Some viewed the lines in random order. To others, the lines were presented from short to long and in two even groupings labeled A and B. Overall, people typically erred by no more than one-fifth of an inch per line in the accuracy of their guesses. Yet those who saw two separate groups of lines on average offered responses that were off by up to an inch for the dividing lines between the groups. A mere categorization sabotaged their grasp of the lines' continuity, leading them to see far more difference between the groups than existed. It was a "simplified exercise in stereotyping," wrote Tajfel, a World War II refugee.

His findings help explain why most Americans agree that diversity is good for the country, yet only one-quarter of adults overall would like their own neighborhood to be more racially mixed, or why Amilah couldn't let go of her outdated understanding of her friend as just a tomboy, as someone like her, not a transgender man. Once we relegate people unlike us to the other side, we fear and shun crossing the vast gap of seeming difference. *They were just a mass of people living their life as a race completely apart from the rest of us*, wrote Nixon, a reluctant proponent at best of civil rights as president. How do we traverse the divides of our own making? Others are the questions so few want to ask. In 2008, the future head of the Leadership Lab thought he had the answers, and he was feeling "really smart."

↵

That year, voters in California overwhelmingly backed the nation's first Black president and on the same day banned gay marriage. The narrow, unexpected passage of Proposition 8 in one of the most liberal states in the union shocked supporters and threw activists into disarray. Veteran canvasser Dave Fleischer flew in from Ohio, where he had been mobilizing for Barack Obama, to join forces with the Leadership Lab, the outreach and research arm of the nonprofit Los Angeles LGBT Center. A compact, muscular man with a shaved head and a Harvard Law School degree, Fleischer is quick to laugh and radiates a seemingly unquenchable intensity.

He grew up a closeted gay Jew in a small Republican town in Ohio. Talking to people who disagree with him is part of his pedigree.

Touching down in Los Angeles, he came up with an idea so unusual that he was later chagrined that it had not occurred to him before. Talk to the opposition, he proposed. Take the increasingly rare step of interacting with the masses who were in effect their out-group, the voters who opposed them. Door-to-door political canvassing long has been considered a poor cousin to media campaigns and a strategy (when used at all) that is deemed best for mobilizing one's own side or "knocking down the base." But Fleischer argued that if they could probe their opponents, they could perfect their message and fire off increasingly honed appeals that would win converts. With a knock and a script, they could turn the *other* into people like them.

All seemed promising at first. A surprising number of voters in opposition neighborhoods were opening their doors and conversing. Skeptical volunteers returned energized from each morning's encounters. Early scripts—nineteen in the first year alone—swelled with clever rebuttals and tailored talking points. "We were clinging to them," recalled a Lab veteran. If religion, marriage, or impressionable children were sticking points, the Lab had a prepared answer. One glance at a pickup truck in the driveway or an opposition sticker on the front door, and they were braced and ready. *Gay couples are honoring the institution of marriage, . . . what's wrong with that?* the canvassers would counter. *Do you wish gay people were a lot less visible?* Use open-ended questions only in a pinch, an early script advised.

Yet while the Lab was talking to voters, they were largely failing to lower their bias. Focusing on their mission, their ask, their rightness, they at first did not see that beyond their perspective was an *other*, waiting to be heard. Crossing the divide, they had closed their eyes and ears. ("How nice it would be," observed Socrates, "if wisdom were the kind of thing that could flow from what is more full into what is more empty.") The first step to opening others' minds would begin with opening their own to an idea that they had refused to accept: allowing out-group members their own hopes, dreams, and individuality. Then in the fall of 2009, Dave Fleischer met Ernest, a widower who stood in his driveway beside the 1966 Mustang that he had lovingly restored for his wife. Caught on one of the Lab's first videos, the conversation marked a coming-out of sorts—for the voter.

As the video begins a few minutes into their conversation, Dave is listening. *I don't have a problem with gay and lesbian rights*, insists Ernest, although he says that he abstained on Proposition 8 and wishes all the fuss over equality would die down. *Quite frankly, are we ever really satisfied with life?* asks Ernest, drawing on a cigarette. *When do you reach a limit?* To this, Dave leaves his script behind and offers a kind of assurance. "It sounds like marriage is incredibly important to you," he suggests. And Ernest warms up, remembering his wife of forty-seven years whose heartbreaking loss seems to him not a decade but rather days ago. Ever so slightly, the "Mustang Man," as the Lab came to call him, swivels to face Dave, and in that moment, he becomes far more than a name on a voter roll, a political opinion, a category.

You can see this literal turning point repeatedly in other Lab encounters, as a conversation deepens and a voter emerges from the shadows to face the canvasser. Two bodies draw just a step closer, and the horizons of the moment expand from a front porch or a driveway to the dynamic world beyond. Dave looked past a label and saw not set-in-stone bigotry but rather potential, and with that, the Mustang Man made a leap. *I want gay people to be happy too*, says Ernest. He mentions his neighbors, a long-time lesbian couple. *They're wonderful.* Next time, he says, he would vote for equality. Then he searches for words, his hand on the car. *I would hope they would find the happiness I had in life.* "That's a beautiful wish," says Dave.

Years of tinkering and experimenting would follow, but the Lab had uncovered a crucial chink in the siege wall of bias. By treating an opponent as an individual, they began to see a person worthy of connection and investigation and so paved the way for the opponent to do the same. The indifference that we extend to an out-group can be punctured with this simple cognitive twist.

Recall how incompletely we often experience out-group faces, coolly averting our eyes from theirs. Yet when White participants in a series of experiments were exhorted to pay attention to what made Black faces unique, their perceptual bias disappeared. Their eyes sought out those of the other, although no explicit suggestion to do so had been made. The faces became far more memorable, even more so than those of White people. And this tiny victory over bias changed people ever so slightly. When asked later to select team partners for a new experiment from a series of photos, participants who had endeavored to individuate the *other* chose almost equally from both groups. They were willing to move from taking a closer look to embarking on a relationship with a person they now saw as fully human.

To cross the divides of our own making, look past a label and see someone: the teen in the hoodie, hiding her vulnerability; the downcast man with a past life beyond sleeping on the streets; the girl waking up to the truth of her masculinity. It's only a start, a first step to the difficult work of countering bias. Yet by the time I landed in Los Angeles, the Lab had begun to unlock gated minds, inspired by Fleischer's unerring faith in the epic importance of the task. Doorstep by doorstep, they were opening up to the mysteries of another and making room for the kind of change that no script could guarantee.

A few hours before the canvass, I join thirty-eight Lab staff and volunteers trickling into borrowed offices near the day's target territory for coffee, bagels, and pre-canvass training. There are newcomers and veterans, mothers of gender-transitioning children, folks of many sexual orientations, and activists visiting from Washington, D.C., and from Washington State. Many volunteers are a bit nervous, and some are plain scared.

The Lab's efforts are gaining attention; the activist world that once shunned their invitations to collaborate now eagerly seeks to learn from them. Yet their endeavors remain far from the norm not just for political campaigns but also in daily life itself. Once engaged, voters often prove thirsty for connection, and some simply hurl invectives. Later, I would watch Deline come out to an elderly man in pajamas planted behind a screen door. "It don't make me hate you," said the voter. "But I feel ashamed that God made you."

Soon the canvassers will hit the streets, pursuing the chance for a daunting meeting without the shield of pat answers or the escape hatch of a two-minute "knock rate." In the wake of the Mustang Man, the Lab threw out 75 percent of its work and the very mention of talking points. Their conversations became scripted only in the loosest sense. At each door that day, the canvassers would seek not just an ear and a vote but also a stranger's willingness to work together to understand one another's worlds.

"So we're going to be in South Los Angeles today, which is an older, predominantly African American community," announces longtime volunteer Nancy Williams, a transgender former teacher with a clarion voice.

The chatter in the room quiets as she offers both an energetic welcome and a gentle admonition born of the Lab's past errors. "We are asking voters to not prejudge people," says Williams. "*We* need to walk that walk." Don't assume that changes of mind track to race, age, gender, or even "a crucifix on the door," the volunteers are told. "It's a mind shift," stresses longtime Lab staffer Laura Gardiner who, along with Deline, is leading the canvass while Fleischer is away. "You might be a little nervous, so you're going to suppress those butterflies," she says. Put down the sunglasses, look up from the clipboard, and smile.

Be unguarded in the most risky of moments when two in opposition first meet, they exhort. By leaving the comforting shelter of the categorizing mind, the true work of an interaction can begin: jointly exploring lived experiences, from the transition of Amilah's friend Che to Ernest's grief for his lost love. Eradicating prejudice demands not just glimpsing a unique, complex human in the *other* but also drawing closer to probe and then try on their perspective, the Lab had learned these seven years. And that is how Amilah slowly came around to a revelation, with Steve Deline at her side.

The angry dog is quiet. The neighbor across the hedge listens intently. *It's just easier*, continues Amilah, to keep calling her now-male friend "she." *There was no coming out.* Gently, Steve gives her a stepping stone. "Probably at work now people call Che 'him,'" he says. What's on the other side—of Che? Steve is asking.

I don't think she cares one way or the other, Amilah insists. *It's more respect for our comfort.* Almost despite herself, she starts to grasp Che's outlook and notice her friend's consideration. Steve eases his way into the story of his former boss, who was shunned by family and discriminated at work for transitioning, and Amilah drops her knowing stance and grows curious. *In your community, what's more important*, she asks, *what people call you or how you feel*, that is, being accepted by others or accepting yourself? "It's both," Steve responds. He talks about the difficulties of coming out. "It's pretty scary," he says, "having one thing to tell everyone in your life that is going to shift every relationship and in unpredictable ways."

They talk a bit more, then he asks, "Have *you* ever been treated differently for who you are?" *I'm Black, so yes*, says Amilah. "Hell yes," barks the neighbor, an older Black man, "have we been treated differently!" A corporate refugee, Amilah says she suffered for taking up what diversity really means, most notably by wearing her hair in cornrows. Standing up in this and other ways caused her to lose her job, she says. *Not to compare myself to the gay and lesbian community, but I felt myself not wearing them because I wanted to make sure other people were comfortable.* At that instant, I think—and is she too thinking?—of Che, who perhaps is afraid to come out to friends whose language, for all their care, keeps others in the shadows, makes people who are different into strangers to themselves.

And that is where Fleischer's assurances, Deline's gentility, and, most of all, the Lab's growing willingness to value the unscripted come into play. ("Being willing to enter into a conversation where we don't know for sure where it's going to end up—that's a big part of deep canvassing," Fleischer later tells me.) At the start, the Lab's leaders had no idea how much patience, pausing, awkwardness—all that we strive to eradicate in today's discourse—would be demanded. Don't rush through the conversations, they tell their volunteers. A mind cannot be forced or even hurried to change. Such a transformation is only ours to make, with the help, if we're lucky, of someone from the other side. By holding up another point of view, Deline allows Amilah a glimpse of where behavior can fall short of belief and how disregard can be as toxic as explicit rejection. *It's more out of respect for our comfort.* The pieces are there, and then he steps back, allowing her to do the last crucial work—what the Lab calls the "pure gold"—of trading her perspective for another's, just as both Dave and the Mustang Man did.

"You know, you shouldn't have to disguise or hide who you are—that's why laws like these exist," Steve says. *Exactly*, said Amilah. She has turned toward Steve. They are working together, ever so slightly dismantling divisions. They are teaching one another, keeping a dynamic moment of mutual exploration going. At last, she emerges a fully onboard "10" on the Lab's scale of support. In the end, each sees someone anew.

⤵

When we take the perspective of another, we can begin to see not just someone's uniqueness but also the fuller texture of a life. We fill in the blank of the label, noticing how they, like we, are far more than sterile categories. We begin to see the overlooked details and contexts that can puncture our assumptions.

Picture a day in the life of "Robert," a young Black man who gives up his seat on the subway for a stranger in need, swears at a sales clerk, eats a sandwich for lunch. Across the hours, his actions are equal parts kindness, hostility, and routine. In one study, White and Asian American participants were shown his photo and told his tale. Those asked to view his behavior objectively later recalled nearly double the moments of aggression, a stereotype long pegged to Black people. But participants who instead were told to visualize what it would be like to see the world through Robert's eyes remembered as many incidents of sweetness as anger. As Amilah newly saw her friend, they recognized Robert as a deeply human mix of contradictions, a good soul perhaps encountering a gamut of daily slights.

Walking in another's shoes: this is the folk wisdom tapped by the Lab and increasingly revealed by science to be a promising counterpoint to prejudice. A milestone in a child's development and a path to social bonding, the act of perspective taking can be most transformative in the dark realm of disregard, when we actively contemplate the experience of the other. It is the cognitive side of empathy, a complex reaching out not just for snatches of feeling but also for fuller understanding. It is mere speculation, a mental plunge in the dark, made all the more difficult the farther apart or the more deeply biased we are. But if we practice this cognitive skill in the spirit of inclusion, imagining the view from the other side can dramatically open our minds.

By taking a few minutes to imagine life as an out-group member or an outcast, people become more willing to sit closer to, work with, and even help that individual *and* similar others, decades of studies show. In one real-world experiment, people who briefly imagined what it would be like to be a refugee fleeing a war-torn country were more likely to write letters to the government supporting asylum for Syrian refugees, according to a study involving five thousand Americans. One-fifth of perspective takers wrote a letter, about 10 percent more than those who simply answered questions about their attitudes toward refugees. Other studies show that perspective taking can lower prejudice and can help people see others as more similar to themselves. By imagining the viewpoint of an elderly man, for example, young people can realize that they too know what it is like to be forgetful. They can gain a foothold on the humanity that they share.

Two mornings later, I meet Fleischer, just returned from London, at the Lab's tiny offices. The first to arrive, he has set out a heaping bowl of cherries for the staff and is perched at a conference table combing over the canvass results: nearly seven hundred and eight-seven doors knocked on, one hundred and thirty new supporters. The Lab is hitting, perhaps even exceeding, the rates of success captured by political scientists David Broockman and Joshua Kalla in their first studies of the Lab's strategy when, among persuaded voters, warmth toward transgender people rose an average of 10 percent and remained so for at least three to four months. Later studies will reveal that deep canvassing conversations evoke both lasting declines in bias and more support for inclusionary policies for immigrants and other out-groups. Not just a feat of political persuasion, the Lab's work is both real-world evidence of perspective taking's potential and a rare breakthrough in decades of efforts to scale back prejudice. Over Fleischer's shoulder, a poster declares, *Discrimination Exists. Discrimination Is Legal. We Can Stop It.*

Still, Fleischer and his team see their work as deeply unfinished. They know how uncertain such encounters can be and how far they have to go. "We are just at the beginning of understanding this," Fleischer tells me. Each new canvass is painstakingly dissected, and volunteers are closely consulted, with hope and with skepticism. No formula will do. ("Hypothesis Man," I privately dub Fleischer.) In coming years, the strategy's creators will continue to hone their work of improvisation, translating their efforts to a range of issues from voter turnout to police reform. They are driven by a central question of our times: how can we make open-mindedness a daily practice, one encounter at a time?

Talk to the opposition, Fleischer said, and then he found a way to inject humanity into the most unpredictable of moments. Look past a label and open up to the mystery of those we dismiss. See the *other* as worthy of investigation and begin an encounter tempered by remaining open to all views. For perspective taking is, in the end, a form of accountability, an astonishing set of brakes that we can, if we choose, offer most potently to one another. When someone shares their point of view, do we take the responsibility to see the world from their perspective? When we extend our own outlook, do we allow space for the other to do the same? Prejudice is at heart a simplification and a retreat that we cannot cure at a distance.

And tolerance begins where we least want to look—in a moment of mutual regard.

That is why the Lab's pioneers are changed profoundly by their practice. Through their work, they learn to refrain from shutting down a friend's opinion or from rapidly judging a point they may have misheard, they tell me. Over time, they can refuse the temptation to retreat into easy assumptions about a bitter older man at the door. As they are opening opposition minds, theirs are opening too. Along with boosting voter tolerance, the practice that the Lab pioneered lowers activists' *own* animosity for the opposition by the equivalent of a decade's worth of national increases in partisan hostility, field experiments show. In our own lives, do we answer the knock of a differing point of view? At stake is far more than a doorstep conversation, far more than the fragile flowering of an open mind.

⊺

Prejudice begins with a glance but flourishes behind the walls that we build to silence and distance one another. Even as the country grows more diverse, most large cities and a rising proportion of suburbs increasingly are segregated into majority single-race communities. Meanwhile, nearly one-third of U.S. students in 2019 attended schools that were made up of 75 percent or more minority youths, up from 18 percent of students a quarter of a century ago. In the melting pot of New York, a Latinx student can graduate from high school without encountering a White classmate. A nation "moving toward two societies . . . separate and unequal," sounded the famous 1967 Kerner Report on racial tensions. Decades later and still deeply divided by race, class, religion, and politics, what do we see of others' lives? What do we hear of their views?

In the summer of 2014, the police slaying of unarmed Black teen Michael Brown in Ferguson, Missouri, set fire to simmering frustrations. That same week, the ranks of non-White adults who had faith in the impartiality of American justice halved to just 16 percent, while White people's belief that U.S. justice was blind edged up a bit to nearly half the population. *Just another funeral, just another boy.* Nearly a decade and a social revolution later, a majority of Black, Asian American, and Hispanic adults felt that much more work was needed to attain racial equality, while just 40 percent of White Americans thought so. *Nothing's really changed—for me.*

How easily does difference slide into opposition and bigotry. With politics distilling along party identity, not ideology, polarization has risen in democracies from New Zealand to India but most dizzyingly so in the United States. The tendency of Americans to characterize people from the opposite party as "selfish" more than doubled in the past half century. Four in five Republicans and Democrats alike say the other party has few or no good ideas. Given the chance, members of both parties prove equally willing to discriminate against each other, experiments show. Asked to pick the winner of a college scholarship, people rarely chose the most qualified candidate if they knew that the applicant was a political other. "The nigger, the fag, the bitch illuminate the border, illuminate what we ostensibly are not," writes Ta-Nehisi Coates. "We name the hated strangers and are confirmed in the tribe." Inhabiting worlds apart, the company we keep and the opinions we seek are becoming stunningly like our own.

We are talking to the mirror. According to a sixteen-nation study, Americans tend to have some of the most politically similar-minded core social circles in the world, a level of homophily that fuels out-party hostility. Only 25 percent of Americans discuss important matters with someone from a different race, ethnicity, or political party. Our core networks are not only homogeneous but also shrinking; they are, as a team of scientists notes, "closing in" on themselves. Less than half of Americans, down from two-thirds a little more than three decades ago, discuss important matters with anyone beyond their own parents, spouses, or children.

Nor are our wider, weaker networks, the folks across the hedgerow or those we befriend or follow online, as likely as a generation ago to be fertile sources of "bridging ties" to challenging viewpoints. Towns and cities are divided not just by race but also increasingly by politics, following a geographic shuffling nicknamed the Big Sort. By 2020, nearly 60 percent of voters, up from one-quarter in 1976, lived in counties where a close presidential contest was won by a landslide. Online, many people are exposed inadvertently and briefly to diverse views, yet the disproportionate noise made by extremists winds up inhibiting deeper "crosscutting" talk. Fewer than one-fifth of social media users regularly engage in such conversations on those platforms. An estimated four in five Facebook friends are like-minded politically, and an equal proportion of retweets are exchanged between those with similar views.

Within the in-group, we do not always agree. Yet withdrawing into circles of mutual affirmation and jockeying to confirm our place in the tribe, we narrow the scope of seeming difference between *people like us*, even as we extend our distance from *them*. This is the law of group polarization, the dark flip side to the yearning for belonging revealed by Tajfel's experiments with simple lines. Across society, proximity and conformity tend to strengthen homogeneity of views, while distance and disregard deepen bias. Like pairs of magnets, in-groups and out-groups repel one another as they gravitate to opposite extremes. In Tajfel's classic study, people saw far more distinction than warranted between the groups of lines and far less within. That is why positive feelings for the in-party have been rising as fast as animosity for the out-party and why tribal differences left to fester may take generations to heal.

Moreover, these deepening schisms unfold at a time of rising reluctance not just to connect with the other side but also to be fully present to other human beings. In one of the first studies comparing virtual and in-person first meetings, scientists brought together seventy pairs of strangers for a twenty-minute encounter that was half spent chatting online and half in person, with results controlled for the order of encounter. Get to know one another, the partners were told. No topics are taboo. In the end, finding something to say and carrying on the conversation proved harder in person, participants reported. The unease could not be escaped, even though studies show that the awkwardness anticipated in real-time conversation generally tends to be lower than people fear. Still, in facing one another, the strangers emerged feeling closer to each other. They read one another's characters more accurately. They enjoyed the meeting more.

Whether they are posting or chatting online, people typically present a premeditated, edited, promotional self. As a result, they tend to focus more often on themselves and overestimate the clarity and frequency of their own contributions. We are our own virtual heroes; the other is subtly demoted. In the first impressions experiment, both sides felt *less* self-conscious while in the same room and saw their partners as less self-centered.*

---

*The study did not include live on-screen communications, but evidence suggests that such encounters, while offering a kind of face-to-face togetherness, nevertheless involve a thinner type of mutual connection.

All connection is a start by any means. Yet we cannot cultivate mutual understanding in a divided world without turning to face the stranger or outcast and making room for their perspectives. We cannot forge lasting ties to those unlike ourselves without shattering the false hope of bias: that we need not change at all.

Talk to the opposition, seek their perspective, and we become willing not just to glimpse another's views but also to accept their right to differ from us. When political scientist Diana Mutz asked people to list as many sound arguments as they could on both sides of a controversy, such as affirmative action, most gave triple the rationales on average for their own views. Those with the most diverse social circles, however, offered nearly as many rationales contrary to their positions as for them. They could see in an opponent a reasoning human taking a legitimately opposing stance. They could make room for both potential commonality and the possibility within discord. Asked for their views on a group that they least liked—gay people, White supremacists—people who regularly engaged in crosscutting talk showed more willingness to support the reviled group's right to teach school, to operate without government surveillance, and to protest.

Even a brief crosscutting conversation, whether face-to-face or online, can boost people's warm feelings toward the other party while increasing their appetite for further encounters, as uncomfortable as they may be. In one study, pairs of opponents who briefly discussed what they disliked about each other's parties wound up talking longer, agreeing more, and rating cross-party dialogue as more important than those who took turns simply praising their own side's policies. Other research suggests that those who regularly experience debate in their social circles are more likely to see both good and bad qualities in out-group members. They become a bit more agnostic, ambivalent, uncertain, and therefore open about what they hold dear.

And who are these daring, willing few? They are the people who are at times openly undecided and therefore reviled as fence-sitters. Consider the partisan whose commitment to the cause we rightly revere. Audacious and strident, they have been the historic instigators of social change from the civil rights movement to the fall of communism. "If they saw more, they would probably not see so keenly," wrote the philosopher John Stuart Mill of those he called "one-eyed . . . systematic half-thinkers." Often a force for good, partisanship nonetheless can slip into "the antithesis of open-mindedness and tolerance," notes Mutz. It can become "a form of prejudice." The most loyal partisans of any political stripe tend to show more hostility toward the other side and are *less* likely in daily life to talk to the opposition. At the extreme, they are mentally rigid and impulsive. In contrast, a hallmark of centrism is a willingness to fully engage, not just skirmish with, the other side.

Yet is the price to be paid for diverse interaction the watering down of our convictions? Is the dark side of an open mind a Hamlet-like inertia? In contrast to long-held assumptions, people who regularly interact with the opposition are on average no less likely to join a protest, turn out to vote, or otherwise be politically engaged, new research reveals. Social diversity leads to political indifference primarily among those who avoid face-to-face conflict, according to Mutz and others. Less politically engaged centrists may talk to the opposition, but they stop short of working through their disagreements. They sideline themselves.

Heed the partisan pushing with surety for change. But in an age of poisonous disregard, do not underestimate those who take a stand without abandoning the promise inherent in our differences. They are, in Mill's words, "complete thinkers," the rare few who face up to all that we increasingly shun: discord, unpredictability, unease. They are the bearers of restraint, driven not by single-minded conviction or by the hostility that now inspires political participation more than love of one's party. They spurn the complacency of both indifference and blind activism and welcome the challenge of not-knowing to further their understanding.

We need this voice among us but most of all within us, reminding us to quell the blinkered conviction that, left unchecked, spirals into prejudice and polarization; inspiring us to consider the unknown sides of a person; encouraging us to stand up for what we see as right while respecting an opponent's right to do so. Somewhere between the path of easy accord for *us* and cold disregard for *them*, there is a middle ground. For only by risking the encounters that we most fear and shun can we begin to discern when we are in the wrong and expand our cognitive horizons. Only by questioning ourselves as much as we question others can we build heights of understanding beyond facile assumptions. This was the lesson that Socrates died trying to teach in the first days of a democracy whose fragility echoes our own. Tolerance, he knew, is the only way that we can shield one another from the dark side of ourselves.

⬇

Picture a barefoot Socrates strolling through the Agora in the heart of golden-age Athens. Merchants, women, travelers, and leading citizens throng the marketplace, buying and selling spices, speeches, fish, and wool. The din of trade, the call of the orator, and the march step of the military echo in the halls of nearby courts and council chambers. From far and wide, cobblers and aristocrats alike come to contribute their voices to the running of the city-state. In democracy, "all things are possible," wrote an admiring nobleman visiting from Athens' archenemy Persia. The West's first experiment in majority rule was heady, noisy—and vulnerable. A popular vote could not protect Athens from simmering divisions that, like silent cracks in the city walls, would turn *demos-kratia* into a realm of hate-filled closed minds.

All this Socrates foresaw and fought. "It's this that will convict me, the prejudice ... of most people," asserted the philosopher at his trial on charges of denying the power of the gods and corrupting the city's youth with his maverick ideas. "This is what's convicted many other good men and, I think, it'll do so in the future." Soon after condemning Socrates to death in 399 BCE, repentant Athenians erected a bronze statue of the martyred philosopher. Fittingly, it graced the Potter's Quarter, the liminal riverside district just outside the city where a dozen years into the Greek Miracle, the son of a stonemason first began pursuing his unique craft: the opening of minds.

"Aren't mistakes . . . due to this ignorance of thinking one knows when one does not?" Socrates once queried a future military commander. "What is virtue?" he asked a young nobleman. Socrates ambled through the streets, bathhouses, workshops, and society's elite circles; he argued alike with prostitutes, artisans, oligarchs, and outcasts. Pressing his needling questions, he held up a new form of heroism born not of brawn but of mind, a vision of each human taking responsibility for the worth of their lives and for the fate of their society. He called his lifework "performing my Herculean labors."

Socrates was a complete thinker, willing to continually test his convictions while goading the people of Athens to do the same. "They told me in plain truth you . . . reduce others to perplexity," the aristocrat Meno once complained to Socrates. And the philosopher replied, "The truth is that I infect them with the perplexity I feel myself." He met with resistance, even violence, and made the powerful squirm, yet he was unafraid to keep searching for better answers, forged from relentless discourse. Forsake the disregard of intolerance, he taught, and we gain the chance not just to do right by another but to create a better self as well.

All his life, Socrates stood apart, eschewing political gain and wealth, even creature comforts. He founded no party or school of philosophy and sought no disciples. He refused to hide behind easy assumptions or blind allegiances. Yet we could not call him indifferent. Each day, he worked in his way for the good of the polis and took a stand when it counted most for what he saw as right. In his later years, the Greek Miracle began to falter, its people divided. Citizens voted to ostracize dissenters. Tightening repression deadened a once-vibrant trade in ideas. That was the tense moment when Socrates stood up in the line of public fire.

It was the late summer of 406 BCE, and six Athenian generals had just returned home from a sea battle with Sparta, victorious yet condemned. Fleeing a storm, the generals had left the dead and wounded behind. For this sacrilege, they faced a hearing before six thousand citizens eager for swift retribution. Putting himself forward for public office for the first time, Socrates was chosen by lottery to lead the day's proceedings. And he alone refused to back down on defending the men's right to fair, individual trials as the crowd bayed to convict both the aging philosopher and the generals of treason. "Talk to and teach each other," Socrates had tried to tell the Athenians. Hear one another out. Save a place in the most contentious of times for not-knowing, for accountability, for the possibility of a changed mind. By the end of the tense day, the Athenians had sided with justice, but the promise was broken by sunrise, a foreshadowing of the time not far off when the city would brand Socrates an outcast.

What is the gift of tolerance? It is far more than a living and a letting be. In the riskiest of moments, we have the potential to see a human worthy of connection, a person bearing perspectives wholly unlike our own. Then if we wish, we may shed the ease of disregard and move forward with the help of those we have shunned. Nascent efforts to lower polarization—civility dialogues, town halls—often seek to muzzle disagreement, a practice that, as political scientist David Broockman told me, "misses the meat of what democratic politics should be about. The whole reason that we have democracy is that there *is* disagreement." When we instead fully engage with the other side, we can achieve a twin accountability: we can stand up for what is right, all the while adjusting our notions of what "right" is. Tolerance is the chance to create with another an evolving understanding. It is a mutual promise to keep learning.

Not long ago, twenty-two liberals and an equal number of conservatives came to a Brown University neuroscience laboratory to watch short videos, including an innocuous nature clip and a high-tension segment of the 2016 vice-presidential election debate. While viewing the debate from inside a brain scanner, people who shared political views reacted similarly—perhaps feeling anger at Mike Pence or heightened attention to Tim Kaine—as shown by their brain scans. The more partisan a person was, the more "neural synchrony" they exhibited with others with the same political views. But the experiment did more than affirm Tajfel's classic work. After probing the scans, the scientists discovered that the most partisan people on either side shared a conviction beyond politics: intolerance of uncertainty. Those who were less willing to inject perplexity into their lives were more in lockstep with their own side and more disconnected from their opponents. They were far from ready to cross the divide.

All around us, doors are closing and siege walls tower higher. Who among us will dare to complete the journey that tolerance can spark? Who is willing to engage in mutual uncertainty-in-action and potentially be changed? Each age has its unsung heroes. Each in a way repeats our sins. Bear witness then to what we all can do when we see possibility where we least expect it. It might happen when we answer a stranger's knock or hear the other out. It might happen when we are mortally tested by another's dark side. What if we stand up for those we hate and take a stand that changes all? If the most partisan among us can do so, perhaps we can too.

↵

She was a sharecropper's daughter and a tenth-grade dropout, a brash and tenacious force in civil rights–era Durham. A single mother abandoned by the man she had wed at age fourteen, Ann Atwater fought for tenants' rights in a city where most of her neighbors lived in ramshackle houses and died on average by age forty. She "had it at the heart" to battle wrong, she said, yet she admitted that hatred motivated her too.

He was a gas station owner just scraping by and the local Ku Klux Klan chief in the supremacist group's reportedly most active state. A vicious bigot and a voice for segregation, C. P. Ellis sought to take the Klan's secretive work public. He was dangerous, Atwater sensed. She was effective, he knew. They met on the streets or in heated city council meetings; he openly packed a gun, and she once drew a knife on him. "We was caught in this web together," she later said. Across the land, the lie of racial harmony built on segregation was crumbling. The boycotts, sit-ins, and marches had begun. In Durham, Atwater and Ellis became lightning rods in a breaking storm.

Decades later, long after he was gone and just weeks before she died, I met Atwater at the "rest home" where she was staying. In long conversations over a spring weekend, she walked me back to that searing time when two in opposition began to understand one another and, as Ellis would later say, "the whole world was openin' up." One day, I sat beside her bed as we nibbled on fried catfish lunches; another morning, we talked as the strains of a gospel church service drifted down the hall. Tall and big-boned, she was forceful even in her hour of frailty.

"How do you help people see that the other side has a point of view?" I asked.

"You don't throw that point of view away," she said resolutely in her deep Carolina drawl. "We use a little bit of mine and a little bit of yours to get where we're trying to get at."

In 1971, the divide seemed unconquerable and hatred was running deep when an intensive series of community meetings called a charrette were planned to defuse tensions over school desegregation. It was Nixon's third year in office. Some saw talking to the other side as the only way to avert violence amid deepening battles for school integration. Others thought the process a sham or simply sought obstruction. Planning sessions nearly broke down for the ten days of meetings to be held at a largely Black elementary school. Then in the midst of it all, the city turned to them—a White man bent on preserving divisions, a Black woman without money or fancy connections—to lead the charrette. At first, neither would address the other. They had ceased long ago to be human to one another. Yet the truth was that they were drawing closer.

Not long before the meetings began, the Great Divide that Ellis treasured had cracked. His clear lines of belonging were muddied by the specter of class. Walking downtown, he had run into a city leader with whom he secretly had been strategizing. Their eyes met, and Ellis put out his hand, but the councilman turned away, all distance and disregard. *How does it feel to be judged?* Steve asked Amilah. *Isn't it a kind of ignorance to think one knows when one does not?* Socrates queried. Once smug within the walls of his perspective, Ellis was left in perplexity, yet he did not turn away. "That's when I began to do some real serious thinkin'," he later said. "I'd look at a Black person walkin' down the street, and the guy'd have raggedy shoes or his clothes would be worn. That began to do somethin' to me inside."

When Martin Luther King was assassinated three years earlier, Ellis had gathered his Klansmen at his gas station and rejoiced into the night. But by the time the charrette opened, he had begun to see the *other* as someone worthy of connection, as a person with a point of view. The first night of the meeting, even as he started to get death threats, he called Atwater and asked her to join him in laying aside their hatred. On the second night, they talked for a while and cried together about their children's futures. And it might have ended there with a bit less bias and an encounter or two. But then he began to retreat into hatred, and that is when, to all's surprise, she stood up and protected him.

Perhaps King's thundering words from a Durham pulpit a decade before inspired her. At White Rock Baptist Church in 1960, the civil rights leader famously gave his blessing to nonviolent protest, to taking action. Then he posed the question beneath all divisive encounters: what do we want from the other? he asked. Must opposition be met with the ruthless pursuit of victory? Seek reconciliation, urged King. "As we protest," he said, "our ultimate aim is not to defeat or humiliate the White man but to win his friendship and understanding." Atwater, who was working then as a housemaid, arrived at the church only in time to see King depart. But years later, she lived out his words at one of the last charrette meetings, when Ellis reverted to the shelter of his old ways.

After she invited a gospel choir to perform, he set up a retaliatory display of Klan paraphernalia: armbands, hate literature, photos of burning crosses. Soon a group of Black teens were heading his way, aiming to tear down his exhibit or worse. Atwater stepped forward and blocked the doorway. *What do you think you're doing? Get away from there! Leave that alone!* she shouted. *You need to read this material, not tear it up! If you want to know where a person is coming from, you got to see what makes him think what he thinks!*

That night, she taught them all the promise of tolerance, the mutual need to keep learning, the glory of restraint. But she did something more. In one instant, she freed Ellis from being forever in the wrong, a wrong that could have been her victory. And she freed herself from being on the other side, from being his enemy. Isn't that, in the end, what happens when we liberate one another from the prisons of our assumptions, when we work together to see in one another not set-in-stone wrong but potential? The philosopher Hannah Arendt argued that human freedom offers the "sheer capacity to begin" anew and is a deeply social condition, requiring the company of others. By protecting Ellis's right to oppose her, Atwater against all odds offered them both the gift of a second chance. Nothing's changed, he tried to say, and she answered: but it could.

At a party to mark the end of the charrette, they stood up together to toast its success. "Some say that by participating, I have lost my effectiveness in the conservative community," Ellis told the crowd. "But I have done what I thought was right." He resigned from the Klan, becoming a pariah to many in his community for his crosscutting work. But this time, he did not retreat. By then a maintenance worker at Duke University, he campaigned to unionize the mostly Black members of the department and later helped lead the chapter. Accused by some of selling out the Black cause for befriending Ellis, Atwater nonetheless battled her whole life for the rights of the oppressed. In the wake of that night, Atwater and Ellis became close friends and, in time, heroes to many.

"It takes a lot of work for people to cross the divide," I suggested to Atwater the first time we spoke.

"No," she quickly countered. "It just takes an 'I will.' That's all. 'I'm ready. I will.' That's all we've got to say."

Talking to the other is one of the most powerful antidotes to prejudice that we know. Roommates of differing races, classmates from historically adversarial religions, and people who interact with different generations or persuasions gain tolerance. There is no formula to this metamorphosis, although working together or being on an equal footing bolsters the process. There is no neat recipe for the artistry of bearing restraint and no ease. Beyond our comfort zone: that is a place we may never seek without an inner struggle. But as experiments and lived experience alike show, the lessons of tolerance are clear: apartness breeds hatred, quickly and easily. Seeing the other up close as a unique human, imagining another's perspective, finding their individuality and your commonality, and learning our limits together can open minds. "Thank God I got to the point," said Ellis, "where I can look past labels."

This practice is more powerful than we may at first realize. Recall how perspective taking can inspire people to sit closer, to work with, and to help both an *other* and their out-group. That is just a start. For if contact and discourse endure and are made to flourish amidst pauses, silence, and disagreement, tolerance spills generously and lastingly beyond the act itself, dozens of studies show. Contact that leads to less bias for one out-group, such as immigrants, also tends to lower prejudice for different but similarly maligned categories of people, such as those who are living unhoused.

Even more remarkably, tolerance can spread across communities among those who do *not* have direct contact with out-group members. Just having a friend who talks to the political opposition likely will lower your hostility for *other* party members and boost your willingness to be closer to them as much as if you had positive contact with the other side, studies show. In one study, the pairing of roommates across race lowered bias not just for those directly involved but also for students across campus for years to come. Once sparked, tolerance can sweep across a neighborhood, a city, or a region, expanding mental horizons far and wide. When two are willing to change, the world indeed opens up.

Ann Atwater's and C. P. Ellis's closing recommendations from the charrette were largely ignored. Their day-to-day work at the margins of society is mostly forgotten. Discrimination still casts an unmistakable shadow in the fraying homes and embattled schools of Durham and beyond. Yet while traveling around the city not long ago, I kept glimpsing a lasting light from their acts of courage.

Leaving Atwater, I drive across town in a pelting rainstorm to a low-slung brick industrial park where a pillar of the city's Black community greets me from behind a massive wooden desk. Brash and young in 1971, Ed Stewart stayed just one night at the charrette, yet again and again, he has seen evidence of its legacy unfold across the city and in his life. "Ann's presence and her tolerance, their tolerance of each other," Stewart tells me, "helped that thinking come to the table, come to the top. They began to [help people] look at persons not as Black and White, but as their fellow man."

Then he recounts a story of restraint and liberation. One day, Stewart drove to a poor coastal region virulently loyal to the Klan where his staff was holding job training classes. Shots had been fired into the rental house where the workers—young, idealistic, Black, and White—lived in Craven County. Pulling into town, Stewart locked eyes with a White man in overalls who was getting out of his dusty car. "To me right there, I knew that was my enemy. . . . He was the guy who did it. I had no reason, I had no evidence, but suddenly he was guilty." Stewart took to carrying a gun each time he came back to the region until one day he realized that both he and the man he saw as his enemy were trapped in a divide of their own making. He stopped carrying the weapon. "There was no need," he tells me. A mind cannot be forced or hurried. The transformation, the miracle of it all, is ours to make. Stewart's voice falls almost to a whisper, and his tall frame bends forward. What Ann Atwater did, he says, *it just gave strength to all of us*.

What do we want from the other? Just what they want from us: a leap into the unknown made safe by a haven called tolerance.

CHAPTER SIX

UNCOMMON GROUND

Uncertainty and the New Right Stuff of Collaboration

> *No one individual knows the whole of the truth,*
> *and no one individual fails entirely. Everyone says*
> *something true about the nature of things.*
> —ARISTOTLE

The tensions came to a head just after Christmas. The three astronauts, all rookies in space, were halfway through nearly three months orbiting Earth aboard Skylab, the first U.S. space station. They were on their way to breaking the record for the longest time living and working in space. Circling the planet every ninety minutes, they shot across the skies, a tiny streak of light visible from Earth in deep evening, a silent reminder of a new era in knowledge seeking.

Yet their odyssey wasn't going well. The astronauts were struggling to keep up with a blistering daily regimen of repairs, briefings, and experiments, including some of the most rigorous extraterrestrial observations to date of Earth and sun. They were already the first team of astronauts to receive a public reprimand while in space for hiding a bout of queasiness. Was this crew, the third and last to inhabit Skylab, up to par, NASA flight controllers wondered?

The astronauts saw things differently, however, and they were about to do what few heroes of those glory days ever dared: question the NASA way. It's time for some "straight words" on the situation, Jerry Carr, the mission's captain, radioed to the ground. "Commander out." The skirmish that would ensue has attained mythical status in the space program, insiders say. It's still being studied half a century later in the run-up to the country's next grand ambitions in space, landing humans once more on the moon and later on Mars. For from this contentious moment emerged a new, more reflective approach to exploring the universe, with implications for how we all work today. The space rebellion of 1973 offers a remarkable window into how we can combat the rising danger of the echo-chamber workplace and cultivate the uncertainty that can turn our differences into collective brilliance.

Carr and his crew fell behind schedule almost before they rocketed into space. Earlier in the year, the first team aboard Skylab had spent most of their month in orbit racing to repair the badly damaged new space station, which had been largely cobbled together from Apollo-era parts. They earned kudos for saving the Skylab program. A second trio, also commanded by an astronaut who had walked on the moon, made up for lost time by sprinting through a grueling scientific workload each day for eight weeks and then cheerfully asking for more. Dubbed the 150-percenters, they were in total sync with the space agency's philosophy of treating missions as "prize fights," recalled Neil Hutchinson, Skylab's flight director and later a space shuttle executive. The order of the day was a "nice, crisp 'yes, sir,' 'no, sir,' turn-it-on, turn-it-off, rigid disciplined flight operations mentality," he said in a NASA oral history. Failing to fall in line with this code was not an option.

The trouble was that Carr, pilot Bill Pogue, and scientist Ed Gibson were allowed almost no time to acclimate to space before being launched into a schedule that in many ways exceeded those of their predecessors. At the last minute, they had been given nearly double the number of science experiments as the other crews by researchers eager to make use of the country's last scheduled foray into space for who knew when. "Everything pushed back onto this last mission," NASA's chief historian Brian Odom told me.

Slowing them further, the crew had moved into a space station—essentially a floating laboratory—left in something of a mess, with many of the craft's 20,000 movable pieces of equipment misfiled or simply left to drift around. Once on board, they sometimes had just ten minutes to race across a spacecraft that was as long as a ten-story building was tall to set up a hastily planned experiment whose execution left no room for error or for the serendipity and deliberation that drives good science. "I don't know what is causing their slowness," NASA's chief of life sciences told reporters. "They may have a feeling of being pushed." One morning, the astronauts tried to save time and sanity by taking turns monitoring the constant barrage of radio traffic from the ground but wound up mistakenly shutting down contact altogether for part of a day. To their dismay, they were later accused in the press of holding a strike.

But it wasn't the long workdays that most put them at odds with their teammates two hundred and seventy miles below. The mission schedule needed adjusting, they knew, but they were as eager as any to do the job. "It's been my feeling that we really do up here need to work at the fastest and most efficient pace," Carr later told the ground. What ultimately spurred their dissent was being treated as marionettes on high, as "cogs in the wheel," says Odom. The crew tried half a dozen times in their first month in orbit to call NASA's attention to the growing disconnect between them and the ground. They received no reply until Carr radioed down his impassioned six-minute audio plea for an air-to-ground meeting. He and his crew were essentially fighting to fully contribute to the mission. "We'd like to be in on the conversation," said Carr. Two days later, they would get their way.

We might assume that we have moved on from swaggering old boys' clubs and times not long ago when men in suits were groomed to think and move as one. It's easy to believe that in a world marked by rising demographic diversity, we have triumphed over the alluring blind allegiance to the group that seemed the norm in Skylab's day. We might think that taking our differences to the streets and to the virtual market square will be the last word in forging ahead together with mutual dignity and respect. We would be wrong. To forge equity and understanding at work and beyond in an era of deep divisions and rising diversity, we must not just build bridges to those we loathe, to "them." We must counter the insularity of *our* side. What is the new right stuff of collaboration? It starts with recognizing the complacency of *we*.

⟱

It's not just in neighborhoods, social circles, and schools that people increasingly mingle with those who look and think like them. Work itself, a realm long seen as the best hope for injecting a diversity of perspectives into daily life, is becoming a place of insidious siloing. The upshot is that due to both context and choice, we stack the deck against difference, mingling at the office party, trading notes, and talking politics (if we do so at all) with people like us.

Picture who works in a company's boardroom versus its cafeteria or in an affluent suburban McDonald's versus a Golden Arches in an inner-city district a few miles away. Despite the increased presence of people of color in many once-predominantly White establishments and professions, overall diversity across organizations has fallen steeply compared with a generation ago. In the U.S. high-tech sector, only about 20 percent of executives are Asian American, and just 5 percent are Hispanic, with African American people holding a similarly tiny slice of top jobs. In many work realms, companies "hire for fit," a euphemism for seeking candidates of similar race, gender, education, or personality traits, such as extroversion. Employees even cluster along similar levels of well-being, according to a study of employees at companies in Spain and Japan. Data from workers who wore sensor badges for two weeks showed that they stood closer to and talked the most to colleagues who felt as socially connected to people and as satisfied with work and life as they were. There *is* a cheerful crowd and a sociable clique at the office—and they want to keep it that way.

At the end of Odysseus's long journey home, he is making his way along the road to his palace to confront the opponents who have been trying to seize his throne. Disguised as a beggar, the warrior-king is accompanied by his personal swineherd, a childhood friend who does not recognize him. As Homer relates in *The Odyssey*, they chance on Odysseus's head goatherd, an accomplice to the plotters. The climax of the story is imminent, and the brief interaction is telling. Also blind to Odysseus's true identity, the goatherd insults the lowly pair as vile birds of a feather. "Dirt finds dirt by the will of god—it never fails!" he snarls before hurrying off to the palace and to his death in the coming battle.

Our love for similar others answers the essential human need for belonging. Being on the same page is our vision of what a group should be. Without homophily, we might be eternal strangers in our own lives. But by relentlessly pursuing alignment, we tend to miss not only the humanity of the other side but also the failings of our own. Odysseus seeks to return to his circle. Still, before doing so, he sets himself apart from friend and foe alike in order to assess the social and political realities of his homeland. He is "an incarnation of the cautious and skeptical investigator," observes the classicist René Nünlist. Whether he is ruling his country, fighting in an epic war, or making his way home, wily Odysseus is a master of joining in while keeping an independent perspective. Contrary to what the goatherd thinks, Odysseus knows well the blinkers we wear when we rush too eagerly toward accord, whether we are fighting for an ancient kingdom or a slice of a modern-day financial pie.

It wasn't long after trading began in the experimental markets that some exchanges started to derail, felled by the pricing bubbles that have sunk fortunes and governments for centuries. Just why this phenomenon plagues financial markets has long been a mystery variously ascribed to mania, confusion, or error. But an international team of social scientists came together in 2014 to test a hidden-in-plain-sight cause of such behavior: the human urge to take almost any excuse to unthinkingly align. The influential study, one outside commentator noted, lays bare the costs of our era's "unmitigated celebration" of cohesion.

The traders in the markets set up in Texas and Singapore were financially savvy. Some were professionals, and most had earned an advanced degree in economics or in finance. Once in the laboratory, they were tested on their acumen to "make sure they understood that to make money in the market you may need to break away from your rivals, do the opposite of what they do," lead researcher Sheen S. Levine, an authority on strategic management and diversity, explained to me. The participants were then divided into six-person markets and given real money to spend as well as detailed information on the performance of each financial asset that they were trading. "They could have done the work to value the assets, to understand what it means to buy cheap and sell high," noted Levine. All but handed a route map to success, some of the groups nevertheless marched lockstep onto a path not of profit but of disaster.

Half of the markets had been set up to be ethnically homogeneous, with members made up solely of each region's dominant Hispanic or Chinese majorities. Others included a minority, such as a person who identified as White or Indian. All of the players carried out their trades on private screens in separate cubicles and *met one another just once for a few minutes* in the waiting room before the experiment began. That brief engineered glimpse of likeness or difference, however, was enough to dramatically change the game.

In ten rounds of trading, ethnically identical groups rapidly lost sight of the assets' fundamental value. Their trades on average wound up being about 60 percent less accurate than those made in diverse groups. Members of homogeneous markets spent more money on each asset than warranted, jumped to accept inflated offers, and eagerly copied one another's mistakes, creating bubbles that burst violently, at times possibly wiping out hundreds and even thousands of dollars in gains. "We had made it very difficult for people to fall in line," said Levine, by keeping traders apart, offering them advance data, and stressing the importance of competitive play. "We designed the study to fail."

But a mere whiff of belonging offered players a group-level heuristic—a powerful cognitive shortcut—for placing too much stock, so to speak, in others' competence and in their own. The result was the dark side of what sociologist Émile Durkheim called "mechanical solidarity," or unity built on homogeneity. In contrast, traders in diverse markets better calibrated prices to true values, behavior that led to less clustered, more thoughtful transactions. In diverse exchanges, bubbles were less frequent and burst more gently. Homogeneity, Levine and colleagues concluded, "discourages people from scrutinizing behavior."

Psychologists call this the "delusion of homogeneity." In bonding like with like, people tend to become careless, overconfident, and out of step with reality. Cohesion feels wonderful and yet can quickly turn into a group opiate. The old-timers gang, the righteous left or right, the inner circle, the soccer mom clique, or street protest loyalists: even a hastily or briefly shared identity or a moment's agreement breeds comforting insularity. A group "operates with a specific kind of logic," the evolutionary biologist Michael Tomasello observes.

And once we settle into the embrace of a unifying view, it becomes increasingly difficult to break away. For just as similarity ushers us toward accord, agreement breeds further perceptions of similarity that, like a pricing bubble, may not be grounded in reality at all. Coming together, we narrow our cognitive horizons to match those of our side, aligning our allegiances and our minds. This is the hidden peril in the ancient story of human belonging, one whose critical neural mechanisms are just beginning to be understood.

Not long ago, decoding the cognitive underpinnings of social interaction was a rudimentary enterprise. The study of how people's minds react to one another was limited largely to snapshots patched together from surveys, interviews, and neuroimages of people's brains as they played games in separate scanners. Even the dynamics of conversation was a research topic that psychologists tended to leave to linguistics and sociology.

Joy Hirsch, a neuroscientist with appointments in three Yale departments, a honeyed voice, and an infectious laugh, spent years searching for the technological means to capture the social brain in live action. A pioneer in neuroimaging, Hirsch saw early potential in functional near-infrared spectroscopy (fNIRS), a brain-scanning technique discovered in the early 1990s that harnesses light rather than the magnetic waves that standard scanners use to map the blood flow signaling brain activity. Combining the portability of an electrocardiogram and the near power of a magnetic resonance scanner, the novel swim cap–style scanning device, Hirsch realized, was perfect for decoding the mentality underlying social interactions. "We're going to develop a new neuroscience of two," Hirsch boldly promised her bosses in 2013. Seven years later, she succeeded, igniting dramatic gains in understanding the mechanisms of togetherness.

"You can see the frontal lobes that look like a band across the head," Hirsch tells me. One snowy winter day, she is walking me through her findings from one of the first neuroimaging studies of live unscripted human discourse. In the experiment, she asked pairs of people wearing fNIRS caps to sit down together and talk about divisive topics, such as whether the death penalty should be banned. On some issues participants agreed, on others not at all. The unscripted interactions were set up to resemble the chance conversations we might have with a stranger on a bus. While on a call, Hirsch and I jointly view a page from the study showing a diagram of a brain sliced into two hemispheres. Sections that ignited when people disagreed, such as the frontal lobes, are colored red. Parts of the brain active during accord are tinted bright blue. There is little overlap in the two sets of brain networks, I notice. We are looking at two remarkably different modes of human thinking, depending on whether people are on the same page.

"When there is a clash of viewpoints, you can see the brain trying to understand what is being said while formulating its response," explains Hirsch. "It's sending and receiving information in, let's say, an energetic manner." At this moment, cognitive networks related to decision making, strategizing, cognitive processing, executive function, and communicating come online. Then she turns my attention to the agreeing brain, which she notes uses less cerebral real estate. "It looks a lot more gentle, like there's not much going on," she observes. The supramarginal gyrus, an area linked to our capacity to understand others' minds, is ignited, as are regions associated with making eye contact or facial expressions, such as smiling. Social harmony, it turns out, is almost sensory. Once we are in cozy alignment with someone, we are not thinking very hard at all.

But what fascinates Hirsch most is how deeply in sync agreeing brains are with one another. During an argument, both you and a friend may be using your frontal lobes, yet the patterns of neuronal firing in these regions are likely quite different. In contrast, when we are thinking as one, a complex array of cognitive activity is correlated, her studies show. In accord, "it's like you're having coffee with your friend," says Hirsch, conjuring up a portrait of a soothing, almost visceral feeling of togetherness. "You're on the same wavelength.... It's comfortable." You are lounging together on the cognitive loveseat of agreement. I gaze at the diagram of the agreeing brain, its familiar cortical folds punctuated by patches of soothing blue, and realize that I am looking at the backstory to the feel-good complacency of *we*. "I'll have what she's having," in-sync brains are saying, few questions asked.

Moreover, this joint view—the "shared mental model" that companies laud—is persistent. When people agree, they carry their unified way of seeing the world from one problem to the next. An unjustified leap in a stock price, then another and another, looks fine if your trading buddies are buying in. A venerated "yes sir, no sir" mindset can seem the gold standard long past its sell-by date. In a study led by Dartmouth social scientist Adam Kleinbaum, groups of three to six people were asked to watch a series of ambiguous movie clips and then get together to reach a consensus on what was going on in the films. Subsequently, their brains showed the same unique patterns of alignment—the same tendency to focus on, for example, car chases—while viewing new, unrelated film snippets. It's as if your film club watched a romance together and then unwittingly saw your next selection, a mystery, as being all about love or as if your oncology team thought that a plan of attack for your cancer seemed just right for the next patient's different case.

"How powerful it is to agree, and once you've established that with someone, how that lingers," says Hirsch. In essence, the brain systems related to coherence "far overwhelm" those we use to explore our differences. And that is a double-edged capacity. Agreeing is both rewarding and risky, a comfort that humans cling to even at enormous cost. Yearning for accord, people are stunningly likely to miss out on the differences between them that literally can save them from a fall.

Discord would seem to have no place on the slopes of Mount Everest, where frigid gale-force winds, the thinnest of air, and shape-shifting terrain can turn a false step into a death sentence. Ascending to the highest point on Earth—known in Tibet as Chomolungma, or Mother Goddess, and in Nepal as Sagarmatha, or Goddess of the Sky—would seem to depend on focusing on commonalities and privileging shared goals, in short on a group-mindedness that psychologists call *collectivism*. "There is no feeling to equal this complete confidence of one man in another," wrote the twentieth-century French mountaineer Maurice Herzog.

Such intense cooperation can be a mark of a culture, a company, or a team. Some countries, including Guatemala and Indonesia, rank high on global scales of collectivism and less so on individualism. In many workplaces, group orientation is seen as a stepping stone to the cohesion that is assumed to be a path to productivity. *Are we all in? Unity is strength!* New lessons from decades of expeditions to the roof of the world, however, show how easily overlooked diverse perspectives can be in high-stakes situations whose outcomes depend on thinking well jointly—not uniformly.

From 1950 to 2013, 60 percent of climbers attempting Everest had never before made an ascent in the Himalayas. At the other extreme, 14 percent of climbers in that period had made three or more climbs in the region. Such a range of experience often resulted in expeditions with diverse knowledge among members, according to a recent study by leading researchers in group dynamics. At the same time, some of the climbing teams with varied expertise stressed a collectivist mindset, according to climber surveys and nationalities. This all-for-one mentality—call it über-team spirit—did not hurt and may have helped one traditional expedition goal: sending one or more people to the summit. After all, the finale of mountaineering is a *conjunctive* group task, akin to moving a friend's sofa or meeting a sales quota, which depends on keeping novices and experts alike progressing in march step toward a single goal.

But an even more important if less celebrated challenge in the high peaks is the complex work of ensuring that all climbers make it up and back alive. Mountaineering teams must closely monitor the weather, their own health, and the state of their equipment and then evaluate these and other variables to choose the safest routes on the slopes, a process made all the more tricky by a modern emphasis on quick, agile, and lightly equipped alpine-style climbs. Climber safety is a *disjunctive* task, involving just the kind of difficult decision making that information-era professionals engage in every day. And in this kind of work, an "overly cooperative" outlook is often not an edge but rather a threat. Knowledge-diverse Everest treks that emphasize group-first values are far more likely to suffer the death of a climber on their team.

Why are people more likely to perish on expeditions that possess the in-house wisdom to protect their own? This finding was based on statistical analyses that are a powerful way to unmask life's larger realities. But to further reveal why a group-first mindset often has steep "collateral damage," the same team of scientists set up their own simulated expedition, this time on the surface of the moon. When planning the way forward, "you'll want to learn from others," a mountaineering guidebook advises. In a group, we have immense trouble doing just that.

Your space vessel crash-landed two hundred miles from the mother ship. How will you and your two fellow astronauts get back? Several hundred adults tried this exercise, which was originally created by a psychologist working with NASA. On half of the teams, people role-played astronauts who had all been to space once before. Other groups were comprised of two rookies and one space veteran who alone had key information on which of two routes across the mountainous lunar landscape was the safest. Before discussing the problem, the threesomes either were primed to think collectively by writing about the benefits of groups or were nudged into an individualistic worldview by writing about the advantages of standing out. Echoing the patterns of failure on Everest, knowledge-diverse groups with a strong *we* stance failed to opt for the longer, safer path back, a choice that placed their teams at high risk.

Most remarkably, it wasn't because such teams considered yet rejected the veteran's crucial ideas. To the scientists' shock, members of diverse but collectivist crews did not even recognize the range of expertise among them, which the scientists discovered by asking participants to recall their team's characteristics. "They didn't even notice the experts were there, which for me is terrifying and bizarre," Lindred Greer, a social scientist who coauthored the research, told me. "When you're focused on the group, liking the group, attracted to the group, that blinds you," said Greer, whose later research and that of others shows that collectivist collaborators have trouble recognizing even visible differences. Once aligned, we do not merely take on a shared view of the world, we begin to treat one another as alike. "As soon as a person is in the midst of a group," the pioneering psychologist Solomon Asch once wrote, "he is no longer indifferent to it."

Bonding is a story that we are eager to tell ourselves, a lens on the world that offers a useful yet often insufficient way to look at things. By cultivating a unified view, people become less willing to challenge one another and to dig deeply into the evidence at hand. They see the world and their collaborators as more alike than in fact they are and tend to expect to agree with their team. This is the flip side of the dangerous human propensity to categorize the *out-group* as all alike and therefore unworthy of one's time and attention. Being on the same page can lead to an equal sin of omission, this time inspired by giving a pass to the foibles and failings of *people like us*.

Humans are not made to go it alone. Belonging is high on Maslow's hierarchy of needs and nearly as essential for survival as physical health and safety. But we are long past an era in human history when simple insularity can serve us well. It is crucial to discover the revelatory uncertainty that follows when our differences are seen, heard, and explored.

↵

From the beginning, NASA prided itself on planning space flights to the microsecond, including every move the astronauts made, whether they "laid a spoon down or turned around or went to the bathroom or moved from one point to another," recalled flight director Neil Hutchinson. "And we did that on purpose because the [early] flights were very finite and very short and there was a great deal of pressure to get an awful lot done." This was Apollo mode, the mindset born of a time when missions were executed with military precision by a "little club" of fighter pilots and engineers deeply cognizant of the high risks, steep costs, and relentless public pressures dogging each trek into the universe.

Carrying this outlook into the Skylab era, crews were sent as much as sixty to seventy feet of teletype instructions a day that they were expected to follow to the letter. For example, new instruments to observe Earth's ocean currents, geological activity, or pollution levels were set up so that astronauts only had to push a button at a prescribed time to capture data. "We had a tough time convincing them that if we saw three-quarters cloud cover, maybe we shouldn't be taking the data," said Gibson, a solar physicist. "They didn't want to let us have that judgment." Recalled Hutchinson, "It got to the point where we could just absolutely control those people. It was like they were robots." At the time, there was fierce internal and public debate over whether actual robots could do the astronaut's job more dependably and cheaply. The unspoken compromise seemed to be to treat humans in space as automatons.

The Skylab rookies, however, were aching to be more than medical guinea pigs, trained handymen, and flag planters, as critical as those early roles were. As Carr later recalled, his team wanted "to exercise judgment and creativity," precisely the skills that were increasingly needed for longer, more complex missions that would focus on studying, not just ducking in and out of, outer space. Eight years before Skylab's launch, NASA somewhat reluctantly had begun to accommodate this new reality by opening up seats on space missions to scientist-astronauts. Still, administrators loyal to Apollo mode wound up micromanaging them as well. Carr put it diplomatically when he said in an in-flight news conference that "people in our line of work—a very technical line of work—are inclined to move along with blinders on. You forget to look around you." He was talking about the new art and science of observing Earth from space, but he was also taking a larger stand. He and his crew were exhorting NASA to heed all voices, as unique and challenging as they might be. The third Skylab team was out of step with ground control for good reason: they were the future of the corps.

The séance, as the crew called it, started over Bermuda and continued on and off for an hour as Skylab passed over ground communication bases scattered across the globe. With the astronauts gathered in their wardroom and high-ranking officials phoning in from Earth, Mission Control's "CapComm," a crew liaison who was typically a fellow astronaut, began with a mea culpa and a surprise.

As the crew suspected, they initially had been scheduled at a pace that surpassed the final days of their predecessors, admitted Dick Truly. ("We just weren't thinking straight," Hutchinson said later.) But after Carr's salvo, flight planners quietly had cut down the workload a bit, and the crew had begun accomplishing just as much as past super-teams. The mission was more than on par, flight controllers discovered, after Carr rattled their blind assurance. ("It took that to hit us on the head," Bob Crippen, another mission CapComm, recalled.) Carr expressed relief. "I understand now why we went off at such a fire-house pace." But neither side was finished. The dialogue had just begun.

Back and forth they went, sparring, negotiating, confessing, and concurring, with NASA periodically prodding for more and faster work and the crew alternatively giving way and holding their ground. Truly warned that Earth observations would be ramping up and added that "to get as much done in that area, it's quite obvious that the only people we have to push on is you." Answered Carr, "We've been ready from day one to play that game." They argued over when and how the crew would exercise or do science or take a moment before bed to reflect and plan ahead, but it was clear that both sides were having their say.

"Nobody down here has any argument at all with giving you the free time you think the crew needs to get your heads together, get prepared for the day, . . . or the next day," ventured Truly. "But if there were times that we could stick a specific [experiment] in there, for instance at 8:30 at night, . . . and pay you back at another time, . . . there's science gain for that."

"Yes, we can appreciate that, too, Dick," retorted Carr, "and the reason why we started hollering is there was just getting to be too much of that."

"Okay," said Truly. "I want to reiterate that . . . the amount of free time that you feel like the crew needs—that's your business and your call."

At another point, Carr ventured an un-Apollo mode suggestion: take noncritical and household tasks off the main schedule and put them on a "shopping list," to be performed as the crew decided. Taken up by ground control, that small change went far in relieving "the automaton-like existence they had been leading for six weeks," notes an official NASA history of Skylab. The showdown then ended with one last mutual victory. "We've tried to answer the questions straight, and when you get any more, we'd like to hear them," concluded Truly. And by the way, he added, don't use the one-way audio recorder, the "voice dump," to express concerns. "We think it's a lot better to talk about it on the air-to-ground," real-time, two-way radio channel, he said, so that when there are issues, we can "have it out." Marvels the official history of Skylab, "The importance of the discussion was that it took place at all."

After that, NASA didn't have to muster half-hearted defenses of the crew to reporters asking about their "lethargy" or "lack of enthusiasm." With a little more freedom, a little more say, the astronauts went on to surpass the overall achievements of the first Skylab missions by multiple measures. "They ran some numbers, and in terms of average work per day, we came out a little ahead of the second crew," Gibson told me with a laugh. Admitted Hutchinson, "You know, they turned out the stuff." The three completed their full allotment of science experiments and observations with flair, then began to concoct their own often-impromptu investigations, for example, studying air as a medium and water's capacity to form perfect spheres in zero gravity. Gibson grew so adept at operating the spaceship's array of intricately coordinated solar telescopes that he could improvise on it as if he were playing "a piano by ear," he recalled. Solar data from the Skylab program provided dramatic new views of the sun's violence and mutability and is still used by scientists today.

There were lessons learned and some forgotten. Astronauts now are given time to adapt when they arrive at the International Space Station, yet they still openly chaff against the micro-scheduling dispensed by the Onboard Short-Term Plan Viewer software, which, as one astronaut laments, "rules our lives." Moments of reflection, if not robustly welcome, are not actually forbidden as they were in early missions, when astronauts' requests to stop in the middle of a space walk to marvel at the vast universe often were met with a curt "that's not why you're there." In recent years, team conflict and the Skylab saga itself have become topics of study at NASA ahead of a planned return to the moon and a future three-year mission to Mars. The final Skylab mission "really taught the ground some lessons for the shuttle programs," says space historian Emily Carney.

Did the space rebellion of 1973 set the stage in some way for humanity's growing recognition of the dynamism of the universe? That might be asking too much of a footnote in history. Yet perhaps three mavericks' long-ago fight for the value of diverse perspectives may still come down to Earth like a ray of light from a distant star that takes years to see. They brought us a step closer to recognizing the wonders of collective uncertainty.

⇾

"Decatur is a very nice town," the man tells his fellow jurors. "But I'm looking at a White judge, a White prosecutor, a flag hanging in the corner with a . . ."

"Don't do that," asserts a man across the table. "Don't go there."

Decades after Skylab and very much back on Earth, we are eavesdropping on deliberations about a sexual assault trial by six jurors assembled in an Ann Arbor, Michigan, courthouse. We are looking for a different kind of verdict, however, from the discourse of that day. How does difference, once unleashed, influence a group? What happens when the blinkers of quick unity are cast off? The locals were taking a break from actual jury duty to participate in a famous psychological experiment that can help uncover the revelations of uncommon ground.

Samuel Sommers, now a noted scholar of bias and diversity, was a University of Michigan graduate student when he began showing up weekly one winter at the Washtenaw County Courthouse to do a little jury selection of his own. With help from two supportive judges, Sommers drew on local jury pools to assemble twenty-nine mock panels, half of which had all-White members and half of which included two Black participants. The groups viewed highlights of a real trial, received official jury instructions, and set out to discuss the case, in which a Black man was accused of raping two White women one night in Georgia. The forensic evidence was suggestive though hardly conclusive, and neither victim could definitively identify her assailant. Nonetheless, in the hour they were afforded to reach a verdict, half the groups far outperformed their peers.

Almost from the beginning, the homogeneous groups became "lazy information processors," Sommers observed. They spent an average of thirty-eight minutes in discussions, 20 percent less time than diverse panels did, and made many more inaccurate statements about the case. There was laughter and joking, markers of what psychologists call a "relationship focus," an effort to bond. "I think you're a plant, you work for them," a middle-aged man teased a young woman who urged caution in their hasty assumptions. They still had differences of opinion; juries, after all, are not set up to forge the cohesion that can erase even the perception of diversity. Still, just the comfort of belonging smoothed the way for racially similar panels to gloss over ambiguities and errors and give an upper hand to the human longing for easy accord.

In contrast, racially mixed jurors were "more comprehensive and re-mained truer to the facts of the case," notes Sommers. These groups not only made fewer inaccurate statements but also corrected their mistakes more often. Importantly, they speculated more often about missing clues. "But we never seen anything in her testimony where she says, 'Yeah, that was the scar I see,'" noted a forty-nine-year-old White man on a mixed panel. "Juries have to be careful when they're deliberating if there's missing information or contradicting information," he warned.

How does diversity slow the rush to collective judgment and inspire a deeper and wider lens on a problem? Do those who bring difference to the table—the Latino man on a jury, the Asian woman trader—just gallop in and set things straight? Social scientists traditionally surmised that di-versity boosts group performance by adding a new perspective, a missing piece of the puzzle. In Sommers's study, Black participants in mixed groups did contribute new information, for example, by raising race-related topics more often than White jurors. But that is not the end of the story. White people on mixed-race juries on average raised more facts from the case overall and cited more missing evidence than people on same-race juries did. Differences, once unmuffled, change the workings of the *entire* group.

The spark of difference shatters the persistent human expectation of sim-ilarity. Suddenly, a puzzle does not seem quite as easy to solve. Difference ushers a group to a new, unfamiliar, and uncertain place, prompting its members to ask, in effect, *If you're not like me, who are you?* ("It took that to hit us on the head.") Attention moves away from bonding, an effort that at least initially is a proven distraction from group problem solving, and toward questioning, probing, and evaluating the situation and one's peers. Sommers compares this shift to how you may feel when entering a staff meeting where you know a contentious topic will be addressed. "You're more at the top of your cognitive game," he tells me.

What follows is a new dynamic that is the opposite of what Asch called the "polluted social process" of overzealous alignment. Differences come alive. Controversial and conflicting opinions are allowed to surface. Only one-third of homogeneous panels in the Ann Arbor study made any mention of race bias, but each time that someone did, the issue was shut down as a topic of conversation. "What does that have to do with it?" a twenty-one-year-old White woman snapped when a fellow juror reiterated that the defendant was Black. A possible rent in the fabric of agreement was hastily patched. *Don't go there.*

In contrast, racial prejudice was raised in nearly two-thirds of diverse juries and then silenced only twice. Liberated from the pressures of homophily and cohesion, groups with acknowledged differences became more willing to probe contested perspectives. Their disagreements were at times vociferous, their dialogue more open-minded. "Diversity is not about harmony," historian Robin Kelley reminds us, "but about unleashing creative dissonance, of being able to see the world in all its complexity." It's about coming together to explore the new, eye-opening realms we find on the other side of blind unity. And yet rarely do we recognize this dynamic as a path to success.

Imagine a room filled with flurries of laughter and excited whispers. A few years ago, dozens of sorority sisters and fraternity brothers assembled to play amateur detective. No nudges were needed this time to inspire cohesion, but just to make sure, banners were hung high trumpeting their group loyalties. The scene was far from a risky financial market or a life-and-death mountain trek, yet these were no college antics. It was a landmark experiment led by scientists who broke ground by questioning the common assumption that differences among us should be hastily smoothed into comforting accord.

The students were divided into teams of three and asked to solve a fictional murder mystery often used as an executive problem-solving exercise. Who pushed the small-town car dealer to his death from his back deck: the disgruntled handyman, the gambling gardener, or the crooked auto parts dealer? After five minutes of discussion, a latecomer joined each group, either from the same social club or from a different, perhaps rival, one. All the clues needed to exonerate two suspects and to implicate a third were woven into the story. But while all-insider groups got the right answer only half the time, three-quarters of diverse teams solved the problem, even if the newcomer had *not* contributed any novel information to the discussion. The outsider–insider teams capitalized on all the available data; by the end, from one-quarter to a remarkable 70 percent of their members who were initially wrong had switched to the correct answer. In contrast, just one-quarter at best or sometimes *no one* in homogeneous groups took this step. "A lot of the [homogeneous] groups agreed right off," coauthor Margaret Neale told me. "'We have the right answer.' Ta da! They were happy and confident—and wrong."

Yet despite their stellar performances, dissimilar groups tended to rate themselves as less effective. Many among these teams reported feeling a bit less bonded with their own sororities and fraternities by the end of the experiment. They recalled having more initial differences over "who did it" than same-club groups did, even though the teams had been set up to have equal levels of conflicting opinions at the start. In other words, mixed teams recognized the friction in their midst yet had trouble seeing this dynamic as beneficial, while those who were bonded overlooked their differences and developed unwarranted swagger.

If groups "do not perceive, attain, or express much disagreement during a discussion, they will . . . believe that they have settled on the right solution," wrote coauthor Katherine Phillips, whose life's work was inspired at age nine by being among the first Black students to integrate a Chicago elementary school in the mid-1990s. In the trenches of collaboration, dissimilar groups feel far less victorious and yet are doubly so. They are struggling in all the right ways not only to find the best solution but also against our mistaken assumptions of what a group should be.

Diversity long has been haunted by the seeming taint of friction. Work teams with a mix of genders, roles, ethnicities, or races report higher levels of conflict and more dissatisfaction. "They like it less," one social scientist notes. "They're less comfortable there." They tend to identify less with the group. For decades, diversity's rough edges have been seen as something to smooth away by stressing commonality or team building, efforts that studies show may help a group bond or feel good but do *not* tend to improve problem-solving performance. "We are family," a big car manufacturer boasts on its website, offering a well-meaning claim that evidence suggests actually tends to make people of color feel less included. "We want to make sure everyone feels like an insider," the diversity chair of a large soft-drink maker tells an interviewer.

But of what use are differences that are papered over or shelved? The loosening of bonds and the spotlighting of disagreements are not lamentable downsides to having differences but are its gifts. This is as true when we see distinctions between us as when we hear them. The friction of dissimilarity, however it is unearthed, provokes members of a group to preserve the capacity most essential to collaboration yet most threatened by accord: the ability to think for themselves.

Consider what happens when someone dares to stand up and disagree. Dissent has been shown to curb groups' strong tendency to discuss knowledge that is already known to all, a narrowing of focus that leaves a "hidden profile" of unique information unshared. Discord inspires collaborators to consider multiple perspectives beyond their shared view, then to take the crucial step of connecting the dots between them. As one research team puts it, the discussion "intensifies." In an analysis of forty years of U.S. Supreme Court cases, levels of such *integrative complexity* were twice as high when a minority of justices dissented. Splits in the courts provoke judges who are writing majority opinions, regardless of their ideology, to give all sides of a case their due. Dissent stimulates thinking "that is wide and curious as well as deep and scrutinizing," asserts Charlan Nemeth, a psychologist who has spent decades tracking the surprising effects of dissent.

In one of her best-known experiments, Nemeth brought three dozen college students into her laboratory for what was purportedly a test of visual perception. Each was paired with another student who was Nemeth's secret confederate. The teams were then asked to name the color of twenty images depicting shades of blue, which the allies promptly labeled green. Some of the participants were led to believe that a majority of people called the samples green; others were told that this was an atypical response. A few participants caved to the green side. Most held their ground. What most fascinated Nemeth, however, was the dramatic effect that mere exposure to dissent had on people's later capacity for originality.

A few minutes after the color-naming task, participants were asked to free-associate words related to the two hues. As we have seen, most people have a great deal of trouble moving past well-worn ideas that first spring to mind. Blue instantly reminds us of *sky*, and *grass* goes hand in hand with green. But after experiencing dissent, people become more adventurous, Nemeth's and other studies reveal. By the second of seven tries, participants in Nemeth's lab were beginning to think of jazz, jeans, and greenbacks (i.e., slang for dollar bills). They showed twice the originality of those exposed to an opposing majority, a condition that usually prompts compliance within a group. They also admired their dissenting partners and rated themselves as more thoughtful when on teams that included outsiders. *Embolden* and *liberated* are not words used lightly in circumspect psychology journals. But that is how many in the field sum up dissent's impact on "the jury room of people's own minds." As the philosopher John Dewey noted, "Conflict is a *sine qua non* of reflection and ingenuity"—even when the messenger of difference is *wrong*.

Cali Williams Yost has seen this transformation again and again in just the kind of workplaces that we might call our own. A strategist who helps firms adopt flexible work options, she often has to restrain leaders who in the name of efficiency try to squelch opposition to their plans to loosen work routines. The leaders want to say, "'We're just going to get onboard and do it!'" Yost tells me. Gently she advises them, "Don't shut down the dissenters. Because what's happening is important," as occurred not long ago at one of her most staid client companies.

"I can still see the faces of everyone in the room," recalls Yost. At a meeting of two dozen leaders and team representatives of a large utility's legal department, a senior executive vocally opposed the top boss's imminent plan to offer various flexible work options to staff. The dissenter, "Jim," helped lead the department's utility fraud investigators, a team of fifty who soon were to be allowed to work from home twice weekly. To everyone's shock and the top boss's ire, Jim announced that he "wasn't going there," mainly because he thought the change would eviscerate the critical information swapping that occurred at the office every morning before investigators headed into the field.

Initially pointed out to Yost as a troublemaker, Jim could have been quickly silenced. Instead, he was given his say then and there. And later in the meeting, a junior investigator unexpectedly spoke up, proposing a virtual knowledge-sharing platform to allow employees to trade information potentially lost in the disconnect of virtual work. The dissenter's zealous objections shook up the group, inspiring a bolder version of the game plan and over time a new departmental willingness to court the friction that seeds innovation. "He was right that the information needed to be shared and wrong that there wasn't another way," said Yost, who counseled the angry department chief after Jim's outburst to go easy on him. "'He's *not* being unsupportive,'" Yost emphasized. It took time, but "now it's become a norm in the organization to say, 'I don't think that is working,'" says Yost. "It's not a problem to say that anymore."

Difference typically doesn't ride in waving the flag of the right answer. It doesn't usher us smoothly and neatly onto a new same page. Instead, difference—be it diversity, dissimilarity, or dissent—jolts a group off the beloved turf of blinkered accord. A powerful new dynamic, a "social effervescence," is sparked by the friction that emerges when differences are acknowledged and unpacked. Members of a diverse school committee, for example, are more likely to call to light a missing or ignored angle of a contentious discussion. An employee who witnesses a colleague oppose a hasty consensus is then emboldened to offer her *own* perspective, be it right or wrong. When I say "yes" and you say "no," we can probe the intricate spaces between these realms and ultimately reach an accord based on a full understanding of the issue and on the airing of *all* views. Here on uncommon ground, disagreement becomes in essence collective uncertainty-in-action. This is a work of courage and of equity. For when we awaken to the distinctions between us, we discover what we should have known all along: the onus of collaboration is on us all.

⬆

Well, do you think it could be impact generated? asks the first scientist.

No, not impact generated, 'cause, they may be a certain, well, I don't know, says another member of the team.

You know, one thing you can say is that maybe these were, that there is a sulfate cement in there, ventures a third researcher.

It's a winter's day in early 2004, and members of one of the most innovative teams in space history are gently arguing. They are part of one hundred or so scientists and engineers who weeks earlier had landed a pair of robotic rovers on Mars, seeking clues to the origins of life and to our own planet's fragile future.

The Mars Explorer Rover (MER) mission was a paragon of collaboration and a harbinger of the multifaceted diversity that marks teams in our day. Varied in specialty, level of expertise, ethnicity, and location, the mission's members worked across time and distance in shifting constellations that formed and re-formed as the work demanded. So as they were looking at Mars, psychologists, sociologists, and computer scientists were looking at them, armed with an arsenal of tools aimed at capturing for the first time the fine-grained dynamics of collaboration. The scientific discourse that seems at first like esoteric rock-talk turns out to be a window on what sociologist Janet Vertesi calls the *productive zone of disagreement*.

At a time when a majority of NASA's missions to Mars had failed, one of the MER rovers had scored a hole in one. *Opportunity* safely settled in a small crater near a piece of exposed bedrock, a formation that offered elated scientists a glimpse of the planet's original infrastructure, or its "geological truth."

On the sixteenth day of *Opportunity*'s time on Mars, the first panoramic color photos of the landing area reached Earth, and the scientists based at the Jet Propulsion Laboratory in Pasadena, California, were digging into them. NASA's goal for the mission was to "follow the water," an essential ingredient for the genesis of life. Was the layered shelf of bedrock near the landing site that the scientists named Eagle Crater, formed by meteorites, ancient volcanic eruptions, or the slow hands of water and wind? Could it be suffused with sulfate salts, minerals left by water coursing through stone? An intense study of the mission's early days by a trio of researchers revealed that roughly one in five of the team's conversations involved brief "micro-conflicts," most of which included expressions of uncertainty.

The best disagreements do not pit people against one another. Good friction is not a clash of entrenched opinions and assumptions, however right or wrong. Proficient collaborators cultivate judicious conflict as a way to discover "what they do not know in order to move forward and innovate," wrote the researchers, who shot four hundred hours of video of the MER team's first ninety days to tease out the secrets of its collaborative skills. "At some point, you want to increase your uncertainty to find what you hadn't thought of before—that's where disagreement comes in," information scientist Joel Chan, a study leader, tells me. This is how the jury realizes what evidence is missing and why an executive's dissent can catalyze a colleague's cognitive daring. MER lead engineer Adam Steltzner calls "holding on to the doubt" a critical part of working "at the edge of what is possible." The MER team's prolific not-knowing led to effective problem solving, particularly of scientific matters, the researchers conclude. It was central to the mission's ultimate success.

Consider the incident of the "dirt folks." In 2007, some of the mission's soil and atmospheric scientists were seeking to investigate mysterious dark streaks seemingly etched by wind-borne dust onto the walls of a crater that the rover *Opportunity* was then examining. But at a teleconferenced planning meeting, a top MER leader challenged the soil scientists' request to begin an in-depth study of the streaks. Is this foray of use to any group but yours? he asked. The public micro-conflict that ensued was awkward yet profitable: scientists across disciplines quickly began to realize that such marks—and the planet's soil itself—perhaps should be more of a shared concern. The mission's "wind streaks campaign," although small scale, nevertheless wound up revealing clues to patterns in the planet's shifting climate. Amidst friction, the surfacing of hidden unknowns—information new to some in the group, fissures in a team's shared mental models—keeps a problem open as evidence accrues while allowing teammates to remain open to one another.

At this critical time, the use of seemingly trifling expressions of uncertainty, such as "maybe," "possibly," or "somewhat," can go far in making disagreement productive. *Hedge words* alert a group that it is on unfamiliar territory and that there is more to know. They help nurture *conversational receptiveness*, a willingness to engage productively with opposing viewpoints. In one series of studies, two hundred and forty senior state and local government executives participating in a management education program discussed controversial topics with a peer with contrasting opinions. Leaders who used hedge words and listened demonstrably to others' views were rated by discussion opponents as having better judgment and as being more effective professionals and prospective teammates than those who offered harsher responses, including words such as *wrong* and *therefore*. Giving voice to not-knowing is particularly crucial in virtual work, where conflict tends to remain unacknowledged due to lower overall levels of information sharing.

During the MER mission's early days, expressions of uncertainty during episodes of micro-friction were followed by the resolution rather than the escalation of conflict, according to the study by Chan and colleagues. *Maybe there is a sulfate cement in there*, a scientist asked early in the mission. And a few days and many disagreements later, the team found this aqueous material in astonishingly high quantities in Eagle Crater's bedrock, one of the final points of proof needed in order to announce the historic news: water had flowed on ancient Mars.

Two years later, a feisty young Princeton sociologist began embedding herself into the working life of the MER project. Due to the rovers' unexpected longevity, the enterprise had by then turned from a ninety-day scientific sprint into a multiyear investigation. Janet Vertesi ultimately studied the team through 2017, nearly the full life of the endeavor. She sat in on tactical planning sessions and coffee klatches, attended scientific conferences and crisis meetings, interviewed top investigators and graduate students alike, and began to make discoveries of her own. The exploration of differences, she realized, is work that cannot be left to chance.

As time passed, the rovers' guardians developed tremendous solidarity with one another. Vertesi calls the team collectivist; their proudly worn lanyard badges, mission tattoos, and logo clothing testified to a strong group identity. But the group counterbalanced the risks of belonging by setting up practices to preserve a culture of conflict, she observed. In the workplace, the jokes and sideline chatter that indicate distracting efforts to privilege bonding over debate were rare, she observed. And every meeting, in person or virtual, ended with the "listening ritual." Are there any other comments, any other perspectives? the meeting host would ask. Far from being antagonistic toward people who then offered a conflicting view, such "countering" was lauded during both workaday interactions and high-level formal meetings. In many organizations, someone who disagrees "can be seen as a pain, a problem, or a jerk," she told me. "But there, you demonstrated that you were a committed member of the team by trying your hardest to bring in alternative perspectives," especially those that no one else had thought of before.

Nevertheless, curbing the innate human longing for cozy cohesion demands constant vigilance and a ceaseless willingness to court uncertainty, the Mars rover team discovered. In 2007, faulty commands were uploaded to one of the rovers, a fiasco that could have led to the demise of a robot worth hundreds of millions of dollars. The project's top leaders put the robot temporarily to sleep, canceled all scientific operations, and gave the entire staff a long weekend off for reflection. Then they called the team's first "all-hands meeting," where they reiterated in person and by teleconference that their work could not progress unless everyone was willing, as the mission's project manager said, "to raise our hand and say, 'I don't know,' 'I don't understand.'"

An assistant with no engineering background should feel free to challenge a lead mission manager if something "looks funny," the principal scientific investigator added. We're known for "the rigor of the questioning we all go through when we are trying something very challenging," he said. "And I'd like to get that back." Then they opened up the call for discussion, and scientists, engineers, students, and support staff debated for two hours about how to better occupy the enlightening space between *yes* and *no*.

"Uncertainty and conflict were how the mission worked," says Vertesi, who watched and listened year after year as the MER team pieced together clues to the history of a distant planet where fiery volcanoes, rippling lakes, and tumbling rivers left their mark billions of years ago. "This is what allowed MER to be able to keep going so long, to be extremely innovative even a decade into the mission," she tells me. "That's why we are still talking about them years later." Almost wistfully, she adds, "They saw themselves as explorers and [the mission] as an adventure and a challenge. . . . It was a very exciting and a very positive place to be."

Positive? Her words may seem at odds with our perceptions of difference and disagreement. By countering others, we rupture the cozy cohesion fueled by similarity and mutual affirmation. Decision making slows. A shared view of the world is at least temporarily shattered. Often, we instead prefer to linger on the loveseat of accord. But when differences are no longer silenced or ignored, something far greater than mere comfort or ease can emerge.

Groups that cultivate judicious conflict, dissent, and mutual criticism tend to be high-performing, growing evidence reveals. A recent study at a company that manages long-term care complexes for elders revealed that employees who frequently experience mild conflict—debate and the expression of differences versus full-on clashes—across departments gain valuable information about coworkers' perspectives from the exchanges. This dynamic leads them to be far more interested, active, excited, and energized both during the encounters and in their jobs overall than coworkers in harmonious settings. (Recall how neuroscientist Joy Hirsch describes the disagreeing brain as operating in an "energetic manner.") In contrast, management teams that experience little conflict lack the "energy" of those that constantly challenge one another, and their firms perform less well, an analysis of Silicon Valley companies reveals.

Groups that skillfully nurture friction to explore what they do *not* know feel unease alongside a sense of challenge. They find inspiration in heeding the voices we so often ignore. Falling on *and* off the same page is essential, after all, to figuring out the world as it is, not as we wish it to be. Asks novelist and essayist Marilynne Robinson, "Where did the idea come from that society should be without strain and conflict, that it could be . . . stable and harmonious?"

There always will be times when we need to still the clamor and see as one. That can be an end goal in collaboration yet should not be the norm. When faced with life's complexities, the succor of hurried agreement lulls us into complacency, blinding us to the distinctions between our and other points of view. Differences brought to life, in contrast, break the spell of assent, propelling a group onto uncommon ground where the exploratory work of not-knowing together can begin. Assumptions are shaken, inaccuracies are caught and corrected, missing evidence surfaces, and multiple perspectives are revealed when we dare to disagree. We emerge with a sense of what we do not know—and with an understanding of true collaboration as more intricate, uncertain, and demanding than we too often would like to admit. Why come together to simply become less than the sum of our remarkable parts? That is the most perilous form of *we*.

⤓

"What did we learn?" asks NASA's chief historian Brian Odom. I am posing just that question to him: what is the legacy of Skylab's last mission?

Odom is a leading voice in the new space history, a scholar as committed to honoring the women and people of color who furthered the wizardry of space exploration as he is to respecting those who deride such forays as pricey joyrides. When I ask him about the lasting impact of the final Skylab mission, however, he at first responds with generalities and pleasantries drawn from the company playbook. But then he mentions, almost to himself, NASA's Day of Remembrance, an annual tribute to the astronauts lost in the worst U.S. space catastrophes. The year that he and I talk, the day coincides with the anniversary of the morning when blind accord about a design flaw led to the deaths of the *Challenger* shuttle crew. And at that, Odom takes off his mask.

"The potential, the power, the courage, whatever you want to call it, to be honest—*that's* the contribution of Skylab's last crew," he says. "That's why discourse matters. If I don't give you honest feedback, if I don't tell you the points of difficulty, we don't learn what we need to know." Dissenters may rub people the wrong way, he says. "But who is the person I need to go to when something matters? Well, it's the person who's going to give me feedback that's not full of crap."

His voice is raised, and I am riveted. "Don't tell me what I want to hear, that's not helping me." Parroting Apollo mode, he continues, "'Yeah we can do whatever experiments you want, on whatever schedule you want.' Okay, then, what did we learn? What did we learn?"

PART IV

ASPIRING MINDS

CHAPTER SEVEN

LIFE AT THE EDGE

Keeping ahead of Precarity and Taming It Too

> *In this short Life that only lasts an hour*
> *How much—how little—is within our power.*
> —EMILY DICKINSON

That Sunday morning, Shaniece Langley heard the screen door open and was on instant alert. Her three-year-old son, Robert, had been slipping outside nearly every day. Despite pleas, locks, and discipline, she would find him on the front porch or by the lone tree in the yard. Their ranch house was just off a highway in the north end of Hobbs, New Mexico, an oil town. Her husband, a pipe fitter, was on call that weekend, his comings and goings unpredictable. Langley shouted to her kids, heard back from her four-year-old daughter, and took off yelling through the house. She found her son clutching his football at the end of the driveway. "I freaked out," she says. "He had his breakdown. I had mine. 'Robert,' I said, 'you can't do that. Momma didn't know what was going to happen.'"

As Langley ends her story, there are murmurs of consolation from a dozen other women seated around a conference table set up in a school gym. They are midway through a parenting course being beta-tested for families of Head Start, the iconic free preschool program. Many are single mothers. A majority live at or near the poverty line in a town at the epicenter of a precarious industry. All are deeply familiar with what it is like to spend their lives, as Langley puts it, "figuring out how we're going to do it from one day to the next" while wanting something far more. Turning on a dime, you might say, unites them.

Set amidst one of the world's most productive oil fields, Hobbs lies just west of Texas at the edge of the High Plains in country that some call "85 percent sky and 15 percent grasslands." Ups and downs have been routine here for nearly a century, but lately, no boom ever quite remedies the last bust. It is getting harder to find steady work with erratic global oil prices, jobs in the fields being automated, and fossil fuels just plain on the wane. A food bank director tells me that most people in town are three paychecks away from knocking at her door. Even in a good year, one-fifth of local kids are food insecure each day. And gathered around the table are moms who are struggling to give their offspring a better future.

There is the convenience store manager who often must leave her three young children alone at night as she fills in at the last minute for revolving door staff. There is the young mother whose car keeps breaking down. In the evenings, she calls around to cage rides to school for her four kids and two younger siblings, then wakes up to chase down the no-shows. In this weekly class, lesson plans often are set aside, and parents meet on into the afternoon, singing what Langston Hughes called the "weary blues." They swap tales of young men in their lives dying violently, days too hectic to give a child a hug, and tinges of fear when a strange car lingers on the street. Mornings for Langley typically have meant waking up late, rushing her children along, forgotten homework, lost tempers. By evening, she often would count the minutes until her kids' bedtime.

And yet there is grace in this room. It doesn't take long to see in the sheer victory of their survival a kind of smarts that few outsiders recognize. That day, the women are lauded warmly for what they do well even as they are being offered a way to move beyond lives of hurry and near misses. In a few years, the class will be rolled out in various iterations to tens of thousands of families across the country. But the lessons of this April morning go far beyond any schoolroom. How can we adapt to rising unpredictability and learn to tame it too? Here in Hobbs, I am witnessing a new resilience born of life at the edge, a stance marked by wary vigilance, dynamic learning, and snatched moments of reflection. This is where the wonders of our uncertainty meet the world's precarity. It is how we can learn to handle what life throws at us and teach our children to do so too.

"I've noticed that Robert, something's off with him," Langley is telling the class. "He's laying down at night but not sleeping. The other day, it was

1:30 in the morning, and I go into his room, and he's just sitting in a corner with the tablet. So we're going to try to do the deep breaths to calm him."

"He's so young, so bright, he wants to express himself, but it sounds like something else is going on?" asks Patricia Grovey, the energetic, no-nonsense director of this preschool and several others in town. She is pushing Langley to think harder, to see the bigger picture.

"Oh yeah, oh yeah," agrees Langley and begins to weep. "There's other things, I know that."

"He needs a little help," says Grovey, "but that doesn't take away from his potential or who he's going to be."

"When he was born, Robert failed his hearing test for a month," says Langley, a sturdy woman with an oval face, a melodic voice, and taut energy. "It was the opposite with his sister. Everything was so easy. She's so calm. . . . 'He's just a boy. He's just a boy,' I told myself. It was an excuse to ignore things."

"You know your children," soothes Grovey. "It's time to do some research. We'll work with it, too." The class moves on, the stories flow, and again and again, Grovey and her staff will emphasize that, as one teacher says, "when things don't go as planned, you get a chance to learn something new. When things don't work, we can get curious."

⟱

For decades, scientists have tried to uncover the roots of poverty's often-toxic impact on young minds. Does the number of traumas experienced by a child, added up like points in a tragic game, later lead to posttraumatic stress disorder? Do lower-income parents speak fewer words each day to their children, and does this matter? Determining how early challenges shape life outcomes is a fiendishly complex puzzle. No single piece holds the key.

But as scientists' attention began to focus on wider systemic factors, not just income or family structure or neglect, a missing link emerged: unpredictability. Lower-income families tend to move more, largely involuntarily. Their child care is routinely disrupted, often due to high costs. Crowded households and volatile schedules can translate to fewer routines at home. Relentlessly not-knowing where the rent money will come from or who will be home tonight or how a parent will react turns out to be a crucial, overlooked influence on the young.

In 2016, a group of scientists began videotaping mothers playing with their babies for just ten minutes. Then they studied the mothers' "sensory signals," the touch, words, and gestures offered to the child, in order to calculate her entropy rate or the level of unpredictability of her behavior. One parent, for example, consistently might speak to her child before showing him a toy, while another might provide these same types of signals but in unpredictable patterns. This fine-grained type of early chaos had not been studied before, yet it can matter more to a baby's development than the quantity or even the type of interactions, Elysia Davis, Laura Glynn, Tallie Baram, and colleagues discovered. In particular, one-year-old infants with unpredictable caregivers often show less ability to "self-regulate" years later. They tend to rush into things, fail to wait when asked to do so, and get frustrated by failure.

The findings should not inspire us to fall back on mother blame. Instead, they offer a new window into how chronic unpredictability, as developmental psychologists say, "gets under a child's skin," sculpting both behavior and the young brain. The hand of chaos at home or in relationships can have a roster of impacts, inhibiting language development or the ability to focus. But most of all, it seems to tip the young toward reactivity or what some scorn as impatience.

In one typical study, five-year-olds whose households had been rated as unstable at age two could not resist peeking at a gift being wrapped for them despite being told not to look. They glanced over their shoulders far faster than children raised with order and quiet. Children of chaos also tend to do poorly at the Pavlovian task of seeing how long they can wait before eating a candy balanced on their tongues. When asked to sort and clean up but not play with a pile of toys, they may dawdle or just plain have fun.

Hearing such stories, we probably can't help but think of the marshmallow test and the dreaded future that reportedly befalls those who fail this challenge. Preschoolers who grab the first treat rather than patiently waiting for a larger reward tend to have lower SAT scores, less self-confidence, and a tendency to yield to temptation, according to studies by Walter Mischel and others. Mischel's famous experiment is not the oracle that it's often taken to be. Many children who fail do fine in life.

The more important question to consider is: could reactivity *not* always be wrong? Cognitive control is crucial to human survival. By discounting the future too steeply, people may wind up saving too little, eating too much junk food, or drinking and driving. But reining in impulse is not a panacea for life's challenges. And in times of chronic flux, the opposite can be true.

When psychology researcher Celeste Kidd first read about the marshmallow test as a student, she found its predictions depressing. At the time, she was volunteering at a crowded shelter in Santa Ana, California, where families shared a communal living space. She recalled, "When one child got a toy or treat, there was a real risk of a bigger, faster kid taking it away. I thought, 'all of these kids would eat the marshmallow right away.'" But as she got to know the children, she began to question the assumption that low self-control was an innate flaw or always irrational. "For a child accustomed to stolen possessions and broken promises, the only guaranteed treats are the ones you already have swallowed," observed Kidd. Perhaps reactivity can be a cogent response to an unreliable world, she thought.

As a graduate student, Kidd set up a series of experiments to test her hunch, with dramatic results. First, she gave twenty-eight four- to six-year-olds from a variety of socioeconomic backgrounds art kits that involved coloring a band of paper to be inserted into the inner rim of a cup. One at a time, the children were told they could use a shabby jar of used crayons or wait for a researcher to return with a "new exciting set of art supplies." The catch was that for half the children, the researcher came back with nothing but an apology. In a second experiment, the same kids were offered one small sticker or a better batch that never materialized.

As you can foresee, by the time these children got to a third experiment, they were in no mood to wait for promised treats. Only one in this group held out a full fifteen minutes for a second marshmallow compared to two-thirds of the kids who had been made to feel that the world was reliable. Kidd did not analyze whether children from lower socioeconomic backgrounds were more reactive; her aim was to see how precarity can lead almost anybody to be opportunistic. (In grown-up versions of such challenges, adults act similarly.) When the future is less assured, says Kidd, "not waiting is the rational choice."

Mischel knew this well. In his early experiments, he showed that children whose lives are marked by an absent father or other upheavals tended to opt for immediate rewards. "Of special interest is how individual differences in relevant expectancies interact with situational variables to determine choice preferences," he wrote. Perhaps Mischel's own admittedly conflicted relationship with control—it took him years to quit smoking—can be traced to lessons he learned about the chanciness of the world while fleeing Nazi-occupied Austria at age eight.

Decades later, a caller to a radio show where Mischel was a guest gave a haunting corroboration of the scientist's work. The sixty-three-year-old Steve related how at age four, he had badly wanted a bright yellow, heavy-duty rain slicker. His mother said that they couldn't afford the coat until her next paycheck but that he could have a cheap plastic version now. "I was willing to wait," recounted Steve, except that his mother often hadn't kept her promises. "I was thinking I might not get any raincoat if I try to wait." He took the cheap one. "And that transparent raincoat, it was torn up in a couple of weeks." The radio host moved on without giving Mischel time to comment. But perhaps he would have gently pointed out to the child-man on the line that he had made the best of the difficult hand that he was dealt.

Why do some children wiggle and sing and sit on their hands, doing all they can to wait for life's later treats? Why do others change course and cut short the chase so soon? The postscript to the marshmallow test is that context matters. The unpredictability that often marks poverty can inspire an inclination to live out the saying, "A bird in the hand is better than two in the bush." And such a response may be not just practical but also wise. Now, in an era of rising unknowns, what more can we learn from those raised in volatility? Could the chaos of poverty spur both a range of cognitive ills *and* unsung strengths?

Not long ago, a young Dutch psychologist was asking himself those very questions. In his early training, Willem Frankenhuis constantly had bumped up against the *deficit model*, the prevalent assumption in his field that children from challenged backgrounds are cognitively damaged and in need of "fixing." (One 2013 scientific paper was titled "The Poor's Poor Mental Power.") While deficits exist, this relentlessly bleak picture didn't jibe with Frankenhuis's teenage experiences hanging out with a tough crowd in Amsterdam. During that time, he had befriended kids who were struggling in school and with the law, yet were stunningly "quick on their feet," says Frankenhuis, an earnest professor who retains a rebellious streak. "The prevailing perspective in psychology focused on which skills they were lacking. It was hard for me to imagine that was the whole story."

An equally formative aspect of his childhood gave him a further clue. From the time Frankenhuis was nine years old on through his teenage years, his biologist father was head of Artis, the venerable Royal Amsterdam Zoo. During that time, his family lived on the grounds of the twenty-five-acre animal park and gardens. "You could see and hear the animals in the morning and evening, and as we walked through the zoo, my father would ask me, 'Why do you think the peacock has those feathers?' or 'Why is this animal doing this?' He would encourage me to think about survival and reproduction and costs and benefits." By the time he earned a PhD in biological anthropology from the University of California, Los Angeles, Frankenhuis realized that the deficit model failed to account for people's capacity to adjust to the demands of their current environment. And the brain, with its vast potential to change its structure and function in response to experience, was the ultimate organ of adaptation.

Natural selection is often thought to be a process that unfolds over generations, a slow chiseling of species-wide traits. But even a single generation or a subgroup—a flock of finches, a regional variation of a plant—can develop characteristics called phenotypes that bolster their fit to a particular ecology. Such evolved traits may have downsides, but the benefits will tend to outweigh the costs, according to evolutionary theory. In areas rife with predators, for example, baby European starlings tend to be underweight so that they can learn to take flight quickly. Young children who have been abused often have an uncanny ability to pick up on the slightest cues of anger. Inspired by these findings, Frankenhuis had a radical idea: not only were his friends supremely suited to their harsh surroundings, but it was unethical for experts to try to erase their unrecognized strengths.

At the time, many social workers, resilience researchers, and psychologists viewed impoverished children's wariness and opportunism as a kind of excusable frailty. They saw such reactivity as a mismatch with the safe, predictable world that everyone should inhabit. What mattered for people in lower-socioeconomic strata were the future skills that they would need in order to fit into the mainstream one day, or so the common thinking went. What counted as beneficial were qualities of mind such as patience or sustained focus that might emerge despite adversity, not due to it.

Frankenhuis's innovation was to see chaos as instead producing adaptive forms of intelligence that were advantageous in times of precarity. What if shortsightedness could be a kind of cunning? he asked. What if impulsivity is at times a marker of agility? He was offering a new lens on the ancient story of human struggle and casting a scientific spotlight on the lived wisdom of people raised in precarity, from runner Jesse Owens and novelist Charles Dickens to Supreme Court justice Sonia Sotomayor.

In 2013, Frankenhuis wrote a paper summarizing the scattered evidence for his nascent theory. His call to arms shifted the course of developmental psychology and caught the eye of University of Utah psychologist Bruce Ellis, a pioneer in evolutionary theories of children's growth. Joining forces, the pair began to interview teenagers, parents, social workers, and fellow academics in Europe and in the United States. What do kids growing up in a world where threat can come without warning have to learn to do well? they asked. What do they do as well as or better than kids across town who have order, resources, and sometimes surfeits of adult attention?

Frankenhuis and Ellis were trying to create the first high-resolution map of what we might call street smarts, and the going was tough. A vast literature in the psychology of poverty offered only a few findings—sometimes accidentally discovered—of chaos-inspired skills, but more often, the research held gaps. As in many disciplines, researchers were under pressure to keep shoring up the scientific consensus, so they tended to dismiss outlier findings as flukes. Some researchers suspected they were missing an alternative perspective but were at a loss to understand how they could shed light on the strengths of people in poverty. Yet through spadework, error, and persistence, Frankenhuis, Ellis, and a widening network of collaborators began to uncover the cognitive skills that humans can develop in tough times.

By the time the young teens came to the University of Minnesota laboratory, they had been living with their adoptive families for most of their lives. But their early experiences in international orphanages, where care was often unreliable and conditions were harsh, had left their mark. In the 2016 experiment, more than four dozen adoptees and another thirty-three children raised in their biological families were told they were going to play an online trust game with an anonymous peer who, unknown to the participants, was a software program.

At the start of each round, a child received six virtual coins that he could hold onto or hand over to the other player, a gesture that would quadruple the competitor's pile. If the other player then reciprocated, the entire stash would be split equally. The child's initial kindness would pay off. But if the other defected and kept the loot, the child would be left with the consolation of a measly three coins. One group of children picked up on key trends in the play far faster than the others. One group was fluent in survival mode.

At first, the digital player seemed all kindness, reciprocating 70 percent of the time, and the adoptees, while initially a tad suspicious, became as willing to share their gains as children with more stable upbringings. But in later rounds, the tables turned, and the other player reciprocated less than one-third of the time. At this point, most non-adopted youth doggedly kept sharing their coins, slow to give up on the idea that the world was safe and predictable. In contrast, adoptees who had lived longer in overseas institutions "promptly changed their behavior" when the other player became punitive. As the scientists observed, "They learned faster."

A spate of discoveries inspired largely by the new "Hidden Talents" paradigm reveals a kind of cognitive agility born from early precarity. Youths raised in upheaval pick up on subtle changes in a fast-evolving situation, such as faint signs of anger or deceit or signals that the time is ripe to cut short their losses. They can do far more than grab the first marshmallow in view. One series of experiments involved young adults who had experienced high rates of family divorce, residential moves, or day-to-day chaos in childhood. (To assess early precarity, participants were asked, for example, questions such as to what extent, "when I woke up, I often didn't know what could happen in my house.") When coaxed to feel that the world was growing more unpredictable via a newspaper article, participants raised in chaos excelled on tests of working-memory updating, the ability to mentally swap out irrelevant data for new, more salient information.

People reared in more chaotic milieu tend to "reallocate their cognitive resources to pressing needs," observes Jennifer Sheehy-Skeffington, a social psychologist studying family precarity. They back-burner a distant future that they "may never come to experience." Just as life's surprises prompt the arousal that inspires learning in us all, so the constant upheaval of precarity can lead youths to become exceptionally attuned to their environment. This is a way of life that few would readily choose, yet it is no less remarkable for being born of necessity. And it is a stance that can save lives.

"Stability, I don't know the definition of," says Justin, a twenty-one-year-old Black man living in straitened circumstances in the Baltimore region. "If you expect one thing and the ball don't roll that way," he says, "Plan B should already be."

In urban communities that systematic injustice has left steeped in poverty, inequality, and violence, young Black men often grow up edgy. "I'm always, like, with it," says Tony, eighteen, another of the Baltimore youths whose skill in the here and now has been studied by researcher Jocelyn Smith Lee for more than a decade. Wherever they are, Justin, Tony, and their peers constantly scan their surroundings and closely read social encounters, displaying a hypervigilance that is a primary symptom of post-traumatic stress disorder, except that in their cases, as Smith Lee and others note, the trauma is ongoing, not past. In one East Baltimore study, Black men reported experiencing the murders of three close kin or peers on average by the time they turned twenty-four years old.

In such milieu, an alertness that can seem threatening to the rest of society is often a protective coping mechanism, researcher Noni Gaylord-Harden has found. To probe the connection, she measured incidents of hyperarousal, such as being jumpy, testy, or constantly checking one's surroundings, in a group of Black teen boys from low-income communities in Chicago. Those who were most highly alert wound up witnessing the least violence over the course of the following year. "Hypervigilance allows them to pick up on cues and clues about the safety of their immediate environment," Gaylord-Harden told me.

Typical youth programs strive to eradicate such reactivity as maladaptive, a process that educators and social workers liken to "getting a cat to retract its claws." But like Frankenhuis, Gaylord-Harden asks, "Are we undermining or disabling needed survival strategies through our intervention efforts?" As importantly, are we as a society ignoring a mindset that all humans may need at times in environments marked by volatility? Full-throttle attunement keeps people right where they should be in situations of high precarity: at the raw edge of change. Says Matt, a nineteen-year-old in Baltimore, "It's a lot of work to keep your life." Frankenhuis and Ellis call the hidden talents that they are bringing to light "stress-adapted skills." Young men on the streets call this kind of agile, electrifying, but often costly way of living and learning being "on point."

In his memoir *The Color of Water: A Black Man's Tribute to His White Mother*, James McBride recalls getting on a bus to go to a summer camp "for the neediest." Clambering into his seat, he noticed that his mother was standing beside a debonair Black man sporting a goatee and full-on leather. His twice-widowed mother had a big heart and a quick temper and worked multiple jobs to raise McBride and his eleven siblings on a shoestring. The children grew up skirmishing for scarce food and sharing beds with rotating casts of their brothers or sisters. McBride described the household as utterly chaotic.

When the little boy next to him on the camp bus proudly pointed out the man in leather as his father and bragged that he was a Black Panther, the young McBride remembered stories of violence associated with the activist group and was flooded with fear for his mother. As the bus pulled away, he turned and without a word punched his astonished seatmate in the jaw.

↵

The brains of children raised in volatility wind up doing just what they need to do to survive. Their cognitive circuitry becomes specialized for picking up on what matters most at a vulnerable time: fleeting opportunities, subtle clues to what's coming next, and, above all, signs of impending danger. Amid high unpredictability, the developing prefrontal cortex, the epicenter of human meaning making, "takes whatever it can from the sensory world—the sights, smells, the sounds of this harsh environment—and crystalizes [this input] into a decision-making platform for threat detection," neuroscientist Takao Hensch, an expert on neural plasticity, tells me. This mindset may be out of step with placid environments, as McBride's temper illustrates. But even more important, this bittersweet cognitive narrowing may leave little room for the wider work of childhood: exploration and wonder.

When all goes well, a developing brain grows into a flexible and efficient matrix of neural connections that serves as the biological basis of increasingly sophisticated thoughts, feelings, and perceptions. To this end, the neocortex, the critical top layer of the brain, thickens in the first year of life as neural connections multiply. Then across the toddler years and on into early adulthood, the cortex reverses course and slowly thins. Weaker or unused synapses are pruned as a child gradually learns what's important in her environment and what can be forgotten.

At the same time, the brain's efficiency is boosted by a speeding up in communications between synapses. In a process called myelination, the axon—the neuronal body that sprouts branch-like connections that send signals to other neurons—becomes ensheathed in a fatty insulation that bolsters synaptic conductivity. The growing brain is streamlining, gaining speed of intraneural communication while nevertheless developing at a leisurely pace in order to allow for the gradual building of rich complexity in its branch-like architecture.

Chronic unpredictability, however, seems to prompt a kind of developmental rush job. Compared to more affluent youths, the cortexes of children from lower-socioeconomic backgrounds often thin early and rapidly, a process that curtails the protracted growth of neural connections built up from a range of experiences. There is some evidence as well of early and excess myelination in people who have suffered trauma, abuse, or poverty as children. Importantly, in boosting neuronal efficiency, myelination prevents new synaptic connections from sprouting between neurons. The sheathing process, in other words, inhibits neuroplasticity, the forging of new neural connections that occurs throughout our lives but particularly in periodic windows in childhood. The besieged young brain is becoming set in its ways.

A developing mind under chronic stress seems to take whatever shortcuts it can to hone a narrow set of survival skills, a process of accelerated development that can shortchange the mind's long-term potential. When University of Pennsylvania scientists fed images of socioeconomically diverse teens' brains into a machine learning algorithm, the program classified half of the boys from challenged backgrounds as adults based on multiple measures of brain structure and function. In comparison, fewer than one-third of their more affluent peers were labeled so. (While less dramatically, the software similarly judged teen girls.) At the same time, the teens with early brain maturation tended to do poorly on tests of cognitive reasoning. Growing up amid chaos may mean cognitively growing up too fast and, in so doing, eroding the cognitive capacity to reason well. It also may mean confronting life a bit too often on your own.

One of the first discoveries of premature cognitive maturation in children of chaos involved the brain networks that help us manage our fears. Across childhood, the prefrontal cortex slowly lays down connections with and then regulates the amygdala, the seat of the brain's ability to detect and regulate environmental threats. Because infants initially lack prowess in managing their responses to life's bumps, parents typically step in to help. By calming a tantrum or soothing away sadness, the parent acts as a "quasi-prefrontal cortex" for the child, says Hensch. Not only do such gestures of solace teach varied paths to mental well-being, but they also prime the young human's cortico-limbic circuitry—the amygdala, prefrontal cortex, hippocampus—to be receptive to trusted voices of experience then and in the future. The adult is signaling, *You can lean on me. You can learn from me.* This is neuroplasticity in action.

Children in volatile environments, however, may have to learn too quickly to dry their own tears. Many young survivors of early adversity show advanced maturing of cortico-limbic circuitry and less of the high anxiety that typically follows such experiences, according to work led by Yale neuroscientist Dylan Gee. This rapid development may enable them to hold it together emotionally during times of adversity. But with this feat, they may turn away from chances to learn a range of new ways to soothe themselves.

Faced with a stressful situation, for example, a majority of young children who have spent time in institutions do not seem to be as soothed by the proximity of an adoptive parent; their amygdala remains highly reactive even in this caring presence, studies show. Consumed by survival mode, they may not have the bandwidth to try out other ways of being long after the bad times are over.

Children reared in unpredictability often keep a wary eye on whatever is new and threatening. Their capacity to stay in sync with rapid change reflects our species' ability to learn in dynamic environments and exemplifies the audacity of human adaptation. Still, the costs of this way of life can be high. Children of precarity may lose what developmental psychologist Alison Gopnik calls the "turbo-charged" plasticity of childhood, a "protected time to extract information from the environment through exploration." All children wonder, all are curious regardless of the harshness of their lives. But the poignant trade-off to growing up on point is a foreshortening of critical opportunities to nurture worlds of thinking beyond reactivity. Survival mode is a short-term victory.

"There is no revolution," Willem Frankenhuis wrote in 2019. Natural selection, he emphasizes, teaches that all adaptations have trade-offs. By uncovering the strengths of people in precarity, he and his collaborators insist they are not trying to put a sunny face on poverty or distract from efforts to tackle its ills, as some accuse. On video calls with me, he visibly squirms at the thought that reporters or even his collaborators will overstate their early findings. "We only know bits and pieces," asserts Frankenhuis, who wins respect from colleagues and critics alike for his transparency and scientific caution. It may take decades to map poverty's strengths, he says, but mounting evidence shows that "something is there."

And increasingly, policymakers, scientists, foundations, and activists are heeding his calls to question the overly clean-cut story of poverty's deficits and rehumanize people whose skills have been denigrated by a society deeply fearful of unpredictability. They argue that the question "What's right with the kids?" isn't a distraction from progress but rather an overdue chance to acknowledge that no single approach to thriving in uncertainty is best.

In 2018, the Museum of Modern Art in New York invited Frankenhuis to contribute a brief video to a daylong salon on friction. "Is there something to be learned from difficulties and risks?" asked the conference's lead organizer, curator Paola Antonelli.

Standing in his Dutch garden, with flowers waving in a June breeze, Frankenhuis holds his wriggling ten-month-old son as he speaks to the camera. "This is my son, Lukas," he begins. If he was growing up in a harsh, unpredictable environment, says Frankenhuis, it's likely that Lukas would not perform well on some cognitive tests. "Decades of psychological research have focused on [this finding]," says Frankenhuis. "In my research, however, I focus on a different question, on the hidden talents of youth growing up in high-adversity conditions."

In little more than a minute, Frankenhuis makes it clear that he is playing the long game. He offers no dramatic claims or fancy jargon for the artsy crowd. "What we need is a well-rounded approach where we understand both the pluses and minuses" to living in precarity. The story is far from complete, he is saying. Can we recognize that lives steeped in unpredictability demand street-smart reactivity *and* a chance to wonder and to explore? Can we see both sides to a question?

Four-year-old Jamar hesitates. In his hand is a card depicting a plain yellow triangle. Arrayed on a pint-sized table before him is a row of four other picture cards. The game he is playing in a north Minneapolis preschool with his teacher and a few classmates seems simple: sort the cards either by color or by shape. In a color round, yellow or blue cards get placed together. When the rules shift, triangles or circles are matched up.

But the game's seeming ease belies its importance. A few minutes of play can predict how well a young child pays sustained attention, listens, and responds, not just reacts, to a problem. Here is where survival mode, as adaptive as it may be, won't do and where children reared in under-resourced settings often fall short. Jamar is a soft-spoken boy wearing a camouflage shirt, jeans, and cornrows. This morning, he is being asked to see two sides of a question, and at first, he is failing.

Initially, the teacher, Laurie Ostertag, gives Jamar a card with a yellow moon on it and asks him to sort by color. None of the cards lying on the table are yellow. Jamar hastily places his card on top of a blue moon. Ostertag then gently walks him back through his choices—*Is this yellow? Is this yellow?*—before coaxing him to place his card in a discard pile. She gives the other children a turn and then offers Jamar an extra chance, this time at sorting by shape.

This is when he pauses, holding his yellow triangle hesitantly over a picture of a tempting yellow flower before placing it gently on a red triangle. "You stopped and you remembered we were playing the shape game," Ostertag says with delight. They high-five. Jamar lifts both arms in the air and does a little wiggle dance in his seat. The magnitude and fragility of his victory are not lost on either teacher or child.

Standing nearby is Philip David Zelazo, a renowned University of Minnesota researcher who has spent his career studying how children can move beyond the confines of constant reactivity. One bitterly cold winter day, he and I are observing classes at two of the preschools, including one in a shelter, where he undertakes experiments and develops interventions, including the program that will bring together the women of Hobbs.

A tall, meditative man, Zelazo is the son of a developmental psychologist who is known for presciently countering past assumptions that infants were largely incapable of conscious thought or abstract reasoning. As a high school student in the 1980s, Zelazo was drawn to the field yet grew frustrated that researchers at the time largely avoided delving into the messy subjectivity of people's inner lives. At college, he set out to write fiction until a scintillating course on the frontal lobes convinced him that a psychologist could do justice to the mind's complexities as well as any novelist. Zelazo did not worry about toiling in his father's shadow. "I always had a sense of how little we knew and how much there was to discover," Zelazo tells me.

As a graduate student at Yale, Zelazo invented the Dimensional Change Card Sort, the game that Jamar was playing and now one of the world's most famous cognitive assessments for children. At the time, educators pursuing the secrets of good learning were starting to focus less on what facts children knew and more on how they used their minds. As part of this shift, they uncovered a trio of attention skills—working memory, cognitive flexibility, and inhibition—called executive function. Children high in these abilities can manage their minds adroitly and so power through school. With the card sort test, Zelazo created an ingenious way to track these hot new skills that teachers and parents increasingly were seeking to teach their charges.

But even as he became a globe-trotting expert on executive function, Zelazo sensed there was more to the question of how kids succeed in school and in life than how well they sit still and pay attention. What he discovered was a promising way to help children of chaos recover the wonder and plasticity that should be the special terrain of the young.

Consider the central mystery of the sorting game: why some children fail to switch gears when the rules change. Like youths who are wired for threat and so too-persistently operate on point, preschoolers raised in precarity often stick with one way of play long past the age when most children can act on a card's hidden-in-plain-sight other dimension.

Intriguingly, this error is not wholly explained by deficits in executive function skills, such as working memory. If you stop and ask children who are sorting erroneously, "Which round—shape or color—are we playing now?," they can tell you exactly what they are *supposed* to be doing while doggedly continuing to err. Nor are they so well practiced in one type of play that they cannot operate any other way, a mindset indicating a lack of cognitive control. Many start to persevere after taking just one turn. What could lift children up and out of a singular view on the world and teach them to confront complex change more thoughtfully? A critical complement to survival mode, Zelazo argues, is reflection.

On my next visit, he and I meet at a crowded Middle Eastern café near his home in St. Paul. As is often the case when Zelazo is talking about the mind, he deigns small talk and for a long while leaves his food untouched. As the lunch hour comes and goes and the restaurant empties, he patiently distills years of unheralded work. Throughout a storied career researching executive function, he refused to set aside his quest to parse the murky complexities of our inner lives. With reflection, however, he had chosen a topic of study so big, so abstract, and so close to the enigma of consciousness that it was considered by many of his peers to be merely philosophical, a term of dismissal in psychology circles. Undeterred, Zelazo quietly worked to flesh out the concept scientifically, discover its neural underpinnings, and map its development in the young, all while dreaming of the day he could take his findings out of the lab and into the lives of children mired in precarity. Now that time was near.

Think of a ship's captain embarking on a journey. To navigate, she might use a sextant, a compass, or a star chart, guidance tools akin to the mind's executive function skills. But for all her skill in wielding these support systems, the captain still must endeavor to fully understand each unexpected or ambiguous problem—a shift in the wind, a sudden squall—that comes her way. According to Zelazo's increasingly influential theories, this cognitive work is achieved by iteratively considering and reconsidering a problem in order to add detail and context to an initially sketchy view. "We start with what's given," he says, "then actively reflect on it, enriching our understanding."

The human brain, with its branching connections and hierarchical structure, is uniquely suited to perform this work, Zelazo explains. Not only are "bottom-up" sensory regions loosely managed by "top-down" frontal lobes, but various sections of the frontal brain themselves are recruited in ascending order of complexity as we build understanding. By learning to coordinate increasingly elaborate constellations of brain networks, a feat that takes years to achieve, children gain the ability to see multiple sides to a question *and* the relations between these different threads of knowledge. After a bit of reflection, a red rabbit suddenly can become in a young child's eyes both a colored object and a kind of animal. This is the epiphany that allows thinkers young and old to, as Zelazo says, "stand on top of the deci-sion tree."

Children who do not reflect while playing the sorting game can keep one rule in mind, such as sorting by color. They can understand the exis-tence of an alternative way to play and even advise someone how to sort by shape. But because they have not mentally connected these two pieces of information, once the rules change, they fall out of step with a new reality.

In speaking to educators, Zelazo often compares reflection to an air traffic control system of the mind. By thinking in this way, you ascend to a meta-view of both the problem and the contents of your mind. "You go from a one-dimensional view—focusing on color or shape but not simul-taneously—to a two-dimensional view, where you can recognize that both effectively are in play but that you're using one and not the other dimension at this moment," he says. You "jump up a level or two in thinking and get serious about a problem." By mining advances in psychology, neuroscience, and consciousness studies, Zelazo is helping reveal the workings of what we call "slow thought." He is unlocking a critical form of uncertainty in action that even as adults we often fail to pursue.

The year that I first visited Zelazo's laboratory was a turning point for him. Not long before Jamar's victory, Zelazo published a series of exper-iments that would inspire the next decade of his career and become the basis for achieving his quest to change lives. He discovered how to teach reflection.

To kick off the studies, Zelazo and his graduate students asked pre-schoolers from middle- and lower-income backgrounds to play the sorting game. Then they invited only those children who had failed the challenge to participate in the actual experiment, which involved playing versions of the game with pictures they had not seen before. Some of the children who had failed the game then just played new rounds by themselves. Others were told if their answers were right or wrong; they were offered the kind of "reinforcement learning"—think gold-star charts—found in many kindergartens.

A third group of children who had initially failed, however, received a transformative lesson. Any time they made a mistake, the experimenter would halt the play, spell out what had gone wrong, ask the child to name which game they were playing, offer a corroborative example, and then ask them to try again, with help if needed. Essentially, they were being taught to reflect on the nature of the task and to connect their branches of knowledge about the game. They were being coached to recognize that their way of thinking in any one moment is just an idea, something they can build on and fine-tune. The outcome was dramatic: mere milliseconds at a panoramic level of thought turned cognitive defeat into success.

Most of the children who had been taught to reflect went on to ace the sorting challenge, with many making no errors at all. Those from the lowest-income households, who typically score in the thirty-eighth percentile nationally on the game, made the most progress. The findings indicate that explicit coaching can boost children's abilities to manage their minds by strengthening the executive function skills that support higher-order thinking. But far more exciting to Zelazo were hints that just twenty minutes of reflection training could help children as young as three years old try out new dimensions of mind.

During the experiment, the children wore skullcaps of electrodes that tracked their neural activity. In particular, Zelazo recorded the N2, a brain wave that accompanies the "oops" moment when we implicitly or explicitly pick up on an error, problem, or ambiguity in the environment. Nearly everyone, even infants, at some level senses the multifaceted nature of life. The question is, will we face up to our uncertainty, our most telling indicator of change? The surge of stress that occurs at this time is a starting point, a physiological firing up that readies us to consider what's gone awry. From there, we can take up uncertainty's invitation to respond, not merely react, to the changing situation.

In Zelazo's study, the children who were taught to reflect had lower levels of N2 activity before and after the rules of the game changed compared with those who failed to switch gears. It's not that they were any less on their toes. Rather, their ability to gain a meta-view helped them to better contend with a cognitive conflict, that is, resolve the "oops" signal and settle more smoothly into a new round of play. (Children trained to reflect also show higher recruitment of their frontal lobes while playing, other research shows.) After the training, moreover, they sharply improved their performance on a highly difficult task for their age-group: discerning another person's mistaken perspective. "Joey moved Susie's doll while she was out of the room," an experimenter would tell a young child. "When she returns, where will Susie think the doll is?" Most preschoolers think that Susie knows where the doll has gone. Those who reflect are better able to explore unexpected points of view.

Could reflective thinking safeguard children of chaos from cognitively growing up too fast? I asked Zelazo. At the time, no one knew if the newly discovered phenomenon of premature brain development in children experiencing adversity could be prevented or reversed. Neuroplasticity was still largely a scientific mystery, although there was intriguing evidence from rodent studies that periods of heightened neural connectivity can be cultivated.

Nevertheless, Zelazo already was looking ahead and connecting the dots. By reflecting, children of chaos likely are building the rich complexity in thinking that can be lost when their brains specialize too fast, he said. "Being in an exploratory mode, being curious, finding it easier to play the new game—that's plasticity," he said. "Reflection is an opening up to possibilities. You are keeping open a kind of child mind when you reflect."

With his landmark work on training reflection in hand and with corroborating evidence emerging from other labs, Zelazo started to take a public stand. He and his closest collaborator, psychologist Stephanie Carlson, began speaking openly about the importance of reflection to educators and to their funders, including the Bezos Family Foundation and the Chan Zuckerberg Initiative. They created a start-up to market a digital version of the sorting game and named the company Reflection Sciences. Next, Zelazo would try a new, risky way to bring his findings deeper into the daily lives of children who too often, as one Minneapolis shelter teacher told me, "do not know what will happen tomorrow."

In the decades leading up to his discoveries, gold-standard interventions to remedy the cognitive impairments of poverty too often were small, costly, highly controlled, and moderately or inconsistently effective. The benefits that emerged usually failed to scale up or to generalize outside the petri dish of the programs themselves. Too often, the interventions sidelined the intricate realities of participants' lives: the intrinsic unpredictability, the lightning tempo, and the relentless demands of days spent in survival mode. For example, typical efforts focused on the needs of either parents *or* children, a siloing that ignored the family interactions that are central to a youngster's world. As well, many in the field were beginning to ask, could promising early scientific findings be better adapted to and even shaped by people in precarity themselves?

In 2013, Zelazo joined a new Harvard University–based initiative created to address these gaps. Frontiers of Innovation was set up to fund "short-cycle" interventions featuring strategies and content that would evolve as evidence of a program's effectiveness emerged. The operating mode would be more akin to Silicon Valley–style fail-fast experimentation than to scripted interventions of the past. In addition, the activist-academics behind the initiative especially encouraged ventures that involved whole families. Working with a respected firm that manages Head Start programs and curricula, Zelazo spent several years creating one of Frontiers of Innovation's first projects, a pioneering approach to teaching reflection to families in precarity. Some of his most important early collaborators would be the women of Hobbs.

Called Ready4Routines, the course that grew out of Zelazo's research ostensibly aims to help families build what William James called "habits of order," the daily routines so often eroded by poverty and chaos. Each participating family receives a pack of activity cards centered on transforming often-tense daily transitions, such as getting ready for school or bedtime, into rhythmic practices. But while important, the routines themselves are simply ingenious entry points into learning how, as the curriculum explains, to "think about what you are doing." Says Zelazo, "It's a stealth course in reflection. Routines are a nice fringe benefit."

During the eight-week class, parents are taught a set of skills—pausing, engaging, encouraging their children, and, most important, reflecting—to call on as they and their children clean up toys or set the table. In this way, simple acts of survival and, by extension, the times when they inevitably go wrong can become something to ponder, to investigate, and to improve. "I thought the class was going to be more like getting us on a schedule, getting us on a schedule," Shaniece Langley told me. "But it is not even just about how we get out of the house or come home. It's about how I react to people at work or in the store, my husband or my mother, how I get things done and what I prioritize and don't. It's gotten so much deeper into other areas of my life."

↑

The room quiets as preschool director Patricia Grovey gets down to business. At the time of my 2018 visit, Hobbs is serving as one of eleven sites across the country where Ready4Routines is being beta-tested and assessed. So far this morning, the mothers have been catching up with one another after spring break, talking of small joys such as a child conquering the monkey bars and of heart-wrenching times like a child wandering away. Now they turn their attention to Grovey. "Let me stop and think—that's reflection," she is saying. "What's working? What isn't working? We're doing all this pausing and engaging and encouraging to reflect." She is underscoring the core message of the course: "In any moment, you have choices."

After a few more introductory words, the women break into small groups to discuss how they are putting their new skills into practice. I join Langley, a couple of other women, and Starr Gibson, the young mother with the breakdown-prone car.

Gibson begins relating her recent terror when her own preschooler slipped out of the house. One minute she could hear Prince playing with his toys, then all went silent; she was instantly on point. When she couldn't find him in the house or on the sidewalk, she first wondered if he had gone to visit Kia, a cousin who often babysat him. "Every weekend, that's their baby." In the thirty seconds that it took her to cross the street, a storm of other possibilities raced through her mind. Could he be hiding? Did he go all the way to her brother's house? She dialed her brother as she walked. He did not pick up.

Dorothy Fields, poet and sage of the group, marvels, "How were you able to stay calm? I mean you weren't a screaming momma, running around, lashing out," as she recalls being once when one of her children took off.

Lost in her recollections, Gibson murmurs, "I started thinking again." What would her child usually do, and what might he do when the usual wasn't his whim? "I know my child, he's not going to just wander," she remembers thinking even as that terrible possibility crossed her mind. She was staying curious amidst her fears, bravely reaching for the meta-view. Says Zelazo, "Taking responsibility for seeing the world one way or another or coming up with a third way—that is the kernel and the insight." Gibson rang Kia's doorbell. There was no answer. She tried again. There was Prince.

"I felt like a bad mom," admits Gibson, nearly in tears.

"It sounds as though you were reflecting." Grovey joins the discussion. "You were considering the way you were approaching the situation. That made you think about some other choices."

The conversation opens up to the whole group and to the other main aim of the class: passing the skill of reflection down to the youngest minds. Grovey continually reminds the women, and they in turn urge one another, to take time to confront life's precarity *with* their children. They are the frontline teachers here. By scaffolding their thinking via reflection, the mothers of Hobbs are learning to teach their children to do so as well.

Gibson speaks up again, telling how her children had rejected her younger siblings when they recently had to move in with her. "It was like, 'Take them home. I don't want them here,'" she relates. "One said, 'This is my bedroom and my bedroom only.'"

"'Listen, I got bunk beds for a reason, there's two of you,'" Gibson patiently explained to her children. She set aside survival mode to walk them through another point of view. "'It's y'all's room now.'"

"'She has her room at Granny's house.'"

"'Well, no, she doesn't,'" she emphasized. Turning to her peers, Gibson concludes, "They're getting used to it now, but at first it was not working out."

"It's getting there, Starr, you're doing good," says Grovey. "You're making them think, you're making them think."

"Reflection is about investigating," adds teacher Angela Green, drawing from her lesson book, "so you can plan, be creative, make it better next time." And that was exactly what Dorothy Fields said that she had, through this class, set out to do.

"I'd been putting it off on the teachers to teach my kids," begins Fields, mother of a six-year-old boy with autism and a four-year-old girl. Recently, her son was being sent home from school repeatedly for acting up. Fields feared that one day, he would drop out, just as she had done. At first, she had no clue what to do, she tells the class. But then she told herself, "Okay, make a solid commitment." Hearing the ferocity in her voice, the women grow still.

"My momma didn't teach me nothing. I left home at fifteen," says Fields. "My children are going to be better than me. I'm going to start a generation where their children are going to be better than *them*. I'm instilling in them—you know what, baby, I don't yet know—but I'm going to help them find it. . . . So that's why I'm here, to start that generational pattern. It's got to start somewhere." The other parents erupt into applause, and Fields continues in tears.

When people see the transformation in her children, she asserts, they will say, "'How did that happen? Where she come from? The ghetto? The projects? Little old her. Momma's barely got an income. Momma's barely scraping it together. But ooh, look at them babies. They're okay.'" There is a beat or two of silence. The women understand her profoundly. This is a high-stakes survival game. Getting stuck in one way of play could cost them their futures and their children's too.

True to the nature of short-cycle interventions, initial results from the first Ready4Routine classes were mixed. Intriguing boosts in children's executive function scores in two pilot experiments did not pan out in a pair of full studies for many possible reasons, including the difficulty of assessing constantly evolving lessons for participants with little time for filling out forms.

Still, by many measures, the overall program was a resounding success. Parents and other caregivers from Hobbs to Jacksonville, Florida, to Las Vegas brought aunts, grandparents, uncles, siblings, and their own grown children to classes. After taking the course, more than 90 percent of participants reported feeling closer to their children, and equal numbers said they got along better as families. By 2022, Acelero Learning was embedding elements of the course into family engagement and other educational programs at the Head Start schools that it operates as well as into its technical assistance work with state and community partners while continuing to develop the materials on its own. The initiatives were reaching up to 40,000 children and families in multiple states. "There's something promising about this," Lori Levine, senior vice president of family engagement at Acelero Learning, told me. "It creates moments of spaciousness and connection in the lives of families."

For his part, Zelazo was torn. As a scientist, he was intent on gathering more data to explore why and how reflection matters in children's lives. But along with many of his colleagues, he increasingly was convinced that change would come to children of chaos only if the field brought science-in-progress out into the world with the help of people in precarity themselves.

"We have a good sense of what reflection is and how it's related to the brain and how it develops," he told me. "We know more than we need to know to make a much bigger difference in children's lives than we are—and that's starting to get frustrating." For the first time in the decade that I had known him, he raised his voice. "Everybody wants to do another study and another study and it's like, how about we just let somebody benefit from all this work?" He was embracing the unpredictable even as he was helping those far out on the precipice of the unknown to step a bit back from that very edge.

Learning to draw close but not too close to raw precarity: this is the remarkable gift that the mothers of Hobbs ultimately learned to offer their children. In a PhD study supervised by Zelazo, Andrei Semenov later showed that parents who had taken Ready4Routines classes became far better at helping their children as needed, no more or less. The caregivers became more *autonomy supportive*, meaning they let their offspring experience challenges on their own while stepping in to help if a task became overwhelming. They allowed them to be on point to a volatile world without going it alone.

In essence, they began teaching their children how to work skillfully, even comfortably, within what psychologists call the "zone of proximal development," the outer horizons of one's understanding, Zelazo tells me excitedly. "That's where the growth in a human occurs. It's like the green tip of a bud on the tree. That's where all the action is happening." In countries as diverse as China and Ghana, children with autonomy-supportive caregivers tend to be more successful, motivated learners who experience higher well-being. In addition, their families are more cohesive. The mothers of Hobbs were helping their young find their place at the edge of the unknown.

For the vigilant teen, the child of chaos, the besieged parent, and the emboldened scientist, the new resilience is a kind of ambidexterity, a capacity to toggle between gauging what's confronting you right now and discovering hidden sides to a question. In volatile times, being full-cylinder on point equips us to stay intimately in sync with change. The rapidly shifting present—the broken-down car, the runaway child, the messy evidence—must be addressed. As the state of our work, our health, our politics, and our earth grows more volatile, we can no longer afford to overlook the critical skills inherent in stress-fueled survival mode or the lessons to be learned from those raised in precarity who do it painfully well.

And yet chaos also must be met with another dimension of mind. By ascending to a panoramic view in thought, we gain the spaciousness needed to look up and ahead. We can adopt the stances of exploration, curiosity, and wonder that elevate us from merely fending off threat after threat.

[↓]

On my last evening in Hobbs, I stop by Shaniece Langley's home. As I drive up in my rented pickup truck, I see a house in seeming fortress mode, with shades drawn, bars on the windows, and a backyard fenced off by a low cinder-block wall. Inside, the dusty living room is dimly lit. I hear a kid's television program and a persistent smoke alarm blaring in distant corners of the house. But Langley greets me warmly and takes me down a hallway to her son's room to see her children play "Simon Says Pick-Up," a class activity that sweetens the housekeeping that she loathes.

"Are you ready to start playing pickup?" she asks Robert, giving him a tickle while grabbing the remote to turn off the Disney Channel. She calls her daughter in and lets her begin.

"Simon says, 'touch your toes,'" says Angelia, a somber girl with long, dark-blonde hair.

"No-o-o," says her mother. "We're playing 'Clean-Up Simon Says,' remember?"

"Simon says, 'Pick up your dinosaurs.'"

"Yes, ma'am. All righty, Robert, you ready to play? You can help him, Lia."

"I don't need no help," asserts the little boy, shaking his ponytail.

"Okay," says Langley, "Simon says, 'Pick up all the dark blue blocks and put them in your train, please.'"

She sends Angelia to her room to start cleaning up, then pivots agilely between the children, stepping in here and there to avert bickering, to revive interest in the game, to solve a small problem—"Mommy, the Play-Doh's all dry!"—or to expand the routine with a little wonder. "What kind of pie do you think this is, Lia? Chocolate? Yum, yum, yum," says Langley, pretending to gobble up a toy slice.

The smoke alarm is still ringing. The cat knocks over a dish or two in the kitchen. But for the moment, Langley is calm. There are still setbacks, explosions, and rushed mornings, yet she is beginning to "take more time with things, to actually make it meaningful while you're doing it," she relates as we sit together in the living room. "I've learned so much more about my kids in these past few weeks," from her son's lingering hearing issues to the unexpected ways that her daughter can step up and help when given a chance. "I am much more aware." Robert wanders in, immersed in a game on a tablet, and nestles beside her on the sofa.

"If you don't see it, you can't fix it, huh Bubba?" she says to him, kissing the top of his head. "You got to see it to fix it. I love you, my handsome man."

"I love you, momma."

Two years after my visit, Langley would become jobless and be evicted from her home. When the pandemic hit, she was selling cable television and internet plans door to door, pregnant with her third child. Her doctor ordered her on bed rest, and the work dried up. Her husband was let go, they separated, and days after giving birth to a baby girl, she was forced out of her house. She then was jobless for a year while living in a rental town house before finding work as a property manager that came with an apartment. Finally, she switched back to better-paying work in internet sales.

All the while as she put out fire after fire, she held onto snatches of reflection like lifelines, she tells me when I call one day. Such moments have kept her going and are, she believes, the building blocks of her children's futures. "If you don't teach your children how to handle life and what gets in your way," says Langley, "they will never think about the things they are doing and the things they are going to do."

Hearing her words, I recall a moment in class when she talked about teaching her children how to ride their bicycles. "It was a couple of hours falling in the driveway," she laughed. "Lia was so adamant, Robert was ready to give up. She finally got the hang of it, and I said to her, 'Now you have to step in in place of me and help him and guide him, encourage him,' and she did. 'I'm so proud of you,' I said to her. Then she would fall again, and I would tell her, 'Everybody makes mistakes. You've got to just get back up. It's okay to try over and over again until you get it.'"

CHAPTER EIGHT

AN I-DON'T-KNOW ROBOT AND THE FUTURE OF UNCERTAINTY

Hope is the story of uncertainty, of coming to terms with the risk involved in not knowing what comes next, which is more demanding than despair and, in a way, more frightening. And immeasurably more rewarding.
—REBECCA SOLNIT

The robot is uncertain, and I am thrilled.

Deep within a sprawling complex of engineering laboratories at Virginia Tech, I am teaching a robotic arm affixed to a table how to do a simple task: use a laser light to "paint" a line across the tabletop. The lesson is hands-on. My aim is to manually move the claw end of the machine along the path that I would like it to take when the robot does the work on its own. Towering curvaceously above me, muscular in its own steely way, such robots are widely used in manufacturing and sometimes in smaller form as smart prosthetics on wheelchairs.

This particular specimen, however, has a revolutionary new capacity. Within seconds of pulling the robot toward me to begin the task, I can feel it come uncannily alive. By gently inflating various armbands distributed along its length, the robot is signaling its uncertainty about how close to the edge of the table I would like it to be. I can then hone my teaching so it can refine its work. This creature can know that it doesn't know and tell me so, qualities that are at the heart of an urgent effort to radically reimagine artificial intelligence and perhaps humanity itself.

In trying to emulate and even surpass human intelligence, AI's designers have long focused on building machines that know just what to do. In most AI to date, humans specify an objective—stack a package, play masterful chess—and the machine learns how to pull it off, ideally free of human guidance. Contending with uncertainty, such as noise in its sensor data or humans in its path, has been treated as a necessary evil, something at best peripheral to the cause.

Operating with this worldview, AI's gee-whiz achievements have piled up, from beating champions at complex strategy games such as Go and spotting a malignant tumor to enabling a self-driving car to traverse a busy city street. In its first few decades on Earth, imperfect, erratic, and yet increasingly powerful AI seemed poised to be able to one day do almost anything we asked.

Yet as AI has become more capable and so more embedded in the real world, cracks in the field's grand ambitions have begun to appear. Social media algorithms are built to doggedly steer humans toward extremist content in order to boost user time spent online. *Objective achieved?* Robots intent on accomplishing their mission are alarmingly tone deaf to humans' shifting needs and to their guidance. A robot arm playing a chess tournament in Moscow drew headlines when it broke the finger of its seven-year-old opponent as he reached for a piece on the board. *Objective achieved?* Facial recognition and medical diagnostic systems and their users often sweep ambiguities and inconsistencies under the rug. Algorithms that categorize facial expressions may diminish human complexity, for example, by labeling a face showing happiness *and* surprise as one or the other. *Objective achieved?*

For all its wonders, AI tends to be woefully misaligned come "run time" with human perspectives, values, and lives. "It is as if the better part of humanity were, in the early twenty-first century, consumed by the task of gradually putting the world—figuratively and literally—on autopilot," observes researcher Brian Christian, author of *The Alignment Problem*. As a result, achieving the field's goal of fully autonomous ultrasmart AI likely will carry grave risks to our species, growing numbers of scientists warn. "Success for my field," says AI pioneer Stuart Russell, "would be the biggest event in human history and perhaps the last."

In crafting a future coexistence with such machines, there will not be just one way forward. But increasingly, designers and researchers alike agree that a crucial piece of the puzzle of making safe, wise systems has been overlooked far too long. Many at the front lines of AI are beginning to prioritize building AI with a capacity to be uncertain as a path to creating intelligent machines that are more honest, adaptable, inclusive, cooperative, and reflective. In a sense, the field is aligning itself with nascent movements across many domains that are recognizing uncertainty as a strength of mind, human or artificial. "Uncertainty is at the heart of what our work is about," says Dylan Losey, the young scientist whose cutting-edge robotics research brought me to Virginia Tech. "It's a critical part of the solution." That day in September, I had at my fingertips a sense of coming change.

As Losey's graduate student Soheil Habibian prepares another test of the painter-robot, I take a look around the bustling laboratory. Beneath a high ceiling bristling with exposed pipes and beams, experimental robots sit and stand, poised to be put through their paces. One will later act out different ways to stack a set of paper plates, in effect asking me multiple-choice questions about my domestic preferences. Another will admit that it does not yet know how best to carry a cup. During my visit, they will learn from me and I from them. In a small way, I am test-driving not only the cutting edge of AI but also the future of uncertainty in an era of flux. The robot is ready, and I turn back to run the task once more, looking for a better way. How near to the edge do I want to be? it asks me again. At that moment, the robot is thinking of tables. I am thinking of the unknown.

[↓]

In 2014, Google shocked many in the AI field by paying $650 million to acquire a London-based AI start-up that had fewer than one hundred employees and no publicly revealed products or services. It was "utterly bewildering" to discover that this under-the-radar firm was valued at such a hefty sum, recalls Michael Wooldridge, then head of Oxford University's computer science department.

Google's acquisition proved prescient a year later when DeepMind published the bombshell innovation of a trained algorithm or "model" that could quickly learn from scratch to conquer dozens of extremely varied Atari video games. Despite knowing nothing in advance of each game's rules and setup, how to shoot, or which objects might move where, the company's "deep q-network" achieved levels of play far exceeding those of expert humans. Given the simple aim of winning, the program set off to make its fortune like a prodigal hero from a fairy tale. Its stunning success in diverse environments was tantalizing evidence that AI could one day rival or exceed humanity's generalized intelligence, not just the kind of narrow, specialized smarts it had achieved to date.

To conquer Atari, DeepMind imbued an artificial neural network—a brain-like layered amalgam of simulated neurons—with the field's most vaunted machine learning strategy, reinforcement learning. Inspired by early theories on how animals learn, reinforcement learning algorithms progress by trial and error. They play a game, for example, tens of thousands of times in order to obtain feedback useful for unearthing the single best path to victory. Actions called policies that are mathematically rewarding to the algorithm are reinforced and repeated, while those that lead further from its goal are abandoned. Such algorithms also constantly predict whether their current state of play will achieve their goal, learning from broken expectations much as our own dopamine networks do. Reinforcement learning is essentially reward-centric. In a nutshell, the Atari-cracking model epitomized the field's longtime ideal of building machines that pursue their aims with a kind of single-minded intensity.

To date, intelligence in AI largely has rested on one major premise: to be smart is to attain one's goals. Whether the machine uses reinforcement learning or another strategy, its raison d'être is to make its actions and decisions servant to its aims. This vision of what is deemed "good" or "rational" in cognition dates back millennia, especially in the West, and also reflects biological truth. After all, organisms would be ill equipped to survive without the capacity to achieve their goals. So it seemed natural that from its outset in the 1950s, the AI field would embrace this definition of smarts as its own. "We build objective-achieving machines, we feed objectives into them, or we specialize them for particular objectives and off they go," says Russell, a University of California, Berkeley, professor and coauthor of the definitive textbook on AI. This approach fueled much of twentieth-century technological progress, he notes. Yet giving a system a mission and letting it take care of the rest is where we begin to see both AI's magic and its risks.

A lone white speedboat in a video game wildly spins around a teal-blue harbor. Around it goes, crashing and burning again and again into other boats, a harbor breakwater, and a series of posts. The boat-racing game that I am watching seems almost laughably simple considering that it is part of an effort by one of the world's leading AI companies to build systems that can one-up deep q-networks by leagues and so take AI steps closer to exhibiting all-purpose human intelligence. Part of OpenAI's Universe project, the algorithm driving the boat is serious business, yet it is also an infamous lesson in how reward-centric AI can go badly wrong.

When Dario Amodei created the AI-driven boat to compete in the racing game, he gave it a seemingly fail-safe objective: score points. Blithely assuming this was the way to win, he didn't look closely at the implications of that objective. But the system did. The boat carried out its marching orders to the letter by slamming into "power-ups," features of the game that offer bonus points. The problem was that in order to score more points, it dropped out of the race. "That's what makes these systems so powerful—they make decisions on their own," says Ava Thomas Wright, a leading philosopher of AI ethics. "That's a feature we love about autonomous systems, but it's also what makes them kind of dangerous, possibly in an existential way."

The solution seems obvious. Give the system better instructions. But a moment's thought will deprive us of that illusion. Beyond ultra-predictable, bubble-world environments, "it is often difficult or infeasible to capture exactly what we want an agent to do," Amodei and his colleague Jack Clark later wrote. Neither designers nor users can account in advance for every wrinkle that AI may face in doing a task or for all the consequences of its resourcefulness. Rushing off to work, you might forget to tell the robot housekeeper not to clean the kids' new aquarium inside *and* out, to the fish's chagrin. Or you might like the fact that your self-driving taxi is forbidden to cross double-yellow lines until a rogue truck suddenly swerves into your lane. *Off they go.*

Already misalignment is very much with us, often causing serious harm. In one recent incident, makers of an algorithm to decide which patients receive extra medical care based people's risk scores on expected per-patient health care costs. But since Black patients, likely due to systemic bias and to patient mistrust, generally get less care and so accrue lower costs than White people who are equally sick, the algorithm wound up disproportionately excluding them from high-risk care programs.

Or consider the algorithms trained to do the natural language processing that is the backbone of online translation, search, and even recruiting. Such systems suggest the next word in the e-mail that you are writing or sift through résumés seeking good candidates for a job. Many do so by calculating how closely any one word or phrase is related to others. "Tea," for example, is closely related to "cup." And according to many such systems, a doctor is a "he," and African American names are unpleasant, studies show.

Such bias in AI often reflects a lack of diversity in the largely Web-based data used to train many algorithms. But remedying that flaw, as important as that is, may not produce algorithmic equity. That is because to boost its chances of realizing its objective—for example, predicting the next word in a sentence—systems prioritize only the most common results. An algorithm trained with diverse examples might successfully recognize that physicians can be female yet overlook the existence of nonbinary doctors. Intent at all costs on optimizing an objective, AI tends to ignore alternate ways of being in the world and so in essence the plurality of human experience.

AI increasingly gets the job done. But creating literal-minded systems with expanding abilities to execute marching orders handed out by innately shortsighted humans is a perilous mix. In concocting his wily speedboat, Amodei decided against simply telling it to win because *that* objective seemed too complicated.

In 2003, the Swedish philosopher Nick Bostrom proposed a thought experiment. Imagine that a superintelligent AI system is told to make paper clips and then does so until Earth and a good portion of outer space are transformed into paper clip–manufacturing facilities. In a field notorious for its false leads and boom-and-bust cycles, his prediction at first seemed laughable. Even as increasingly robust neural networks began to fuel impressive machine learning gains, many in the field continued to treat any mention of AI's potential existential dangers as unrealistic or unhelpful to the cause. "A lot of the alarmism comes from people not working directly at the [front lines of AI], so they think a lot about more science-fiction scenarios," scoffed DeepMind cofounder Demis Hassabis. "I don't think it's helpful when you use very emotive terms because it creates hysteria."

By the early 2020s, however, AI's rising capabilities, while perennially hyped and deeply fallible, were of deepening concern to the field. A British company was poised to make a computer with 100 million times faster processing capacity than the average laptop. A single DeepMind agent called Gato could play Atari, stack blocks, caption photos, and chat, while OpenAI's headline-making ChatGPT, although far from unbiased or accurate, could generate business strategies and answer questions in clear prose. The annual value of global venture capital investment in AI firms grew from $3 billion in 2012 to $207 billion less than a decade later. An aggregate of expert forecasts estimated that there was a 50 percent chance that AI could outperform humans in any task by 2060.

A dream once thought impossible seemed on the horizon, bringing with it the potential for both transformative benefits, such as higher living standards or a cure for cancer, and a scaling up of the alignment problem to terrifying heights. In his book *The Precipice*, philosopher Toby Ord paints a vivid picture of just one way in which AI might plausibly endanger humanity. By constantly self-improving while controlling millions of internet systems, general AI could take over the world's resources, from human capital to the vast mineral wealth under the sea. Most alarmingly, Ord notes that "AI would be practically impossible to destroy."

Unstoppability—that is where superhuman intelligence separates irrevocably from its human creators and where the amusing spectacle of the rogue toy boat begins to resemble a science fiction nightmare come to life. AI would not need an instinct for survival or a soupçon of consciousness to defy us. It likely will thwart efforts to amend its goals or to turn it off because doing so would counter its mandate to optimize its objectives above all. It would interpret any attempt to shut it down as "a form of incapacitation which would make it harder to achieve high reward," writes Ord.

The high-stakes risks inherent in achieving superhuman AI, as well as the lack of a parachute in our leap toward such a goal, are major reasons why issues of safety and control have become urgent priorities in a field once intent on simply achieving might. In 2023, more than 1,500 technology leaders and researchers urged a global pause in furthering the most advanced AI, saying developers are "locked in an out-of-control race to develop and deploy ever more powerful digital minds that no one—not even their creators—can understand, predict or reliably control." No longer can humans afford to imbue AI with an objective and then step back and, as one designer says, "just pray and depend on the magic."

↵

In warning of AI's risks, scientists often mention "The Sorcerer's Apprentice." Although the story has been told worldwide since at least the fourth century BCE, in our day it likely conjures up Disney's classic animated version. In that film, in the absence of his wizard boss, Mickey Mouse casts a spell on a broom to make it fetch pails of water only to lose control of the rogue tool. On his return, the furious sorcerer chastises Mickey for using magic beyond his capabilities. The movie represents one of two major versions of the saga, notes Jack Zipes, a world-renowned scholar of folktales, fairy tales, and critical theory, in his recent anthology of the tale. In this type, the humiliated youth remains manacled to his ignorance.

Far more prevalent throughout history, however, is the tale of the rebellious apprentice. In this variation, the naive hero's burgeoning knowledge awakens him (or far more rarely, her) to his state of powerlessness. He rises up and liberates himself (and in some tales the community as well) from the wizard's tyranny. This version pits a novice who is struggling to learn and to grow against a hoarder of secrets who, perhaps like standard AI, works only for his own ends. The story depicts the "life-and-death struggle to know ourselves, our desires, and our talents," Zipes writes.

But when I press Zipes one day to reveal exactly how the rebellious youth overcomes the sorcerer, he demurs. The story does not offer formulas for success, nor is the hero's metamorphosis any less important than the reader's, he tells me. As readers, we come to the narrative and perhaps all of life with mistaken assumptions—that the tale you know is the only version of a story, that knowledge is for an elite few. "So, what the tale helps us to do," says Zipes, "is see that we *don't* see the world all that clearly." In order to liberate ourselves and to progress, "we have to shed the blindness that we have." The puzzle of how to do so is ours to solve.

In the six years that Zipes spent gathering, translating, and studying the tales, he was at first amazed and even a bit bewildered by his deepening fascination with the story. "It gradually became clear to me why I had become infatuated with these tales," he writes. "They have given me some signs of hope when it seemed that we were living in hopeless times."

One winter evening in 2014, just as DeepMind was pushing forward with its breakthrough work on Atari, Stuart Russell was riding the Paris Metro.

He was on his way to a rehearsal for a choir that he had joined while living in the French capital during a sabbatical from Berkeley.

That evening, he was listening to the piece that he would be practicing, Samuel Barber's *Agnus Dei*, the composer's choral arrangement of his haunting *Adagio for Strings*. At the time, Russell's research focused largely on ways to spur robot algorithms to better maximize their reward function. Yet he had begun to give credence to rising calls, still from mostly outside the field, to address humanity's potential collision course with AI. He recently had expressed his growing concern publicly for the first time in a lecture at a small British museum. But one question was preying on him. How could the peril be averted?

Swept up in the sublime music, Russell had a breathtaking idea. AI should be built to support ineffable human moments like this one. Instead of delegating an objective to a machine and then stepping back, designers should make systems that will work *with* us to realize both our complex, shifting goals and our values and preferences. "It just sprang into my mind that what matters, and therefore what the purpose of AI was, was in some sense the aggregate quality of human experience," he later recalled. And in order to be constantly learning what humans want or need, AI must be uncertain, Russell realized. "This is the core of the new approach: we remove the false assumption that the machine is pursuing a fixed objective that is perfectly known."

Talking with me by video call one autumn day in 2022, Russell elaborates. Once the machine is uncertain, it can start working with humans instead of "just watching from above." If it doesn't know how the future should unfold, AI becomes teachable, says Russell, a thin, dapper man with a manner of speaking that is somehow both poetical and laser precise. A key part of his Paris epiphany, he says, "was realizing that actually [AI's] state of uncertainty about human objectives is permanent." He pauses. "To some extent, this is how it's going to be for humans too. We are not born with fixed reward functions."

A few weeks later, I meet up virtually with Anca Dragan, an energetic Berkeley roboticist who is a protégé of Russell's and one of a growing number of high-profile scientists turning his vision for reimagining AI into algorithmic reality.

"One of my biggest lessons over the past five years or so has been that there's a tremendous amount of power for AI in being able to hold appropriate uncertainty about what the objective should be," she tells me. *Power?* I ask. She explains that by making AI "a little bit more humble, a little bit more uncertain, all of a sudden magical things happen" for both the robot *and* the human. Together, we begin watching two illustrative bits of video whose banality, like the toy boat scene, belies their importance.

In the first clip filmed during experiments in her laboratory, we watch as a robot arm swings into action, carrying a coffee cup several feet high above a table. Almost immediately, a graduate student in a red T-shirt tries to push the arm lower. "It's Ellis's favorite mug," says Dragan, describing the hypothetical scenario inspiring the research, "and he doesn't like it that the robot is holding it so high up because if it drops, it will break." As Ellis pushes, the robot doesn't fight or freeze. But as soon as he lets go—"this is the interesting part," says Dragan—the robot promptly bounces back up, reclaiming its initial trajectory. This is how AI traditionally has treated the human—as a pesky obstacle on the road to fulfilling the gospel of its objective, says Dragan. The robot views Ellis as an unknown to be ignored, skirted, or eliminated in order to get the job done. I watch as he gives the imperturbable machine a final two-fingered poke before standing back, looking a little defeated.

In what is known as the classical period of AI, early systems by necessity were built to operate in a kind of utopian world that was clear-cut, predictable, and fully understood. In order to make the first algorithms work, designers had to, as Dragan says, "cut off a tiny piece of the world, put it in a box, and give it to a robot." By the 1980s, however, scientists realized that if they were to create systems for real-world use, they needed to grapple with the unpredictability of life.

To meet this challenge, computer scientist Judea Pearl famously turned to Bayes' theorem, an Enlightenment-era mathematical system for dealing with uncertainty by constantly updating one's prior beliefs with new evidence. By investing AI with probabilistic capabilities, Pearl enabled systems to weigh various actions against both the current state of the world and a range of possible futures before deciding on the best route to maximizing a reward. He gave AI wiggle room. Yet the foundational premise of the work remained the same. Unknowns—whether a hesitant pedestrian in a crosswalk, an unanswerable search engine query, or a coffee drinker with ideas of his own—are best summarily dispatched en route to realizing an objective. When Ellis lets go, the coast is clear. The robot knows just what to do.

In the next clip, Ellis tries again. But this time, he only has to push the arm down once before stepping back and watching, one hand nonchalantly in his pocket, as the robot glides by a few inches above the table. Suddenly, the system is doing not what *it* wants but something far more in line with what Ellis prefers. The maneuver is over in less than a minute, and the inner workings of the robot's metamorphosis are hidden from view. But I can clearly see that this time, the robot has learned something about carrying coffee, about human priorities, and about aligning with intelligences other than its own. As the robot completes the task, Ellis nods approvingly to someone off camera. He looks relieved.

This is the new paradigm of what Russell calls "human-compatible AI." Gone is the fallacy of the known fixed objective, whether it is given in advance—"win points"—or, as is the case with a strategy called inverse reinforcement learning, pieced together by the system from initial training demonstrations that in effect say "carry the coffee this way." (In the latter scenario, a robot may accept a correction while in training, but once it is deployed, it will remain undeterred from its objective.) As Ellis experienced, most standard robots cannot learn on the fly.

In contrast, uncertain AI can adapt in the moment to what we want it to do. Imbued with probabilistic reasoning about its aims or other equivalent mathematical capabilities, the system dwells in "a space of possibilities," says Dragan. A push is not an obstacle to getting its way but a hint of a new, likely better direction to go.* The human is not an impediment but a teacher and a teammate. Perhaps most important, human-compatible AI likely will be open to being shut down if it senses that it might not be on the right track, preliminary studies suggest. A human wish to turn the robot off is just another morsel of information for a system that knows that it does not know. "That's the big thing that uncertainty gives you, right, you're not sure of yourself anymore, and you realize you need more input," says Dragan gleefully. "Uncertainty is the key foundation upon which alignment can rest."

---

*What happens if the robot is bumped by accident? To limit erroneous learning by the robot, Dylan Losey, Andrea Bajcsy, and Anca Dragan created "one-at-a-time learning." In a robot imbued with this capability, a human push changes only one section of a robot's approach to a task. In this way, robots gain knowledge incrementally and cumulatively—and a bump from the family dog doesn't cause a household robot to suddenly relearn everything that it has been taught.

In initial user studies, people working with uncertain robots achieve better task performance with less time and effort. They view such systems as more seamlessly collaborative and sensitive to their needs. "The robot seemed to quickly figure out what I cared about," said one participant. In one experiment, when a physically present robot verbally expressed uncertainty about a thorny moral dilemma, people saw it as more intelligent than one that asserted that it was sure of what to do.

The music that helped set the stage for Stuart Russell's vision of a new AI celebrates the liminality and the ambiguity of life. One of the world's most-heard pieces of modern classical music, Barber's *Adagio for Strings* unfolds in a single brief movement suffused with moments of suspense and dissonance. Critic Johanna Keller writes that the piece seems to convey "the effect of a sigh, or courage in the face of tragedy, or hope" and ends on a note of uncertainty. She writes, "In around eight minutes the piece is over, harmonically unresolved, never coming to rest."

↑

At Virginia Tech, I at last meet up with an I-Don't-Know robot. But unlike Ellis, I am working with a system whose uncertainty is an open book. In Losey's lab, I discover the critical complement to making AI better at knowing that it does not know: creating systems that also admit to their uncertainty.

The painter-robot sports three sets of armbands, called soft haptic displays, at the base, in the middle, and near the end of its five-foot length. As I guide it through its work of drawing a line down the table, the robot tells me where in the task it is unsure by inflating specific bands associated with particular aspects of the process. If it is unsure about the angle to hold its claw-like "end effector," for example, it inflates the bottom-most armbands in each set with a soft *woosh*. In this way, I can get a read on whether the robot is catching on no matter where I place my hands. "You can actually touch the robot's uncertainty," Losey tells me. "You can feel in real time as you move it how confused it is."

If uncertainty enables an AI system to be open to our suggestions, then AI that can also show its unsureness will allow us to know where *we* stand in our increasingly high-stakes interactions with such machines. A cycle of questions and answers on both sides can result. "When a robot can let a person know, 'hey, this is where I am at, this is what I've learned,' or 'this is my best guess but I am a little bit uncertain so take that with a grain of salt'—*that's* what I'm working for," says Losey, a scientist with a rapid-fire pace of speaking and a somber intensity.

The research is critical, he and others believe, because not only does standard AI fall woefully short in its understanding of humanity, but *we* in turn know less and less about the complex black-box systems that increasingly manage our lives. "Even as a designer, often I have no clue what's going to happen next with [standard] robots," Losey admits. "I have to press play and hope that what I see is what I want to see." The question is, he says, "how can we open that box?"

How and why does AI succeed or fail? Why did the model conclude that one person was worthy of parole, a job interview, or a loan while a similar candidate was not? We often do not know in part because AI operates in abstract mathematical terms that rarely correspond to human ideas and language. In addition, the more astonishing AI's achievements have become, the more opaque they are to human understanding. After being handily defeated at Go by an AI program, one shocked world champion said AlphaGo's extraordinary strategic play revealed that "not a single human has touched the edge of the truth of Go."

Slowly, the creation of openly uncertain systems is becoming a key part of global efforts to make explainable and transparent AI. It is not enough to bring to light what AI *knows*, for example, by exposing which reward objective or data set was used in training an algorithm. To work with AI, to anticipate its moves, to gauge its strengths and ours, to parse the magic, we also should understand what it does *not* know, leading scientists assert. Dozens of frontline laboratories worldwide are working to build AI that can speak a language of uncertainty that humans can readily comprehend.

Some robots show people on-screen hypothetical scenarios about their next moves, in effect asking, "Should I move closer to or further from the stove?" or "Should I avoid a certain intersection on my way to fetch coffee?" Others play a kind of robot charades. In Losey's lab, a standing robot often used in warehouses acted out for me a plethora of sometimes indecipherably similar ways for it to stack dishes. Its thoroughness raised unresolved research questions, such as how much and what kinds of uncertainty a system should display or how AI's incertitude can interact productively with ours.

"It's not just a question of robot uncertainty," says Laura Blumenschein, a soft robotics expert who cocreated the haptic arm. "It's a question of human–robot systems and the combined uncertainty within them."

Beyond robots, openly uncertain AI models have shown promise for use in medical diagnosis systems and already are being used to bolster AI-assisted drug discovery. For example, to address rising bacterial resistance to drugs, a new kind of model created by Yoshua Bengio and other top researchers in Canada has shown exciting potential to identify synthetic peptides, that is, small proteins that might be turned into new antibiotics. Instead of relying on pattern recognition to settle on one best answer, Generative Flow Networks explore less obvious paths in the data to uncover numerous possible answers, in this case candidate peptides that can be tested further by models and humans alike.

"The whole point is that we want to keep in mind many possible explanations—we want to account for uncertainty," says Nikolay Malkin of Mila, the Quebec-based leading AI research institute where the algorithm was created. And by operating reflectively rather than relying on simplifying and opaque snap judgments, the new models shed light on both a problem's deeper causal intricacies and their own decision-making processes. The system's uncertainty can be an engine of transparency.

For many scientists, moreover, constructing AI that admits its uncertainty is not just a safety feature, a path to adaptability, a practicality. It is a matter of right and wrong.

Julian Hough is a British computer scientist with a rising reputation and a kindly demeanor. Building on his expertise in linguistics, Hough creates AI that engages with people verbally in order to coordinate on a task or detect signs of Alzheimer's disease. The longer he has been in the field, however, the more concerned he has become about the pretense of certainty traditionally built into the machine.

"The reality is they are never certain—100 percent certain—about anything," Hough tells me on a video call. A tiny ambiguity in the environment, such as a person walking a bicycle or a sticker on a stop sign, can stymie a robot's visual sensors. A frail person with a shaky hand can confuse a robot learning to carry coffee. Yet by sidelining and downplaying its uncertainty in order to get the job done, standard AI essentially has been designed to "pretend to be confident when it is not, to pretend to understand things that it doesn't," says Hough. Such systems routinely leap to judgments—*that's probably not a pedestrian*—while ignoring less likely possibilities—*it's a gal walking a bike!*—and tend to offer a single explanation when many interpretations may be valid. The result has been misalignment *and* a kind of masquerade, argues Hough. Since 2017, his research has centered on creating AI that drops its mask of certainty.

After eighteen months of intensive work, Hough created a robot arm whose gestures slow in direct proportion to the degree of its uncertainty. In one series of experiments, people guided the robot as it solved a simple puzzle. If the machine was completely unsure whether to pick up a green or a blue piece, it would move toward one of the pieces at half speed. In this way, it could make progress on the task while enabling the human to, as linguists say, "repair" the interaction if need be.

In contrast to Losey's pioneering use of touch as a kind of complex code between human and robot, Hough invested his robot, created with computational linguist David Schlangen, with body language that people intuitively can recognize. And despite using a far more simple system than Losey's, participants in Hough's studies easily could infer the robot's incertitude. Both systems speak a language of uncertainty—in different dialects but each no less fluently. As his work gains attention, Hough is turning the algorithm behind his robot into a *modeling uncertainty tool kit*, a kind of mathematical template for investing a range of agents with the capacity to be openly unsure. "Uncertainty is a really powerful tool," he says.

Before we part, Hough offers a final word of warning. Any time that uncertainty is swept under the rug, he cautions, "it won't be going away. It's just going to be hidden in dangerous ways and basically hidden by system designers." By way of example, he describes a scenario. "Say a cop robot is looking for a suspect, and it has 60 percent confidence in one person, but it's been programmed to act at any level beyond 50 percent confidence. If it does not express its level of doubt, that's very dangerous. It could have fatal consequences." By 2022, robots were being used by U.S. police and private entities to patrol factories, parks, and hospitals even as public debate grew over the possible use of police robots equipped with lethal force.

This is a watershed moment in the history of AI. Uncertainty is at the heart of efforts to create systems that can better align with human aims. Still, there is no easy blueprint for reimagining humanity's most powerful and dangerous invention to date. "It's hard to argue with Russell's principles," says leading computer scientist Adrian Weller, "but the devil is in the detail."

For example, how are humans to serve as role models and guides to AI if people don't always behave as they intend? We might say that we don't want that slice of cake yet minutes later go ahead and help ourselves. Or how should an eager-to-learn diagnostic system assist a doctor whose judgment is more often wrong than not? What happens when preferences conflict on a robot–human team or across a hybrid machine–human society? Such questions spur contentious debate—and rightfully so. To ensure that AI systems better know us and we them, we must welcome constant negotiations between human and machine and among ourselves. In this endeavor, as in so many, uncertainty will help us to get it right—slowly, iteratively, thoughtfully.

Perhaps even more important, who will *we* as humans become as we draw closer to uncertain machines? Human preferences are both difficult to decipher and plastic. They are shaped by society, relationships, accidents of experience, and increasingly by technology itself. Our malleability may mean that ultrasmart, uncertain AI may try to mold our preferences to make them easier to satisfy even as it works with us. The magic may yet carry risks.

Yet agents designed to flourish in a space of possibilities also might offer a remarkable lesson in how to do so. A robot that is perennially unsure about what to do, that is curious and ever questioning, is in learning mode. A gentle push from a human is just the hint of a better next move, not a new certainty. An ambiguity in the data is no longer something to be hidden. And by engaging with unsure AI, perhaps *we* will increasingly recognize the value in not-knowing, in keeping an open mind. "My experience is that if an artificial agent, like a robot, communicates some type of behavior," says Hough, "then the people who are interacting with it are more likely to allow that kind of behavior themselves."

One day, AI may hold up a mirror to our better selves, inspiring us to wield the power of uncertainty and to admit it. Already, as leading scientists work to build humble, honest robots, many are realizing that imbuing AI with such qualities helps them to cultivate these skills within themselves. "Uncertainty," Dragan tells me, "teaches you a little bit of what to aspire to."

The visionary Victorian mathematician Ada Lovelace did not believe that the world's first digital computer would be able to think for itself. In her prescient analysis of the wider implications of Charles Babbage's plans for the Analytical Engine, Lovelace wrote in 1843 that "it can do whatever we know how to order it to perform."

Still, although she may have failed to fully anticipate the future reach of AI, Lovelace recognized what Babbage did not: his computer was far more than a machine that, as Lovelace wrote, "weaves algebraical patterns just as [a] loom weaves flowers and leaves." The machine could process *any* information representable by algebraic symbols, she wrote, hinting at the computer's future facility with language or images. In so doing, the computer could spark insight by presenting knowledge in unexpected ways. Through its work, she wrote presciently, "the relations and the nature of many subjects . . . are necessarily thrown into new lights."

⬇

The costs of clinging to a pretense of certainty in our technologies and across our lives are mounting. Too often in corridors of power, across media channels, and around the kitchen table, people trade airtight convictions that admit neither to the fresh air of fact nor to the winds of amendment. It has become common and even lauded to retreat from the discomfort of a measure of complexity or an alternative point of view. Calls for dismantling mistaken assumptions of the past are stymied by hatred, paralysis, and fear, while complex crises are flamed by a reliance on knee-jerk solutions. Uncertainty is no grand panacea for the ills of our era. Yet simply by realizing that at any given moment we might *not* know, we begin to free ourselves from the destruction wrought by a closed mind.

Already, tendrils of change are unfurling. No longer is it quite as taboo for a doctor, a lawyer, or a politician to publicly admit to being unsure. Some medical students are being taught to bolster their diagnostic skill by admitting to patient and colleague alike if they do not yet know. No longer is it an automatic career killer for a young scientist to explore the remarkable ways in which the human mind finds solace and wisdom in pausing, in reverie, or in simply doing "nothing" at all. By investigating the hidden strengths of people living in precarity, scholars are countering the idea that humans flourish only amid predictability. And one day sooner than you imagine, you might work side by side with a robot that will ask you good questions and admit to its uncertainty, all while expecting that you in turn will do so too.

In an era of flux, we are a long way from fully realizing the wisdom of working at the edge of the unknown. But the makings of a seismic shift in humanity's approach to *not*-knowing are emerging. It is not outrageous—and increasingly it is necessary—to ponder a future in which our uncertainty can save humanity. And it is not too soon to begin working toward this end. What is the future of uncertainty? Like hope, it is something that we must endeavor to bring into our lives again and again.

↵

At the close of one of my conversations with Jack Zipes, he mentions to my surprise that most of the "Sorcerer's Apprentice" stories, especially the ones that feature a rebellion, do not have neat, clear, happily-ever-after endings. Just as in more than one-third of all fairy tales and folktales, we do not quite know what will happen in the end. If there is a marriage, will it be happy? Will emancipation from the tyrant bring lasting peace?

"There is an ending, but that ending is a beginning," says Zipes, a joyful octogenarian who himself looks a bit like a benevolent wizard. "That's what our lives are about." From this nebulous starting point, "it's up to us—[reader and character alike]—to form something new," he says. "There's an uncertainty at the end of most of the tales." And as he speaks, I think to myself, that is what makes them so true.

NOTES

Author's Note: Interviews that were carried out during an in-person visit, by video call, or by e-mail are designated as such; all others were by telephone. The titles (i.e., professor, executive director) of interviewees were current at the time of an interview.

EPIGRAPH

vii   **"I know" seems to describe . . . I knew.":** Ludwig Wittgenstein, *On Certainty*, ed. G. E. M. Anscombe and G. H. von Wright, trans. Denis Paul and G. E. M. Anscombe (Malden, MA: Blackwell, 1969, 1975), sec. 3e, 12.

INTRODUCTION

xi   **On the night before:** Gary Younge, *The Speech: The Story behind Dr. Martin Luther King Jr.'s Dream* (Chicago: Haymarket Books, 2015), 1–2; Drew D. Hansen, *The Dream: Martin Luther King, Jr., and the Speech That Inspired a Nation* (New York: Ecco, 2003), 65, 68–69. I am indebted to Gary Younge's brilliant analysis of the speech and its context.

        sought extra counsel: Younge, *The Speech*, 102; Hansen, *The Dream*, 66–69.

        "Everyone had a . . . predetermined angle": Clarence B. Jones and Stuart Connelly, *Behind the Dream: The Making of the Speech That Transformed a Nation* (New York: Palgrave Macmillan, 2011), 59.

        leaders were deeply divided: Younge, *The Speech*, 34–35.

        King reworked his speech: Hansen, *The Dream*, 71.

        "promissory note": Martin Luther King Jr., "I Have a Dream" (Speech to the March on Washington, Washington, DC, August 28, 1963), Transcript from Archival Research, Catalog-Identifier 2602934, National Archives and Records Administration.

        In closing, it would have been: Gary Younge, "The Speech: Fifty Years after the March on Washington, Dr. King's Famous Words Remain Misrepresented," *The Nation*, August 14, 2013, 18; Hansen, *The Dream*, 153, 171. According to

Hansen, some activists were disappointed that King did not use the occasion of the speech to make specific demands.

xi   **"nebulous":** Younge, *The Speech*, 159.

"ethereal": Taylor Branch, *Parting the Waters: America in the King Years, 1954–63* (New York: Simon and Schuster, 1988), 887, quoting unnamed critics.

"undefined": Eric J. Sundquist, *King's Dream* (New Haven, CT: Yale University Press, 2009), 4.

King rose to lead: Branch, *Parting the Waters*, 185.

"neat and tidy": King quoted in Branch, 872.

"the type of activist who . . . finite agenda": Younge, "The Speech: Fifty Years after the March on Washington."

xii   **"Go back [home] knowing somehow . . . be changed":** Martin Luther King, "I Have a Dream."

"That day, for a moment . . . kingdom real.": James Baldwin, *No Name in the Street* (New York: Vintage Books, 2007), 140.

"We Demand Freedom of Mind": Younge, "The Speech," 3.

"Not knowing whether building . . . modern rights are built": Younge, "The Speech: Fifty Years after the March on Washington," 18.

"began the long overdue . . . idea of itself": Hansen, *The Dream*, 227.

fluency—literally bring a smile: Daniel Kahneman, *Thinking, Fast and Slow* (New York: Farrar, Straus and Giroux, 2011), 132.

Keats called "half knowledge": John Keats, Letter to George and Tom Keats, December 21–27, 1817, (45), *The Letters of John Keats, 1814–1821*, ed. Hyder Edward Rollins (Cambridge, MA: Harvard University Press, 1958), 194.

It's a proven psychological finding: Archy O. de Berker et al., "Computations of Uncertainty Mediate Acute Stress Responses in Humans," *Nature Communications* 7, no. 1 (March 29, 2016): 10996, https://doi.org/10.1038/ncomms10996.

xiii   **persuasive arguer:** Zakary L. Tormala and Derek D. Rucker, "Attitude Certainty: Antecedents, Consequences and New Directions," *Consumer Psychology Review* 1, no. 1 (2018): 72–89.

the most capable student: Sidney D'Mello et al., "Confusion Can Be Beneficial for Learning," *Learning and Instruction* 29 (February 1, 2014): 153–70.

xiv   **the resilient physician:** Tania D. Strout et al., "Tolerance of Uncertainty: A Systematic Review of Health and Healthcare-Related Outcomes," *Patient Education and Counseling* 101, no. 9 (September 2018): 1518–37.

***and* patient:** Ivan R. Molton et al., "Pilot Intervention to Promote Tolerance for Uncertainty in Early Multiple Sclerosis," *Rehabilitation Psychology* 64 (2019): 339–50.

xiv   **the nimble executive:** Nils Plambeck and Klaus Weber, "CEO Ambivalence and Responses to Strategic Issues," *Organization Science* 20 (December 1, 2009): 993–1010; Naomi B. Rothman et al., "Understanding the Dual Nature of Ambivalence: Why and When Ambivalence Leads to Good and Bad Outcomes," *The Academy of Management Annals* 11 (2017): 33–72.

more romantically inviting: Erin R. Whitchurch, Timothy D. Wilson, and Daniel T. Gilbert, "'He Loves Me, He Loves Me Not . . .': Uncertainty Can Increase Romantic Attraction," *Psychological Science* 22, no. 2 (February 1, 2011): 172–75.

"So far as man . . . except upon a maybe.": William James, "Is Life Worth Living?," in William James, *The Will to Believe: And Other Essays in Popular Philosophy* (New York: Dover, 1960), 59.

"All kind of narratives . . . to quake": Carol Anderson quoted in Amy Harmon and Audra D. S. Burch, "White Americans Say They Are Waking Up to Racism. What Will It Add Up To?," *New York Times*, June 22, 2020, https://www .nytimes.com/2020/06/22/us/racism-white-americans.html.

"spurious precision": John Kay and Mervyn King, "The Radical Uncertainties of Coronavirus," *Prospect Magazine*, March 30, 2020, https://www.prospect magazine.co.uk/magazine/coronavirus-model-uncertainty-kay-king.

"begins to look quaint": Helga Nowotny, *The Cunning of Uncertainty* (Cambridge: Polity, 2016), 129.

categorize uncertainty largely into two main types: Craig Fox and Gülden Ülkümen, "Distinguishing Two Dimensions of Uncertainty," in *Perspectives on Thinking, Judging and Decision-Making*, ed. Wibecke Brun et al. (Oslo: Universitetsforlaget, 2011).

xv   **the "probabilistic turn":** Mike Oaksford and Nick Chater, *Bayesian Rationality: The Probabilistic Approach to Human Reasoning* (Oxford: Oxford University Press, 2006), 68; for an excellent discussion of the history of probability theory, see Daniel R. DeNicola, *Understanding Ignorance: The Surprising Impact of What We Don't Know* (Cambridge, MA: MIT Press, 2017), 168–72.

"taming of chance": Ian Hacking, *The Taming of Chance* (Cambridge: Cambridge University Press, 1990). Hacking was not the first to use this phrase but explicitly did so to convey efforts to control chance through statistical means. My thanks go to C. Dalrymple-Fraser for help in understanding Hacking's use of the phrase.

associated with full ignorance: DeNicola, *Understanding Ignorance*, 167–70, 161.

realized the limits of your knowledge: Paul K. J. Han, *Uncertainty in Medicine: A Framework for Tolerance* (New York: Oxford University Press, 2021); Paul K. J. Han, William M. P. Klein, and Neeraj K. Arora, "Varieties of Uncertainty in Health Care: A Conceptual Taxonomy," *Medical Decision Making: An*

International Journal of the Society for Medical Decision Making 31, no. 6 (2011): 828–38. While Han focuses on uncertainty in medicine, his writings offer cogent discussions of the topic that are useful for all readers.

xv   **Enter the innate drive:** Jerome Kagan, "Motives and Development," *Journal of Personality and Social Psychology* 22 (1972): 51–66.

"Thought hastens toward . . . force the pace": John Dewey, *The Quest for Certainty: A Study of the Relation of Knowledge and Action* (New York: Minton, Balch, 1929), 227.

xvi   **Remarkably, even the psychology field:** Michael Smithson, "Psychology's Ambivalent View of Uncertainty," in *Uncertainty and Risk: Multidisciplinary Perspectives*, ed. Gabriele Bammer and Michael Smithson (London: Earthscan, 2008), 205–18; Michael Smithson, "The Many Faces and Masks of Uncertainty," in Bammer and Smithson, eds., *Uncertainty and Risk*, 13–26; Plambeck and Weber, "CEO Ambivalence and Responses to Strategic Issues."

Consider the executives who: Plambeck and Weber, "CEO Ambivalence and Responses to Strategic Issues."

Widely seen as enacted hastily: Author interview with Klaus Weber (professor of management and organizations, Northwestern University), July 30, 2020.

"We actually ran the analysis . . . some fluke": Interview with Klaus Weber.

"There's a reality out . . . *not* binary": Interview with Klaus Weber.

xvii   **Plato compared to a charioteer:** Plato, "Phaedrus," *Plato, in Twelve Volumes*, ed. Harold North Fowler (Cambridge, MA: Harvard University Press, 1975), 1:246a–c.

brain systems dealing with cognitive control: Amitai Shenhav, Matthew M. Botvinick, and Jonathan D. Cohen, "The Expected Value of Control: An Integrative Theory of Anterior Cingulate Cortex Function," *Neuron* 79, no. 2 (July 24, 2013): 217–40.

"A remarkable aspect . . . rarely stumped.": Kahneman, *Thinking, Fast and Slow*, 97.

"conflict processing": Matthew Botvinick et al., "Conflict Monitoring and Cognitive Control," *Psychological Review* 108, no. 3 (2001): 624–52.

xviii **measure a fluted column with a straight edge:** Aristotle, "Nichomachean Ethics," book 5, in *Aristotle: In Twenty-Three Volumes*, Loeb Classical Library (Cambridge, MA: Harvard University Press, W. Heinemann, 1970), 1037b, 30–32.

"sense of unusualness": Phrase used by Plambeck and Weber, "CEO Ambivalence and Responses," based on research by Christina Fong, "The Effects of Emotional Ambivalence on Creativity," *Academy of Management Journal* 49, no. 5 (October 2006): 1016–30.

xviii   **alert to what's new and better able to learn:** Adrian R. Walker et al., "The Role of Uncertainty in Attentional and Choice Exploration," *Psychonomic Bulletin & Review* 26, no. 6 (December 1, 2019): 1911–16.

Working memory, the capacity: Daniel Randles et al., "Searching for Answers in an Uncertain World: Meaning Threats Lead to Increased Working Memory Capacity," *PLoS One* 13, no. 10 (October 3, 2018): e0204640, https://doi .org/10.1371/journal.pone.0204640.

The brain is directing . . . good form of stress.: Achim Peters, Bruce S. McEwen, and Karl Friston, "Uncertainty and Stress: Why It Causes Diseases and How It Is Mastered by the Brain," *Progress in Neurobiology* 156 (September 2017): 164–88.

"And it's very useful . . . deeper and deeper.": Unnamed former student of Kahneman's quoted in Michael Lewis, *The Undoing Project: A Friendship That Changed Our Minds* (New York: Norton, 2017), 52.

"I am going to show you . . . a dog or a cat.": E. Frenkel-Brunswik, "Intolerance of Ambiguity as an Emotional and Perceptual Personality Variable," *Psychological Issues* 8, no. 3 (1949, 1974): 58–91. Frenkel-Brunswik's original paper paraphrases the methodology of her experiment, but a 1956 study quotes the directions given to participants. See Sheldon Korchin and Harold Basowitz, "The Judgment of Ambiguous Stimuli as an Index of Cognitive Functioning in Aging," *Journal of Personality* 25, no. 1 (1956): 81–96.

xix   **"a preference to escape into . . . seems definite":** Frenkel-Brunswik, "Intolerance of Ambiguity," 130.

willing to stay open to it: For a discussion see Naomi B. Rothman and Shimul Melwani, "Feeling Mixed, Ambivalent, and in Flux: The Social Functions of Emotional Complexity for Leaders," *Academy of Management Review* 42, no. 2 (April 2017): 259–82.

Those who shun the indefinite . . . chaos and surprise.: Adrian Furnham and Joseph Marks, "Tolerance of Ambiguity: A Review of the Recent Literature," *Psychology* 4, no. 9 (August 22, 2013): 717–28; Adrian Furnham, "Ambiguity Intolerance," in *Oxford Encyclopedia of Health and Risk Message Design and Processing*, ed. Roxanne Parrott (Oxford: Oxford University Press, 2017). See also R. Nicholas Carleton, "The Intolerance of Uncertainty Construct in the Context of Anxiety Disorders: Theoretical and Practical Perspectives," *Expert Review of Neurotherapeutics* 12 (January 9, 2014), 937–47, and author interviews with Nicholas Carleton (professor of psychology, Regina University, Canada), March 27 and November 29, 2019, and March 11, 2020.

"cognitive map," "rigidly defined tracks": Frenkel-Brunswik, "Intolerance of Ambiguity as an Emotional and Perceptual Personality Variable," 129.

curious, flexible thinkers: Haley Jach and Luke Smillie, "To Fear or to Fly to the Unknown: Tolerance for Ambiguity and Big Five Personality Traits," *Journal of Research in Personality* 79 (2019): 67–78.

xx   **have more gray matter:** Dandan Tong et al., "Association between Regional White and Gray Matter Volume and Ambiguity Tolerance: Evidence from Voxel-Based Morphometry," *Psychophysiology* 52, no. 8 (August 2015): 983–89.

And while political conservatives: John R. Hibbing, Kevin B. Smith, and John R. Alford, "Differences in Negativity Bias Underlie Variations in Political Ideology," *Behavioral and Brain Sciences* 37, no. 3 (June 2014): 297–307; author interview with John Hibbing (professor of political science, University of Nebraska), August 3, 2020.

Situation and context matter: Arne Roets et al., "The Motivated Gatekeeper of Our Minds: New Directions in Need for Closure Theory and Research," in *Advances in Experimental Social Psychology*, vol. 52, ed. James M. Olson and Mark P. Zanna (Cambridge, MA: Academic Press, 2015), 221–83.

Picture a laboratory experiment: Matthew Fisher et al., "The Influence of Social Interaction on Intuitions of Objectivity and Subjectivity," *Cognitive Science* 41, no. 4 (May 2017): 1119–34.

"I can absolutely see that point": Matthew Fisher et al., "The Tribalism of Truth," *Scientific American* 318, no. 2 (January 16, 2018): 50–53.

They were no less confident: Fisher et al., "The Influence of Social Interaction." See also Lauren B. Cheatham and Zakary L. Tormala, "The Curvilinear Relationship between Attitude Certainty and Attitudinal Advocacy," *Personality and Social Psychology Bulletin* 43 (2017): 3–16.

xxi   **From such a vantage point:** Matthew Fisher and Frank Keil, "Arguing to Win or Learn: Contrasting Mindsets Revealed by Situational Constraints," unpublished study. See also Zakary Tormala and Derek Rucker, "How Certainty Transforms Persuasion," *Harvard Business Review*, September 2015, 96–103. Research by Tormala and Rucker shows that uncertainty can be persuasive in marketing messaging if communicated by an expert and when highlighting possibility, such as the future potential of a product or job candidate.

"We don't have a home-run . . . some easy intervention": Author interview with Paul K. J. Han (senior research scientist, National Institutes of Health), August 2020.

"If both arguers refuse to . . . can take place": Matthew Fisher and Frank C Keil, "The Trajectory of Argumentation and Its Multifaceted Functions," in *The Psychology of Argument: Cognitive Approaches to Argumentation and Persuasion*, ed. Fabio Paglieri (London: College Publications, 2016), 1–15. This chapter discusses the 2016 study.

When a lull arises: Transcripts from the 2016 experiments provided to the author by Matthew Fisher, December 30, 2018; Mark Felton et al., "Arguing Collaboratively: Argumentative Discourse Types and Their Potential for Knowledge Building," *British Journal of Educational Psychology* 85 (May 14, 2015): 372–86; author interview with Mark Felton (professor of teacher education, San José State University), December 20, 2018.

xxi   **the metaphors typically used:** Smithson, "The Many Faces and Masks of Uncertainty," in Bammer and Smithson, *Uncertainty and Risk*, 13–25, esp. 17–18.

xxii   **"cramped and ultimately brittle experience":** Jerome Ravetz, "Preface," in Bammer and Smithson, *Uncertainty and Risk*, xvi.

        video cropped to shock: Caitlin Flanagan, "The Media Botched the Covington Catholic Story," *The Atlantic*, January 23, 2019, https://www.theatlantic .com/ideas/archive/2019/01/media-must-learn-covington-catholic-story/581 035; Michael Massing, "Was the Media Biased against the Covington Students," *The Guardian*, February 27, 2019, https://www.theguardian.com /commentisfree/2019/feb/27/media-covington-students-bias.

        A mere quarter of online posts: Maria Glenski, Corey Pennycuff, and Tim Weninger, "Consumers and Curators: Browsing and Voting Patterns on Reddit," *IEEE Transactions on Computational Social Systems* 4, no. 4 (December 2017): 196–206; Maksym Gabielkov et al., "Social Clicks: What and Who Gets Read on Twitter?," *Performance Evaluation Review* 44, no. 1 (June 14, 2016): 179–92.

        Instead, calls for restraint: James Fallows, "The Confrontation on the Mall," *The Atlantic*, January 21, 2019, https://www.theatlantic.com/ideas /archive/2019/01/imagining-injustices-confrontation-mall/622223; Monica Hesse, "The Covington Students and the Calculated Art of Making People Uncomfortable," *Washington Post*, January 23, 2019, https://www .washingtonpost.com/lifestyle/style/the-covington-students-and-the-cal culated-art-of-making-people-uncomfortable/2019/01/23/817ffbba-1e8f -11e9-8e21-59a09ff1e2a1_story.html.

        A columnist who urged uncertainty: Frank Bruni, "Covington and the Pundit Apocalypse," *New York Times*, January 23, 2019, A23.

        "fierce urgency of now," "dignity and discipline": Martin Luther King Jr., "I Have a Dream."

xxiii   **A fifth of Democrats . . . as not fully human.:** Nathan Kalmoe and Lilliana Mason, "Lethal Mass Partisanship: Prevalence, Correlates, and Electoral Contingencies" (paper presented at the American Political Science Conference, 2019). Note: The figures include those who lean toward one party or another.

        "detachment of commitment": Jerome Bruner, "The Conditions for Creativity," in Jerome Bruner, *On Knowing: Essays for the Left Hand*, 2nd ed. (Cambridge, MA: Belknap Press, 1962, 1979), 23–24.

        "A pause is not . . . nothing happens": Vinod Menon quoted in Lisa Krieger, "When the Music Stops, the Brain Gets Going," *The Mercury News*, August 2, 2007, https://www.mercurynews.com/2007/08/02/when-the-music -stops-the-brain-gets-going.

xxiii   **In a pioneering experiment, Menon:** Devarajan Sridharan et al., "Neural Dynamics of Event Segmentation in Music: Converging Evidence for Dissociable Ventral and Dorsal Networks," *Neuron* 55, no. 3 (August 2, 2007): 521–32.

xxiv   **Long ago, the Roman statesman:** Cicero, *Academica*, 2.54; author e-mail communication with Tobias Reinhardt (professor of Latin language and literature, Oxford University), June 3, 2020. Also author e-mail communication with Charles Brittain (professor of classics and philosophy, Cornell University), May 29–30, 2020.

quest for certainty: Dewey, *The Quest for Certainty*.

the cosmos is expanding: Alan P. Lightman, *Searching for Stars on an Island in Maine* (New York: Pantheon Books, 2018), 12–15.

xxv   **believe that technology has boosted:** Cary Funk, Brian Kennedy, and Elizabeth Sciupac, "U.S. Wary of Biomedical Technologies to Enhance Human Abilities," *Pew Research Center Report*, July 26, 2019, 99–100. Note: The study reports that roughly half of Americans say technology has had a mostly positive effect on society. Only 10 percent of this group cite increased knowledge, curiosity, and understanding as a positive attribute of technology, while a majority cite ease and speed of access to information.

Trust in many major institutions: "Navigating a Polarized World: Edelman Trust Barometer 2023," Edelman Trust Institute, January 15, 2023, https://www.edelman.com/trust/2023/trust-barometer. Also data from "General Social Survey 1972–2018 (SDA4.0)," shared with the author by Tom Smith of the National Opinion Research Center/University of Chicago, May 7, 2019.

as a fear of the unknown: R. Nicholas Carleton, "Fear of the Unknown: One Fear to Rule Them All?," *Journal of Anxiety Disorders* 41 (2016): 5–21.

"a realm no longer . . . of questions": Daniel J. Boorstin, *Cleopatra's Nose: Essays on the Unexpected*, ed. Ruth Frankel Boorstin (New York: Random House, 1994), 17.

xxvi   **By the time the world's foremost:** Unless otherwise noted, sources for the DNA story are Thomas Hager, *Force of Nature: The Life of Linus Pauling* (New York: Simon & Schuster, 1995); Horace Freeland Judson, *The Eighth Day of Creation: Makers of the Revolution in Biology* (New York: Simon and Schuster, 1979); Matt Ridley, *Francis Crick: Discoverer of the Genetic Code* (New York: Atlas Books/HarperCollins, 2006); James D. Watson, *The Double Helix: A Personal Account of the Discovery of the Structure of DNA*, ed. Gunther S. Stent (New York: Norton, 1980); Matthew Cobb, *Life's Greatest Secret: The Race to Crack the Genetic Code* (New York: Basic Books, 2015), 106; and David Ewing Duncan, *Masterminds: Genius, DNA, and the Quest to Rewrite Life* (New York: Harper Perennial, 2006).

"It was just a matter of time.": Linus Pauling quoted in Hager, *Force of Nature*, 415.

xxvii   **A brilliant young chemist:** Cobb, *Life's Greatest Secret*, 106. See also Matthew Cobb and Nathaniel Comfort, "What Watson and Crick Really Took from Franklin," *Nature* 616 (April 27, 2023), 657–660. Note: In telling of this discovery, I have highlighted the contrast between Pauling's hubris and Crick and Watson's willingness to embrace uncertainty as a cognitive strength. My intent is not to sideline the work of Rosalind Franklin, whose significant contributions are at last coming to light. At first, Franklin largely studied a precise form of DNA in solution not found in nature, a choice that briefly led her to conclude that the molecule was not helical. By early 1953, she had achieved several key insights, such as how DNA could specify proteins, yet she was not able to pull the pieces of the puzzle together before Crick and Watson did so through, as Cobb and Comfort note, "their own iterative approach." Contrary to lore, Crick and Watson did not obtain Franklin's data by underhanded means; rather their bosses shared it between their labs. However, Crick and Watson did not explicitly get permission from Franklin and Wilkins before using their X-ray data to corroborate the discovery. As well, while Crick and Watson did acknowledge Franklin's contributions in their first scientific papers on DNA in 1953–1954, they did so belatedly and minimally. Watson's wrongful portrait of Franklin in his 1968 memoir *The Double Helix* further set the stage for a denigration of her achievements that has taken decades to dispel.

    "We could not at all see . . . relevant point of view.": Francis Crick, *What Mad Pursuit: A Personal View of Scientific Discovery* (New York: Basic Books, 1988), 75.

    "I have practically no doubt . . . beautiful one.": Pauling quoted in Hager, *Force of Nature*, 420.

xxviii   **"I don't know":** Pauling quoted in Francis Crick, "LP + C + 2NP ≠ DNA," *New York Times Magazine*, January 1, 1995.

    "making no assumptions . . . from time to time": Crick, *What Mad Pursuit*, 60.

    "behind the data to their meaning": Horace Freeland Judson, "The Theorist," *Nature* 443, no. 7114 (October 26, 2006): 917–19.

    retired in shame: Amy Harmon, "James Watson Had a Chance to Salvage His Reputation on Race. He Made Things Worse," *New York Times*, January 1, 2019, D1.

CHAPTER 1

3   **"Whoever cannot seek . . . an impasse.":** Heraclitus, *Fragments: The Collected Wisdom of Heraclitus*, trans. Brooks Haxton (New York: Viking, 2001), 7.

    three-pound organ, home to 13 percent: "Liver: Anatomy and Functions," November 19, 2019, https://www.hopkinsmedicine.org/health/conditions -and-diseases/liver-anatomy-and-functions.

3   **Thought by the ancient Greeks:** Derek Collins, "Mapping the Entrails: The Practice of Greek Hepatoscopy," *American Journal of Philology* 129, no. 3 (2008): 319–40.

I listen in, preparing: Author visit, interviews with Carol-anne Moulton (associate professor of general surgery and staff surgeon, University of Toronto), Toronto, September 15–18, 2013.

4   **"Most of our business . . . are like that.":** Author visit, interviews with senior surgeon (anonymous), September 15–18, 2013.

But if they mistakenly: Michal Grat et al., "Intraoperative Injuries during Liver Resection: Analysis of 1,005 Procedures," *Hepatology International* 6, no. 2 (June 14, 2011): 498–504.

Articles in the field: Michael C. Lowe and Michael I. D'Angelica, "Anatomy of Hepatic Resectional Surgery," *Surgical Clinics of North America* 96, no. 2 (April 2016): 183–95.

"Surgeons must be very careful . . . the Culprit - Life!": Emily Dickinson, "Surgeons Must Be Very Careful" (156), in *The Poems of Emily Dickinson*, ed. R. W. Franklin (Cambridge, MA: Harvard University Press, 1998).

5   **"All of the pressures . . . side of production":** Peter Pronovost quoted in Sandra G. Boodman, "The Pain of Wrong Site Surgery," *Washington Post*, June 20, 2011, E1.

"make it go away," "then we're done": Author interview with Paul K. J. Han (senior scientist, National Institutes of Health), August 2020.

Speed matters, for the: Hang Cheng et al., "Prolonged Operative Duration Is Associated with Complications: A Systematic Review and Meta-Analysis," *Journal of Surgical Research* 229 (September 2018): 134–44.

6   **Fire chiefs make 80 percent:** Gary A. Klein, *Sources of Power: How People Make Decisions* (Cambridge, MA: MIT Press, 1998), 4.

En route to the world Chess Olympiad: Fernand Gobet, "Adriaan de Groot: Marriage of Two Passions," *ICGA Journal* 29, no. 4 (January 1, 2006): 236–43; John Saunders, "Chess Magazine at War," *Chess News*, February 2011, 30–32.

7   **Masters nearly always chose:** Gobet, "Adriaan de Groot," 239; Philip E. Ross, "The Expert Mind," *Scientific American*, August 2006, 64–71; Adriaan de Groot, *Thought and Choice in Chess* (Amsterdam: Amsterdam University Press, 1946).

Grandmasters calculate an average: Guillermo Campitelli and Fernand Gobet, "Adaptive Expert Decision Making: Skilled Chess Players Search More and Deeper," *International Computer Games Association Journal* 27, no. 4 (2004): 209–16.

Shown a chessboard: William Chase and Herbert Simon, "Perception in Chess," *Cognitive Psychology* 4 (1973): 55–81. This article describes and confirms de Groot's findings on this score. See also Paul J. Feltovich, Michael J. Prietula, and K. Anders Ericsson, "Studies of Expertise from Psychological Perspectives," in *The Cambridge Handbook of Expertise and Expert Performance*, ed. K. Anders Ericsson et al. (Cambridge: Cambridge University Press, 2006), 41–68.

7   **memory "chunked" in meaningful patterns:** Chase and Simon, "Perception in Chess," 56.

To a grandmaster, twenty-six game: Gobet, "Adriaan de Groot, 240."

"Intuition is nothing more . . . than recognition": Herbert A Simon, "What Is an 'Explanation' of Behavior?," *Psychological Science* 3, no. 3 (1992), 150–61, esp. 155.

One repertoire of quick thought: Daniel Kahneman and Gary Klein, "Conditions for Intuitive Expertise: A Failure to Disagree," *The American Psychologist* 64, no. 6 (September 2009): 515–26, esp. 519–21.

This is the gift of knowledge: Michael I. Posner, "The Expert Brain," in *Expertise and Skill Acquisition: The Impact of William G. Chase*, ed. James Staszewski (New York: Psychology Press, 2013), 244–59.

8   **de Groot helped inspire a vision of the mind:** Vittorio Busato, "In Memoriam: Adriaan Dingeman de Groot (1914–2006)," *APS Observer* 19, no. 11 (November 1, 2006), https://www.psychologicalscience.org/observer/in-memoriam-adriaan-dingeman-de-groot-1914-2006.

Cognition became seen as computation: George A. Miller, "The Cognitive Revolution: A Historical Perspective," *Trends in Cognitive Sciences* 7 (2003): 141–44; Gerd Gigerenzer and Daniel G. Goldstein, "Mind as Computer: Birth of a Metaphor," *Creativity Research Journal* 9, no. 2–3 (1996): 131–44.

Years of experience are often weakly: K. Anders Ericsson, Michael J. Prietula, and Edward Cokely, "The Making of an Expert," *Harvard Business Review* 85, no. 7/8 (July/August 2007): 114–21.

senior auditors were worse: Sarah E. Bonner and Barry L. Lewis, "Determinants of Auditor Expertise," *Journal of Accounting Research* 28 (1990): 1–20.

The patients of more experienced: John J. Norcini, Harry R. Kimball, and Rebecca S. Lipner, "Certification and Specialization: Do They Matter in the Outcome of Acute Myocardial Infarction?," *Academic Medicine* 75, no. 12 (December 2000): 1193–98.

9   **What we experience first:** Dana R. Carney and Mahzarin R. Banaji, "First Is Best," *PLoS One* 7, no. 6 (June 27, 2012): e35088, https://doi.org/10.1371/journal.pone.0035088.

Exposure to early evidence: Robert Lawson, "Order of Presentation as a Factor in Jury Persuasion," *Kentucky Law Journal* 56, no. 1 (1968): 523–53. Christine Ruva et al., "Timing and Type of Pretrial Publicity Affect Mock-Jurors'

220   NOTES

Decisions and Predecisional Distortion," *Journal of Psychology and Behavioral Sciences* 2, no. 4 (2012): 108–19.

9   **When expert chess players:** Merim Bilalić, Peter McLeod, and Fernand Gobet, "Why Good Thoughts Block Better Ones: The Mechanism of the Pernicious Einstellung (Set) Effect," *Cognition* 108, no. 3 (September 2008): 652–61.

Instead, these microcosms of the brain . . . by our complex surroundings.: Author e-mail communication with Michael I. Posner (professor of psychology, University of Oregon), December 19, 2013.

10   **As a graduate student visiting:** Karl Duncker, *On Problem-Solving*, trans. Lynne S. Lees (Washington, DC: American Psychological Association, 1945).

"productive problems—with beautiful solutions": Max Wertheimer quoted in D. Brett King, Michaella Cox, and Michael Wertheimer, "Karl Duncker: Productive Problems with Beautiful Solutions," in *Portraits of Pioneers in Psychology*, ed. Gregory Kimble and Michael Wertheimer (Washington, DC: American Psychological Association, 1998), 3:163–78.

Fascinated by the uncharted: Duncker, *On Problem-Solving*, 9.

"a certain heuristic value," "little to do with thinking": Duncker quoted in King, Cox et al., *Portraits of Pioneers in Psychology*, 170.

In Duncker's best-known experiment: Duncker, *On Problem-Solving*, 86–94.

"When the crucial object . . . fallen from their eyes.'": Duncker, *On Problem-Solving*, 88.

lose sight of "essential aspects": Duncker, *On Problem-Solving*, v.

Admiralty initially turned down: Alfred Gollin, "The Wright Brothers and the British Authorities, 1902–1909," *The English Historical Review* 95, no. 375 (1980): 293–320, esp. 317.

hospitals treated donated blood as primarily: Stephen Hall briefly refers to this practice in his book *Commotion in the Blood: Life, Death and the Immune System* (New York: Henry Holt, 1997): 164–65. Further detail and context came from author interview with John R. Hess (professor of laboratory medicine and pathology, University of Washington), February 27, 2023. Also author e-mail communications with H. W. Reesink (former medical director, Red Cross Blood Bank Amsterdam), February 27, 2023, and with Pieter van der Meer (senior scientist, Sanquin Research, the Netherlands), March 1, 2023. My thanks to Michael Duffy for initially pointing me to the example.

"a costly side effect": Margaret Anne Defeyter and Tim P. German, "Acquiring an Understanding of Design: Evidence from Children's Insight Problem Solving," *Cognition* 89, no. 2 (September 1, 2003): 133–55.

10   **"cognitive entrenchment"**: Erik Dane, "Reconsidering the Trade-Off between Expertise and Flexibility: A Cognitive Entrenchment Perspective," *Academy of Management Review* 35, no. 4 (October 2010): 579–603.

11   **tested children on a kid-friendly version**: Tim P. German and Margaret Anne Defeyter, "Immunity to Functional Fixedness in Young Children," *Psychonomic Bulletin and Review* 7, no. 4 (2000): 707–12. Note: Duncker first carried out his experiments in the mid-1920s, although his major opus *On Problem-Solving* was not published until 1945.

given the hint of a box placed: Michael I. Posner, "Search Strategies and Problem Solving," in Michael I. Posner, *Cognition: An Introduction*, 2nd ed. (Glenview, IL: Scott Foresman & Co., 1973), 147–79, esp. 155–56.

"an answer, any answer": Arie Kruglanski, "Motivations for Judging and Knowing: Implications for Causal Attribution," in *The Handbook of Motivation and Cognition: Foundation of Social Behavior*, ed. E. T. Higgins and R. M. Sorrentino (New York: Guilford Press, 1990), 2:333–68, esp. 337.

September 11 attacks or from a hip high-tech: Edward Orehek et al., "Need for Closure and the Social Response to Terrorism," *Basic and Applied Social Psychology* 32 (2010): 279–90.

"They were craving certainty": Author interview with Arie Kruglanski (professor of psychology, University of Maryland), December 28, 2013.

12   **"gatekeeper of our minds"**: Arne Roets et al., "The Motivated Gatekeeper of Our Minds: New Directions in Need for Closure Theory and Research," in *Advances in Experimental Social Psychology*, ed. James M. Olson and Mark P. Zanna (New York: Academic Press, 2015), 52:221–83.

carryover mode: Paul J. Feltovich, Rand J. Spiro, and Richard L. Coulson, "Issues of Expert Flexibility in Contexts Characterized by Complexity and Change," in *Expertise in Context: Human and Machine*, ed. Paul Feltovich, Kenneth Ford, and Robert Hoffman (Cambridge, MA: MIT Press, 1997), 125–46. Note: By calling this a mode of operation, I am extending their discussion of how experts "carry over" routinized information into new situations, a practice that can be, as they note, "reductive of reality."

In 1817, a London surgeon: Biographical material on Keats drawn mainly from Nicholas Roe, *John Keats: A New Life* (New Haven, CT: Yale University Press, 2012); Andrew Motion, *Keats* (New York: Farrar, Straus and Giroux, 1998); and Robert Gittings, *John Keats* (London: Heinemann, 1968).

Decades before the first use of anesthesia: F. González-Crussi, *A Short History of Medicine* (New York: Modern Library, 2007), 34–39; Roy Porter, ed., *The Cambridge History of Medicine* (Cambridge: Cambridge University Press, 2006), 180–200.

"rash in the extreme": Astley Cooper comment about William Lucas in Stanley Plumly, *Posthumous Keats: A Personal Biography* (New York: Norton, 2008), 192.

13   **His breakthrough began with a visit:** Roe, *John Keats*, 150–53; Grant Scott, *The Sculpted Word: Keats, Ekphrasis, and the Visual Arts* (Hanover, NH: University Press of New England, 1994), 45–67.

At the time, some in the arts: Scott, *The Sculpted Word*, 47–48.

His lines begin to celebrate: For an excellent discussion of the importance of these sonnets in Keats's poetry and life, see Roe, *John Keats*, 151–53.

In a letter to his brothers: John Keats, "Letter to George and Tom Keats, Dec. 21–27, 1817" (45), in *The Letters of John Keats, 1814–1821*, ed. Hyder Edward Rollins (Cambridge, MA: Harvard University Press, 1958).

"making up his Mind about every thing": John Keats, "Letter to George and Georgiana Keats" (213), September 24, 1819, in Rollins, *The Letters of John Keats*. Written later than Keats's first mention of negative capability, the letter illustrates the deep, lasting impact that the concept had on Keats.

***negative capability*:** For further discussions of negative capability, see Li Ou, *Keats and Negative Capability* (London: Continuum, 2009), esp. 4–5, 188, and Lionel Trilling, "The Poet as Hero: Keats in His Letters," in *The Opposing Self: Nine Essays in Criticism* (New York: Viking Press, 1955), 3–48, esp. 28–33.

14   **"never events":** Thomas Rodziewicz, Benjamin Houseman, and John E. Hipskind, *Medical Error Reduction and Prevention*, Open-Access E-Book (Treasure Island, FL: StatPearls Publishing, 2022), 12.

15   **"It's something we fear . . . what uncertainty means.":** Carol-anne Moulton, "Behind the Curtain: Surgical Judgment beyond Cognition," lecture at Morristown Medical Center, Morristown, NJ, May 9, 2013.

"slowing down when you should": Carol-anne Moulton et al., "Slowing Down When You Should: A New Model of Expert Judgment," *Academic Medicine* 82, no. 10 (October 2007): S109–16.

"you can actually be in charge of the moment": Moulton, lecture at Morristown Medical Center.

"So many surgeons talk about . . . where things go wrong": Moulton, lecture at Morristown Medical Center.

She recounts a tight spot: Author interviews with Carol-anne Moulton, March 6 and October 11, 2014.

16   **Situations that are clear, repetitive:** Daniel Kahneman, *Thinking, Fast and Slow* (New York: Farrar, Straus and Giroux, 2011), 59.

"many experts aren't problem solving . . . *have* the answer": Moulton, lecture at Morristown Medical Center.

Consider the case of a group: Jenny Rudolph and D. B. Raemer, "Diagnostic Problem Solving during Simulated Crises in the OR," *Anesthesia and Analgesia* 98, no. 5S (2004): S34. See also Jenny W. Rudolph, J. Bradley Morrison, and John S. Carroll, "The Dynamics of Action-Oriented Problem Solving: Linking Interpretation and Choice," *Academy of Management Review* 34, no. 4 (2009): 733–56.

16   **"It's hard to switch tracks . . . miles an hour":** Cameron Kyle-Sidell quoted in Cameron Kyle-Sidell interview by John Whyte, "Do COVID-19 Vent Protocols Need a Second Look?," Medscape, April 6, 2020, https://www.med scape.com/viewarticle/928156. See also Philippe Rola et al., "Rethinking the Early Intubation Paradigm of COVID-19: Time to Change Gears?," *Clinical and Experimental Emergency Medicine* 7, no. 2 (June 2020): 78–80.

by an infection that typically: Luciano Gattinoni et al., "COVID-19 Does Not Lead to a 'Typical' Acute Respiratory Distress Syndrome," *American Journal of Respiratory and Critical Care Medicine* 201, no. 10 (May 15, 2020): 1299–1300.

Anticipating that such compromised: Author interview with Cameron Kyle-Sidell (critical care physician), September 8, 2020; Heidi Ledford, "Why Do COVID Death Rates Seem to Be Falling?," *Nature* 587, no. 7833 (November 11, 2020): 190–92.

doctors placed up to 90 percent: Data cited in Hannah Wunsch, "Mechanical Ventilation in COVID-19: Interpreting the Current Epidemiology," *American Journal of Respiratory Critical Care Medicine* 202, no. 1 (2020): 1–21. Original data from Safiya Richardson et al., "Presenting Characteristics, Comorbidities, and Outcomes among 5700 Patients Hospitalized with COVID-19 in the New York City Area," *JAMA* 323 (2020): 2052–59. See also Giacomo Grasselli, Alberto Zangrillo, and Alberto Zanella, "Baseline Characteristics and Outcomes of 1591 Patients Infected with SARS-COV-2 Admitted to ICUs of the Lombardy Region, Italy," *JAMA* 323, no. 16 (2020): 1574–81.

"For a while that was the only . . . when to intubate them": Interview with Kyle-Sidell. Also e-mail communication with Cameron Kyle-Sidell, September 24, 2020.

17   **Many of the sick:** Gattinoni et al., "COVID-19 Does Not Lead to a 'Typical' Acute Respiratory Distress Syndrome."

And many fared poorly: Author interview with Kyle-Sidell.

"The patterns I . . . didn't make sense": Kyle-Sidell, quoted in Whyte, "Do COVID-19 Vent Protocols Need a Second Look?"

Yet his urgings and those of others: Gattinoni et al., "Reply by Gattinoni et al. to Hedenstierna et al., to Maley et al., to Fowler et al., to Bhatia and Mohammed, to Bos, to Koumbourlis and Motoyama, and to Haouzi et al.," *American Journal of Respiratory and Critical Care Medicine* 202, no. 4 (August 15, 2020): 628–30.

less aggressive breathing supports: Thomas Voshaar et al., "Conservative Management of COVID-19 Associated Hypoxaemia," *ERJ Open Research* 7, no. 1 (January 2021): 00026–02021, https://doi.org/10.1183/23120541.000 26-2021.

In July 2020, about a fifth of: Intensive Care National Audit and Research Centre, "ICNARC Report on Covid-19 in Critical Care: England, Wales, and

Northern Ireland," February 17, 2023, esp. 72, 82. Also author video interview with David Harrison (senior statistician, ICNARC), March 3, 2023. Note: ICNARC is an independent, nonprofit scientific research institute. The data did not include Scotland. From July 2020 to late 2022, the rate of COVID-19 patients being put on mechanical ventilators in their first twenty-four hours in intensive care fluctuated between 20 and 40 percent.

17   **a reduction attributed in part:** This point comes from numerous interviews and academic sources. For example, a review study reports that roughly 20 percent of the reduction in mortality rates among hospitalized COVID-19 patients between March and August in the United Kingdom (minus Northern Ireland) could be explained by increasingly treating patients with less invasive respiratory supports and with steroids. Annemarie Docherty et al., "Changes in In-Hospital Mortality in the First Wave of Covid-19: A Multicentre Prospective Observational Cohort Study Using the WHO Clinical Characterisation Protocol UK," *Lancet Respiratory Medicine* 9, no. 7 (July 2021): 773–85.

"When you move away . . . the unknown.": Interview with Cameron Kyle-Sidell.

The elite few anesthesiologists: Rudolph et al., "The Dynamics of Action-Oriented Problem Solving."

18   **The most crucial time:** Author e-mail communication with Michael I. Posner, December 19, 2013. Posner, "Search Strategies and Problem Solving," 149–50.

"progressive deepening": de Groot, *Thought and Choice in Chess*, 171–73, 266–74.

"forever testing what they think they know," "their resting state is not certainty": Roger L. Martin, *The Opposable Mind: How Successful Leaders Win through Integrative Thinking* (Boston: Harvard Business School Press, 2007), 127.

Imagine you are a seasoned: This scenario is drawn from Joyce Osland, "Expert Cognition and Sensemaking in the Global Organization Leadership Context: A Case Study," in *Informed by Knowledge: Expert Performance*, ed. Kathleen Mosier and Ute Fischer (New York: Psychology Press, 2011), 23–40, and author interview with Joyce Osland (executive director, Global Leadership Advancement Center, School of Global Innovation and Leadership, San José State University), April 26, 2021.

19   **Strategic business decisions:** Paul C. Nutt, "Expanding the Search for Alternatives during Strategic Decision-Making," *Academy of Management Perspectives* 18, no. 4 (2004): 13–28. See also Paul Nutt, *Why Decisions Fail: Avoiding the Blunders and Traps That Lead to Debacles* (Oakland, CA: Berrett-Koehler, 2002).

"routine experts": Giyoo Hatano and Kayoko Inagaki, "Two Courses of Expertise," in *Child Development and Education in Japan*, ed. Harold Stevenson,

Azuma Hiroshi, and Kenji Hakuta (New York: W. H. Freeman, 1986), 262–72. Hatano and Inagaki reportedly were the first to write about the concepts of "routine" and "adaptive" expertise.

19   **"creeping intuition bias":** Ericsson et al., "The Making of an Expert," 5.

"comfort zone of their achievement": Ericsson et al., "The Making of an Expert," 5.

"adaptive experts": For an excellent discussion, see John Bransford, Ann Brown, and Rodney Cocking, eds., "How Experts Differ from Novices," in *How People Learn: Brain, Mind, Experience, and School* (Washington, DC: National Academies Press, 1994), 31–50. See also Hatano and Inagaki, "Two Course of Expertise," 266.

In the operating room, good: Carol-anne Moulton et al., "Slowing Down to Stay Out of Trouble in the Operating Room: Remaining Attentive in Automaticity," *Academic Medicine* 85, no. 10 (October 2010): 1571–77.

In domains from medicine to physics: T. J. Nokes, C. D. Schunn, and Michelene Chi, "Problem Solving and Human Expertise," in *International Encyclopedia of Education* (Amsterdam: Elsevier, 2010), 265–72.

the best chess players opted: Jerad H. Moxley et al., "The Role of Intuition and Deliberative Thinking in Experts' Superior Tactical Decision-Making," *Cognition* 124 (2012): 72–78.

20   **"You're in a different . . . gathering the information.":** Author interview with Carol-anne Moulton, November 30, 2022.

barely correlate with intelligence: Keith Stanovich and Richard West, "What Intelligence Tests Miss," *The Psychologist*, February 2014, 80–83.

One-third to two-fifths of Americans: Cary Funk et al., "Trust and Mistrust in Americans' Views of Scientific Experts," Pew Research Center, August 2019, 33, https://www.pewresearch.org/science/2019/08/02/trust-and -mistrust-in-americans-views-of-scientific-experts.

21   **By the time scientific findings are made:** Hans Peter Peters and Sharon Dunwoody, "Scientific Uncertainty in Media Content," *Public Understanding of Science* 25, no. 8 (2016): 893–908. See also Jakob Jensen et al., "Communicating Uncertain Science to the Public: How Amount and Source of Uncertainty Impact Fatalism, Backlash, and Overload," *Risk Analysis* 37, no. 1 (January 2017): 40–51.

"People have had enough of experts": U.K. Justice Secretary Michael Gove quoted in Sam Coates and Michael Savage, "I Can't Guarantee Everyone Will Keep Their Jobs, Admits Gove," *The Times*, June 4, 2016.

"Look at the mess . . . experts that we have": Then-President Donald Trump quoted in Nick Gass, "Trump: 'The Experts Are Terrible,'" *Politico*, April 4, 2016, https://www.politico.com/blogs/2016-gop-primary -live-updates-and-results/2016/04/donald-trump-foreign-policy-experts -221528.

21   **"a world permeated by error":** David Esterly, *The Lost Carving: A Journey to the Heart of Making* (New York: Penguin Books, 2012), 238.

By seeking to extend—not just apply: For discussions, see Bransford et al., "How Experts Differ from Novices," 46–48, and Maria Mylopoulos and Glenn Regehr, "Cognitive Metaphors of Expertise and Knowledge: Prospects and Limitations for Medical Education," *Medical Education* 41 (2007): 1159–65.

"arrested development": K. Anders Ericsson, "Deliberate Practice and Acquisition of Expert Performance: A General Overview," *Academic Emergency Medicine* 15, no. 11 (November 2008): 988–94, esp. 991.

tend to overprescribe antibiotics: Lucy Brookes-Howell et al., "Understanding Variation in Primary Medical Care: A Nine-Country Qualitative Study of Clinicians' Accounts of the Non-Clinical Factors That Shape Antibiotic Prescribing Decisions for Lower Respiratory Tract Infection," *BMJ Open* 2, no. 4 (August 22, 2012): e000796, https://doi.org/10.1136/bmjopen-2011-000796; Malin Andre et al., "Uncertainty in Clinical Practice: An Interview Study with Swedish GPs on Patients with Sore Throat," *BMC Family Practice* 17 (May 18, 2016): Article 56, https://doi.org/10.1186/s12875-016-0452-9.

shy from treating underserved patients: Sharon Wayne et al., "The Association between Intolerance of Ambiguity and Decline in Medical Students' Attitudes toward the Underserved," *Academic Medicine* 86, no. 7 (July 2011): 877–82.

fall prey to the anxiety and depression: Jason Hancock and Karen Mattick, "Tolerance of Ambiguity and Psychological Well-Being in Medical Training: A Systematic Review," *Medical Education* 54, no. 2 (February 2020): 125–37; Georga P. E. Cooke, Jenny A. Doust, and Michael C. Steele, "A Survey of Resilience, Burnout, and Tolerance of Uncertainty in Australian General Practice Registrars," *BMC Medical Education* 13, no. 2 (January 7, 2013), https://doi.org/10.1186/1472-6920-13-2.

22   **"unhealthy reaction to uncertainty":** Arabella Simpkin, "Embracing Uncertainty: Could There Be a Blueprint from Covid-19?," *The BMJ Opinion*, April 16, 2020, https://blogs.bmj.com/bmj/2020/04/16/embracing-uncertainty-could-there-be-a-blueprint-from-covid-19.

The care that cardiologists dispense: David Katerndahl, Robert Wood, and Carlos Roberto Jaén, "Family Medicine Outpatient Encounters Are More Complex Than Those of Cardiology and Psychiatry," *Journal of the American Board of Family Medicine* 24, no. 1 (2011): 6–15.

"This is what the residents . . . why are they unhappy": Author interviews with Deborah Taylor (psychologist, Central Maine Medical Center), July 3, 2020, and April 27, 2021.

a fear of the uncertainty: Author interview with Donald Woolever (family medicine specialist-physician, Central Maine Medical Center), July 6, 2020.

"I was hoping . . . out of my textbook": Author interview with Nupur Nagrare (family medicine physician), July 11, 2020. Also author e-mail communication with Nupur Nagrare, July 14–15, 2020.

22   **"We set them up for that":** Interview with Deborah Taylor, July 3, 2020.

To the trainees' initial dismay: Deborah Taylor et al., "A Pilot Study to Address Tolerance of Uncertainty among Family Medicine Residents," *Family Medicine* 50, no. 7 (July 2018): 531–38.

"to make things muddier and messier . . . the obvious": Interview with Deborah Taylor, April 27, 2021.

"We reframed the learning . . . lightbulbs going on.": Author interview with Bethany Picker (physician and medical director, Central Maine Medical Center's Family Medicine Residency Program), July 1, 2020.

In one year, the subtle but: Taylor et al., "A Pilot Study to Address Tolerance of Uncertainty among Family Medicine Residents."

23   **"It was reiterated to us . . . expectations of yourself.":** Interview with Nupur Nagrare.

"When you value uncertainty . . . as the picture changes.": Interview with Bethany Picker.

try considering the opposite: Charles Lord, Mark Lepper, and Elizabeth Preston, "Considering the Opposite: A Corrective Strategy for Social Judgment," *Journal of Personality and Social Psychology* 47, no. 6 (December 1984): 1231–43. For recent confirmation of the findings, see Aleksey Korniychuk and Eric Luis Uhlmann, "Rebiasing: Managing Automatic Biases over Times," *Frontiers in Psychology* 13 (2022): 914174, doi:10.3389/fpsyg.2022.914174. Note: I adapted and expanded on the extrovert–introvert challenge used in one of the experiments in Lord et al.

24   **Sometimes called "Fermi-izing":** Philip E. Tetlock and Dan Gardner, *Superforecasting: The Art and Science of Prediction* (New York: Crown Publishers, 2015), 278–79.

"flush ignorance into the open": Tetlock and Gardner, *Superforecasting*, 278.

"thoughtfulness and uncertainty and even indecisiveness": Carol-anne Moulton, "Peeking behind the Curtain: Surgical Judgment beyond Cognition," American College of Surgeons Olga M. Jonasson Lecture, Chicago, 2012. Also author interview with Carol-anne Moulton, October 26, 2012.

"There's a world of difference . . . not where we should be.": Interview with Carol-anne Moulton, November 30, 2022.

25   **"When you're uncertain . . . that's when you care.":** Interview with Moulton, October 26, 2012.

CHAPTER 2

27   **"What I like . . . to deceive you.":** C. S. Lewis, *Surprised by Joy: The Shape of My Early Life* (New York: HarperCollins, 2017), 217.

27   **no one was working on:** B. Jack Copeland, ed., *The Essential Turing: Seminal Writings in Computing, Logic, Philosophy, Artificial Intelligence, and Artificial Life, plus the Secrets of Enigma* (Oxford: Oxford University Press, 2004), 257.

Deemed unbreakable . . . victory or defeat.: Stephen Budiansky, *Blackett's War: The Men Who Defeated the Nazi U-Boats and Brought Science to the Art of Warfare* (New York: Alfred A. Knopf, 2013), 110.

"Everything happening . . . the outcome": Winston Churchill quoted in Budiansky, *Blackett's War*, 246.

a third of the globe's merchant shipping: Andrew Hodges, *Alan Turing: The Enigma* (Princeton, NJ: Princeton University Press, 2012), 186.

28   **In one 1940 foray, U-boats . . . out of Cape Breton.:** Budiansky, *Blackett's War*, 136.

In October of that year: S. W. Roskill, *The War at Sea, 1939–1945*, rev. ed. (London: Naval and Military Press, 2004), 1:614–18, appendices Q–R.

"battle of wits": Stephen Budiansky, *Battle of Wits: The Complete Story of Codebreaking in World War II* (New York: Free Press, 2000).

In the interwar era . . . into seeming randomness.: David Kahn, *Seizing the Enigma: The Race to Break the German U-Boat Codes, 1939–1943* (Boston: Houghton Mifflin, 1991), 31–48.

"The submarine should . . . with in 1917": Navy Report quoted in Roskill, *The War at Sea*, 1:34.

"Our goal must . . . in this belief": Dönitz quoted in Peter Padfield, *Dönitz, the Last Führer: Portrait of a Nazi War Leader* (London: V. Gollancz, 1984), 209.

did not include a single cryptanalyst: Hodges, *Alan Turing*, 188.

learning the enemy's whereabouts: Commander of U.K. Home Fleet quoted in Hodges, Andrew Hodges, *Alan Turing*, 189.

29   **"I could have it to myself":** Turing quoted in Patrick Mahon, "History of Hut 8 to December 1941," in Copeland, *The Essential Turing*, 279. Mahon was a Bletchley Park code breaker.

"decision problem": A. M. Turing, "On Computable Numbers, with an Application to the Entscheidungsproblem," *Proceedings of the London Mathematical Society* 42, ser. 2, no. 1 (1936): 230–65. I am indebted to Mark Sprevak and Jack Copeland for help with the intricacies of the decision problem. Author e-mail communication with Mark Sprevak (senior lecturer and associate professor of philosophy, University of Edinburgh), January 9, 2023. Author e-mail communication with Jack Copeland (distinguished professor, University of Canterbury, New Zealand, and director of the Turing Archive for the History of Computing), January 7 and 9, 2023.

"A.M. Turing," wrote . . . certain questions.": Unnamed examiner for the mathematics part of the United Kingdom's Higher School Certificate, likely writing in 1929, quoted in Hodges, *Alan Turing*, 38.

29   **"that most important faculty . . . interest from others":** Alan Turing, *Alan Turing's Systems of Logic: The Princeton Thesis*, ed. Andrew Appel (Princeton, NJ: Princeton University Press, 2012), 116.

That year, a sultry . . . behind blackout curtains.: Budiansky, *Battle of Wits*, 122; Budiansky, *Blackett's War*, 111.

30   **His research-driven theory:** George Mashour et al., "Conscious Processing and the Global Neuronal Workspace Hypothesis," *Neuron* 105, no. 5 (March 4, 2020): 776–98; Lucia Melloni et al., "Making the Hard Problem of Consciousness Easier," *Science* 372, no. 6545 (May 28, 2021): 911–12.

I waited two hours: Author visit, interview with Stanislas Dehaene (professor of experimental cognitive psychology, Collège de France), Gif-Sur-Yvette, France, June 27, 2014. Also author visit, interview with Stanislas Dehaene, Boston, August 31, 2014.

31   **There were "blindsight" patients:** David Concar, "Out of Sight into Mind," *New Scientist*, September 5, 1998, 38–41.

People with "spatial neglect" . . . blazing dwelling.: J. C. Marshall and P. W. Halligan, "Blindsight and Insight in Visuo-Spatial Neglect," *Nature* 336, no. 6201 (December 1988): 766–67.

"What is two plus two?": Dehaene tells the story of Mr. N in Stanislas Dehaene and Laurent Cohen, "Two Mental Calculation Systems: A Case Study of Severe Acalculia with Preserved Approximation," *Neuropsychologia* 29, no. 11 (1991): 1045–54; Stanislas Dehaene, *The Number Sense: How the Mind Creates Mathematics* (New York: Oxford University Press, 1997), 163–65.

32   **"miniature mock-ups . . . faithful to reality":** Stanislas Dehaene, *How We Learn: Why Brains Learn Better Than Any Machine . . . for Now* (New York: Viking, 2020), 5.

predictive processing: J. Benjamin Hutchinson and Lisa Feldman Barrett, "The Power of Predictions: An Emerging Paradigm for Psychological Research," *Current Directions in Psychological Science* 28, no. 3 (June 2019): 280–91.

"Playing the notes . . . kind of begun.": Cleveland Symphony Orchestra interview with first horn Nathaniel Silberschlag, "Nathaniel Silberschlag on Beginning Brahms Piano Concerto No. 2," YouTube, March 16, 2022, https://www.youtube.com/watch?v=acDzjYBC_GQ.

In contrast to insects: Davide Filingeri and George Havenith, "Human Skin Wetness Perception: Psychophysical and Neurophysiological Bases," *Temperature* 2, no. 1 (February 3, 2015): 86–104.

Moreover, raw sensory data: Dehaene, *How We Learn*, 6; Jan W. Brascamp and Steven K. Shevell, "The Certainty of Ambiguity in Visual Neural Representations," *Annual Review of Vision Science* 7 (September 15, 2021): 465–86.

33   **"carefully controlled hallucination":** Lisa Feldman Barrett, *Seven and a Half Lessons about the Brain* (Boston: Houghton Mifflin Harcourt, 2020),

71; Andy Clark, "Perception as Controlled Hallucination," interview with *The Edge*, June 6, 2019, https://www.edge.org/conversation/andy_clark -perception-as-controlled-hallucination.

33   **Such uncanny experiences . . . are largely harmless.:** Mascha M. J. Linszen et al., "Occurrence and Phenomenology of Hallucinations in the General Population: A Large Online Survey," *Schizophrenia* 8, no. 1 (April 23, 2022): 1–11.

Many early Greek philosophers: Brascamp and Shevell, "The Certainty of Ambiguity in Visual Neural Representations," 472–73.

One prominent theory: Robert McQuaid, "Ibn al-Haytham, the Arab Who Brought Greek Optics into Focus for Latin Europe," *Advances in Ophthalmology and Visual System* 9, no. 2 (April 12, 2019): 44–51. J. Benjamin Hutchinson and Lisa Feldman Barrett note Ibn al-Haytham's contributions in Hutchinson and Barrett, "The Power of Predictions," 291. I thank Lisa Feldman Barrett for source suggestions on Ibn al-Haytham and Dharmakīrti (see below).

In his seven-volume . . . created in the eye.: Brascamp and Shevell, "The Certainty of Ambiguity," 472–73; Jim Al-Khalili, *The House of Wisdom: How Arabic Science Saved Ancient Knowledge and Gave Us the Renaissance* (New York: Penguin Books, 2011),152–63.

Still, his nascent understanding: McQuaid, "Ibn al-Haytham," 47–49.

Dharmakīrti, a leading seventh-century: John Dunne, "Key Features of Dharmakīrti's Apoha Theory," in *Apoha: Buddhist Nominalism and Human Cognition*, ed. Mark Siderits, Tom J. F. Tillemans, and Arindam Chakrabarti (New York: Columbia University Press, 2011), 84–108. Dharmakīrti's contributions are noted in Hutchinson and Barrett, "The Power of Predictions," 291.

34   **"radically distorts our experience of the world":** Dunne, "Key Features of Dharmakīrti's Apoha Theory," 102.

"things that are actually . . . were the same": Dunne, "Key Features of Dharmakīrti's Apoha Theory," 102.

Thought, they teach: The Dalai Lama, "My Encounter with Science," in *Science and Philosophy in the Indian Buddhist Classics, Vol. 2: The Mind*, ed. Thupten Jinpa, trans. Dechen Rochard and John Dunne (Somerville, MA: Wisdom Publications, 2020), 1–21, esp. 11–12.

Chances are this incongruity: Simon van Gaal et al., "Can the Meaning of Multiple Words Be Integrated Unconsciously?," *Philosophical Transactions of the Royal Society of London. Series B, Biological Sciences* 369, no. 1641 (May 5, 2014): 20130212, https://doi.org/10.1098/rstb.2013.0212.

"then your neurons . . . prepared you to act": Barrett, *Seven and a Half Lessons*, 75.

35   **"degree of absurdity":** Stanislas Dehaene, *Consciousness and the Brain: Deciphering How the Brain Codes Our Thoughts* (New York: Viking, 2014), 73.

35   **Although people only consciously:** van Gaal et al., "Can the Meaning of Multiple Words."

The extraordinary work of signaling: Mélanie Strauss et al., "Disruption of Hierarchical Predictive Coding during Sleep," *Proceedings of the National Academy of Sciences* 112, no. 11 (March 17, 2015): E1353–62, https://doi.org/10.1073/pnas.1501026112.

36   **This is why babies:** Aimee E. Stahl and Lisa Feigenson, "Observing the Unexpected Enhances Infants' Learning and Exploration," *Science* 348, no. 6230 (April 4, 2015): 91; Aimee Stahl and Lisa Feigenson, "Violations of Core Knowledge Shape Early Learning," *Topics in Cognitive Science* 11, no. 1 (January 2019): 136–53.

"No surprise, no learning": Dehaene, *How We Learn*, 205.

Mr. N became so upset: Robert Kunzig, "A Head for Numbers," *Discover*, July 1, 1997, https://www.discovermagazine.com/the-sciences/a-head-for-numbers; Dehaene, *The Number Sense*, 163–65.

"Words are spinning . . . scarcely a meaning," "Wild fragments . . . rare flashes.": Tristan Tzara, "Approximate Man," in *Approximate Man and Other Writings*, trans. Mary Ann Caws, (Boston: Black Widow Press, 2005), 23–108. For further analysis, see Marius Hentea, *TaTa Dada: The Real Life and Celestial Adventures of Tristan Tzara* (Cambridge, MA: MIT Press, 2014), 227–29.

37   **The release of powerful neurotransmitters . . . control our focus.:** Chang-Hao Kao et al., "Functional Brain Network Reconfiguration during Learning in a Dynamic Environment," *Nature Communications* 11, no. 1 (April 3, 2020): 1682, https://doi.org/10.1038/s41467-020-15442-2; author interview with Joseph Kable (professor of psychology, University of Pennsylvania), July 1, 2022.

Bursts of dopamine help: Sabrina Trapp, J. P. O'Doherty, and Lars Schwabe, "Stressful Events as Teaching Signals for the Brain," *Trends in Cognitive Sciences* 22, no. 6 (June 2018): 475–78; Bahareh Taghizadeh et al., "Reward Uncertainty Asymmetrically Affects Information Transmission within the Monkey Fronto-Parietal Network," *Communications Biology* 3, no. 1 (October 21, 2020): 594.

"Hey, there's something to be learned here . . . is adaptive.": Interview with Joseph Kable.

attentional priority: Jacqueline Gottlieb et al., "Curiosity, Information Demand and Attentional Priority," *Current Opinion in Behavioral Sciences* 35 (2020): 83–91.

In particular, specialist neurons: Nicholas C. Foley et al., "Parietal Neurons Encode Expected Gains in Instrumental Information," *Proceedings of the National Academy of Sciences* 114, no. 16 (April 18, 2017): E3315–23, https://doi.org/10.1073/pnas.1613844114.

38   **In a groundbreaking series of studies:** Mattias Horan, Nabil Daddaoua, and Jacqueline Gottlieb, "Parietal Neurons Encode Information Sampling Based on Decision Uncertainty," *Nature Neuroscience* 22, no. 8 (August 2019): 1327–35; author e-mail communication with Mattias Horan (physician and neuroscience PhD student, Sainsbury Wellcome Centre, London), April 2 and 6, 2022.

"Uncertainty is another . . . of knowledge": Author interview with Jacqueline Gottlieb (professor of neuroscience and principal investigator at Zuckerman Institute, Columbia University), May 5, 2022.

focused arousal: Horan et al., "Parietal Neurons Encode Information Sampling Based on Decision Uncertainty."

"licenses you to say . . . that new data": Interview with Joseph Kable; Matthew R. Nassar et al., "An Approximately Bayesian Delta-Rule Model Explains the Dynamics of Belief Updating in a Changing Environment," *Journal of Neuroscience* 30, no. 37 (2010): 12366–78.

"You want to be . . . unpredictable situations": Author interview with Robb Rutledge (assistant professor of psychology, Yale University), July 1, 2022.

In 2016, Rutledge and: Archy O. de Berker et al., "Computations of Uncertainty Mediate Acute Stress Responses in Humans," *Nature Communications* 7, no. 1 (March 29, 2016): 10996, https://doi.org/10.1038/ncomms10996.

39   **"We're hard-wired . . . hate uncertainty":** Marc Lewis, "Why We're Hardwired to Hate Uncertainty," *The Guardian*, Opinion section, April 4, 2016, https://www.theguardian.com/commentisfree/2016/apr/04/uncertainty-stressful-research-neuroscience.

In addition, the neurotransmitter acetylcholine . . . a tricky game.: Amy Bland and Alexandre Schaefer, "Different Varieties of Uncertainty in Human Decision-Making," *Frontiers in Neuroscience* 6, no. 85 (2012): 1–11.

Norepinephrine also is a barometer: Kristin Kaduk and Fadila Hadj-Bouziane, "Insights into the Role of Noradrenaline in Effortful Decisions," *PLoS Biology* 20, no. 2 (February 22, 2022): e3001545, https://doi.org/10.1371/journal.pbio.3001545; Nicolas Borderies et al., "Pharmacological Evidence for the Implication of Noradrenaline in Effort," *PLoS Biology* 18, no. 10 (October 12, 2020): e3000793, https://doi.org/10.1371/journal.pbio.3000793. Note: Norepinephrine is also called noradrenaline.

"We are not simply . . . teaches itself": Dehaene, *How We Learn*, xx.

40   **"singular talent of our species":** Dehaene, *How We Learn*, xx.

humans routinely give up: Maja Brydevall et al., "The Neural Encoding of Information Prediction Errors during Non-Instrumental Information Seeking," *Scientific Reports* 8, no. 1 (April 17, 2018): 6134, https://doi.org/10.1038/s41598-018-24566-x.

There are limits to this inquisitiveness: Caroline J. Charpentier, Ethan S. Bromberg-Martin, and Tali Sharot, "Valuation of Knowledge and Ignorance in Mesolimbic Reward Circuitry," *Proceedings of the National Academy of Sciences* 115, no. 31 (July 31, 2018): Article 6134, https://doi.org/10.1073/pnas.1800547115.

40   **"laser-like focus ... immediate utility":** Zachary Wojtowicz, Nick Chater, and George Loewenstein, "The Motivational Processes of Sense-Making," in *The Drive for Knowledge: The Science of Human Information Seeking*, ed. Charley M. Wu, Eric Schulz, and Irene Cogliati Dezza (Cambridge: Cambridge University Press, 2022), 3–30, esp. 5. Also author interview with George Loewenstein (professor of economics and psychology, Carnegie Mellon University), April 11, 2022.

"strictly a means to material ends": Wojtowicz et al., "The Motivational Processes of Sense-Making."

monkeys repeatedly had opted to find out: Ethan S. Bromberg-Martin and Okihide Hikosaka, "Midbrain Dopamine Neurons Signal Preference for Advance Information about Upcoming Rewards," *Neuron* 63, no. 1 (July 16, 2009): 119–26.

41   **In both humans and their primate:** Wolfram Schultz, "Dopamine Reward Prediction Error Coding," *Dialogues in Clinical Neuroscience* 18, no. 1 (March 2016), 23–32.

In a 2015 experiment: Tommy Blanchard, Benjamin Hayden, and Ethan Bromberg-Martin, "Orbitofrontal Cortex Uses Distinct Codes for Different Choice Attributes in Decisions Motivated by Curiosity," *Neuron* 85, no. 3 (2015): 602–14.

"Evolution has endowed ... Often very little.": Author interview with Ethan Bromberg-Martin (senior scientist, Department of Neuroscience, Washington University School of Medicine in St. Louis), April 4, 2022.

42   **"balance the immediate ... investing in knowledge":** Wojtowicz et al., "The Motivational Processes of Sense-Making," 4.

"We're exactly the sort ... seeking out prediction error.": Author interviews with Ethan Bromberg-Martin, March 30 and April 4, 2022.

43   **capturing a little gray circle:** Dean Mobbs et al., "Choking on the Money: Reward-Based Performance Decrements Are Associated with Midbrain Activity," *Psychological Science* 20, no. 8 (August 2009): 955–62.

reward-driven distraction: Dorottya Rusz, Erik Bijleveld, and Michiel A. J. Kompier, "Reward-Associated Distractors Can Harm Cognitive Performance," *PLoS One* 13, no. 10 (2018): e0205091, https://doi.org/10.1371/journal.pone.0205091. See also Dorottya Rusz et al., "Reward-Driven Distraction," *Psychological Bulletin* 146, no. 10 (2020): 872–79.

When the trophy: Erik Bijleveld, Ruud Custers, and Henk Aarts, "When Favourites Fail: Tournament Trophies as Reward Cues in Tennis Finals," *Journal of Sports Sciences* 29, no. 13 (October 2011), 1463–70.

43   **"cue words":** Peter Gröpel and Christopher Mesagno, "Choking Interventions in Sports: A Systematic Review," *International Review of Sport and Exercise Psychology* 12, no. 1 (January 2019): 176–201. Also author e-mail communication with Christopher Mesagno (senior lecturer, sports and exercise psychology, Victoria University, Melbourne City, Australia), June 7, 2021.

"focus on every play": Chris Stankovich, "Using Cue Words for Improved Mental Toughness and Athletic Success," *The Sports Doc: Chalk Talk with Dr. Chris Stankovich* (blog), August 15, 2011, https://drstankovich.com /using-cue-words-for-improved-mental-toughness-and-athletic-success.

"the quiet eye": Gröpel and Mesagno, "Choking Interventions in Sports," 190.

44   **This is the infamous Trier:** Andrew Allen et al., "The Trier Social Stress Test: Principles and Practice," *Neurobiology of Stress* 6 (February 2017): 113–26.

"People don't realize . . . minutes is": Author interview with Jeremy Jamieson (associate professor of psychology, University of Rochester), June 8, 2022.

People who are taught: Jeremy P. Jamieson et al., "Optimizing Stress Responses with Reappraisal and Mindset Interventions: An Integrated Model," *Anxiety, Stress, and Coping* 31, no. 3 (May 2018): 245–61.

Its release in the wake of surprise: Jamieson et al., "Optimizing Stress Responses."

Blood flow is constricted: Jamieson et al., "Optimizing Stress Responses"; Jeremy P. Jamieson, Matthew K. Nock, and Wendy Berry Mendes, "Mind over Matter: Reappraising Arousal Improves Cardiovascular and Cognitive Responses to Stress," *Journal of Experimental Psychology. General* 141, no. 3 (August 2012): 417–22.

People who learn to reappraise: David S. Yeager et al., "A Synergistic Mindsets Intervention Protects Adolescents from Stress," *Nature* 607, no. 7919 (July 2022): 512–20.

45   **tough math class:** Jeremy P. Jamieson et al., "Reappraising Stress Arousal Improves Performance and Reduces Evaluation Anxiety in Classroom Exam Situations," *Social Psychological and Personality Science* 7 (2016): 579–87.

graduate school admissions exam: Jeremy P. Jamieson et al., "Turning the Knots in Your Stomach into Bows: Reappraising Arousal Improves Performance on the GRE," *Journal of Experimental Social Psychology* 46, no. 1 (January 1, 2010): 208–12.

They have a more open posture: Jamieson et al., "Mind over Matter."

It ebbs and flows: David M. Lydon-Staley, Perry Zurn, and Danielle S. Bassett, "Within-Person Variability in Curiosity during Daily Life and Associations with Well-Being," *Journal of Personality* 88, no. 4 (August 2020): 625–41. Also author e-mail communication with David Lydon-Staley, April 8, 2022.

"frisk about and rove about": Philo, *The Works of Philo: Complete and Unabridged, (Agriculture) Section VII*, trans. Charles Duke Yonge (Peabody,

MA: Hendrickson Publishers, 1993). For an in-depth treatment of styles of curiosity, see Perry Zurn, "Busybody, Hunter, Dancer: Three Historical Models of Curiosity," in *Toward New Philosophical Explorations of the Epistemic Desire to Know*, ed. Marianna Papastephanou (Newcastle upon Tyne: Cambridge Scholars Publishing, 2019), 26–48.

46   **browse Wikipedia for a few minutes:** David M. Lydon-Staley et al., "Hunters, Busybodies and the Knowledge Network Building Associated with Deprivation Curiosity," *Nature Human Behaviour* 5, no. 3 (March 2021): 327–36.

willingness to tolerate the stress: Todd B. Kashdan et al., "The Five-Dimensional Curiosity Scale: Capturing the Bandwidth of Curiosity and Identifying Four Unique Subgroups of Curious People," *Journal of Research in Personality* 73 (2018): 130–49; Paul J. Silvia, "Appraisal Components and Emotion Traits: Examining the Appraisal Basis of Trait Curiosity," *Cognition and Emotion* 22, no. 1 (2008): 94–113.

neural roots of curiosity: Lieke van Lieshout et al., "Induction and Relief of Curiosity Elicit Parietal and Frontal Activity," *Journal of Neuroscience* 38 (2018): 2816–17; Blanchard et al., "Orbitofrontal Cortex Uses Distinct Codes for Different Choice Attributes in Decisions Motivated by Curiosity"; Charpentier et al., "Valuation of Knowledge and Ignorance in Mesolimbic Reward Circuitry."

"It's not that curious . . . from doing it.": Author interview with Paul Silvia (professor of social psychology, University of North Carolina Greensboro), May 3, 2022.

Highly curious people are drawn to: Todd B. Kashdan et al., "How Are Curious People Viewed and How Do They Behave in Social Situations? From the Perspectives of Self, Friends, Parents, and Unacquainted Observers," *Journal of Personality* 81, no. 2 (April 2013), 142–54; Paul Silvia and Alexander Christensen, "Looking Up at the Curious Personality: Individual Differences in Curiosity and Openness to Experience," *Current Opinion in Behavioral Sciences* 35 (2020): 1–6.

Being consistently inquisitive . . . meaningful moments each day.: Kashdan et al., "The Five-Dimensional Curiosity Scale," 138.

Curious people tend to be playful: Kashdan et al., "How Are Curious People Viewed"; Silvia and Christensen, "Looking Up at the Curious Personality."

"curious eyes": Evan Risko et al., "Curious Eyes: Individual Differences in Personality Predict Eye Movement Behavior in Scene-Viewing," *Cognition* 122, no. 1 (January 2012): 86–90; Adrien Baranes, Pierre-Yves Oudeyer, and Jacqueline Gottlieb, "Eye Movements Reveal Epistemic Curiosity in Human Observers," *Vision Research* 117 (December 1, 2015): 81–90.

Stress tolerance is the facet: Kashdan et al., "The Five-Dimensional Curiosity Scale," 145.

47   **"but are unlikely . . . and explore"**: Todd Kashdan et al., "The Five Dimensions of Curiosity," *Harvard Business Review*, September–October 2018, 58–60.

The crisp look and click-driven feel: Benjamin Storm and Julia Soares, "Memory in the Digital Age," in *Oxford Handbook of Human Memory*, vol. 1, ed. Anthony Wagner and Michael Kahana (New York: Oxford University Press, in press).

Moreover, the results . . . minimizes surprise.: Benjamin C. Storm, "Thoughts on the Digital Expansion of the Mind and the Effects of Using the Internet on Memory and Cognition," *Journal of Applied Research in Memory and Cognition* 8 (2019): 29–32.

"Web search engines . . . are complex": Kevyn Collins-Thompson, Preben Hansen, and Claudia Hauff, "Search as Learning: Report from Dagstuhl Seminar 17092," *Dagstuhl Reports* 7, no. 2 (2017): 135–62, esp. 135.

"Through online search . . . information oyster": Daniel Russell, *The Joy of Search: A Google Insider's Guide to Going beyond the Basics* (Cambridge, MA: MIT Press, 2019), 5.

After even a brief online search: Stephanie Pieschl, "Will Using the Internet to Answer Knowledge Questions Increase Users' Overestimation of Their Own Ability or Performance?," *Media Psychology* 24, no. 1 (January 2, 2021): 109–35; Matthew Fisher, Mariel K. Goddu, and Frank C. Keil, "Searching for Explanations: How the Internet Inflates Estimates of Internal Knowledge," *Journal of Experimental Psychology: General* 144, no. 3 (2015): 674–87; Evan F. Risko et al., "On the Prospect of Knowing: Providing Solutions Can Reduce Persistence," *Journal of Experimental Psychology: General* 146, no. 12 (2017): 1677–93.

In one set of five experiments: Matthew Fisher, Adam H. Smiley, and Tito L. H. Grillo, "Information without Knowledge: The Effects of Internet Search on Learning," *Memory* 30, no. 4 (2022): 375–87.

48   **This false confidence:** Johannes von Hoyer, Joachim Kimmerle, and Peter Holtz, "Acquisition of False Certainty: Learners Increase Their Confidence in the Correctness of Incorrect Answers after Online Information Search," *Journal of Computer Assisted Learning* 38, no. 3 (2022): 833–44.

"Search as Learning": Collins-Thompson et al., "Search as Learning"; Johannes von Hoyer et al., "The Search as Learning Spaceship: Toward a Comprehensive Model of Psychological and Technological Facets of Search as Learning," *Frontiers in Psychology* 13 (2022): 827748, https://www.frontiersin.org/articles/10.3389/fpsyg.2022.827748.

"our eyes deceive us": Sarah McGrew et al., "The Challenge That's Bigger Than Fake News: Civic Reasoning in a Social Media Environment," *American Educator* 41, no. 3 (Fall 2017): 4–9.

48   **As a graduate student:** Sam Wineburg and Sarah McGrew, "Lateral Reading and the Nature of Expertise: Reading Less and Learning More When Evaluating Digital Information," *Teachers College Record: The Voice of Scholarship in Education* 121, no. 11 (November 2019): 1–40.

49   **"taking bearings":** McGrew et al., "The Challenge That's Bigger Than Fake News," 9; author interview with Sarah McGrew (assistant professor, Department of Teaching and Learning, University of Maryland), November 1, 2019.

        In 2022, Google's Daniel Russell: Daniel Russell, "Search Mastery Speaker Series: Dan Russell, Senior Research Scientist for Search Quality and User Happiness, Google Inc." (University of Maryland School of Information Studies, College Park, 2021), Virtual Talk, https://www.youtube.com/watch?v=CVQKSdiEqQU.

50   **"don't signal . . . give an answer":** Daniel Russell, "What Do You Need to Know to Use a Search Engine? Why We Still Need to Teach Research Skills," *AI Magazine* 36, no. 4 (Winter 2015): 61–70, esp. 68.

        "But there's an . . . worth noticing": Russell, *The Joy of Search*, 279 (emphasis in the original).

        In the fall, a U-boat: Robert K. Massie, *Castles of Steel: Britain, Germany, and the Winning of the Great War at Sea* (New York: Ballantine Books, 2003), 161–62.

        By March, German submarines: Marc Milner, *Battle of the Atlantic* (Gloucestershire: Tempus/Vanwell Publishing, 2003), 30.

        only thing that had really frightened him: W. L. S. Churchill, *The Second World War: Their Finest Hour* (New York: Mariner Books/Houghton Mifflin, 1949, 1986): 2:529.

        "gnawed my bowels": W. L. S. Churchill, *The Second World War: The Grand Alliance* (New York: Mariner Books/Houghton Mifflin, 1949, 1986): 3:106.

        At Bletchley Park, there: Hodges, *Alan Turing*, 186.

        So far, Turing's team: Hodges, *Alan Turing*, 188–89.

        "You know the Germans . . . you ever will.": Denniston quoted in Kahn, *Seizing the Enigma*, 118.

        pondered the intellectual implications: Hodges, *Alan Turing*, 435.

51   **"The cryptographer, like all . . . to the unknown":** Christopher Morris, "Navy Ultra's Poor Relations," in *Codebreakers: The Inside Story of Bletchley Park*, ed. F. H. Hinsley and Alan Stripp (Oxford: Oxford University Press, 1993), 231–45, esp. 232.

        its mirror-like symmetry: Kahn, *Seizing the Enigma*, 105.

51   **"The popular view … lines of research.":** A. M. Turing, "Computing Machinery and Intelligence," *Mind* 59, no. 236 (October 1, 1950): 433–60, esp. 442.

He had an inheritance: My brief explanation of the Polish and British work on Enigma is drawn largely from Budiansky, *Battle of Wits*, 96–103, 124–31; Hodges, *Alan Turing*, 170–85; and Kahn, *Seizing the Enigma*, 52–65, 92, 100. See also Ralph Erskine, "Breaking German Naval Enigma on Both Sides of the Atlantic," in *Action This Day*, ed. Ralph Erskine and Michael Smith (New York: Bantam, 2003), 174–96. See also e-mail communication with Jack Copeland.

dubbed the "Bomba": Note: Although no one really knows why the machines carried these monikers, the Polish Bomba was reportedly named for a layered ice-cream cake popular in Europe. The U.K. Bombe, in turn, apparently was named for the Polish machine. Author e-mail communication with David Kenyon (research historian, Bletchley Park), January 9–10, 2023.

52   **forerunner to the modern search engine:** Hodges, *Alan Turing*, xvi.

"Computing machines aren't … infallible at all": Turing comment in Alan Turing, Richard Braithwaite, Geoffrey Jefferson, and Max Newman, "Can Automatic Calculating Machines Be Said to Think?," BBC Radio, January 14, 1952; transcript published in Copeland, *The Essential Turing*, 487–506.

"there is no virtue … from data": Turing, "Computing Machinery and Intelligence," 451.

"Machines take me … great frequency": Turing, "Computing Machinery and Intelligence," 450.

Still, Turing's visionary work: Budiansky, *Blackett's War*, 163; Kahn, *Seizing the Enigma*, 279.

If Turing had not: Jack Copeland et al., eds., *The Turing Guide* (Oxford: Oxford University Press, 2017), 83.

53   **"special evidence of insufficient security":** Admiral Ludwig Stummel's July 1944 report on possible breaches in German Naval Enigma is quoted in a postwar U.K. study written by a U.S. Navy officer. See Lt. Col. K. W. McMahan, "Naval SIGINT: The German Navy's Use of Special Intelligence and Reactions to Allied Use" (Government Code and Cypher School: circa 1945), 7:160, 166. The report was generously digitized and shared with the author by Robert Simpson (librarian, National Cryptologic Museum, Fort Meade, MD), January 10, 2023.

"impatient of pompousness … any kind": Bletchley Park cryptographer and international chess master Hugh Alexander quoted in Hodges, *Alan Turing*, 204.

building electrical circuits: Malcolm MacPhail recollection in Hodges, *Alan Turing*, 137–38. MacPhail, a Canadian physicist, met Turing in the late 1930s at Princeton University, where Turing created an encryption machine while studying for his PhD.

53   **"I see! I see!":** Hodges, *Alan Turing*, 233.

how complex patterns and forms: Andrew L. Krause et al., "Introduction to 'Recent Progress and Open Frontiers in Turing's Theory of Morphogenesis,'" *Philosophical Transactions of the Royal Society A: Mathematical, Physical and Engineering Sciences* 379, no. 2213 (December 27, 2021): 20200280, https://doi .org/10.1098/rsta.2020.0280.

"Processes that are . . . be unlearnt": A. M. Turing, "Computing Machinery and Intelligence," 459. Note: Turing wrote "hundred per cent." I have edited for clarity.

died at the age: Pathology reports indicate that Turing died from cyanide poisoning, and a coroner ruled the death a suicide. But Turing archive director Jack Copeland argues that the coroner's investigation was not thorough and that the case is not clear-cut. Turing used cyanide in chemistry experiments carried out in a home laboratory and so could have accidentally ingested the poison. Further complicating the picture is the fact that, amidst Cold War hysteria, many in government circles deemed gay men who were privy to state secrets, as Turing was, to be security risks. The "jury is out" on whether his death was suicide, accidental, or even foul play, writes Copeland. See Jack Copeland and Jonathan Bowen, "Life and Work," in Copeland et al., *The Turing Guide*, 14–17.

"candour and comprehension . . . to breathe": Lyn Irvine, "Foreword to the First Edition," in Sara Turing, *Alan M. Turing: Centenary Edition* (Cambridge: Cambridge University Press, 1959, 2012), xxi. Note: Lyn Newman often published under Irvine, her maiden name.

"strangely fresh eyes": Hodges, *Alan Turing*, 264.

CHAPTER 3

57   **Not knowing is . . . without result.:** Ann Hamilton, "Making Not Knowing," in *Learning Mind: Experience into Art*, ed. Mary Jane Jacob and Jacquelynn Baas (Berkeley: University of California Press, 2010), 67–73, esp. 68–69.

Late one night: Author visit, interview with Nam Nguyen (research assistant, Robert Stickgold Sleep Laboratory, Harvard University Medical School), November 14–15, 2010.

58   **"diffuse cortical inhibition":** Jeffrey M. Ellenbogen et al., "The Sleeping Brain's Influence on Verbal Memory: Boosting Resistance to Interference," *PLoS One* 4, no. 1 (2009): e4117, https://doi.org/10.1371/journal.pone.0004117.

58   **Hints of the mind's nocturnal:** Eugene Aserinsky and Nathaniel Kleitman, "Regularly Occurring Periods of Eye Motility, and Concomitant Phenomena during Sleep," *Science* 118, no. 3062 (September 4, 1953): 273–74.

But for decades, most of sleep: Ellenbogen et al., "The Sleeping Brain's Influence on Verbal Memory."

These are the night's slow hours: Penelope A. Lewis, *The Secret World of Sleep: The Surprising Science of the Mind at Rest* (New York: St. Martin's Press, 2013), 7–9.

"I startled awake . . . telling us something.": Author interview with Robert Stickgold (professor of psychiatry, Harvard Medical School), December 6, 2015.

Stickgold famously validated: Robert Stickgold et al., "Replaying the Game: Hypnagogic Images in Normals and Amnesics," *Science* 290, no. 5490 (October 13, 2000): 350–53.

59   **"These are the kind . . . asterisk next to":** Author visit, interview with Robert Stickgold, November 15, 2010.

"memory evolution": Matthew P. Walker and Robert Stickgold, "Overnight Alchemy: Sleep-Dependent Memory Evolution," *Nature Reviews Neuroscience* 11, no. 3 (March 2010): 218.

60   **"frankly experimental operation":** William Beecher Scoville and Brenda Milner, "Loss of Recent Memory after Bilateral Hippocampal Lesions," *Journal of Neurology, Neurosurgery, and Psychiatry* 20, no. 1 (February 1957): 11.

Scoville hoped that by: Scoville and Milner, "Loss of Recent Memory after Bilateral Hippocampal Lesions," 11.

"striking and totally . . . recent memory": Scoville and Milner, "Loss of Recent Memory after Bilateral Hippocampal Lesions," 12–13.

61   **"forgot daily events . . . they occurred":** Larry R. Squire, "The Legacy of Patient H.M. for Neuroscience," *Neuron* 61, no. 1 (January 1, 2009): 6–9, esp. 6.

"Every day is alone . . . from a dream.": Brenda Milner, Suzanne Corkin, and H. L. Teuber, "Further Analysis of the Hippocampal Amnesic Syndrome: 14-Year Follow-Up Study of H.M.," *Neuropsychologia* 6, no. 3 (1968): 215–34, esp. 217.

At the time, memory: Squire, "The Legacy of Patient H.M.," 7.

Unlike frantic amnesic movie: Milner et al., "Further Analysis of the Hippocampal Amnesic Syndrome"; Scoville and Milner, "Loss of Recent Memory after Bilateral Hippocampal Lesions."

Like H.M., such patients: Wilder Penfield and Brenda Milner, "Memory Deficit Produced by Bilateral Lesions in the Hippocampal Zone," *AMA Archives of Neurology and Psychiatry* 79, no. 5 (May 1, 1958): 475–97.

61   **"some secondary . . . storage of information":** Milner et al., "Further Analysis of the Hippocampal Amnesic Syndrome," 232.

62   **These were the connections:** "In Profile: Matt Wilson," MIT News, Massachusetts Institute of Technology, October 19, 2009, https://news.mit.edu/2009/profile-wilson.

      Scientists previously had recorded: Author e-mail communication with Matthew Wilson (professor of neuroscience, Massachusetts Institute of Technology), December 1, 2022.

      By leaving the microphone on: Matthew Wilson and Bruce McNaughton, "Reactivation of Hippocampal Ensemble Memories during Sleep," *Science* 265, no. 5172 (July 29, 1994): 676–79.

      If replay is interrupted: Gabrielle Girardeau et al., "Selective Suppression of Hippocampal Ripples Impairs Spatial Memory," *Nature Neuroscience* 12, no. 10 (October 2009): 1222–23.

      just as H.M. proved to be: Milner et al., "Further Analysis of the Hippocampal Amnesic Syndrome," 232.

      In time, the mysteries: Daniel B. Rubin et al., "Learned Motor Patterns Are Replayed in Human Motor Cortex during Sleep," *Journal of Neuroscience* 42, no. 25 (June 1, 2022): 5007–20.

      Early proof in humans: Delphine Oudiette et al., "Evidence for the Re-Enactment of a Recently Learned Behavior during Sleepwalking," *PLoS One* 6, no. 3 (March 21, 2011): e18056, https://doi.org/10.1371/journal.pone.0018056.

63   **The greater the magnitude:** Arielle Tambini and Lila Davachi, "Persistence of Hippocampal Multivoxel Patterns into Postencoding Rest Is Related to Memory," *Proceedings of the National Academy of Sciences* 110, no. 48 (November 11, 2013): 19591–96.

      Interrupt these silent rehearsals: Jai Y. Yu and Frank M. Loren, "Hippocampal-Cortical Interaction in Decision Making," *Neurobiology of Learning and Memory* 117 (January 2015): 34–41.

      healthy older adults and Alzheimer's patients: Jessica Alber, Sergio Della Sala, and Michaela Dewar, "Minimizing Interference with Early Consolidation Boosts 7-Day Retention in Amnesic Patients," *Neuropsychology* 28, no. 5 (September 2014): 667–75.

      People who pause quietly: Michaela Dewar et al., "Boosting Long-Term Memory via Wakeful Rest: Intentional Rehearsal Is Not Necessary, Consolidation Is Sufficient," *PLoS One* 9, no. 10 (October 15, 2014): e109542, https://doi.org/10.1371/journal.pone.0109542; Erin Wamsley, "Memory Consolidation during Waking Rest," *Trends in Cognitive Sciences* 23, no. 3 (March 2019): 171–73; Markus Martini et al., "Wakeful Resting and Memory Retention: A Study with Healthy Older and Younger Adults," *Cognitive Processing* 20, no. 1 (February 1, 2019): 125–31.

63   **flew there to confirm:** Author e-mail communication with Sergio Della Sala (professor of human cognitive neuroscience, University of Edinburgh), November 20, 2015.

Memory making seems to be opportunistic: Sara Mednick et al., "An Opportunistic Theory of Cellular and Systems Consolidation," *Trends in Neurosciences* 34, no. 10 (October 2011): 504–14.

steep drop in the neurotransmitter acetylcholine: M. E. Hasselmo, "Neuromodulation: Acetylcholine and Memory Consolidation," *Trends in Cognitive Sciences* 3, no. 9 (1999): 351–59; Gordon Feld and Jan Born, "Neurochemical Mechanisms for Memory Processing during Sleep: Basic Findings in Humans and Neuropsychiatric Implications," *Neuropsychopharmacology* 45 (2020): 31–44.

hippocampus dims its communications: Author e-mail communication with Kenneth Norman (professor of computational and theoretical neuroscience and professor of psychology and neuroscience, Princeton University), December 20, 2022.

64   **After its discovery as a center:** D. J. Willshaw, P. Dayan, and R. G. M. Morris, "Memory, Modelling and Marr: A Commentary on Marr (1971) 'Simple Memory: A Theory of Archicortex,'" *Philosophical Transactions of the Royal Society of London. Series B, Biological Sciences* 370 (April 19, 2015): 20140383, https://doi.org/10.1098/rstb.2014.0383.

Hippocampal neurons are both: Sam McKenzie et al., "Hippocampal Representation of Related and Opposing Memories Develop within Distinct, Hierarchically Organized Neural Schemas," *Neuron* 83, no. 1 (July 2, 2014): 202–15. Also author interview with Howard Eichenbaum (professor of psychological and brain sciences, Boston University), September 4, 2015, and author e-mail communication with Howard Eichenbaum, September 2, 2015.

Patterns of hippocampal reactivation: McKenzie et al., "Hippocampal Representation of Related and Opposing Memories Develop within Distinct, Hierarchically Organized Neural Schemas"; John Lisman et al., "Viewpoints: How the Hippocampus Contributes to Memory, Navigation, and Cognition," *Nature Neuroscience* 20, no. 11 (2017): 1434–47.

"elements [to] function together . . . open-ended learning.": Zeb Kurth-Nelson et al., "Replay and Compositional Computation," *Neuron* 111, no. 4 (2023): 454–69.

To glimpse the deep connectivity: Lila Davachi and Anthony D. Wagner, "Hippocampal Contributions to Episodic Encoding: Insights from Relational and Item-Based Learning," *Journal of Neurophysiology* 88, no. 2 (August 2002): 982–90.

65   **Knowledge is held within:** Suzanne Nalbantian, Paul M. Matthews, and James L. McClelland, "Memory as a Constructive Process: The Parallel Distributed Processing Approach," in *The Memory Process: Neuroscientific and Humanistic*

Perspectives (Cambridge, MA: MIT Press, 2010), 129–51; author interview with James L. McClelland (professor of social sciences, Stanford University), July 9, 2015.

65   **Even trying to recall or imagine:** Michael Craig, Sergio Della Sala, and Michaela Dewar, "Autobiographical Thinking Interferes with Episodic Memory Consolidation," *PLoS One* 9, no. 4 (April 15, 2014): e93915, https://doi .org/10.1371/journal.pone.0093915. See also Kate Brokaw, "Resting State EEG Correlates of Memory Consolidation," *Neurobiology of Learning and Memory* 130 (2016): 17–25.

Invalided out of the war: D. E. Broadbent, "Frederic Charles Bartlett, 1886– 1969," *Biographical Memoirs of Fellows of the Royal Society* 16 (November 1970): 1–13.

"eliminate associations": Bartlett's paraphrase of a colleague's observation in Frederic Charles Bartlett, *Remembering: A Study in Experimental and Social Psychology* (New York: Cambridge University Press, 1932), 5.

"Uniformity and simplicity . . . organic response": Bartlett, *Remembering*, 3–4.

66   **unusual series of experiments:** For background on Bartlett's work on "War of the Ghosts," see Bartlett, *Remembering*, 64–94, and Alison Winter, *Memory: Fragments of a Modern History* (Chicago: University of Chicago Press, 2012), 197–224, esp. 210–18.

"fixed and changeless 'traces'": Bartlett, *Remembering*, xviii.

writings largely forgotten: Winter, *Memory*, 198.

"effort after meaning": Bartlett, *Remembering*, 20, 45.

"ceaseless struggle . . . rapid change": Bartlett, *Remembering*, 314.

In his most famous study: Bartlett, *Remembering*, 64–94. Quotes are from Bartlett's version of the story.

Listeners changed details: Bartlett, *Remembering*, 72.

67   **"strung together and stored within":** Bartlett, *Remembering*, 201.

"persist as an isolated . . . patchwork," "active organisation," "living, momentary setting": Bartlett, *Remembering*, 201.

also called mental models: Regarding the subtle differences but strong foundational similarity between mental models and schema, see also Andrew M. Colman, *A Dictionary of Psychology*, 4th ed. (Oxford: Oxford University Press, 2015); Rick Busselle, "Schema Theory and Mental Models," in *The International Encyclopedia of Media Effects* (Hoboken, NJ: Wiley-Blackwell, 2017), 1–8, https://doi.org/10.1002/9781118783764.wbieme0079; author e-mail communication with Kenneth Norman; and author e-mail communication with Rick Busselle (associate professor, School of Media and Communication, Bowling Green State University), November 18, 2022.

67   *Memory as a Building . . . meaningful order.*: Seamus Heaney, "Settings," in Seamus Heaney, *Seeing Things* (New York: Farrar, Straus and Giroux, 1991), 75.

"**low road**": A term used by Neisser and Winograd to describe naturalistic science. Ulric Neisser and Eugene Winograd, eds., *Remembering Reconsidered: Ecological and Traditional Approaches to the Study of Memory* (Boston: Cambridge University Press, 1995), 2; see also Winter, *Memory*, 221.

pioneered the discovery: Broadbent, "Frederic Charles Bartlett, 1886–1969," 4; "Obituary: Frederic Charles Bartlett," *The Lancet* 294, no. 7625 (October 18, 1969), 855–56.

teach the cortex which memories: Dhairyya Singh, Kenneth A. Norman, and Anna C. Schapiro, "A Model of Autonomous Interactions between Hippocampus and Neocortex Driving Sleep-Dependent Memory Consolidation," *Proceedings of the National Academy of Sciences* 119, no. 44 (2022): e2123432119, https://doi.org/10.1073/pnas.2123432119.

The brain "is asking . . . new memories": Author visit, interview with Robert Stickgold.

What *resonates* with what we: Marlieke T. R. van Kesteren et al., "How Schema and Novelty Augment Memory Formation," *Trends in Neurosciences* 35, no. 4 (April 2010): 211–19.

If a nascent memory is consistent: van Kesteren et al., "How Schema and Novelty Augment Memory Formation"; James McClelland, "Incorporating Rapid Neocortical Learning of New Schema-Consistent Information into Complementary Learning Systems Theory," *Journal of Experimental Psychology, General* 142, no. 4 (November 2013): 1190–210.

68   **could recall John F. Kennedy's:** Milner et al., "Further Analysis of the Hippocampal Amnesic Syndrome," 217–18.

"**secret quality**": Winter, *Memory*, 213. Note: According to Alison Winter, Bartlett used the phrase in his dissertation and credited it to a Robert Louis Stevenson essay in which the Scottish writer muses on how memory abstracts the gist of a subject over time. See Winter, *Memory*, 213, and Robert Louis Stevenson, "An Autumn Effect," in *Nineteen Modern Essays*, ed. John Galsworthy (New York: Longmans, Green and Co., 1926), 134–35.

discover how pairs of patterns: Jeffrey M. Ellenbogen et al., "Human Relational Memory Requires Time and Sleep," *Proceedings of the National Academy of Sciences* 104, no. 18 (May 2007): 7723–28.

69   **learning to navigate a virtual town:** Michael Craig et al., "Wakeful Rest Promotes the Integration of Spatial Memories into Accurate Cognitive Maps," *Hippocampus* 26, no. 2 (February 2016): 185–93.

a concealed rule for solving: Michael Craig, Georgina Ottaway, and Michaela Dewar, "Rest on It: Awake Quiescence Facilitates Insight," *Cortex* 109

(December 2018): 205–14; Célia Lacaux et al., "Sleep Onset Is a Creative Sweet Spot," *Science Advances* 7, no. 50 (December 8, 2021): eabj5866, https://doi.org/10.1126/sciadv.abj5866.

69   **the secret grammar of a made-up language:** Ullrich Wagner et al., "Sleep Inspires Insight," *Nature* 427, no. 6972 (January 2004): 352–55.

These visions, especially the: Antonio Zadra and Robert Stickgold, *When Brains Dream: Exploring the Science and Mystery of Sleep* (New York: Norton, 2021), 124.

"understand possibilities": Zadra and Stickgold, *When Brains Dream*, 115.

"Mount Everest of memory": Psychiatrist and savant syndrome expert Darold Treffert quoted in Bruce Weber, "Kim Peek, Inspiration for 'Rain Man,' Dies at 58," *New York Times*, December 27, 2009, A30.

found abstract concepts largely incomprehensible: Darold Treffert and Daniel Christensen, "Inside the Mind of a Savant," *Scientific American* 293, no. 6 (December 2005): 108–13.

Solomon Shereshevsky, known: A. R. Luria, *The Mind of a Mnemonist: A Little Book about a Vast Memory* (Cambridge, MA: Harvard University Press, 1987), 33–34, 116.

"To think is to forget differences . . . only details.": Jorge Luis Borges, "Funes, the Memorious," in *Object Lessons: The Paris Review Presents the Art of the Short Story*, ed. Lorin Stein and Sadie Stein (New York: Picador, 2012), 123–35, esp. 134.

70   **Charles Darwin is dreaming.:** My main sources on Darwin are E. J. Browne, *Darwin's Origin of Species: A Biography* (New York: Atlantic Monthly Press, 2006); E. Janet Browne, *Charles Darwin: Voyaging* (Princeton, NJ: Princeton University Press, 1996); Charles Darwin, *On the Origin of Species*, ed. Joseph Carroll (New York: Broadview Press, 2003); Carl Zimmer, *Evolution: The Triumph of an Idea* (New York: Harper Perennial, 2006); and John van Wyhe, "Mind the Gap: Did Darwin Avoid Publishing His Theory for Many Years?," *Notes and Records of the Royal Society* 61, no. 2 (May 22, 2007): 177–205.

"a sort of a shock": George Darwin quoted in Browne, *Charles Darwin*, 130.

"mental riotings," "do monkeys cry": Browne, *Darwin's Origin of Species*, 42.

"Dreamt somebody . . . in French": Howard E. Gruber, *Darwin on Man: A Psychological Study of Scientific Creativity*, ed. Paul H. Barrett (New York: E. P. Dutton, 1974), 238, 336; original from Charles Darwin, "Notebook N: Metaphysics and Expression 1838–1839," Cambridge University Library, Darwin Collection, 1260, http://darwin-online.org.uk.

"each word distinctly," "each word separately . . . general sense": Darwin quoted in Gruber, *Darwin on Man*, 336.

71   **"We see nothing . . . lapses of ages.":** Darwin quoted in Zimmer, *Evolution*, 48.

The French zoologist: Zimmer, *Evolution*, 28–29.

Chinese physician Li Shizhen's: James Poskett, *Horizons: The Global Origins of Modern Science* (New York: HarperCollins, 2022), 209.

But the British scientific: Zimmer, *Evolution*, 30; Browne, *Charles Darwin*, 362.

Man from monkeys?: Darwin quoted in Browne, *Darwin's Origin of Species*, 42.

more trifling, the better: Darwin was notable for his interest in minute facts. See Darwin's letter to naturalist Leonard Jenyns, October 12, 1844, in Charles Darwin, *Charles Darwin's Letters: A Selection, 1825–1859*, ed. Frederick Burkhardt (Cambridge: Cambridge University Press, 1996), 85.

"the great effect," "multiplication of little means": Charles Darwin, "Darwin's Notebooks on Transmutation of Species, Part II, Second Notebook C, February to July 1838," ed. Gavin de Beer, *Bulletin of the British Museum (Natural History)*, Historical Series 2, no. 3 (May 1960): 75–118, esp. 75. Also quoted in Gruber, *Darwin on Man*, 114.

"My memory is extensive, yet hazy": Charles Darwin, *The Autobiography of Charles Darwin: 1809–1882*, ed. Nora Barlow (New York: Norton, 1993), 140–41.

"without fail and at once": Darwin, *The Autobiography of Charles Darwin*, 123.

"For I had found . . . favorable ones.", "golden rule": Darwin, *The Autobiography of Charles Darwin*, 123.

72   **urges colleagues to be similarly open:** Darwin, Letter to J. S. Henslow, November 10, 1839, in Darwin, *Charles Darwin's Letters*, 69.

an effort dubbed Hamlet-like: John van Wyhe discusses this issue in his seminal essay. See van Wyhe, "Mind the Gap."

determined to do the monumental work: van Wyhe, "Mind the Gap"; see also Joseph Carroll, "Introduction," in Darwin, *On the Origin of Species*, and author interview with John van Wyhe, December 1, 2015.

"I believe there exists . . . or discovery": Darwin to J. S. Henslow, April 1, 1848, in Darwin, *Charles Darwin's Letters*, 99.

"central, undisclosed hub": Browne, *Charles Darwin*, 363.

few intensive rounds of work: Mason Currey, "Charles Darwin," in *Daily Rituals: How Artists Work* (New York: Knopf/Doubleday, 2013), 162–66; Tim M. Berra, *Charles Darwin: The Concise Story of an Extraordinary Man* (Baltimore: Johns Hopkins University Press, 2008), 47.

then stepped back: van Wyhe, "Mind the Gap," 186, 195.

swivels his focus for years: Browne, *Charles Darwin*, 367.

72 **"to be thoroughly digested":** Browne, *Charles Darwin*, 408.

73 **The order of argument:** Browne, *Charles Darwin*, 437.

"I gained much by my delay in publishing . . . lost nothing by it.": Darwin, *The Autobiography of Charles Darwin*, 124; Browne, *Darwin's Origin of Species*, 50. Note: Increasingly, historians argue that Darwin was wise to delay publishing *Origin of Species* in order to marshal his formidable evidence and his complex arguments.

book's only illustration: Browne, *Darwin's Origin of Species*, 74.

I think: Charles Darwin, "Darwin's Notebooks on Transmutation of Species, Notebook B, July 1837–October 1837," B36, Cambridge University Library Darwin Collection.

Split a first-grade: Rachel Seabrook, Gordon D. A. Brown, and Jonathan E. Solity, "Distributed and Massed Practice: From Laboratory to Classroom," *Applied Cognitive Psychology* 19, no. 1 (2005): 107–22.

74 **obscure math problem:** Doug Rohrer and Kelli Taylor, "The Effects of Overlearning and Distributed Practice on the Retention of Mathematics Knowledge," *Applied Cognitive Psychology* 20 (2006): 1209–24.

Swahili–English word pairs: Mary A. Pyc and Katherine A. Rawson, "Testing the Retrieval Effort Hypothesis: Does Greater Difficulty Correctly Recalling Information Lead to Higher Levels of Memory?," *Journal of Memory and Language* 60, no. 4 (2009): 437–47; author interview with Katherine Rawson (professor of psychological sciences, Kent State University), November 16, 2015.

whale and *mammal*: Nate Kornell, Matthew Jensen Hays, and Robert A. Bjork, "Unsuccessful Retrieval Attempts Enhance Subsequent Learning," *Journal of Experimental Psychology: Learning, Memory, and Cognition* 35, no. 4 (July 2009): 989–98.

75 **victories cut short:** For further discussions, see Scott Small, *Forgetting: The Benefits of Not Remembering* (New York: Crown, 2021), 8; Norman J. Slamecka and Jacobo Fevreiski, "The Generation Effect When Generation Fails," *Journal of Verbal Learning and Verbal Behavior* 22 (1983): 153–63; and Blake Richards and Paul Frankland, "The Persistence and Transience of Memory," *Neuron: Perspective* 94, no. 6 (2017): 1071–84.

master's thesis of surgeon-scientist: Carol-anne E. Moulton et al., "Teaching Surgical Skills: What Kind of Practice Makes Perfect? A Randomized, Controlled Trial," *Annals of Surgery* 244, no. 3 (September 2006): 400–409.

76 **"You can definitely . . . see a struggle.":** Author interview with Carol-anne Moulton, November 20, 2015. All quotes by Moulton from this section are from this interview.

When a device: Betsy Sparrow, Jenny Liu, and Daniel M. Wegner, "Google Effects on Memory: Cognitive Consequences of Having Information at Our

Fingertips," *Science* 333, no. 6043 (August 5, 2011): 776–78; Megan O. Kelly and Evan F. Risko, "Revisiting the Influence of Offloading Memory on Free Recall," *Memory and Cognition* 50, no. 4 (May 2022): 710–21.

76   **The very act of searching online:** Xiaoyue Liu et al., "Internet Search Alters Intra- and Inter-Regional Synchronization in the Temporal Gyrus," *Frontiers in Psychology* 9 (2018): 260. See also Elizabeth Marsh and Suparna Rajaram, "The Digital Expansion of the Mind: Implications of Internet Usage for Memory and Cognition," *Journal of Applied Research in Memory and Cognition* 8 (2019): 1–8, https://doi.org/10.1016/j.jarmac.2018.11.001.

"using the internet . . . and reconsolidation": Benjamin C. Storm, "Thoughts on the Digital Expansion of the Mind and the Effects of Using the Internet on Memory and Cognition," *Journal of Applied Research in Memory and Cognition* 8 (2019): 29–32, esp. 31.

77   **In one study of 2,300 Chinese youths:** Xiaojing Li et al., "Youths' Habitual Use of Smartphones Alters Sleep Quality and Memory: Insights from a National Sample of Chinese Students," *International Journal of Environmental Research and Public Health* 18, no. 5 (March 2021): 2254.

"spaciousness of uncertainty": Rebecca Solnit, *Hope in the Dark: Untold Histories, Wild Possibilities* (New York: Nation Books, 2004), xiv.

Chris Gustin raises his hand: Author studio visit, interview with Chris Gustin (ceramics artist), August 13, 2015.

breath: Daniel Rhodes, *Pottery Form* (Radnor, PA: Chilton Book Co., 1976), 150.

"It's the not-knowing . . . own understanding.": Author visit, interview with Chris Gustin, June 22, 2015.

78   **"leather-hard":** Rhodes, *Pottery Form*, 111.

"The evolution . . . be endured.": Rhodes, *Pottery Form*, 237.

A product of channeled: Rhodes, *Pottery Form*, 22–23.

nest building, "forces the potter . . . dream a little," "moving, organic . . . of finality.": Rhodes, *Pottery Form*, 176.

"impertinent": Cate McQuaid, "'Chris Gustin: Masterworks in Clay,' at Fuller Craft Museum," *Boston Globe*, December 8, 2012, https://www.bostonglobe.com/arts/2012/12/08/chris-gustin-masterworks-clay-fuller-craft-museum/OVpoESwGc6kZ4iFzgA3Y9H/story.html.

Few have the patience . . . inherent freedom: Rhodes, *Pottery Form*, 176.

79   **"You may have one sense . . . don't know you.":** Interview with Chris Gustin, June 22, 2015.

"Coming back is . . . months ago.": Interview with Gustin, August 13, 2015.

79   **"It's hard to stand back ... much in control.":** Interview with Gustin, June 22, 2015.

"I need that ... the edge.": Author visits, interviews with Chris Gustin, June 22 and July 23, 2015.

80   **"Okay, that makes ... because you evolve.":** Studio visit, interview with Chris Gustin, August 13, 2015.

"searches in the byways": Rhodes, *Pottery Form*, 237.

CHAPTER 4

81   **"Invention, it must ... out of chaos.":** Mary Shelley, *Frankenstein: The 1818 Text* (New York: Penguin Classics, 2018), 240.

Most resistant bacteria ... again and again: Author e-mail communication with Kyle Allison (Systems Biology Fellow, Columbia University), May 27, 2015.

Popping up in all manner of bacteria: Ed Yong, "Sleeper Cells: How to Fight Bacteria That Play Dead," *New Scientist*, 213, No. 2858 (March 31, 2012): 40–42.

82   **felt elated and relieved:** The story of the discovery comes from author visit, interview with Kyle Allison (PhD student in biomedical engineering, Boston University), May 28, 2010, and author interview with Kyle Allison (Systems Biology Fellow, Columbia University), March 28, 2015. Also multiple author interviews with Jim Collins, cited below.

"That's brilliant ... stunning result.": Author visit, interview with Jim Collins (professor of biomedical engineering, Boston University), May 28, 2010. Note: Unless otherwise indicated, all quotes from the Collins–Allison meeting and from Collins thereafter are from this visit.

An editor at a prestigious journal: The research was published in Kyle R. Allison, Mark P. Brynildsen, and James J. Collins, "Metabolite-Enabled Eradication of Bacterial Persisters by Aminoglycosides," *Nature* 473, no. 7346 (2011): 216–20.

"It can't be done ... up the good work.": Author visit, interview with Kyle Allison, February 22, 2015.

genetic toggle switch: Timothy S. Gardner, Charles R. Cantor, and James J. Collins, "Construction of a Genetic Toggle Switch in Escherichia Coli," *Nature* 403, no. 6767 (January 2000): 339–42.

power probiotics refitted with biosensors: Ning Mao et al., "Probiotic Strains Detect and Suppress Cholera in Mice," *Science Translational Medicine* 10, no. 445 (June 13, 2018): eaao2586, https://doi.org/10.1126/scitranslmed.aao2586.

83   **His cheap, paper-based:** Keith Pardee et al., "Paper-Based Synthetic Gene Networks," *Cell* 159, no. 4 (November 6, 2014): 940–54; Keith Pardee et al., "Rapid, Low-Cost Detection of Zika Virus Using Programmable Biomolecular Components," *Cell* 165, no. 5 (May 19, 2016): 1255–66.

discovery of the first new antibiotic: Felix Wong et al., "Benchmarking AlphaFold-Enabled Molecular Docking Predictions for Antibiotic Discovery," *Molecular Systems Biology* 18, no. 9 (September 2022): e11081, https://doi .org/10.15252/msb.202211081; Lawrence Tabak, "Using AI to Find New Antibiotics Still a Work in Progress," *NIH Director's Blog*, September 13, 2022, https://directorsblog.nih.gov/2022/09/13/using-ai-to-find-new-antibiotics -still-a-work-in-progress.

"Jim really understands . . . people to be inactive?": Author visit, interview with Kyle Allison, February 22, 2015.

topic was largely overlooked: Jonathan Smallwood and Jonathan W. Schooler, "The Restless Mind," *Psychological Bulletin* 132 (2006): 946–58. Note: Smallwood and Schooler write that they could not find a single mention of mind wandering in the cognitive psychology texts of the time.

84   **"perceptual decoupling":** Benjamin Baird et al., "The Decoupled Mind: Mind-Wandering Disrupts Cortical Phase-Locking to Perceptual Events," *Journal of Cognitive Neuroscience* 26 (2014): 2596–2607.

Up to two minutes: Erik D. Reichle, Andrew E. Reineberg, and Jonathan W. Schooler, "Eye Movements during Mindless Reading," *Psychological Science* 21, no. 9 (September 2010): 1300–1310; Pablo Oyarzo, David Preiss, and Diego Cosmelli, "Attentional and Meta-Cognitive Processes Underlying Mind Wandering Episodes during Continuous Naturalistic Reading Are Associated with Specific Changes in Eye Behavior," *Psychophysiology* 59, no. 4 (2022): e13994, doi:10.1111/psyp.13994.

blinking more rapidly: Daniel Smilek, Jonathan Carriere, and J. Allan Cheyne, "Out of Mind, Out of Sight: Eye Blinking as Indicator and Embodiment of Mind Wandering," *Psychological Science* 21, no. 6 (June 1, 2010): 786–89.

their pupils dilate: Michael S. Franklin et al., "Window to the Wandering Mind: Pupillometry of Spontaneous Thought while Reading," *Quarterly Journal of Experimental Psychology* 66, no. 12 (2013): 2289–94.

their reading pace slows: Tom Foulsham, James Farley, and Alan Kingstone, "Mind Wandering in Sentence Reading: Decoupling the Link between Mind and Eye," *Canadian Journal of Experimental Psychology* 67, no. 1 (March 2013): 51–59.

related to processing visual input: Meichao Zhang et al., "Perceptual Coupling and Decoupling of the Default Mode Network during Mind-Wandering and Reading," *eLife* 11 (2022): e74011, https://doi.org/10.7554/eLife.74011.

84   **settled into a cozy chair:** Daniel J. Schad, Antje Nuthmann, and Ralf Engbert, "Your Mind Wanders Weakly, Your Mind Wanders Deeply: Objective Measures Reveal Mindless Reading at Different Levels," *Cognition* 125, no. 2 (November 1, 2012): 179–94; author e-mail communication with Daniel Schad (doctoral candidate, University of Potsdam, Germany), March 20, 2015.

The Red-Headed League: Jonathan Smallwood, Merrill McSpadden, and Jonathan W. Schooler, "When Attention Matters: The Curious Incident of the Wandering Mind," *Memory and Cognition* 36, no. 6 (September 2008): 1144–50.

"frequency effect": Foulsham et al., "Mind Wandering in Sentence Reading."

85   **60 percent of fatal crashes:** Data from an analysis of national police reports by Erie Insurance Inc., "Can You Guess Our Biggest Driving Distraction?," accessed December 21, 2022, https://www.erieinsurance.com/blog/distracted -driving-study-2018.

Studies in China and France: Cédric Gil-Jardiné et al., "The Distracted Mind on the Wheel: Overall Propensity to Mind Wandering Is Associated with Road Crash Responsibility," *PLoS One* 12, no. 8 (August 3, 2017), https://doi .org/10.1371/journal.pone.0181327; Weina Qu et al., "The Relationship between Mind Wandering and Dangerous Driving Behavior among Chinese Drivers," *Safety Science* 78 (October 1, 2015): 41–48.

"She looks as if . . . do not see it.": Charlotte Brontë, *Jane Eyre* (London: Penguin Classics, 2006), 62.

The word *daydream*: Debra Gettelman, "'Making Out' Jane Eyre," *ELH* 74, no. 3 (2007): 557–81, 560.

stood *The Daydreamer*: Nikolaus Pevsner, *High Victorian Design: A Study of the Exhibits of 1851* (London: Faber & Faber, 2011), 19–20, 84.

"dreaming always—never accomplishing": Florence Nightingale quoted in Gettelman, "'Making Out' Jane Eyre," 561.

"private theater . . . of her illness": Josef Breuer, "Case 1-Fraulein Anna O," in *The Freud Reader*, ed. Peter Gay (New York: Norton, 1995), 61–77, 62.

"childish and illicit": Sigmund Freud, "The Creative Writer and Daydreaming," in Sigmund Freud, *The Uncanny*, trans. David McLintock (New York: Penguin Books, 2003), 23–34, esp. 27.

"We are repelled . . . cool towards them": Freud, "The Creative Writer and Daydreaming," 33.

screen U.S. Army recruits: Lila Thulin, "The First Personality Test Was Developed during World War I," *Smithsonian Magazine*, September 23, 2019, https://www.smithsonianmag.com/history/first-personality-test-was-de veloped-during-world-war-i-180973192.

85   **"Does your mind . . . bother you?":** M. J. Papurt, "A Study of the Woodworth Psychoneurotic Inventory with Suggested Revision," *Journal of Abnormal and Social Psychology* 25, no. 3 (1930): 335–52.

86   **"sweetly reasonable man":** James L. Jarrett, "Review of *Daydreaming and Fantasy* by Jerome Singer," *British Journal of Educational Studies* 25, no. 3 (1977): 297–98.

In 1965, Jerome Singer: John Antrobus, Jerome Singer, and Stanley Greenberg, "Studies in the Stream of Consciousness: Experimental Enhancement and Suppression of Spontaneous Cognitive Processes," *Perceptual and Motor Skills* 23 (October 1, 1966): 399–417.

He admitted freely: Jerome Singer, *Daydreaming: An Introduction to the Experimental Study of Inner Experience* (New York: Random House, 1966), 14–25; Scott Barry Kaufman, "Conversation on Daydreaming with Jerome L. Singer," *Beautiful Minds* (blog), December 10, 2013, https://blogs.scientificamerican.com/beautiful-minds/conversation-on-daydreaming-with-jerome-l-singer.

87   **"It was difficult . . . calling their friends":** John Antrobus, "Toward a Neurocognitive Processing Model of Imaginal Thought," in *At Play in the Fields of Consciousness: Essays in Honor of Jerome Singer*, ed. Jefferson Singer and Peter Salovey (Mahwah, NJ: Lawrence Erlbaum Associates, 1999), 3–28.

"the powerful unfinished business": Jerome Singer, "Experimental Studies of Daydreaming and the Stream of Thought," in *The Stream of Consciousness*, ed. Kenneth Pope and Jerome Singer (New York: Plenum Press, 1978), 187–223.

up to nearly half of their waking lives: Matthew A. Killingsworth and Daniel T. Gilbert, "A Wandering Mind Is an Unhappy Mind," *Science* 330, no. 6006 (November 12, 2010): 932.

out of the Dark Ages: Randy Buckner, Jessica Andrews-Hanna, and Daniel Schacter, "The Brain's Default Network," *Annals of the New York Academy of Sciences* 1124, no. 1 (April 1, 2008): 1–38, esp. 15.

His candor and sensibility: Jarrett, "Review of Daydreaming and Fantasy."

A state of mind deemed just static: Randy Buckner, "The Serendipitous Discovery of the Brain's Default Network," *NeuroImage* 62, no. 2 (August 15, 2012): 1137–45.

kept a folder on his desk: Buckner, "The Serendipitous Discovery of the Brain's Default Network."

88   **up to 80 percent of the brain's energy:** Marcus E. Raichle, "The Brain's Dark Energy," *Science* 314, no. 5803 (November 24, 2006): 1249–50.

Less than 10 percent of visual: Raichle, "The Brain's Dark Energy."

one-fifth of the brain: Author interview with Olaf Sporns (professor of psychological and brain science, Indiana University), January 27, 2015.

88   **A long-overlooked 1995 study:** Nancy C. Andreasen et al., "Remembering the Past: Two Facets of Episodic Memory Explored with Positron Emission Tomography," *American Journal of Psychiatry* 152, no. 11 (November 1995): 1576–85.

"When the brain/mind . . . complex parts": Andreasen et al., "Remembering the Past," 1583.

Debate grew so heated: Interview with Olaf Sporns, January 27, 2015.

this widely distributed network: Jonathan Smallwood et al., "The Default Mode Network in Cognition: A Topographical Perspective," *Nature Reviews Neuroscience* 22, no. 8 (August 2021): 503–13; Jessica R. Andrews-Hanna et al., "Functional-Anatomic Fractionation of the Brain's Default Network," *Neuron* 65, no. 4 (February 2, 2010): 550–62.

89   **far from the brain's sensorimotor:** Smallwood et al., "The Default Mode Network in Cognition."

end of many cognitive information processing: Smallwood et al., "The Default Mode Network in Cognition."

What were you thinking . . . forget where you were?: Video interview with study participant by Mary Helen Immordino-Yang, University of California, Los Angeles. Viewed by author at the University of Southern California, February 20, 2015.

one of the first longitudinal studies: Information on the "Longitudinal, Cross-Cultural Project on Adolescents' Brains and Psychosocial Development" can be found at the Immordino-Yang Lab, USC Center for Affective Neuroscience, Development, Learning, and Education, https://candle.usc.edu.

Many of their parents: Author interview with Mary Helen Immordino-Yang (professor of psychology and education and chair in humanistic psychology, University of Southern California), October 7, 2017. See also Rebecca Gotlieb, Xiao-Fei Yang, and Mary Helen Immordino-Yang, "Concrete and Abstract Dimensions of Diverse Adolescents' Social-Emotional Meaning-Making, and Associations with Broader Functioning," *Journal of Adolescent Research*, 1–36, https://doi.org/10.1177/07435584221091498.

"I have to prepare . . . divide this up?": Video interview with study participant by Mary Helen Immordino-Yang.

90   **"palliative effect":** Veronika Engert, Jonathan Smallwood, and Tania Singer, "Mind Your Thoughts: Associations between Self-Generated Thoughts and Stress-Induced and Baseline Levels of Cortisol and Alpha-Amylase," *Biological Psychology* 103 (December 2014): 283–91.

Nearly half of our mental: David Stawarczyk, Helena Cassol, and Arnaud D'Argembeau, "Phenomenology of Future-Oriented Mind-Wandering Episodes," *Frontiers in Psychology* 4, article 425 (July 16, 2013): 1–12. https://doi.org/10.3389/fpsyg.2013.00425. See also Arnaud D'Argembeau, "Mind

Wandering and Self-Referential Thought," in *The Oxford Handbook of Spontaneous Thought: Mind-Wandering, Creativity, and Dreaming*, ed. Kieran C. R. Fox and Kalina Christoff (Oxford: Oxford University Press, 2018), 181–91.

90   **Our thoughts turn to the future:** Arnaud D'Argembeau, Olivier Renaud, and Martial Van Der Linden, "Frequency, Characteristics and Functions of Future-Oriented Thoughts in Daily Life," *Applied Cognitive Psychology* 25, no. 1 (2011): 96–103.

Setting out to explore: Engert et al., "Mind Your Thoughts."

Even negative future-oriented daydreams: Florence J. M. Ruby et al., "How Self-Generated Thought Shapes Mood: The Relation between Mind-Wandering and Mood Depends on the Socio-Temporal Content of Thoughts," *PLoS One* 8, no. 10 (October 23, 2013): e77554, https://doi.org/10.1371 /journal.pone.0077554.

91   **very often we are loosely sketching out:** D'Argembeau et al., "Frequency, Characteristics and Functions of Future-Oriented Thoughts in Daily Life," 99.

calling on the "inner speech": Julie Demblon and Arnaud D'Argembeau, "The Organization of Prospective Thinking: Evidence of Event Clusters in Freely Generated Future Thoughts," *Consciousness and Cognition: An International Journal* 24 (2014): 75–83, https://doi.org/10.1016/j.concog.2014.01.002.

no further than later that day: D'Argembeau et al., "Frequency, Characteristics and Functions of Future-Oriented Thoughts in Daily Life."

Any time that we step away: Diana I. Tamir and Jason P. Mitchell, "The Default Network Distinguishes Construals of Proximal versus Distal Events," *Journal of Cognitive Neuroscience* 23, no. 10 (October 2011): 2945–55.

if you imagine that you are working remotely: Adam Waytz, Hal E. Hershfield, and Diane I. Tamir, "Mental Simulation and Meaning in Life," *Journal of Personality and Social Psychology* 108, no. 2 (February 2015): 336–55.

"You're moving in . . . ways of being in my mind": Author visit, interview with Mary Helen Immordino-Yang, February 19–20, 2015.

co-activated with the executive brain: Kalina Christoff et al., "Experience Sampling during fMRI Reveals Default Network and Executive System Contributions to Mind Wandering," *Proceedings of the National Academy of Sciences* 106, no. 21 (May 26, 2009): 8719–24.

92   **parts of the frontoparietal control network:** Matthew L. Dixon et al., "Heterogeneity within the Frontoparietal Control Network and Its Relationship to the Default and Dorsal Attention Networks," *Proceedings of the National Academy of Sciences* 115, no. 7 (February 13, 2018): E1598–1607, https://doi.org/10.1073/pnas.1715766115.

a second frontoparietal subsystem: Dixon et al., "Heterogeneity within the Frontoparietal Control Network and Its Relationship to the Default and Dorsal Attention Networks."

92   **In 2013, Tania Singer:** Jonathan Smallwood, Florence Ruby, and Tania Singer, "Letting Go of the Present: Mind-Wandering Is Associated with Reduced Delay Discounting," *Consciousness and Cognition* 22, no. 1 (2013): 1–7.

93   **"let go of the present":** Smallwood et al., "Letting Go of the Present."

        In Walter Mischel's marshmallow: Harriet Nerlove Mischel and Walter Mischel, "The Development of Children's Knowledge of Self-Control Strategies," *Child Development* 54, no. 3 (1983): 603–19, esp. 609; Walter Mischel, *The Marshmallow Test: Why Self-Control Is the Engine of Success* (New York: Bantam, 2014), 34, 37; Walter Mischel and Nancy Baker, "Cognitive Appraisals and Transformation in Delay Behavior," *Journal of Personality and Social Psychology* 31, no. 2 (1975): 254–61; author e-mail communication with Ozlem Ayduk (chair of psychology, University of California, Berkeley), January 20, 2023.

        "transcendent thinking": Rebecca Gotlieb, Xiao-Fei Yang, and Mary Helen Immordino-Yang, "Default and Executive Networks' Roles in Diverse Adolescents' Emotionally Engaged Construals of Complex Social Issues," *Social Cognitive and Affective Neuroscience* 17, no. 4 (April 1, 2022): 421–29.

        The most promising and motivated: Author interview with Mary Helen Immordino-Yang, January 22, 2015, and visit, interview with Immordino-Yang, February 19–20, 2015. References an ongoing study by Immordino-Yang.

        "Daydreaming is a . . . play them out": Scott Barry Kaufman, interview with Mary Helen Immordino-Yang, "A Defense of Daydreaming," *Radio Times* (WHYY, October 28, 2013).

        "It's really about mental flexibility": Author visit, interview with Immordino-Yang, February 19–20, 2015.

94   **Adolescents who displayed:** Gotlieb et al., "Default and Executive Networks' Roles in Diverse Adolescents' Emotionally Engaged Construals of Complex Social Issues."

        had more complex daydreams: Author interview with Mary Helen Immordino-Yang, November 23, 2022.

        And over time, those teens . . . their identities.: Rebecca Gotlieb, Xiao-Fei Yang, and Mary Helen Immordino-Yang, "Diverse Adolescents' Transcendent Thinking Predicts Young Adult Psychosocial Outcomes via Brain Network Development," preprint, 10.31234/osf.io/cj6an.

        She first outlined her concerns: Mary Helen Immordino-Yang, Joanna A. Christodoulou, and Vanessa Singh, "Rest Is Not Idleness: Implications of the Brain's Default Mode for Human Development and Education," *Perspectives on Psychological Science* 7, no. 4 (July 1, 2012): 352–64.

        Already, high-technology use: Logan E. Annisette and Kathryn D. Lafreniere, "Social Media, Texting, and Personality: A Test of the Shallowing Hypothesis," *Personality and Individual Differences* 115 (September 1, 2017):

154–58, https://doi.org/10.1016/j.paid.2016.02.043; Paul Trapnell and Lisa Sinclair, "Texting Frequency and the Moral Shallowing Hypothesis" (poster presentation at the annual meeting of the Society for Personality and Social Psychology, San Diego, CA, 2012).

94   **"I worry that . . . in your life.":** Interview with Immordino-Yang, "A Defense of Daydreaming."

95   **"The drapes are white . . . anything else.":** Author interview with Alysia Burbidge (high school student), March 24, 2015.

We meet at a noodle: Author visit, interview with Alysia Burbidge, February 20, 2015, Los Angeles.

"I daydream . . . for the future": Author visit, interview with Burbidge. All quotes from Burbidge are from this interview unless indicated otherwise.

"Yeah . . . feel complete.": Author interview with Alysia Burbidge, January 24, 2015.

96   **"imagination is more . . . the entire world":** Albert Einstein quoted in George S. Viereck, "What Life Means to Einstein," *Saturday Evening Post*, October 26, 1929, 17, 110, 113–14, 117.

97   **Extra noise essentially nudges:** Frank Moss and Kurt Wiesenfeld, "The Benefits of Background Noise," *Scientific American* 273, no. 2 (August 1995): 66–69.

"alternate uses test": J. P. Guilford, "Creativity: Yesterday, Today and Tomorrow," *Journal of Creative Behavior* 1, no. 1 (1967): 3–14.

Our potential . . . this simple measure.: Mark A. Runco and Selcuk Acar, "Divergent Thinking as an Indicator of Creative Potential," *Creativity Research Journal*, 24, no. 1 (2012): 66–75; Jonathan A. Plucker, "Is the Proof in the Pudding? Reanalyses of Torrance's (1958 to Present) Longitudinal Data," *Creativity Research Journal* 12, no. 2 (1999): 103–14; Roger Beaty et al., "A First Look at the Role of Domain-General Cognitive and Creative Abilities in Jazz Improvisation," *Psychomusicology: Music, Mind, and Brain*, 23, no. 4 (2013): 262–68.

98   **A landmark series of investigations:** Ken Gilhooly et al., "Divergent Thinking: Strategies and Executive Involvement in Generating Novel Uses for Familiar Objects," *British Journal of Psychology* 98, no. 4 (November 2007): 611–25.

"Does the examinee . . . channels of thought?": J. P. Guilford, "Creativity," *American Psychologist* 5 (1950): 444–54, esp. 452.

creative people's knowledge networks: Yoed N. Kenett, David Anaki, and Miriam Faust, "Investigating the Structure of Semantic Networks in Low and High Creative Persons," *Frontiers in Human Neuroscience* 8, no. 407 (2014): 1–17; Yoed N. Kenett et al., "Flexibility of Thought in High Creative Individuals Represented by Percolation Analysis," *Proceedings of the National Academy of Sciences* 115, no. 5 (2018): 867–72; Marcela Ovando-Tellez et al., "Brain Connectivity–Based Prediction of Real-Life Creativity Is Mediated by Semantic Memory Structure," *Science Advances* 8 (2022): eabl4294, https://www.science.org/doi/pdf/10.1126/sciadv.abl4294.

98   **Scientists neuroimaging divergent:** Roger E. Beaty et al., "Creativity and the Default Network: A Functional Connectivity Analysis of the Creative Brain at Rest," *Neuropsychologia* 64 (November 2014): 92–98.

99   **a vibrating insole:** Attila Priplata et al., "Vibrating Insoles and Balance Control in Elderly People," *The Lancet* 362, no. 9390 (October 2003): 1123–24; "Vibrating Insoles Could Aid Strenuous Walking and Improve Athletic Performance," *Wyss Institute* (blog), May 2, 2016, https://wyss.har vard.edu/news/vibrating-insoles-could-aid-strenuous-walking-improve -athletic-performance.

      "I think people . . . against our culture.": Author visit, interview with Jim Collins (professor of bioengineering, Massachusetts Institute of Technology), February 5, 2015. Also author interview with Jim Collins, December 2, 2022.

100   **"It was a shock":** Author visit, interview with Ahmad "Mo" Khalil (Howard Hughes Medical Institute Postdoctoral Fellow, Department of Biomedical Engineering, Boston University), Boston University, May 28, 2010.

      "We weren't quite sure . . . something from it": Author visit, interview with Kyle Allison, May 28, 2010.

      "Idleness is looked . . . almost demonized.": Author visit, interview with Ahmad Khalil, May 28, 2010.

      as incompetent if they paused: Naomi B. Rothman, Elizabeth A. Wiley, and Malia Mason, "The Downside of Deliberation: Why Decision Makers Who Deliberate Lose Influence," *Academy of Management Proceedings* 2016, no. 1 (2016): 14610, https://doi.org/10.5465/ambpp.2016.228.

      disfluencies in speech: Michael Erard, *Um . . . : Slips, Stumbles, and Verbal Blunders, and What They Mean* (New York: Anchor, 2008), 7–8, 135, 254.

      The more people stare: B. B. Meskin and Jerome Singer, "Daydreaming, Reflective Thought, and Laterality of Eye Movements," *Journal of Personality and Social Psychology* 30, no. 1 (July 1974): 64–71; Smilek et al., "Out of Mind, Out of Sight."

101   **One winter's day, I made:** Author visit to the Sketchbook Project, Brooklyn, NY, February 25, 2015. Note: In 2023, the Sketchbook Project, which later was renamed the Brooklyn Art Library and relocated to Florida, shut down because it was "no longer sustainable," according to founder Steven Peterman. The sketchbooks were being donated to museum collections or returned to owners.

      Picture the sketchbook, held: Miriam Stewart, "Curating Sketchbooks: Interpretation, Preservation, Display," in *Recto Verso: Redefining the Sketchbook*, ed. Angela Bartram et al. (New York: Routledge, 2016), 163–76.

101   **"It's like looking . . . to sketchbooks.":** Author interview with Miriam Stewart (curator, Harvard University Art Museums, Cambridge, MA), March 15, 2015.

primi pensieri: Deanna Petherbridge, "The Persistent Cult of the Sketch," in *The Primacy of Drawing* (New Haven, CT: Yale University Press, 2010): 27–45, esp. 27. Petherbridge notes that there is an equivalent term for "first-thought sketches" in many languages.

people were given four: Masaki Suwa et al., "Seeing into Sketches: Regrouping Parts Encourages New Interpretations," in *Visual and Spatial Reasoning in Design II*, ed. John S. Gero, Barbara Tversky, and Terry Purcell (Sydney: Key Centre of Design Computing and Cognition, 2001), 207–19, esp. 216–17.

102   **"Confused things rouse . . . new inventions":** Leonardo da Vinci quoted in E. H. Gombrich, *Norm and Form: Studies in the Art of the Renaissance* (Chicago: University of Chicago Press, 1966, 1985), 62.

see in the messy indeterminate: Jonathan Fish and Stephen Scrivener, "Amplifying the Mind's Eye: Sketching and Visual Cognition," *Leonardo* 23, no. 1 (1990): 117–26.

Scattered, broken up: Paolo Galluzzi, "The Strange Vicissitudes of Leonardo's Manuscripts," in *The Courier* (Paris: UNESCO, 1974), 5–7. Galluzzi was then director of the Biblioteca Leonardiana, Vinci, Italy. See also Kenneth Clark, *Leonardo da Vinci* (Cambridge: Cambridge University Press, 1939), 2.

"unfinished quality . . . is provisional": Charles Nicholl, *Leonardo da Vinci: Flights of the Mind* (New York: Viking, 2011), 418.

"The mind in an instant . . . east to west.": Leonardo da Vinci, *Codex Atlanticus*, fol. 204v-a., cited in Nicholl, *Leonardo da Vinci*, 402.

"So, reader, you need not . . . to another.": Leonardo da Vinci quoted in Nicholl, *Leonardo da Vinci*, 418.

Even the staff draft: Author interview with Steven Peterman (founder of the Sketchbook Project), February 27, 2015.

103   **Some people just don't finish:** Author interview with Steven Peterman.

"The very best will grab this and go": Author visit, interview with Jim Collins, May 28, 2010, and interview with Jim Collins, December 2, 2022.

For his youthful discovery: Francis Collins, "Creative Minds: Searching for Solutions to Chronic Infection," *NIH Director's Blog*, September 22, 2015, https://directorsblog.nih.gov/2015/09/22/creative-minds-searching-for -solutions-to-chronic-infection; "NIH Early Independence Award: Isolation and Systems-Level Characterization of Persistent Bacteria," NIH RePORTER, accessed December 21, 2022, https://reporter.nih.gov/project -details/1DP5OD019792-01.

103   **His innovation to pair:** Christopher R. Rosenberg, Xin Fang, and Kyle R. Allison, "Potentiating Aminoglycoside Antibiotics to Reduce Their Toxic Side Effects," *PLoS One* 15, no. 9 (2020): e0237948, https://doi.org/10.1371/journal .pone.0237948.

"All those times . . . had been before.": Author visit, interview with Kyle Allison, February 22, 2015.

CHAPTER 5

107   **"It is dangerous . . . secure world.":** Teju Cole, *Open City* (New York: Random House, 2011), 200.

"If you were voting": All quotes from this conversation come from author visit, interviews at the Leadership Lab canvass led by Steve Deline (field organizer, Leadership Lab), May 7, 2016.

108   **Dozens of state laws:** "Past LGBT Nondiscrimination and Anti-LGBT Bills across the Country," American Civil Liberties Union Fact Sheet, accessed June 2016 and February 2022, https://www.aclu.org /lgbt-nondiscrimination-and-anti-lgbt-bills-across-country.

Nearly four in ten Americans: Pew Research Center, "Attitudes on Same-Sex Marriage," May 14, 2019, https://www.pewforum.org/fact-sheet /changing-attitudes-on-gay-marriage.

similar numbers believe that immigrants: Jens Manuel Krogstad, "On Views of Immigrants, Americans Largely Split along Party Lines," Pew Research Center, September 30, 2015, https://www.pewresearch.org/fact-tank/2015/09/30 /on-views-of-immigrants-americans-largely-split-along-party-lines.

with most blaming individual: Pew Research Center, "Report: On Views of Race and Inequality, Blacks and Whites Are Worlds Apart," June 27, 2016, https://www.pewresearch.org/social-trends/2016/06/27/on -views-of-race-and-inequality-blacks-and-whites-are-worlds-apart.

"hugs the easy way . . . cannot understand": Richard Wright, *Black Boy (American Hunger): A Record of Childhood and Youth* (New York: Harper Perennial, 1944, 2020), 272.

In Houston, a campaign: Marie-Amélie George, "Framing Trans Rights," *Northwestern University Law Review* 13, no. 3 (2019): 178–97; Manny Fernandez and Alan Blinder, "Houston Rights Measure Is Undone by a Strategy Built around Bathrooms," *New York Times*, November 5, 2015, A17.

Two-thirds of transgender . . . discrimination, you know: Jaime Grant, Lisa Mottet, and Justin Tanis, "Injustice at Every Turn: A Report of the National Transgender Discrimination Survey," National Center for Transgender Equality and National Gay and Lesbian Task Force, 2016.

108   **Not long before, a landmark:** David Broockman and Joshua Kalla, "Durably Reducing Transphobia: A Field Experiment on Door-to-Door Canvassing," *Science* 352, no. 6282 (2016): 220–24. Note: The study was carried out during a canvassing operation in Florida run by the Lab and SAVE, a Miami LGBT organization, in order to test the effects of the Lab's innovative canvassing techniques.

   The findings "stand alone": Elizabeth Levy Paluck, "How to Overcome Prejudice," *Science* 352, no. 6282 (2016): 147.

   "They blew me away": Author interview with David Broockman (assistant professor, Stanford University), June 6, 2016.

   While only one-tenth of . . . 1998 to 2012.: Broockman and Kalla, "Durably Reducing Transphobia."

110   **More than 70 percent:** Author visit, interview with Dave Fleischer (director, Leadership Lab, Los Angeles LGBT Center), May 9, 2016.

   With a glance.: Brent Hughes et al., "Neural Adaptation to Faces Reveals Racial Outgroup Homogeneity Effects in Early Perception," *Proceedings of the National Academy of Sciences* 116, no. 29 (July 16, 2019): 14532–37.

   Seeing a face brings to life: Jennifer Kubota, Mahzarin Banaji, and Elizabeth Phelps, "The Neuroscience of Race," *Nature Neuroscience* 15, no. 7 (2012): 940–48.

   Register an in-group . . . fall quiet.: Alexandra Golby et al., "Differential Responses in the Fusiform Region to Same-Race and Other-Race Faces," *Nature Neuroscience* 4, no. 8 (2001): 845–50.

   Encountering people we see . . .and human-like.): Kurt Hugenberg et al., "The Face of Humanity: Configural Face Processing Influences Ascriptions of Humanness," *Social Psychological and Personality Science* 7, no. 2 (2016): 167–75. Also author interview with Kurt Hugenberg (professor of psychological and brain sciences, Indiana University), July 15, 2016.

   In contrast, a face from an out-group: Kerry Kawakami et al., "An Eye for the I: Preferential Attention to the Eyes of Ingroup Members," *Attitudes and Social Cognition* 107, no. 1 (2014): 1–20; Kerry Kawakami et al., "Impact of Perceived Interpersonal Similarity on Attention to the Eyes of Same-Race and Other-Race Faces," *Cognitive Research* 6, no. 68 (2021): 1–16.

   ten times better memory: Golby, "Differential Responses in the Fusiform Region," 846.

   "cognitive disregard": Kurt Hugenberg and Donald Sacco, "Social Categorization and Stereotyping: How Social Categorization Biases Person Perception and Face Memory," *Social and Personality Psychology Compass* 2, no. 2 (2008): 1052–72.

111   **"may not be 'faces'. . . same intensity":** Kubota, "The Neuroscience of Race," 943.

111   **While their brains were monitored:** Luca Vizioli, Guillaume Rousselet, and Roberto Caldara, "Neural Repetition Suppression to Identity Is Abolished by Other-Race Faces," *Proceedings of the National Academy of Sciences* 107, no. 46 (November 16, 2010): 20081–86.

the "category level": Kubota, "The Neuroscience of Race," 943. See also Kurt Hugenberg et al., "Social Categorization Influences Face Perception and Face Memory," in *Oxford Handbook of Face Perception*, ed. Andrew Calder et al. (New York: Oxford University Press, 2011), 245–61.

can occur in virtual realms: Nicholas Epley and Justin Kruger, "When What You Type Isn't What They Read: The Perseverance of Stereotypes and Expectancies over E-Mail," *Journal of Experimental Social Psychology* 41 (2005): 414–22.

The only time I really saw … as individuals.: Richard Nixon quoted in Jonathan Aitken, *Nixon: A Life* (Washington, DC: Regnery, 1994), 78. Aitken cites as an original source Richard Nixon, *Dictated Recollections of Early Years*, 1975, Folio F, 22–23.

step away from dehumanization: Brittany Cassidy et al., "Configural Face Processing Impacts Race Disparities in Humanization and Trust," *Journal of Experimental Social Psychology* 73 (2017): 111–24.

112   **In the 1963 series:** Henri Tajfel and A. L. Wilkes, "Classification and Quantitative Judgement," *British Journal of Psychology* 54, no. 2 (1963): 101–14.

"simplified exercise in stereotyping": Tajfel and Wilkes, "Classification and Quantitative Judgement," 113.

His findings help explain. . . to be more racially mixed: Juliana Horowitz, "Report: Americans See Advantages and Challenges in Country's Growing Racial and Ethnic Diversity," Pew Research Center, May 8, 2019, 5–6, 11.

They were just a mass … rest of us: Richard Nixon quoted in Aitken, *Nixon: A Life*, 78.

a reluctant proponent: Dean Kotlowski, *Nixon's Civil Rights: Politics, Principles, and Policy* (Cambridge, MA: Harvard University Press, 2001).

banned gay marriage: The California ban lasted until 2013 when a U.S. Supreme Court ruling paved the way for a 2022 law mandating federal recognition of same-sex marriage. "A Time Line of the Legalization of Same Sex Marriage in the US," Georgetown Law Library, https://guides.ll.georgetown. edu/c.php?g=592919&p=4182201.

113   **Touching down in Los Angeles:** Author interview with Dave Fleischer, April 15, 2016; Author visit, interview with Dave Fleischer, May 9, 2016.

"We were clinging to them": Author interview with Laura Gardiner (national mentoring coordinator, Leadership Lab), April 29, 2016.

113   *Gay couples are honoring . . . a lot less visible?:* Quotes from a March 7, 2009, Lab canvassing script, one of several shared with the author by Dave Fleischer, 2016.

failing to lower their bias: Author e-mail communication with Dave Fleischer, December 27, 2022.

"How nice it would be . . . more empty.": Socrates, *Symposium*, in *Plato in Twelve Volumes*, trans. Harold N. Fowler (Cambridge, MA: Harvard University Press, 1925), 9:175d–e.

Then in the fall of 2009: Video of Ernest–Fleischer conversation provided to the author by the Leadership Lab, June 29, 2016.

114   **Recall how incompletely we:** Kawakami, "An Eye for the I."

115   **Lab threw out 75 percent of its work:** Author interview with Dave Fleischer, June 29, 2016.

"So we're going to be: All quotes related to the training session are from author visit, interviews with participants and Leadership Lab staff, May 7, 2016.

117   **"Being willing to enter . . . deep canvassing":** Author interview with Dave Fleischer, March 23, 2022.

By holding up another point: Joshua Kalla and David Broockman, "Which Narrative Strategies Durably Reduce Prejudice? Evidence from Field and Survey Experiments Supporting the Efficacy of Perspective-Getting," *American Journal of Political Science* 67, no. 1 (2023): 185–204. This paper attributes changes of mind to "perspective-getting," or telling an out-group story to a voter. In Kalla and Broockman's view, this type of narrative activates mechanisms such as self–other merging and attributional thinking, that is, understanding the other's experience. This process is essentially what I witnessed and what can be thought of as the gateway to perspective taking.

118   **Picture a day in the life:** Andrew Todd, Adam Galinsky, and Galen Bodenhausen, "Perspective Taking Undermines Stereotype Maintenance Processes: Evidence from Social Memory, Behavior Explanation and Information Solicitation," *Social Cognition* 30, no. 1 (2012): 94–108.

promising counterpoint to prejudice: Andrew Todd and Adam Galinsky, "Perspective-Taking as a Strategy for Improving Intergroup Relations: Evidence, Mechanisms, and Qualifications," *Social and Personality Psychology* 8, no. 7 (2014): 374–87; William Cox and Patricia Devine, "The Prejudice Habit-Breaking Intervention: An Empowerment-Based Confrontation Approach," in *Confronting Prejudice and Discrimination: The Science of Changing Minds and Behaviors*, ed. Robyn Mallett and Margo Monteith (London: Academic Press, 2019), 249–74.

made all the more difficult: Claudia Sassenrath, Sara Hodges, and Stefan Pfattheicher, "It's All about the Self: When Perspective Taking Backfires," *Current Directions in Psychological Science* 25, no. 6 (2016): 405–10. Imagining the view of an opponent can even make him seem more threatening.

118   **By taking a few minutes:** Cynthia Wang et al., "Perspective-Taking Increases Willingness to Engage in Intergroup Contact," *PLoS One* 9, no. 1 (2014): e856681. Note: Part of this study took place in Singapore. C. Daniel Batson et al., "Empathy, Attitudes and Action: Can Feeling for a Member of a Stigmatized Group Motivate One to Help the Group?," *Personality and Social Psychology Bulletin* 28, no. 12 (2002): 1656–66.

       refugee fleeing a war-torn country: Claire Adida, Adeline Lo, and Melina Platas, "Perspective Taking Can Promote Short-Term Inclusionary Behavior toward Syrian Refugees," *Proceedings of the National Academy of Sciences* 115, no. 38 (September 4, 2018): 9521–26. See also Gábor Simonovits, Gábor Kézdi, and Péter Kardos, "Seeing the World through the Other's Eye: An Online Intervention Reducing Ethnic Prejudice," *American Political Science Review* 112, no. 1 (2017): 186–93. The latter study used a perspective-taking game to reduce prejudice against Roma in Hungary.

       By imagining the viewpoint of an elderly: Adam Galinsky and Gordon Moskowitz, "Perspective-Taking: Decreasing Stereotype Expression, Stereotype Accessibility and In-Group Favoritism," *Journal of Personality and Social Psychology* 78, no. 4 (2000): 708–24. This effect is called "self–other merger."

119   **warmth toward transgender people rose:** Broockman and Kalla, "Durably Reducing Transphobia."

       Later studies will reveal: Joshua Kalla and David Broockman, "Reducing Exclusionary Attitudes through Interpersonal Conversation: Evidence from Three Field Experiments," *American Political Science Review* 114, no. 2 (2020): 410–25.

       translating their efforts: Kalla and Broockman, "Which Narrative Strategies," 1. See also Jennifer Medina, "A New Strategy to Persuade Voters: Listen Carefully. And Don't Hurry," *New York Times*, October 20, 2021, A22.

120   **Lab's pioneers are changed:** Interview with Laura Gardiner, April 29, 2016, and author visit, interview with Gardiner, May 7, 2016; author visit, interview with Steve Deline, May 7, 2016.

       lowers activists' *own* animosity: Joshua Kalla and David Broockman, "Voter Outreach Campaigns Can Reduce Affective Polarization among Implementing Political Activists: Evidence from Inside Three Campaigns," *American Political Science Review* 116, no. 4 (2022): 1516–22.

       most large cities and a rising proportion: Stephen Menendian, Samir Gambhir, and Arthur Gailes, "The Roots of Structural Racism: Twenty-First Century Racial Residential Segregation in the United States," Othering & Belonging Institute/University of California, Berkeley, June 30, 2021, https://belonging.berkeley.edu/roots-structural-racism#footnoteref1_hu hayiq; Domenico Parisi, Daniel Lichter, and Michael Taquino, "Remaking Metropolitan America? Residential Mobility and Racial Integration in the Suburbs," *Socius* 5 (2019): 1–18.

120   **Meanwhile, nearly one-third of U.S. students:** National Center for Education Statistics/Digest of Education Statistics, "Number and Percentage Distribution of Public Elementary and Secondary School Students by Percentage of Minority Enrollment in the School and Student's Racial/Ethnic Group, Fall 1995 through Fall 2019," Table 216.50; author e-mail communication with Grady Wilburn (statistician, National Center for Education Statistics), February 17–18, 2022.

In the melting pot: Halley Potter and Kimberly Quick, "A New Wave of School Integration," The Century Foundation, February 9, 2016.

"moving toward two societies . . . separate and unequal": National Advisory Commission on Civil Disorders, report, February 29, 1968, 1, https://www.ncjrs.gov/pdffiles1/Digitization/8073NCJRS.pdf.

That same week, the ranks of: Robert Jones, "Self-Segregation: Why It's So Hard for Whites to Understand Ferguson," *The Atlantic*, August 21, 2014, citing an American Values Survey by the Public Religion Research Institute, 2016.

Nearly a decade and a: Carroll Doherty, "Deep Divisions in Americans' Views of the Nation's Racial History and How to Address It," Pew Research Center, August 12, 2021, 5–7.

121   **polarization has risen in democracies:** Thomas Carothers and Andrew O'Donohue, eds., *Democracies Divided: The Global Challenge of Political Polarization* (Washington, DC: Brookings Institution Press, 2019). See also Levi Boxell et al., "Cross-Country Trends in Affective Polarization," NBER Working Paper No. 26669, November 2021.

opposite party as "selfish": Shanto Iyengar, Gaurav Sood, and Yphtach Lelkes, "Affect, Not Ideology: A Social Identity Perspective on Polarization," *Public Opinion Quarterly* 76, no. 3 (2012): 405–31.

few or no good ideas: Carroll Doherty, Jocelyn Kiley, and Nida Asheer, "Partisan Antipathy: More Intense, More Personal," Pew Research Center, October 2019, 12.

Given the chance, members: Shanto Iyengar, "Fear and Loathing across Party Lines: New Evidence on Group Polarization," *American Journal of Political Science* 59, no. 3 (July 2015): 690–707, esp. 699.

"The nigger, the fag, . . . in the tribe.": Ta-Nehisi Coates, *Between the World and Me* (New York: Spiegel and Grau, 2015), 60.

According to a sixteen-nation study: Paul Beck and Mariano Torcal, "Discussion Network Contributions to Affective Polarization," Working Paper, December 2022. Note: Similarity in views is measured as shared support for a party or country leader. Nearly one-half of U.S. voters were in complete accord with their two closest confidantes on the 2020 presidential election, up from one-third of Americans in 2016. Also author e-mail communications with Paul Beck, January 28 and 31 and December 27, 2022.

121   **Only 25 percent of Americans discuss:** Keith Hampton et al., "Social Isolation and New Technology: How the Internet and Mobile Phones Impact Americans' Social Networks," Pew Internet and American Life Project, November 2009, 27. See also Diana Mutz, *Hearing the Other Side: Deliberative Versus Participatory Democracy* (Cambridge: Cambridge University Press, 2006), 41. Note: Studies suggest that people tend to interpret the word *discuss* similarly whether or not the context is online.

Our core networks are: Miller McPherson, Lynn Smith-Lovin, and Matthew Brashears, "Social Isolation in America: Changes in Core Discussion Networks over Two Decades," *American Sociological Review* 71, no. 3 (June 2006): 353–75.

"closing in" on themselves: McPherson et al., "Social Isolation in America," 371.

discuss important matters with: Keith Hampton, "Social Isolation and New Technology," 7, 23–24.

nicknamed the Big Sort: Bill Bishop, *The Big Sort: Why the Clustering of Like-Minded America Is Tearing Us Apart* (New York: Houghton Mifflin, 2008).

By 2020, nearly 60 percent: Bill Bishop, "For Most Americans, the Local Presidential Vote Was a Landslide," *Daily Yonder*, December 17, 2020, https://dailyyonder.com/for-most-americans-the-local-presidential-vote-was-a-landslide/2020/12/17.

Online, many people are exposed: Pablo Barberá, "Social Media, Echo Chambers and Political Polarization," in *Social Media and Democracy: The State of the Field and Prospects for Reform*, ed. Nathaniel Persily and Joshua Tucker (Cambridge: Cambridge University Press, 2020), 34–55.

noise made by extremists: Chris Bail, *Breaking the Social Media Prism: How to Make Our Platforms Less Polarizing* (Princeton, NJ: Princeton University Press, 2019), 10.

Fewer than one-fifth of social media users: Kyle Heatherly, Yanqin Lu, and Jae Kook Lee, "Filtering Out the Other Side? Cross-Cutting and Like-Minded Discussions on Social Networking Sites," *New Media and Society* 19, no. 8 (2017): 1271–89. Also author e-mail communication with Kyle Heatherly (PhD candidate in mass communication, Indiana University), February 2, 2022.

An estimated four in five Facebook: Eytan Bakshy, Solomon Messing, and Lada Adamic, "Exposure to Ideologically Diverse News and Opinion on Facebook," *Science* 348, no. 623 (2015): 1130–32. Note: This is among those who reveal their political affiliations.

equal proportion of retweets: Pablo Barberá, "Birds of the Same Feather Tweet Together: Bayesian Ideal Point Estimation Using Twitter Data," *Political Analysis* 23 (2015): 76–91.

122   **law of group polarization:** Tajfel and Wilkes, "Classification and Quantitative Judgement."

122   **Across society, proximity:** For an example of this effect among judges, see Cass Sunstein, "The Law of Group Polarization," *Journal of Political Philosophy* 10, no. 2 (2002): 175–95.

positive feelings for the in-party: Doherty et al., "Partisan Antipathy," 23–24.

comparing virtual and in-person first meetings: Bradley Okdie et al., "Getting to Know You: Face-to-Face versus Online Interactions," *Computers in Human Behavior* 27 (2011): 153–59.

awkwardness anticipated in real-time conversation: Amit Kumar and Nicholas Epley, "It's Surprisingly Nice to Hear You: Misunderstanding the Impact of Communications Media Can Lead to Sub-Optimal Choices of How to Connect with Each Other," *Journal of Experimental Psychology* 150, No. 3 (2021): 595–607.

tend to focus more often on themselves: Suzanne Weisband and Leanne Atwater, "Evaluating Self and Others in Electronic and Face-to-Face Groups," *Journal of Applied Psychology,* 84, no. 4 (1999): 632–39.

overestimate the clarity and frequency: Justin Kruger et al., "Egocentrism over Email: Can We Communicate as Well as We Think?," *Journal of Personality and Social Psychology* 89, no. 6 (2005): 925–36. See also Weisband and Atwater, "Evaluating Self and Others in Electronic and Face-to-Face Groups."

123   **When political scientist Diana Mutz:** Mutz, *Hearing the Other Side*, 69–74.

support the reviled group's right: Diana Mutz, "Cross-Cutting Networks: Testing Democratic Theory in Practice," *American Political Science Review* 96, no. 1 (2002): 111–26.

Even a brief crosscutting: Eran Amsalem, Eric Merkley, and Peter John Loewen, "Does Talking to the Other Side Reduce Inter-Party Hostility? Evidence from Three Studies," *Political Communication* 39, no. 1 (2021): 61–78.

discussed what they disliked: Erik Santoro and David Broockman, "The Promise and Pitfalls of Cross-Partisan Conversations for Reducing Affective Polarization: Evidence from Randomized Experiments," *Science Advances* 8 (2022): eabn5515.

who regularly experience debate: Casey Klofstad, Anand Sokhey, and Scott McClurg, "Disagreeing about Disagreement: How Conflict in Social Networks Affects Political Behavior," *American Journal of Political Science* 57, no. 1 (2013): 120–34. See also Amsalem et al., "Does Talking to the Other Side Reduce Inter-Party Hostility?," 4.

And who are these: Mutz, *Hearing the Other Side*, 33.

"If they saw more … systematic half-thinkers.": John Stuart Mill, "Bentham," in John Stuart Mill, *Mill on Bentham and Coleridge* (London: Chatto & Windus, 1838, 1950), 65.

124   **"the antithesis of open-mindedness and tolerance," "a form of prejudice":** Mutz, *Hearing the Other Side*, 128–29.

show more hostility: Doherty, "Partisan Antipathy," 6. See also Kalla and Broockman, "Voter Outreach Campaigns Can Reduce Affective Polarization among Implementing Political Activists."

less **likely in daily life:** Mutz, *Hearing the Other Side*, 16, 32. See also Heatherly et al., "Filtering Out the Other Side?," 1271–89.

mentally rigid and impulsive: Leor Zmigrod, "The Cognitive and Perceptual Correlates of Ideological Attitudes: A Data-Driven Approach," *Philosophical Transactions of the Royal Society B* 376 (2021): 20200424.

no less likely to join a protest: Klofstad et al., "Disagreeing about Disagreement," 128, 132.

Social diversity leads to: Mutz, *Hearing the Other Side*, 123.

"complete thinkers": Mill, "Bentham," 65.

125   **Merchants, women, travelers:** Bettany Hughes, *The Hemlock Cup: Socrates, Athens and the Search for the Good Life* (New York: Random House, 2010), 161–62. See also James Whitley, *The Archeology of Ancient Greece* (Cambridge: Cambridge University Press, 2001), 191, 331–37, 359.

"all things are possible": Quoted in Herodotus, *The Histories*, trans. A. D. Godley (Cambridge, MA: Harvard University Press, 1920), 3.80.6.

"It's this that will ... so in the future.": Socrates, *The Apology*, in *Plato in Twelve Volumes*, trans. Harold N. Fowler (Cambridge, MA: Harvard University Press, 2014): 1:28a–28b.

erected a bronze statue: Hughes, *The Hemlock Cup*, 71–74, 354.

"Aren't mistakes . . . one does not": Plato, *Alcibiades*, in *Plato in Twelve Volumes*, trans. W. R. M. Lamb (Cambridge, MA: Harvard University Press, 1986), 12:117d.

"What is virtue": *Meno*, in *The Collected Dialogues of Plato, Including the Letters*, ed. Edith Hamilton and Huntington Cairns, trans. W. K. C. Guthrie (Princeton, NJ: Princeton University Press, 1961), 79c.

Socrates ambled through the: Kostas Vlassopoulos, "Free Spaces: Identity, Experience, and Democracy in Classical Athens," *The Classical Quarterly* 57, no. 1 (2007): 33–52, esp. 40–42; Karl Jaspers, *The Great Philosophers: Socrates, Buddha, Confucius, Jesus* (New York: Harcourt, Brace and World, 1962, 1995), 31.

"performing my Herculean labors": *The Apology*, in *Plato in Twelve Volumes*, 1:22a.

"They told me in plain truth ... perplexity I feel myself.": *Meno*, in Hamilton and Cairns, *The Collected Dialogues of Plato*, 80a–c.

126   **He founded no party ... no disciples.:** Jaspers, *Great Philosophers*, 17. See also James Miller, *Examined Lives: From Socrates to Nietzsche* (New York: Farrar, Straus and Giroux, 2011), 23.

    Greek Miracle began to falter: Hughes, *The Hemlock Cup*, 16, 262.

    It was the late summer: Hughes, *The Hemlock Cup*, 306–8; Xenophon, *Hellenica* 1.7.16–33, 1.7.11–13, trans. C. L. Brownson (Cambridge, MA: Harvard University Press, 1918); Donald Kagan, *The Peloponnesian War* (New York: Penguin Books, 2003): 463–66; Plato, *Apology* 32b–d, in *Plato in Twelve Volumes.*

    "Talk to and teach each other": *Apology*, 19d2, translated by Robert Sobak, "Sokrates among the Shoemakers," *Hesperia* 84 (2015): 669–712, 698.

127   **"misses the meat . . . *is* disagreement":** Author interview with David Broockman, April 6, 2022.

    Not long ago, twenty-two liberals: Jeroen van Baar et al., "Intolerance of Uncertainty Modulates Brain-to-Brain Synchrony during Politically Polarized Perception," *Proceedings of the National Academy of Sciences* 118, no. 20 (2021): e2022491118.

    She was a sharecropper's daughter: Virginia Bridges, "Durham Civil Rights Activist Ann Atwater Dies at 80," *The News & Observer*, Durham, NC, June 20, 2016.

128   **died on average by age forty:** Osha Gray Davidson, *The Best of Enemies: Race and Redemption in the New South* (Chapel Hill: University of North Carolina Press, 1996, 2007), 38. The book is an excellent source on the story.

    "had it at the heart": Ann Atwater, "Extended Interview with Ann Atwater," Robert Korstad (emeritus professor of public policy and history, Duke University), no date given, in "Ann Atwater Archive," School for Conversion, https://www.schoolforconversion.org/extended-interview-with-ann-atwater.

    group's reportedly most active state: Sociologist John Salter quoted in Robert Korstad and James Leloudis, *To Right These Wrongs: The North Carolina Fund and the Battle to End Poverty and Inequality in 1960s America* (Chapel Hill: University of North Carolina Press, 2011), 314.

    "We was caught in this web together": Ann Atwater interviewed in "An Unlikely Friendship," documentary directed by Diane Bloom (Durham, NC: Alexander Street Press, Filmmakers Library, 2003).

    I met Atwater at: Author visit, interviews with Ann Atwater (Housing Rights Activist, Durham, NC), April 22 and 24, 2016.

    "the whole world was openin' up": C. P. Ellis, oral history interview, in Studs Terkel, *American Dreams Lost and Found* (New York: Pantheon, 1980), 209.

129   **"That's when I began ... to me inside.":** Terkel, *American Dreams*, 205.

    "As we protest ... friendship and understanding.": Martin Luther King Jr., "A Creative Protest," in *The Papers of Martin Luther King Jr.: Threshold of a New*

Decade, January 1959–December 1960, ed. Clayborne Carson et al. (Berkeley: University of California Press, 2005), 5:367–70.

129 **After she invited a:** Davidson, *The Best of Enemies*, 279–81.

130 ***What do you think . . . what he thinks!*:** Atwater quoted in Davidson, *The Best of Enemies*, 280–81.

"sheer capacity to begin": Hannah Arendt, "What Is Freedom," in *Between Past and Future* (New York: Penguin Books, 2006): 146–47, 169. See also Kimberley Curtis, *Our Sense of the Real: Aesthetic Experience and Arendtian Politics* (Ithaca, NY: Cornell University Press, 1999), 138–55. Curtis offers a helpful discussion of how Atwater's actions fit into Arendt's views.

"Some say that . . . thought was right.": C. P. Ellis quoted in Davidson, *The Best of Enemies*, 286.

one of the most powerful antidotes: J. Nicole Shelton, Jennifer Richeson, and John Dovidio, "Biases in Interracial Interactions: Implications for Social Policy" in *Behavioral Foundations of Public Policy*, ed. Eldar Shafir (Princeton, NJ: Princeton University Press, 2012), 32–51. See also Elizabeth Levy Paluck, Seth Green, and Donald Green, "The Contact Hypothesis Re-Evaluated," *Behavioural Public Policy* 3, no. 2 (2019): 129–58, and Elizabeth Levy Paluck, "Prejudice Reduction: Progress and Challenges," *Annual Review of Psychology* 72 (2021): 532–60.

Roommates of differing races: Colette Van Laar et al., "The Effect of University Roommate Contact on Ethnic Attitudes and Behavior," *Journal of Experimental Social Psychology* 41 (2005): 329–45.

classmates from historically adversarial: Alexandra Scacco and Shana Warren, "Can Social Contact Reduce Prejudice and Discrimination? Evidence from a Field Experiment in Nigeria," *American Political Science Review* 112, no. 3 (2018): 654–77. After some interventions, like this one, participants show continued bias in attitude surveys yet less overall discrimination and higher tolerance toward the out-group. The findings underscore that contact is not a panacea but is linked to crucial progress in lowering prejudice.

131 **"Thank God I got to . . . look past labels.":** C.P. Ellis quoted in Terkel, *American Dreams*, 205.

For if contact and discourse: Oliver Christ et al., "Contextual Effect of Positive Intergroup Contact on Outgroup Prejudice," *Proceedings of the National Academy of Sciences* 111, no. 11 (2014): 3996–4000; Rose Meleady et al., "On the Generalization of Intergroup Contact: A Taxonomy of Transfer Effects," *Current Directions in Psychological Science* 28, no. 5 (2019): 430–35.

different but similarly maligned categories: Thomas Pettigrew, "Secondary Transfer Effect of Contact: Do Intergroup Contact Effects Spread to Noncontacted Outgroups?," *Social Psychology*, 40, no. 2 (2009): 55–65.

131   **Just having a friend:** Magdalena Wojcieszak and Benjamin Warner, "Can Interparty Contact Reduce Affective Polarization? A Systematic Test of Different Forms of Intergroup Contact," *Political Communication* 37, no. 6 (2020): 789–811.

pairing of roommates across race: Van Laar, "The Effect of University Roommate Contact," 337.

"Ann's presence and her tolerance . . . fellow man.": All further quotes from Stewart are from author visit, interview with Ed Stewart (president/chief executive officer, UDI-Community Development Corporation), April 22, 2016.

CHAPTER 6

133   **"No one individual . . . nature of things.":** Aristotle, *Metaphysics,* 993a28–b2, quoted in Robert Sobak, "Sokrates among the Shoemakers," *Hesperia* 84 (2015): 669–712, 672.

receive a public reprimand: John Noble Wilford, "Skylab Astronauts Are Reprimanded in First Day Aboard," *New York Times,* November 18, 1973. See also Henry Cooper, *A House in Space* (New York: Holt, Rinehart and Winston, 1976), 38.

"straight words": Jerry Carr quoted in W. David Compton and Charles Benson, *Living and Working in Space: A History of Skylab* (Washington, DC: NASA, 1983), 327.

"Commander Out.": Cooper, *A House in Space,* 129.

134   **attained mythical status:** Author e-mail communication with a former space shuttle flight director who spoke on condition of anonymity, November 16, 2020.

"prize fights," "nice, crisp . . . operations mentality": Neil B. Hutchinson interviewed by Kevin Rusnak, NASA Johnson Space Center Oral History Project, Houston, TX, June 5, 2000, 14, 17. Hereafter, all quotes by Hutchinson are from this oral history unless otherwise indicated.

no time to acclimate: John Uri, "NASA History: The Real Story of the Skylab 4 'Strike' in Space," November 16, 2020, https://www.nasa.gov/feature/the-real-story-of-the-skylab-4-strike-in-space. Note: There were four total Skylab missions: one unmanned rocket launch called Skylab 1 and then three missions with astronauts aboard. Thus, the third crewed mission was called Skylab 4.

double the number of science experiments: Henry Cooper, "A Reporter at Large: Life in a Space Station," *The New Yorker,* August 30, 1976, 76, 54.

"Everything pushed back onto this last mission": Author interview with Brian Odom (then acting, now NASA chief historian), January 28, 2021.

134 **left in something of a mess:** Thomas Canby, *Skylab, Outpost on the Frontier of Space* (Washington, DC: National Geographic Society, 1974), 464.

they sometimes had just ten minutes: Cooper, "A Reporter at Large," 59.

135 **"I don't know ... being pushed.":** Charles Berry quoted in Reuters, "Lethargy of Skylab 3 Crew Is Studied," *New York Times*, December 12, 1973, 14. Note: This article erroneously calls the crew "Skylab 3."

One morning, the astronauts: Skylab astronaut Edward Gibson interviewed by Carol Butler, December 1, 2000, Houston, TX, NASA Johnson Space Center Oral History Project, 18.

of holding a strike: Edward Gibson quoted in the documentary *Searching for Skylab: America's Forgotten Triumph*, directed by Dwight Steven-Boniecki (1080 Virtual Media Consulting, 2019).

"It's been my ... most efficient pace": Jerry Carr quoted in "Skylab Air-to-Ground Voice Transcription," Tape 365-02/T-535 (December 30, 1973), 6/2808.

"cogs in the wheel": Author interview with Brian Odom, January 28, 2021.

The crew tried half a dozen times: Compton and Benson, *Living and Working in Space*, 322–24.

They received no reply: Compton and Benson, *Living and Working in Space*, 327.

"We'd like to be in on the conversation": Carr quoted in Cooper, *A House in Space*, 129.

136 **stack the deck against difference:** Byungkyu Lee and Peter Bearman, "Political Isolation in America," *Network Science Special Issue: Ego Networks* 8, no. 3 (2020): 333–55. Also author e-mail communication with Byungkyu Lee (assistant professor of sociology, Indiana University), January 20, 2021.

Despite the increased presence: John-Paul Ferguson and Rembrand Koning, "Firm Turnover and the Return of Racial Establishment Segregation," *American Sociological Review* 83, no. 3 (2018): 445–74. Also author e-mail communication with John-Paul Ferguson (associate professor of organizational behavior, McGill University), January 20, 2021.

In the U.S. high-tech sector: U.S. Equal Employment Opportunity Commission, "Diversity in High Tech," report based on 2014 statistics, accessed February 2, 2023, https://www.eeoc.gov/special-report/diversity-high-tech.

"hire for fit": In-Sue Oh et al., "Do Birds of a Feather Flock, Fly, and Continue to Fly Together?," *Journal of Organizational Behavior* 39 (2018): 1347–66.

Employees even cluster along: Joseph Chancellor et al., "Clustering by Well-Being in Workplace Social Networks: Homophily and Social Contagion," *Emotion* 17, no. 8 (2017): 1166–80.

136   **"Dirt finds dirt . . . never fails":** Homer, *The Odyssey*, trans. Robert Fagles (New York: Penguin Books, 1996), 17.237.

137   **"an incarnation of . . . skeptical investigator":** René Nünlist, "'If in Truth You Are Odysseus': Distrust and Persuasion in the *Odyssey*," *Symbolae Osloenses* 89, no. 1 (2015): 2–24, esp. 24.

  It wasn't long after trading: Sheen S. Levine et al., "Ethnic Diversity Deflates Price Bubbles," *Proceedings of the National Academy of Sciences* 52 (2014): 18524–29. Note: Since stock trading often involves subjective judgments, participants in Levine's study instead traded financial assets with a known distribution of returns, a condition that made it possible for them to calculate expected value with ease. This allowed the scientists to gain a more precise read on how the traders performed.

  "unmitigated celebration": Alejandro Portes, "Downsides of Social Capital," *Proceedings of the National Academy of Sciences* 111, no. 52 (December 2014): 18407–8.

  "make sure they understood . . . what they do": Author interview with Sheen S. Levine (assistant professor of organizations, strategy, and international management, University of Texas at Dallas), February 22, 2021. Hereafter, all quotes by Levine are from this interview unless otherwise indicated.

138   **"mechanical solidarity":** Émile Durkheim, *The Division of Labor in Society* (New York: Free Press, 2014), 57.

  the "delusion of homogeneity": Katherine Phillips and Evan Apfelbaum, "Delusions of Homogeneity? Reinterpreting the Effects of Group Diversity," in *Looking Back, Moving Forward: A Review of Group and Team-Based Research* (Bingley: Emerald Group Publishing, 2012), 15:185–207.

  "operates with a specific kind of logic": Michael Tomasello, "The Origins of Human Morality," *Scientific American* 319, no. 3 (September 2018): 70–75.

139   **Even the dynamics of conversation:** Rachel Nuwer, "People Literally Don't Know When to Shut Up—or Keep Talking—Science Confirms," *Scientific American*, March 1, 2021, https://www.scientificamerican.com/article /people-literally-dont-know-when-to-shut-up-or-keep-talking-science-con firms. Adam Mastroianni et al., "Do Conversations End When People Want Them To?," *Proceedings of the National Academy of Sciences* 118, no. 10 (2021): 1–9.

  "We're going to . . . neuroscience of two": Author interview with Joy Hirsch (professor of psychiatry and professor of comparative medicine and neuroscience, Yale University School of Medicine), April 1, 2021. Hereafter, all quotes by Hirsch are from this interview.

  first neuroimaging studies of live: Joy Hirsch et al., "Interpersonal Agreement and Disagreement during Face-to-Face Dialogue: An fNIRS Investigation," *Frontiers in Human Neuroscience* 14 (2021): 606397.

140   **brains showed the same unique patterns:** Beau Sievers et al., "How Consensus-Building Conversation Changes Our Minds and Aligns Our Brains," unpublished working paper. Also author e-mail communication with Adam Kleinbaum, November 12, 2020.

141   **"There is no feeling . . . in another":** Maurice Herzog, *Annapurna* (Guilford, CT: Lyons Press, 1950), 26.

　　　Such intense cooperation . . . less so on individualism.: H. C. Triandis, *Individualism and Collectivism* (London: Routledge, 1995, 2018). Country data is from the firm started by pioneering collectivism researcher Geert Hofstede, Hofstede Insights, https://www.hofstede-insights.com/country-comparison. See also Jackson Lu, Peter Jin, and Alexander English, "Collectivism Predicts Mask Use during COVID-19," *Proceedings of the National Academy of Sciences* 118, no. 23 (2021): e2021793118, https://doi.org/10.1073/pnas.2021793118.

　　　From 1950 to 2013: Jennifer Chatman et al., "Blurred Lines: How the Collectivism Norm Operates through Perceived Group Diversity to Boost or Harm Group Performance in Himalayan Mountain Climbing," *Organization Science* 30, no. 2 (2019): 235–59.

　　　Such a range of experience: Chatman et al., "Blurred Lines."

142   *conjunctive* **group task:** Stefan Schulz-Hardt and Felix Brodbeck, "Group Performance and Leadership," in *Introduction to Social Psychology*, ed. Miles Hewstone et al. (Berlin: Springer, 2012), 265–89, esp. 267–68.

　　　Mountaineering teams must closely: Julie Rak, "Social Climbing on Annapurna: Gender in High-Altitude Mountaineering Narratives," *English Studies in Canada* 33, no. 1 (2008): 109–46.

　　　"overly cooperative": Jennifer Chatman quoted in Laura Counts, "Himalayan Climber Research Nets Outstanding Paper Award," Stanford University press release, July 8, 2020.

　　　"you'll want to learn from others": Craig Connally, *The Mountaineering Handbook: Modern Tools and Techniques That Will Take You to the Top* (Camden, ME: Ragged Mountain Press/McGraw-Hill, 2004), 342.

　　　Your space vessel crash-landed . . . get back?: Chatman et al., "Blurred Lines."

143   **"They didn't even notice . . . that blinds you":** Author interview with Lindred Greer (professor of management and organizations, Ross School of Business, University of Michigan), January 11, 2021.

　　　collectivist collaborators have trouble: David Daniels et al., "Spillover Bias in Diversity Judgement," *Organizational Behavior and Human Decision Processes* 139 (2017): 92–105.

　　　"As soon as . . . indifferent to it.": Solomon Asch, *Social Psychology* (New York: Oxford University Press, 1987), 483.

　　　They see the world and: Phillips and Apfelbaum, "Delusions of Homogeneity?," 193.

144   **"little club":** Hutchinson interviewed by Rusnak, NASA Johnson Space Center Oral History Project, 14.

sent as much as sixty to seventy feet: Cooper, "A Reporter at Large," 128.

"We had a tough . . . have that judgment.": Gibson interviewed by Carol Butler, NASA Johnson Space Center Oral History Project, 11.

"to exercise judgment and creativity": Jerry Carr, letter to William C. Schneider, October 8, 1975, in William Schneider, "Skylab Lessons Learned as Applicable to a Large Space Station," NASA Technical Memorandum (Washington, DC: NASA, 1976), 152.

"people in our line . . . look around you": Cooper, *House in Space*, 167–68.

145   **But after Carr's salvo:** Cooper, *House in Space*, 87–88.

"It took that to hit us on the head": Skylab CapComm Bob Crippen quoted in David Hitt, Owen Garriott, and Joe Kerwin *Homesteading Space: The Skylab Story* (Lincoln: University of Nebraska Press, 2008), 360.

"I understand now why . . . fire-house pace.": Carr quoted in "Skylab Air-to-Ground Voice Transcription," Tape 365-01/T-534 (December 30, 1973), 6/2800.

"to get as much done . . . on is you": Truly quoted in "Skylab Air-to-Ground Voice Transcription," Tape 365-02/T-535, 3/2805.

"We've been ready . . . play that game.": Carr, "Skylab Air-to-Ground Voice Transcription," Tape 365-02/T-535, 4/2806.

"Nobody down here has any argument . . . and your call.": Truly and Carr, "Skylab Air-to-Ground Voice Transcription," Tape 365-02/T-535, 4/2804-05.

146   **"the automaton-like existence . . . for six weeks":** Compton and Benson, *Living and Working*, 329.

"We've tried to answer . . . have it out.": Truly, "Skylab Air-to-Ground Voice Transcription," Tape 365-02/T-535, 5/2807.

"The importance of . . . place at all.": Compton and Benson, *Living and Working*, 328.

"lethargy" or "lack of enthusiasm": Reuters, "Lethargy of Skylab 3 Crew." Also anonymous reporters quoted asking about astronauts' "lack of enthusiasm" at a NASA press conference in the *Searching for Skylab* documentary.

"They ran . . . ahead of the second crew": Author interview with Edward Gibson (Skylab astronaut and science pilot), December 7, 2020.

The three completed their full allotment: Jerry Carr interviewed by Kevin Rusnak, NASA Johnson Space Center Oral History Project, Huntsville, AL, October 25, 2000, 14.

"a piano by ear": Edward Gibson, "Introduction," in *A New Sun: The Solar Results from Skylab*, by John Eddy (Washington, DC: NASA, 1979), xii–xviii.

146   **Solar data from the Skylab . . . still used by scientists today.**: Author interview with Leon Golub (senior astrophysicist, Center for Astrophysics/ Harvard-Smithsonian), January 24, 2021.

"rules our lives": Scott Kelly, *Endurance: A Year in Space, a Lifetime of Discovery* (New York: Knopf, 2017), 70–71. Also author e-mail communication with Jay Chladek (space historian), January 23, 2021.

"that's not why you're there": Author interview with Brian Odom, January 28, 2021.

topics of study at NASA: Lauren Landon, *Evidence Report: Risk of Performance and Behavioral Health Decrements due to Inadequate Cooperation, Coordination, Communication, and Psychosocial Adaptation within a Team* (Houston, TX: Lyndon B. Johnson Space Center/NASA, 2016), 7.

147   **"really taught . . . shuttle programs"**: Author interview with Emily Carney (independent space historian), December 2, 2020.

"*Decatur is a very nice town . . . Don't go there.*": Mock jurors quoted in Samuel Sommers, "On Racial Diversity and Group Decision Making: Identifying Multiple Effects of Racial Composition on Jury Deliberation," *Interpersonal Relations and Group Processes* 90, no. 4 (2006): 597–612.

Samuel Sommers, now a: Sommers, "On Racial Diversity." Also author interview with Samuel Sommers (professor of psychology, Tufts University), December 7, 2020.

"lazy information processors": Sommers, "On Racial Diversity," 609.

148   **"I think you're a plant . . . for them"**: Transcripts of experiment shared with the author by Sommers. This dialogue is from Jury 4, Juror 3, 21.

"But we never seen . . . contradicting information": Transcript of experiment shared with the author by Sommers. This dialogue is from Jury 18, Juror 4, 34, 38.

a proven distraction from group problem solving: Kathleen O'Connor and Josh Arnold, "Sabotaging the Deal: The Way Relational Concerns Undermine Negotiators," *Journal of Experimental Social Psychology* 47, no. 6 (2011): 1167–72. See also Roy Baumeister and Mark Leary, "The Need to Belong: Desire for Interpersonal Attachments as a Fundamental Human Motivation," *Psychological Bulletin* 117, no. 3 (1995): 497–529.

149   **"polluted social process"**: Solomon Asch, "Opinions and Social Pressure," *Scientific American* 193, no. 5 (1955): 31–35.

"What does that have to do with it?": Transcript from Sommers, "On Racial Diversity," Jury 4, Juror 8, 10.

Liberated from the pressures: Sarah Gaither et al., "Mere Membership in Racially Diverse Groups Reduces Conformity," *Social Psychological and Personality Science* 9, no. 4 (2018): 402–10.

149 **"Diversity is not . . . all its complexity.":** Robin Kelley, "Visualizing Race" (keynote speech at the Macalester College American Studies Conference, St. Paul, MN, February 2007).

Imagine a room filled: Author interview with Margaret Neale (professor of management, emerita, Stanford University Graduate School of Business), December 17, 2020. The subsequent quote by Neale is from this interview.

It was a landmark experiment: Katherine Phillips, Katie Liljenquist, and Margaret Neale, "Is the Pain Worth the Gain? The Advantages and Liabilities of Agreeing with Socially Distinct Newcomers," *Personality and Social Psychology Bulletin* 35, no. 3 (2009): 336–50. Note: There were two hundred and twenty total participants divided into numerous sessions.

a fictional murder mystery: Garold Stasser and William Titus, "Pooling of Unshared Information in Group Decision-Making: Biased Information Sampling during Discussion," *Journal of Personality and Social Psychology* 48, no. 6 (1985): 1467–78.

150 **"do not perceive . . . right solution":** Phillips and Apfelbaum, "Delusions of Homogeneity?," 196.

"They like it . . . less comfortable there.": Evan Apfelbaum interview by Martha Mangelsdorf, "The Trouble with Homogenous Teams," *MIT Sloan Management Review* 59, no. 2 (2018): 43–47, esp. 46.

For decades, diversity's rough edges: Cameron Klein et al., "Does Team Building Work?" *Small Group Research* 40 (2009): 181–222; interview with Lindred Greer.

151 **make people of color feel less included:** Unpublished research discussed in author interview with Lindred Greer.

Dissent has been shown to: Stefan Schulz-Hardt et al., "Group Decision Making in Hidden Profile Situations: Dissent as a Factor for Decision Quality," *Journal of Personality and Social Psychology* 91, no. 6 (2006): 1080–93.

"intensifies": Stefan Schulz-Hardt and Andreas Mojzisch, "How to Achieve Synergy in Group Decision Making: Lessons to Be Learned from the Hidden Profile Paradigm," *European Journal of Social Psychology* 23 (2012): 305–43.

In an analysis of forty years: Deborah Gruenfeld, "Status, Ideology, and Integrative Complexity on the U.S. Supreme Court: Rethinking the Politics of Political Decision Making," *Journal of Personality and Social Psychology* 68, no. 1 (1995): 5–20.

"that is wide and curious . . . deep and scrutinizing": Charlan Nemeth, *In Defense of Troublemakers: The Power of Dissent in Life and Business* (New York: Basic Books, 2010), 111.

In one of her best-known experiments: Charlan Nemeth and Julianne Kwan, "Originality of Word Associations as a Function of Majority vs. Minority Influence," *Social Psychology Quarterly* 48, no. 3 (1985): 277–82. Author e-mail communication with Charlan Nemeth (professor of psychology, University of California, Berkeley), March 4, 2021.

152   **"the jury room of people's own minds"**: Matthew Hornsey and Jolanda Jetten, "Stability and Change within Groups," in *The Oxford Handbook of Social Influence*, ed. Stephen Harkins, Kipling Williams, and Jerry Burger (Oxford: Oxford University Press, 2014), 299–315.

"Conflict is a *sine qua* . . . reflection and ingenuity": John Dewey, *Human Nature and Conduct: An Introduction to Social Psychology* (New York: Modern Library, 1922), 300.

"'We're just going to . . . and do it!'": Author interviews with Cali Williams Yost (flexible work consultant), March 6 and 29, 2021. Hereafter, all quotes from Yost are from these interviews unless otherwise indicated.

153   **"social effervescence"**: Serge Moscovici and Gabriel Mugny, "Minority Influence," in *Basic Group Processes*, ed. Paul Paulus (New York: Springer, 1983), 41–64.

Well, do you think . . . ventures a third researcher.: Mars Explorer Mission scientists quoted in Susannah Paletz, Joel Chan, and Christian Schunn, "Uncovering Uncertainty through Disagreement," *Applied Cognitive Psychology* 30, no. 3 (2016): 387–400.

one of the most innovative: A. J. S. Rayl, "The Mars Exploration Rovers Update: The Final Report," The Planetary Society, April 26, 2019, https://www .planetary.org/articles/03-mer-update-the-final-report.

154   **tools aimed at capturing for the first time**: Nale Lehmann-Willenbrock and Ming Chiu, "Igniting and Resolving Content Disagreements during Team Interactions: A Statistical Discourse Analysis of Team Dynamics at Work," *Journal of Organizational Behavior* 39 (2018): 1142–62.

productive zone of disagreement: Author interview with Janet Vertesi (professor of sociology, Princeton University), January 4, 2021.

"geological truth": Steve Squyres *Roving Mars: Spirit, Opportunity, and the Exploration of the Red Planet* (New York: Hyperion Books, 2005), 295.

Was the layered shelf of bedrock: Note: Given the anonymity granted to the scientists by the Carnegie Mellon team, it's impossible to be absolutely certain of the exact location being discussed by the scientists in the quoted dialogue. However, we know that the dialogue occurred on the sixteenth day of *Opportunity*'s mission, and this and other evidence suggests that they were most likely discussing sedimentary rocks near or on a location called "Robert E" on Stone Mountain in Eager Crater. Author e-mail communication with Matthew Golombek (senior research scientist, Jet Propulsion Laboratory), January 7 and 15, 2021. See also Squyres, *Roving Mars*, 307.

An intense study of the mission's: Paletz et al., "Uncovering Uncertainty," 394.

154   **"what they do not . . . and innovate"**: Paletz et al., "Uncovering Uncertainty," 388.

"At some point, you . . . disagreement comes in": Author interview with Joel Chan (assistant professor, College of Information Studies, University of Maryland, College Park, formerly of Carnegie Mellon University), November 11, 2020.

"holding on to the doubt": Adam Steltzner with William Patrick, *The Right Kind of Crazy: A True Story of Teamwork, Leadership, and High-Stakes Innovation* (New York: Portfolio Books, 2016), 48.

155   **"at the edge of what is possible"**: Adam Steltzner interviewed by Megan Gambino, "What Landing a Rover on Mars Teaches You about Leadership and Teamwork," *Smithsonian*, January 11, 2016, https://www.smithsonianmag.com/innovation/what-landing-rover-mars-teaches-you-about-leadership-teamwork-180957751.

Consider the incident of the "dirt folks.": Janet Vertesi, *Shaping Science: Organizations, Decisions, and Culture on NASA's Teams* (Chicago: University of Chicago Press, 2020), 110–11; J. R. Johnson et al., "Surface Changes Observed by Mars Exploration Rovers," paper presented to the Joint European Planetary Science Congress and DPS, 6, EPSC-DPS2011-1205-2 (2011), 1–2. Author e-mail communication with Jeffrey Johnson (MER associate principal investigator and principal professional scientist, Johns Hopkins University Applied Physics Laboratory), January 20–21, 2023.

conversational receptiveness: Michael Yeomans et al., "Conversational Receptiveness: Expressing Engagement with Opposing Views," *Organizational Behavior and Human Decision Processes* 160 (2020): 131–48. Author e-mail communication with Michael Yeoman (assistant professor of strategy and organizational behavior, Imperial College Business School, London), January 21, 2023.

government executives participating in a: Yeomans et al., "Conversational Receptiveness," 136–38.

156   **water had flowed on ancient Mars:** NASA, "Opportunity Rover Finds Strong Evidence Meridiani Planum Was Wet," March 2, 2004, https://www.jpl.nasa.gov/news/opportunity-rover-finds-strong-evidence-meridiani-planum-was-wet.

The exploration of differences: Vertesi, *Shaping Science*; author interview with Janet Vertesi.

calls the team collectivist: Vertesi, *Shaping Science*, 99.

jokes and sideline chatter: Vertesi, *Shaping Science*, 106.

"can be seen as a pain . . . alternative perspectives": Author interview with Vertesi.

In 2007, faulty commands: Scientists quoted in Vertesi, *Shaping Science*, 112–13.

157 **"Uncertainty and conflict . . . positive place to be.":** Author interview with Vertesi.

distant planet where fiery volcanoes: Kenneth Chang, "The Water on Mars Vanished. This Might Be Where It Went," *New York Times*, March 23, 2021.

frequently experience mild conflict: Gergana Todorova, Julia Bear, and Laurie Weingart, "Can Conflict Be Energizing? A Study of Task Conflict, Positive Emotions, and Job Satisfaction," *Journal of Applied Psychology* 99, no. 3 (2014): 451–67. Also author interview with Laurie Weingart (professor of organizational behavior and theory, Tepper School of Business, Carnegie Mellon University), November 10, 2020.

158 **In contrast, management teams:** Kathleen Eisenhardt et al., "Conflict and Strategic Choice: How Top Management Teams Disagree," *California Management Review* 39, no. 2 (1997): 42–62.

"Where did the idea . . . stable and harmonious?": Marilynne Robinson, "Puritans and Prigs," in *The Death of Adam: Essays on Modern Thought*, by Marilynne Robinson (New York: Houghton Mifflin, 1998), 164.

"What did we learn?": All quotes in this section are from author interview with Brian Odom, January 28, 2021.

Day of Remembrance: NASA's annual Day of Remembrance usually takes place on the last Thursday of January and pays homage to the three worst catastrophes in NASA's history: the *Apollo I* fire, which claimed the lives of three astronauts on January 27, 1967; the postlaunch breakup of the space shuttle *Challenger*, in which seven astronauts died on January 28, 1986; and the breakup of the shuttle *Columbia*, in which the seven-member crew died on February 1, 2003. Source: Author e-mail communication with Sean Potter (NASA media relations specialist), March 5, 2021.

CHAPTER 7

163 **"In this short Life . . . within our power.":** Emily Dickinson, "In This Short Life," in *The Complete Poems of Emily Dickinson*, ed. Thomas Johnson (Boston: Little, Brown, 1976), 1287.

"I freaked out . . . going to happen.": Author visits, interviews with Shaniece Langley and other participants in Ready4Routines classes at Child and Family Services Inc., Hobbs, NM, April 2–4, 2018.

A majority live at or near the poverty: Andrei Semenov, "Ready4Routines Final Report—2019," unpublished report shared with the author by Semenov, July 18, 2021.

"figuring out . . . to the next": Author interview with Shaniece Langley (property manager), September 7, 2021.

164 **"85 percent sky and 15 percent grasslands"**: Stephen Bogener, "High and Dry on the Llano Estacado," talk to the West Texas Historical Association, February 26, 2010. Note: According to Bogener, the exact phrase may have been his, but the saying reflects a sentiment shared by many locals and travelers in the region for generations. Author interview with Stephen Bogener (independent historian), January 3, 2023.

   erratic global oil prices: Peter Nagle and Kaltrina Temaj, "Oil Prices Remain Volatile amid Demand Pessimism and Constrained Supply," *World Bank Blog*, December 16, 2022.

   jobs in the fields being automated: Garrett Golding and Sean Howard, "Spotlight: Oil Patch Productivity Rises, Jobs Vanish," in *Southwest Economy* (Dallas, TX: Federal Reserve Bank of Dallas, 2021), 18.

   fuels just plain on the wane: Duane Dickson et al., "The Future of Work in Oil, Gas, and Chemicals," *Deloitte Insights*, October 5, 2020.

   A food bank director: Author interview with Renee Madron (executive director, Isaiah's Soup Kitchen, Hobbs, NM), September 1, 2021.

   are food insecure: Rachel Moskowitz, "Poverty in New Mexico: 2019," *Labor Market Review* 50, no. 2 (April 2, 2021): 10–11. See also Craig Gundersen et al., "Map the Meal Gap 2020: Food Insecurity Estimates at the County Level," Feeding America, 2015–2020, https://www.feedingamerica.org/sites/default /files/2020-06/Map%20the%20Meal%20Gap%202020%20Combined%20 Modules.pdf.

   "the weary blues": Langston Hughes, "The Weary Blues," in *The Weary Blues* (New York: Knopf, 2015, 1954), 5–6.

165 **tend to move more:** Ian Lundberg and Louis Donnelly, "A Research Note on the Prevalence of Housing Eviction among Children Born in U.S. Cities," *Demography* 56, no. 1 (February 2019): 391–404. See also Matthew Desmond, Carl Gershenson, and Barbara Kiviat, "Forced Relocation and Residential Instability among Urban Renters," *Social Service Review* 89, no. 2 (June 2015): 227–62.

   child care is routinely disrupted: Alejandra Ros Pilarz, Heather Sandstrom, and Julia Henly, "Making Sense of Childcare Instability among Families with Low Incomes: (Un)desired and (Un)planned Reasons for Changing Childcare Arrangements," *RSF: The Russell Sage Foundation Journal of the Social Sciences* 8, no. 5 (2022): 120–42; Kaitlin Moran, "Examining Childcare Instability and Transition Patterns in Low-Income, Urban Neighborhoods in the United States: A Qualitative Study," *Child Care in Practice* 27, no. 1 (2019): 35–53.

166 **In 2016, a group of scientists began videotaping:** Elysia Davis et al., "Across Continents and Demographics, Unpredictable Maternal Signals Are Associated with Children's Cognitive Function," *eBioMedicine* 46 (2019): 256–63.

166   **This fine-grained type of early chaos:** Elysia Davis et al., "Exposure to Unpredictable Maternal Signals Influences Cognitive Development across Species," *Proceedings of the National Academy of Sciences* 114, no. 39 (September 26, 2017): 10390–95.

can matter more to a baby's: Karen Smith and Seth Pollak, "Early Life Stress and Neural Development: Implications for Understanding the Developmental Effects of COVID-19," *Cognitive Affective Behavioral Neuroscience* 22, no. 4 (2022): 643–54.

"gets under a child's skin": Author video interview with Willem Frankenhuis (associate professor of psychology, Utrecht University, and senior researcher, Max Planck Institute for the Study of Crime, Security and the Law, Freiburg, Germany), August 12, 2021.

could not resist peeking: Anne Martin, Rachel Razza, and Jeanne Brooks-Gunn, "Specifying the Links between Household Chaos and Preschool Children's Development," *Early Child Development Care* 182, no. 10 (2012): 1247–63.

do poorly at the Pavlovian: Dana McCoy and C. Cybele Raver, "Household Instability and Self-Regulation among Poor Children," *Journal of Child Poverty* 20, no. 2 (2014): 131–52.

When asked to sort: McCoy and Raver, "Household Instability and Self-Regulation among Poor Children"; Radiah Smith-Donald et al., "Preliminary Construct and Concurrent Validity of the Preschool Self-Regulation Assessment for Field-Based Research," *Early Childhood Research Quarterly* 22, no. 2 (2007): 173–87.

the marshmallow test: Walter Mischel and Ralph Metzner, "Preference for Delayed Reward as a Function of Age, Intelligence, and Length of Delay Interval," *Journal of Abnormal and Social Psychology* 64, no. 6 (1962): 425–31.

lower SAT scores: Walter Mischel, Yuichi Shoda, and Monica Rodriguez, "Delay of Gratification in Children," *Science* 244, no. 4907 (1989): 933–38.

less self-confidence: Walter Mischel, Yuichi Shoda, and Philip Peake, "The Nature of Adolescent Competencies Predicted by Preschool Delay of Gratification," *Journal of Personality and Social Psychology* 54, no. 4 (1988): 687–96.

tendency to yield to temptation: Yuichi Shoda, Walter Mischel, and Philip Peake, "Predicting Adolescent Cognitive and Social Competence from Preschool Delay of Gratification: Identifying Diagnostic Condition," *Developmental Psychology* 26, no. 6 (1990): 978–86.

not the oracle that it's: Walter Mischel, *The Marshmallow Test: Mastering Self-Control* (Boston: Little, Brown, 2014), 9, 274.

167   **"When one child got . . . right away.'":** Celeste Kidd quoted in "The Marshmallow Study Revisited: Delaying Gratification Depends as Much

on Nurture as on Nature," University of Rochester press release, October 11, 2012.

167   **"For a child accustomed . . . have swallowed":** Celeste Kidd, Holly Palmeri, and Richard Aslin, "Rational Snacking: Young Children's Decision-Making on the Marshmallow Task Is Moderated by Beliefs about Environmental Reliability," *Cognition* 126, no. 1 (2013): 109–14, esp. 111.

As a graduate student: Kidd et al., "Rational Snacking."

"not waiting is the rational choice": Kidd quoted in "The Marshmallow Study Revisited."

marked by an absent father: Walter Mischel, "Father-Absence and Delay of Gratification: Cross-Cultural Comparisons," *Journal of Abnormal and Social Psychology* 63 (1961): 116–24.

"Of special interest . . . choice preferences": Walter Mischel, "Processes in Delay of Gratification," *Advances in Experimental Social Psychology* 7 (1974): 249–92, esp. 257.

168   **Perhaps Mischel's own . . . at age eight.:** Mischel, *The Marshmallow Test*, 327.

Decades later, a caller to a radio: Walter Mischel interviewed by Diane Rehm, "Walter Mischel: The Marshmallow Test," *The Diane Rehm Show*, WAMU Radio, October 1, 2014. Quotes by Steve are from this show.

deficit model: For a discussion of the deficit model, see Bruce Ellis et al., "Beyond Risk and Protective Factors: An Adaptation-Based Approach to Resilience," *Perspectives on Psychological Science* 12, no. 4 (2017): 561–87.

One 2013 scientific paper: Kathleen Vohs, "The Poor's Poor Mental Power," *Science* 341, no. 6149 (2013): 969–70.

"quick on their feet . . . the whole story": Author video interview with Willem Frankenhuis, July 1, 2021.

169   **"You could see and hear . . . costs and benefits.":** Interview with Willem Frankenhuis, July 1, 2021.

Natural selection is often: Ellis et al., "Beyond Risk and Protective Factors," 562; Willem Frankenhuis, Karthik Panchanathan, and Daniel Nettle, "Cognition in Harsh and Unpredictable Environments," *Current Opinion in Psychology* 7 (2016): 76–80.

But even a single generation: Bruce Ellis et al., "Hidden Talents in Harsh Environments," *Development and Psychopathology* 34, no. 1 (2022): 95–113.

In areas rife with predators: Ondi Crino and Creagh Breuner, "Developmental Stress: Evidence for Positive Phenotypic and Fitness Effects in Birds," *Journal of Ornithology* 156 (2015): 389–98.

Young children who have been abused: Seth Pollak et al., "Development of Perceptual Expertise in Emotion Recognition," *Cognition* 110, no. 2 (2009): 242–47.

169   **unethical for experts:** Frankenhuis et al., "Cognition in Harsh and Unpredictable Environments," 78.

a kind of excusable frailty: Author interview with Alysse Loomis (children's trauma specialist and assistant professor, College of Social Work, University of Utah), August 31, 2021. Author interview with Bruce Ellis (professor of developmental psychology and health psychology, University of Utah), July 29, 2021.

Frankenhuis's innovation was to: Willem Frankenhuis and Carolina de Weerth, "Does Early-Life Exposure to Stress Shape or Impair Cognition?," *Current Directions in Psychological Science* 22, no. 5 (2013): 407–12.

170   **In 2013, Frankenhuis wrote a paper:** Frankenhuis and de Weerth, "Does Early-Life Exposure to Stress Shape or Impair Cognition?"

What do kids growing . . . of adult attention?: Interviews with Bruce Ellis, July 29, 2021, and Willem Frankenhuis, July 9, 2021.

under pressure to keep shoring up: Interview with Frankenhuis, July 9, 2021.

Some researchers suspected they: Bruce Ellis and unnamed audience member discussion during Q&A after Ellis talk at the Fourth Annual Conference on "Child Protection and Well-Being: New Frontiers in the Biology of Stress, Maltreatment, and Trauma," Penn State Social Science Research Institute, September 30–October 1, 2015, https://www.youtube.com/watch?v=uv8b7subqz8. Also interview with Frankenhuis, July 1, 2021.

By the time the young teens: Clio Pitula et al., "To Trust or Not to Trust: Social Decision-Making in Post-Institutionalized, Internationally Adopted Youth," *Developmental Science* 20, no. 3 (2017): 1–15, 10.1111.

171   **"promptly changed their behavior," "They learned faster":** Pitula et al., "To Trust or Not to Trust," 8, 10.

experienced high rates of family divorce, residential: Ethan Young et al., "Can an Unpredictable Childhood Environment Enhance Working Memory? Testing the Sensitized-Specialization Hypothesis," *Interpersonal Relations and Group Processes* 114, no. 6 (2018): 891–908.

"reallocate their cognitive resources to pressing needs": Jennifer Sheehy-Skeffington, "Inequality from the Bottom Up: Toward a 'Psychological Shift' Model of Decision Making under Socioeconomic Threat," in *Social Psychology of Inequality*, ed. Jolanda Jetten and Kim Peters (New York: Springer, 2019): 213–31, esp. 219; author video interview with Jennifer Sheehy-Skeffington, June 25, 2021.

"may never come to experience": Jennifer Sheehy-Skeffington, "Decision-Making Up against the Wall," in *Socio-Economic Environment and Human Psychology: Social, Ecological and Cultural Perspectives*, ed. Ayse Uskul and Shigehiro Oishi (New York: Oxford University Press, 2018), 105–28, esp. 120.

172   **"Stability, I don't know ... should already be.":** Justin quoted in Kevin Roy and Jocelyn Smith Lee, "Ghosting in Safe Relational Spaces: Young Black Men and the Search for Residence," *Journal of Applied Developmental Psychology* 70 (July–September 2020): 101193, https://doi.org/10.1016.j.appdev.2020.101193.

"I'm always, like, with it": Jocelyn Smith and Desmond Patton, "Posttraumatic Stress Symptoms in Context: Examining Trauma Response to Violent Exposures and Homicide Death among Black Males in Urban Neighborhoods," *American Journal of Orthopsychiatry* 86, no. 2 (2016): 212–23.

murders of three close kin: Jocelyn Smith, "Unequal Burdens of Loss: Examining the Frequency and Timing of Homicide Deaths Experienced by Young Black Men across the Life Course," *American Journal of Public Health* 105, no. S3 (2015): S483–90.

To probe the connection: Jenny Phan et al., "Hyperarousal and Hypervigilance in African American Male Adolescents Exposed to Community Violence," *Journal of Applied Developmental Psychology* 70 (2020): 101168, https://doi.org/10.1016/j.appdev.2020.101168.

"Hypervigilance allows ... immediate environment": Author interview with Noni Gaylord-Harden (professor of psychological and brain science, Texas A&M University), June 15, 2021.

"getting a cat to retract its claws": Phrase discussed in Ellis et al., "Beyond Risk and Protective Factors," 565.

"Are we undermining . . . our intervention efforts?": Noni Gaylord-Harden, "Staying Ready, Staying Vigilant, Staying Safe: Hyperarousal and Hypervigilance in African American Male Adolescents Exposed to Community Violence," briefing paper for the Council on Contemporary Families, April 26, 2021.

"It's a lot of work to keep your life": Matt quoted in Smith and Patton, "Posttraumatic Stress Symptoms in Context," 220.

being "on point": Smith and Patton, "Posttraumatic Stress Symptoms in Context," 219; Laura Abrams and Diane Terry, "'You Can Run but You Can't Hide': How Formerly Incarcerated Young Men Navigate Neighborhood Risks," *Children and Youth Services Review* 47 (2014): 61–69, esp. 65. Note: The term is also used in prisons. See Lauren C. Porter, "Being 'On Point': Exploring the Stress-Related Experiences of Incarceration," *Society and Mental Health* 9, no. 1 (2019): 1–17, https://doi.org/10.1177/2156869318771439.

173   **In his memoir:** James McBride, *The Color of Water: A Black Man's Tribute to His White Mother* (New York: Riverhead Books, 1996), 34–36.

"takes whatever it can ... for threat detection": Author interview with Takao Hensch (professor of molecular and cellular biology and professor of neurology

[Children's Hospital], Center for Brain Science, Harvard University), August 23, 2021.

173   **When all goes well, a developing brain:** Rebecca Reh et al., "Critical Period Regulation across Multiple Timescales," *Proceedings of the National Academy of Sciences* 117, no. 38 (2020): 23242–51; Ursula Tooley, Danielle Bassett, and Allyson Mackey, "Environmental Influences on the Pace of Brain Development," *Nature Reviews Neuroscience* 22 (2021): 372–84.

174   **In a process called myelination:** Joan Stiles and Terry Jernigan, "The Basics of Brain Development," *Neuropsychology Review* 20, no. 4 (2010): 327–48.

The growing brain is streamlining: Stiles and Jernigan, "The Basics of Brain Development."

often thin early and rapidly: Tooley et al., "Environmental Influences on the Pace of Brain Development," 372–73.

evidence as well of early and excess myelination: Tooley et al., "Environmental Influences on the Pace of Brain Development," 378.

The sheathing process, in other: Takao Hensch interviewed by Bridget Kendall, "Plasticity," *The Forum*, BBC News-World Service, May 17, 2015.

classified half of the boys: Raquel Gur et al., "Burden of Environmental Adversity Associated with Psychopathology, Maturation, and Brain Behavior Parameters in Youths," *JAMA Psychiatry* 76, no. 9 (2019): 966–75. Author e-mail communication with Raquel Gur (professor of psychiatry, neurology, and radiology, University of Pennsylvania Perelman School of Medicine), September 8, 2021.

One of the first discoveries: Bridget Callaghan and Nim Tottenham, "The Stress Acceleration Hypothesis: Effects of Early-Life Adversity on Emotion Circuits and Behavior," *Current Opinion in Behavioral Science* 7 (2016): 76–81.

175   **"quasi-prefrontal cortex":** Author interview with Takao Hensch, August 23, 2021.

Not only do such gestures: Dylan Gee and Emily Cohodes, "Influences of Caregiving on Development: A Sensitive Period for Biological Embedding of Predictability and Safety Cues," *Current Directions in Psychological Science* 30, no. 5 (2021): 376–83. Also author interview with Dylan Gee (associate professor of psychology and psychiatry, Yale University), June 25, 2021.

show advanced maturing of cortico-limbic: Alexis Brieant, Lucinda Sisk, and Dylan Gee, "Associations among Negative Life Events, Changes in Cortico-Limbic Connectivity and Psychopathology in the ABCD Study," *Developmental Cognitive Neuroscience* 52 (2021): 101022.

Faced with a stressful situation: Bridget Callaghan et al., "Decreased Amygdala Reactivity to Parent Cues Protects against Anxiety Following Early Adversity: An Examination across Three Years," *Biological Psychiatry: Cognitive Neuroscience and Neuroimaging* 4, no. 7 (2019): 664–71.

175   **"turbo-charged" plasticity:** Alison Gopnik, "Childhood as a Solution to Explore-Exploit Tensions," *Philosophical Transactions of the Royal Society B* 375, no. 1803 (2020): 20190502.

"There is no revolution": Willem Frankenhuis and Daniel Nettle, "The Strengths of People in Poverty," *Current Directions in Psychological Science* 29, no. 1 (2020): 16–21, esp. 19.

176   **not trying to put a sunny face:** Bruce Ellis et al., "Beyond Risk and Protective Factors," 561. Also author interview with Frankenhuis, July 9, 2021.

"We only know bits and pieces . . . something is there.": Interview with Frankenhuis, July 9, 2021. He and his colleagues express caution in many papers. For example, see Willem Frankenhuis, Ethan Young, and Bruce Ellis, "The Hidden Talents Approach: Theoretical and Methodological Challenges," *Trends in Cognitive Sciences* 24, no. 7 (2020): 569–81.

In 2018, the Museum: Willem Frankenhuis, "Video Contribution," *Salon 26: Friction* (conference at the Museum of Modern Art, New York, June 27, 2018), http://momarnd.moma.org/salons/salon-26-friction-2.

177   **Four-year-old Jamar hesitates:** Author visit, interviews with teachers and students at a preschool run by the Family Partnership, Burnsville, MN, January 22, 2013.

A few minutes of play: Sabine Doebel and Philip David Zelazo, "A Meta-Analysis of the Dimensional Change Card Sort: Implications for Developmental Theories and the Measurement of Executive Function in Children," *Developmental Review* 38 (2015): 241–68.

presciently countering past assumptions: Philip R. Zelazo and Philip D. Zelazo, "The Emergence of Consciousness," in *Consciousness: At the Frontiers of Neuroscience*, ed. Herbert Jasper et al. (Philadelphia: Lippincott-Raven, 1998), 149–65.

178   **"I always had a sense . . . to discover":** Author interview with Philip Zelazo (developmental psychologist, neuroscientist, and professor, Institute of Child Development, University of Minnesota), September 7, 2011.

Zelazo invented the Dimensional Change: Philip David Zelazo, "Age-Related Changes in the Execution of Explicit Rules: The Roles of Logical Complexity and Executive Function" (PhD diss., Yale University, 1993), ProQuest Dissertations Publishing, 9331574.

Children high in these abilities: Philip David Zelazo et al., "Development of Executive Function in Early Childhood," *Monographs of the Society for Research in Child Development Serial 274* 68, no. 3 (2003): vii–137.

If you stop and ask children: Interview with Zelazo, September 7, 2011.

Nor are they so well practiced: Natasha Kirkham, Loren Cruess, and Adele Diamond, "Helping Children Apply Their Knowledge to Their Behavior on a Dimension-Switching Task," *Developmental Science* 6, no. 5 (2003): 449–76.

179   **chosen a topic of study so big:** Author interview with Stephanie Carlson (development psychologist and professor, Institute of Child Development, University of Minnesota), June 23, 2017. Author interview with Kristen Lyons (former postdoc of Philip David Zelazo), June 2017.

iteratively considering and reconsidering: Philip David Zelazo, "Executive Function: Reflection, Iterative Reprocessing, Complexity, and the Developing Brain," *Developmental Review* 28 (2015): 55–68.

"We start with . . . our understanding.": Author visit, interviews with Philip David Zelazo, April 7, 2016.

By learning to coordinate: Philip Zelazo and William Cunningham, "The Development of Iterative Reprocessing: Implications for Affect and Its Regulation," in *Developmental Social Cognitive Neuroscience*, ed. P. D. Zelazo et al. (Mahwah, NJ: Lawrence Erlbaum Associates, 2010), 81–98. See also Zelazo, "Executive Function."

180   **"stand on top of the decision tree":** Author interview with Philip David Zelazo, June 16, 2017.

"You go from a . . . at this moment": Interview with Zelazo, June 16, 2017.

"jump up a level . . . about a problem": Author interviews with Philip David Zelazo, June 16, 2017, and July 23, 2021.

To kick off the studies: Stacey Espinet, Jacob Anderson, and Philip David Zelazo, "Reflection Training Improves Executive Function in Preschool-Age Children: Behavioral and Neural Effects," *Developmental Cognitive Neuroscience* 4 (2013): 3–15.

181   **recorded the N2:** Stacey Espinet, Jacob Anderson, and Philip David Zelazo, "N2 Amplitude as a Neural Marker of Executive Function in Young Children: An ERP Study of Children Who Switch versus Perseverate on the Dimensional Change Card Sort," *Developmental Cognitive Neuroscience* 2, suppl. 1 (2012): S49–58.

higher recruitment of their frontal: Yusuke Moriguchi and Kazuo Hiraki, "Neural Origin of Cognitive Shifting in Young Children," *Proceedings of the National Academy of Sciences* 106, no. 14 (2009): 6017–21.

182   **"Being in an exploratory . . . when you reflect.":** Author interview with Philip David Zelazo, October 18, 2021.

He and his closest: Author interview with Stephanie Carlson, June 23, 2017.

"do not know what will happen tomorrow": Author interview with Nichol Siedow (preschool teacher, "People Serving People" Crisis Response and Emergency Shelter), Minneapolis, MN, January 22, 2013.

small, costly, highly controlled, and moderately: Jack Shonkoff and Philip Fisher, "Rethinking Evidence-Based Practice and Two-Generation Programs to Create the Future of Early Childhood Policy," *Developmental Psychopathology* 25, no. 402 (2013): 1635–53.

183   **Called Ready4Routines:** Andrei Semenov and Philip David Zelazo, "Mindful Family Routines and the Cultivation of Executive Function Skills in Childhood," *Human Development* 63 (2019): 112–31. See also Andrei Semenov, "Ready4Routines: Improving Child Executive Function Skills through Autonomy-Supportive Parent-Child Reflective Routines" (PhD diss., University of Minnesota, 2021), provided to the author by Semenov. Note: The first classes were held in 2016.

"habits of order": William James, *The Letters of William James,* ed. Henry James (Boston: Atlantic Monthly Press, 1920), 1:148.

"It's a stealth course . . . fringe benefit.": Author visit, interviews with Zelazo, April 7, 2016.

"I thought the class . . . areas of my life.": Author visit, interview with Shaniece Langley (enrollment specialist, Child and Family Services Inc.), April 3, 2018.

184   **"Taking responsibility . . . kernel and the insight.":** Author interview with Zelazo, July 23, 2021.

186   **initial results from the first:** Semenov, "Ready4Routines," 58–62.

After taking the course: Semenov, "Ready4Routines," 60.

By 2022, Acelero Learning: Author interviews with Lori Levine (senior vice president of family engagement, Acelero Learning), January 3, 2018, and July 21, 2021.

"There's something . . . lives of families.": Author interview with Levine, July 21, 2021.

187   **"We have a . . . benefit from all this work?":** Author interview with Philip David Zelazo, July 23, 2021.

In a PhD study supervised by: Semenov, "Ready4Routines," 5–6.

autonomy supportive: Rebecca Distefano et al., "Autonomy-Supportive Parenting and Associations with Child and Parent Executive Function," *Journal of Applied Developmental Psychology* 58 (2018): 77–85.

"zone of proximal development": Lev Vygotsky, "Thinking and Speech," in *The Collected Works of L. S. Vygotsky,* ed. Robert Rieber and Aaron Carton (New York: Plenum Press, 1987), 1:39–285. Note: Vygotsky's original term described what children can do with a little help as they learn to operate independently, but, as Zelazo notes, the concept more broadly refers to the fact that humans learn best by operating on the outer edge of what they know.

"That's where the growth . . . action is happening.": Visit, interview with Zelazo, April 7, 2016.

In countries as diverse as . . . motivated learners: Cecilia Cheung et al., "Controlling and Autonomy-Supportive Parenting in the United States and China: Beyond Children's Reports," *Child Development* 87, no. 6 (2016):

1992–2007; Kristine Marbell and Wendy Grolnick, "Correlates of Parental Control and Autonomy Support in an Interdependent Culture: A Look at Ghana," *Motivation and Emotion* 37, no. 1 (2013): 79–92. See also Mireille Joussemet, Renée Landry, and Richard Koestner, "A Self-Determination Theory Perspective on Parenting," *Canadian Psychology* 49, no. 3 (2008): 194–200.

187 **experience higher well-being:** Cheung et al., "Controlling and Autonomy-Supportive Parenting in the United States and China."

families are more cohesive: Andreas Neubauer et al., "A Little Autonomy Support Goes a Long Way: Daily Autonomy-Supportive Parenting, Child Well-Being, Parental Need Fulfillment, and Change in Child, Family and Parent Adjustment across the Adaptation to the COVID-19 Pandemic," *Child Development* 92, no. 5 (2021): 1679–97, esp. 1695. Note: This study was carried out in Germany.

189 **Two years after my visit:** Author interviews with Shaniece Langley, September 7, 2021, and January 2, 2022.

CHAPTER 8

191 **"Hope is the . . . more rewarding.":** Rebecca Solnit, *Hope in the Dark: Untold Histories, Wild Possibilities* (Chicago: Haymarket Books, 2016), 7.

widely used in manufacturing and sometimes: Author interview with Dylan Losey (assistant professor of mechanical engineering, Virginia Tech University), August 21, 2022.

By gently inflating various: Antonio Alvarez Valdivia et al., "Wrapping Haptic Displays around Robot Arms to Communicate Learning," *IEEE Transactions on Haptics* 16, no. 1 (2023): 57–72.

192 **Social media algorithms:** Sheera Frenkel and Cecilia Kang, *An Ugly Truth: Inside Facebook's Battle for Domination* (New York: Harper, 2021); Brandi Geurkink et al., "YouTube Regrets: A Crowdsourced Investigation into YouTube's Recommendation Algorithm," Mozilla Foundation, July 7, 2021; Manoel Horta Ribeiro et al., "Auditing Radicalization Pathways on YouTube," in *FAT*'20: Proceedings of the 2020 Conference on Fairness, Accountability, and Transparency*, January 2020, 131–41, https://doi.org/10.1145/3351095.3372879; Jack Nicas, "How YouTube Drives People to the Internet's Darkest Corners," *Wall Street Journal*, February 7, 2018.

A robot arm playing: Des Bieler, "Chess-Playing Robot Breaks Finger of 7-Year-Old Boy during Match," *Washington Post*, July 24, 2022, https://www.washingtonpost.com/sports/2022/07/24/chess-playing-robot-breaks-finger-7-year-old-boy-during-match.

Facial recognition and medical: De'Aira Bryant et al., "Multi-Dimensional, Nuanced and Subjective: Measuring the Perception of Facial Expressions," in

IEEE/CVF Conference on Computer Vision and Pattern Recognition, New Orleans, LA, 2022, 20900–909, https://doi.org/10.1109/CVPR52688.2022.02026; author video interview with Ayanna Howard (dean of the College of Engineering, Ohio State University), September 1, 2022. Note: It is common for AI systems to register expressions simplistically, but in addition, AI often is trained on data from humans who are themselves taught to label facial expressions as singular, that is, happy *or* surprised, sad *or* fearful. Finally, even when AI does report complexity in an expression—that is, that a face is highly likely to be amused but might be showing awe—end users "use the dominant output as a default," Howard told me.

192   **"It is as if the better ... on autopilot":** Brian Christian, *The Alignment Problem: Machine Learning and Human Values* (New York: Norton, 2020), 12.

"Success for my field ... and perhaps the last.": Stuart Russell, "Living with Artificial Intelligence, the Biggest Event in Human History," BBC Reith Lecture 1 of 4 (Alan Turing Institute, British Library, London, broadcast on BBC Radio 4, December 1, 2021), https://www.bbc.co.uk/programmes/m001216j.

193   **"Uncertainty is at the heart . . . of the solution.":** Author interview with Dylan Losey, August 21, 2022.

In 2014, Google shocked many: Samuel Gibbs, "Google Buys UK Artificial Intelligence Startup DeepMind for £400m," *The Guardian*, January 27, 2014, https://www.theguardian.com/technology/2014/jan/27/google-acquires-uk-artificial-intelligence-startup-deepmind.

"utterly bewildering": Michael Wooldridge, *A Brief History of Artificial Intelligence: What It Is, Where We Are, and Where We Are Going* (New York: Flatiron Books, 2021), 123.

Google's acquisition proved prescient: Volodymyr Mnih et al., "Human-Level Control through Deep Reinforcement Learning," *Nature* 518, no. 7540 (February 2015): 529–33. DeepMind also released an early paper on the project at the Neural Information Processing Systems Deep Learning Workshop in late 2013.

Despite knowing nothing: Stuart Russell, *Human Compatible: Artificial Intelligence and the Problem of Control* (New York: Penguin Books, 2020), 56.

194   **evidence that AI could one day rival:** Toby Ord, *The Precipice: Existential Risk and the Future of Humanity* (New York: Hachette Books, 2020), 141.

Such algorithms also constantly predict: Christian, *The Alignment Problem*, 138–42.

"We build objective-achieving ... off they go": Russell, "Living with Artificial Intelligence, the Biggest Event in Human History."

195   **When Dario Amodei created:** Dario Amodei and Jack Clark, "Faulty Reward Functions in the Wild," *OpenAI* (blog), December 22, 2016, https://openai.com/blog/faulty-reward-functions.

Blithely assuming this was: Christian, *The Alignment Problem*, 9–10.

"That's what makes . . . existential way.": Author interview with Ava Thomas Wright (assistant professor of philosophy, California Polytechnic State University), August 26, 2022.

"it is often difficult . . . agent to do": Amodei and Clark, "Faulty Reward Functions in the Wild."

In one recent incident . . . high-risk care programs.: Ziad Obermeyer et al., "Dissecting Racial Bias in an Algorithm Used to Manage the Health of Populations," *Science* 366, no. 6464 (October 25, 2019): 447–553; author e-mail communication with Ziad Obermeyer (associate professor of health policy and management, University of California, Berkeley School of Public Health), November 9, 2022.

196   **a doctor is a "he":** Tolga Bolukbasi et al., "Man Is to Computer Programmer as Woman Is to Homemaker? Debiasing Word Embeddings," in *Proceedings of the 30th International Conference on Neural Information Processing Systems*, Barcelona, Spain, December 5, 2016, 4356–64; Nikhil Garg et al., "Word Embeddings Quantify 100 Years of Gender and Ethnic Stereotypes," *Proceedings of the National Academy of Sciences* 115, no. 16 (April 17, 2018): E3635–44, https://doi.org/10.1073/pnas.1720347115.

African American names are unpleasant: James Zou and Londa Schiebinger, "Design AI so That It's Fair," *Nature* 559, no. 7714 (July 12, 2018): 324–26.

systems prioritize only the most common results: Zou and Schiebinger, "Design AI so That It's Fair"; author interview with James Zou (assistant professor of biomedical data science, Stanford University), October 6, 2022.

Amodei decided against: Christian, *The Alignment Problem*, 10.

In 2003, the Swedish philosopher: Nick Bostrom, "Ethical Issues in Advanced Artificial Intelligence," in *Science Fiction and Philosophy: From Time Travel to Superintelligence*, ed. Susan Schneider (Malden, MA: Wiley-Blackwell, 2009), 277–84. Essay originally published in 2003.

In a field notorious for: Wooldridge, *A Brief History of Artificial Intelligence*, 5.

"A lot of the alarmism . . . creates hysteria.": Demis Hassabis quoted in "Special Report/Ethics: Frankenstein's Paperclips," *The Economist* 419, no. 8995 (June 25, 2016), 13.

A British company was poised: "The World That Bert Built: Huge 'Foundation Models' Are Turbo-Charging AI Progress," *The Economist* 443, no. 9300 (June 11, 2022), 17–20.

196   **A single DeepMind agent:** Scott Reed et al., "A Generalist Agent," *Transactions on Machine Learning Research*, August 17, 2022, 1–27.

197   **while OpenAI's headline-making ChatGPT:** "ChatGPT: Optimizing Language Models for Dialogue," *OpenAI* (blog), November 30, 2022, https://openai.com/blog/chatgpt; Cade Metz, "Chatbots Can Amaze, but Also Lie," *New York Times*, December 12, 2022, B1.

The annual value of global: Roland Tricot, "Venture Capital Investments in Artificial Intelligence: Analyzing Trends in VC in AI Companies from 2012 through 2020," OECD Digital Economy Papers, No. 319, September 2021, 5; author e-mail communication with the OECD's AI Team, January 20, 2023.

An aggregate of expert forecasts: Katja Grace et al., "Viewpoint: When Will AI Exceed Human Performance? Evidence from AI Experts," *Journal of Artificial Intelligence Research* 62, no. 1 (May 1, 2018): 729–54.

In his book *The Precipice*: Ord, *The Precipice*, 146–48.

"AI would be . . . to destroy.": Ord, *The Precipice*, 147.

"a form of incapacitation . . . high reward": Ord, *The Precipice*, 145. Multiple AI insiders have made this point.

In 2023, more than: Future of Life Institute, "Pause Giant AI Experiments: An Open Letter," March 29, 2023, https://futureoflife.org/open-letter/pause-giant-ai-experiments. The Future of Life Institute is a U.S.-based nonprofit that advocates for safe use of transformative technologies. For an early warning, see Stephen Hawking, Max Tegmark, and Stuart Russell, "Transcending Complacency on Superintelligent Machines," *HuffPost*, April 19, 2014, https://www.huffpost.com/entry/artificial-intelligence_b_5174265.

"just pray and depend on the magic": Christopher Manning, "Lecture 2, Word Vector Representations," Stanford University School of Engineering, April 3, 2017, 20:23, https://www.youtube.com/watch?v=ERibwqs9p38. I am indebted to Brian Christian for this example. See Christian, *The Alignment Problem*, 36.

198   **In warning of AI's risks:** For examples, see Norbert Wiener, *God and Golem, Inc: A Comment on Certain Points Where Cybernetics Impinges on Religion* (Cambridge, MA: MIT Press, 1964), 57–58, and Russell, "Living with Artificial Intelligence, the Biggest Event in Human History."

Although the story has been told: Jack Zipes, ed., *The Sorcerer's Apprentice: An Anthology of Magical Tales* (Princeton, NJ: Princeton University Press, 2017), 3.

Disney's classic animated version: "The Sorcerer's Apprentice," in *Fantasia*, directed by Norman Ferguson et al., produced by Walt Disney (Walt Disney Productions, 1941), animated feature film.

one of two major versions: Zipes, *The Sorcerer's Apprentice*, 12–18.

198   **Far more prevalent throughout history:** Author interview with Jack Zipes (scholar of folktales, fairy tales, and critical theory and professor emeritus, University of Minnesota), October 11, 2022.

"life-and-death . . . our talents": Zipes, *The Sorcerer's Apprentice*, 28.

The story does not offer . . . all that clearly.": Author interview with Jack Zipes, October 26, 2022.

"It gradually became . . . hopeless times.": Zipes, *The Sorcerer's Apprentice*, xi.

One winter evening in 2014: Stuart Russell, "Living with Artificial Intelligence: Beneficial AI and a Future for Humans," BBC Reith Lecture 4 of 4 (National Innovation Center for Data, Newcastle upon Tyne, broadcast on BBC Radio 4, December 22, 2021); author video interview with Stuart Russell (professor of computer science, University of California, Berkeley), August 30, 2022; author e-mail communication with Stuart Russell, November 8, 2022.

199   **He recently had expressed:** Stuart Russell, "The Future of (Artificial) Intelligence," (Contextual Lecture Series: Ideas That Changed the World, Dulwich Picture Gallery, Dulwich, UK, November 26, 2013).

"It just sprang into . . . human experience": Stuart Russell quoted in Natalie Wolchover, "Artificial Intelligence Will Do What We Ask. That's a Problem," *Quanta Magazine*, January 30, 2020, https://www.quantamagazine.org/artificial-intelligence-will-do-what-we-ask-thats-a-problem-20200130.

"This is the core . . . perfectly known.": Russell, "Living with Artificial Intelligence: Beneficial AI and a Future for Humans."

"just watching from above": Author interview with Stuart Russell, August 30, 2022.

"was realizing that . . . reward functions": Author interview with Stuart Russell, August 30, 2022.

"One of my biggest . . . magical things happen": Author video interview with Anca Dragan (associate professor of electrical engineering and computer science, University of California, Berkeley), August 17, 2022. Hereafter, all quotes by Dragan are from this interview unless indicated.

200   **watching two illustrative bits of video:** Video clips from Andrea Bajcsy et al., "Learning Robot Objectives from Physical Human Interaction," in *Proceedings of the 1st Annual Conference on Robot Learning*, Mountain View, CA, 2017, 217–26, https://www.youtube.com/watch?v=I2YHT3giwcY.

"cut off a tiny . . . to a robot": Anca Dragan, "Putting the Human into the AI Equation," in *Possible Minds: Twenty-Five Ways of Looking at AI*, ed. John Brockman (New York: Penguin Press, 2019), 134–42, esp. 137.

needed to grapple with: Author interview with Laura Blumenschein (assistant professor of mechanical engineering, Purdue University), September 18,

2022. This theme was reiterated in many of my interviews with roboticists and scientists involved in AI.

200   **turned to Bayes' theorem:** Judea Pearl, "Reverend Bayes on Inference Engines: A Distributed Hierarchical Approach," *Proceedings of the Second AAAI Conference on Artificial Intelligence* (Pittsburgh, PA: AAAI Press, 1982), 133–36.

201   **"human-compatible AI":** Russell, *Human Compatible*.

Imbued with probabilistic reasoning about its aims: Note: How exactly can a robot be built to be unsure? To create robots that are uncertain about their objectives, scientists have mainly adopted the Bayesian statistical tools that also help such systems deal with unpredictability in the world. Imagine that a robot is handing a cup of coffee to a person, says roboticist Andrea Bajcsy. Traditionally, the robot would be designed in advance to carry all cups the same way, that is, typically quickly in order to be efficient. In contrast, an uncertain robot that uses Bayesian reasoning to be unsure about its objectives can know there are different possibilities, that is, a probability distribution, about how to move cups. At first, it may believe with 90 percent probability that cups should be moved fast. But after getting feedback from a human user—ouch!—that she prefers slower, spill-proof movements, the robot learns that there is only a 30 percent probability that a fast handover is preferred. "By maintaining uncertainty about how to do the task, the robot detected that its original understanding of the task (moving mugs fast) was not correct," says Bajcsy. This all seems a far cry from how we sense uncertainty, yet such advances in robotics are inspired by studying how human brains learn, especially via predictive processing.

"a space of possibilities": Author video interview with Anca Dragan, August 17, 2022.

open to being shut down: Russell, *Human Compatible*, 196–200; Dylan Hadfield-Menell et al., "The Off-Switch Game," in *Proceedings of the 26th International Joint Conference on Artificial Intelligence* (Melbourne: AAAI Press, 2017), 220–27.

202   **In initial user studies . . . time and effort.:** Valdivia et al., "Wrapped Haptic Display for Communicating Physical Robot Learning"; Shaunak Mehta and Dylan Losey, "Unified Learning from Demonstrations, Corrections, and Preferences during Physical Human-Robot Interaction" (preprint, arXiv, July 7, 2022), http://arXiv.org/abs/2207.03395; Bajcsy et al., "Learning Robot Objectives from Physical Human Interaction," 217.

seamlessly collaborative and sensitive: Dylan Losey et al., "Physical Interaction as Communication: Learning Robot Objectives Online from Human Corrections," *International Journal of Robotics Research* 41, no. 1 (January 2022): 20–44, esp. 37; Valdivia et al., "Wrapped Haptic Display for Communicating Physical Robot Learning."

202   **"The robot seemed . . . cared about":** Study participant quoted in Dylan Losey et al., "Physical Interaction as Communication," 37.

uncertainty about a thorny moral: Carolin Strassmann et al., "Moral Robots? How Uncertainty and Presence Affect Humans' Moral Decision Making," in *Communications in Computer and Information Science*, ed. Constantine Stephanidis and Margherita Antona (New York: Springer International Publishing, 2020), 488–95.

suspense and dissonance: Violinist Ida Kavafian quoted in Johanna Keller, "An Adagio for Strings, and for the Ages," *New York Times*, March 7, 2010, AR21.

"the effect of a sigh . . . or hope," "In around . . . coming to rest.": Keller, "An Adagio for Strings."

"You can actually . . . confused it is.": Author visit, interview with Dylan Losey, September 8, 2022.

"When a robot can let . . . working for": Interview with Dylan Losey, August 21, 2022.

203   **"Even as a designer . . . want to see.":** Interview with Losey, August 21, 2022.

"how can we open that box?": Dylan Losey, "Interactive, Inclusive, and Revealing Robot Learners" (virtual departmental seminar for the University of Virginia, Purdue University, University of Illinois at Urbana-Champaign Human-Centered Autonomy Lab, and Virginia Tech Center for Human-Computer Interaction, October 22, 2021), https://www.youtube.com/watch?v=eWK5Or6sjSc.

AI operates in abstract mathematical: Author visit, interview with Dylan Losey, September 8, 2022.

"not a single human . . . truth of Go": Ke Jie quoted in Eva Dou and Olivia Geng, "Humans Mourn Loss after Google Is Unmasked as China's Go Master," *Wall Street Journal*, January 5, 2017.

To work with AI: For further discussion, see Umang Bhatt et al., "Uncertainty as a Form of Transparency: Measuring, Communicating, and Using Uncertainty," in *Proceedings of the 2021 AAAI/ACM Conference on AI, Ethics, and Society* (New York: Association for Computing Machinery, 2021), 401–13.2021 Note: As Bhatt et al. point out, uncertainty as a form of transparency is not a panacea, but if well calibrated and well communicated, it can bolster a machine's fairness, accuracy, and effectiveness.

Dozens of frontline laboratories: Estimate offered by Dylan Losey in author interview, November 3, 2022.

on-screen hypothetical scenarios: Yuchen Cui and Scott Niekum, "Active Reward Learning from Critiques," in *2018 IEEE International Conference on Robotics and Automation* (Brisbane, Australia, 2018), 6907–14, https://doi

.org/10.1109/ICRA.2018.8460854; author interview with Scott Niekum (associate professor, College of Information and Computer Science, University of Massachusetts Amherst), August 11, 2022.

203   **In Losey's lab, a standing robot:** Soheil Habibian, Ananth Jonnavittula, and Dylan P. Losey, "Here's What I've Learned: Asking Questions That Reveal Reward Learning," *ACM Transactions on Human-Robot Interaction* 11, no. 4 (September 8, 2022): 1–28.

204   **"It's not just . . . uncertainty within them.":** Interview with Laura Blumenschein, September 18, 2022.

use in medical diagnosis systems: James M. Dolezal et al., "Uncertainty-Informed Deep Learning Models Enable High-Confidence Predictions for Digital Histopathology," *Nature Communications* 13, no. 1 (November 2, 2022): 6572; Tyler J. Loftus et al., "Uncertainty-Aware Deep Learning in Healthcare: A Scoping Review," *PLoS Digital Health* 1, no. 8 (August 10, 2022): e0000085, https://doi.org/10.1371/journal.pdig.0000085. Regarding uncertainty-aware AI in military coalitions, see also Richard Tomsett et al., "Rapid Trust Calibration through Interpretable and Uncertainty-Aware AI," *Patterns* 1, no. 4 (July 10, 2020): 100049, https://doi.org/10.1016/j.patter.2020.100049.

For example, to address rising bacterial: Moksh Jain et al., "Biological Sequence Design with GFlow Nets," in *Proceedings of the 39th International Conference on Machine Learning*, PMLR 162 (Baltimore, 2022), 1–16; Emmanuel Bengio et al., "Flow Network Based Generative Models for Non-Iterative Diverse Candidate Generation," in *Advances in Neural Information Processing Systems* (Red Hook, NY: Curran Associates, 2021), 27381–94; Yoshua Bengio, "Generative Flow Networks," (blog) March 5, 2022, https://yoshuabengio.org/2022/03/05/generative-flow-networks; author e-mail communications with Yoshua Bengio (professor at Université de Montréal and founder and scientific director of Mila, the Quebec AI Institute), September 1 and 9, 2022, and November 9, 2022; author e-mail communications with Nikolay Malkin (postdoctoral researcher, Mila-Quebec AI Institute); Emmanuel Bengio (senior machine learning scientist, Recursion Pharmaceuticals); Moksh Jain (graduate researcher, Mila-Quebec AI Institute), September 20–22, 2022, and October 3 and 20, 2022.

"The whole point . . . want to account for uncertainty": Author interview with Nikolay Malkin (postdoctoral researcher, Mila-Quebec AI Institute), September 15, 2022.

"The reality is . . . about anything": Author video interview with Julian Hough (lecturer, School of Electrical Engineering and Computer Science, Queen Mary University of London), September 1, 2022. All quotes are from this interview unless otherwise indicated.

A tiny ambiguity: Melanie Mitchell, "Artificial Intelligence Hits the Barrier of Meaning," *New York Times*, November 5, 2018; Kevin Eykholt et al.,

"Robust Physical-World Attacks on Deep Learning Models," in *Proceedings of the IEEE Conference on Computer Vision and Pattern Recognition* (New York: IEEE, 2018), 1625–34.

204   **A frail person with a shaky:** Ananth Jonnavittula and Dylan P. Losey, "I Know What You Meant: Learning Human Objectives by (Under)Estimating Their Choice Set," *2021 IEEE International Conference on Robotics and Automation* (New York: IEEE Press, 2021).

205   **After eighteen months of:** Julian Hough and David Schlangen, "It's Not What You Do, It's How You Do It: Grounding Uncertainty for a Simple Robot," in *Proceedings of the 2017 ACM/IEEE International Conference on Human-Robot Interaction* (New York: Association for Computing Machinery, 2017), 274–82.

used by U.S. police: Ronnie Wendt, "Electronic Law Enforcement," *Law Enforcement Technology* 47, no. 3 (May 2020): 8–12; Katie Flaherty, "Real-Life RoboCop Was at the Scene of a Crime. Then It Moved On," NBC News, accessed January 3, 2023, https://www.nbcnews.com/tech/tech-news/robocop-park -fight-how-expectations-about-robots-are-clashing-reality-n1059671.

"It's hard to argue . . . in the detail.": Adrian Weller comments in "AI: A Future for Humans?," *BBC Radio 4: Rutherford and Fry on Living with AI*, December 22, 2021.

206   **serve as role models and guides:** Russell, *Human Compatible*, 177. This issue is widely discussed in the field.

What happens when preferences conflict: Russell, Reith Lecture 4, "Beneficial AI and a Future for Humans."

increasingly by technology itself: R. Nicholas Carleton et al., "Increasing Intolerance of Uncertainty over Time: The Potential Influence of Increasing Connectivity," *Cognitive Behaviour Therapy* 48, no. 2 (2019): 121–36; Shahabedin Sagheb et al., "Towards Robots that Influence Humans over Long-Term Interactions," in *Proceedings of the IEEE International Conference on Robotics and Automation (ICRA)*, London, May 29–June 2, 2023, in press.

mold our preferences: Russell, Reith Lecture 4, "Beneficial AI and a Future for Humans."

Lovelace did not believe: James Essinger, *Ada's Algorithm: How Lord Byron's Daughter Ada Lovelace Launched the Digital Age* (Brooklyn, NY: Melville House, 2015), 173; Christopher Hollings, Ursula Martin, and Adrian Rice, *Ada Lovelace: The Making of a Computer Scientist* (Oxford: Bodleian Library, University of Oxford, 2018), 82.

207   **"it can do whatever . . . to perform":** Augusta Ada King, Countess of Lovelace, "Notes by the Translator," in L.F. Menabrea, "Sketch of the Analytical Engine," trans. Augusta Ada King, Countess of Lovelace, in *Scientific Memoirs, Selected from the Transactions of Foreign Academies of Science and Learned Societies, and*

from Foreign Journals, vol. 3, ed. Richard Taylor (London: R. and J. E. Taylor, 1843), Note G, 722. She is commonly known as Ada Lovelace.

207   **"weaves algebraical . . . and leaves":** Lovelace, "Notes by the Translator," Note A, 696.

"the relations and the . . . new lights": Lovelace, "Notes by the Translator," Note G, 722; author e-mail communication with Adrian Rice (professor of mathematics, Randolph-Macon College), November 8, 2022.

208   **Just as in more than one-third:** Interview with Jack Zipes, October 26, 2022.

ACKNOWLEDGMENTS

Writing a book is an uncertain enterprise. Along the way, there are twists and wrong turns, plenty of suspense, seeming dead ends, and winding paths that unexpectedly lead to clarity. Over the years of its creation, this book in particular provoked, intrigued, delighted, and unsettled me. In short, to write about uncertainty is to be given the chance to experience life at its fullest. For that, I am grateful.

I was fortunate to have extraordinary guides to the mysteries of uncertainty and to the intricacies of the mind. In particular, I am indebted to Mike Posner for generously sharing his insights with me and to Phil Zelazo for extensive conversations that helped shape this work.

My deep thanks also go to many others who invited me into their lives and answered innumerable questions, often over the course of multiple interviews: Carol-anne Moulton, Stanislas Dehaene, Willem Frankenhuis, Chris Gustin, Jim Collins, Mary Helen Immordino-Yang, Dave Fleischer, Shaniece Langley, Dylan Losey, and Jack Zipes. During my travels, I appreciated the time and help offered by the senior surgeon, Robert Stickgold, Alysia Burbidge, the late Ann Atwater, Diane Bloom, Stephanie Carlson, Steve Deline, and Patricia Grovey.

For patiently schooling me in their areas of expertise, I am grateful to Yoshua Bengio, Ethan Bromberg-Martin, Emily Carney, Noshir Contractor, Anca Dragan, Noni Gaylord-Harden, Dylan Gee, Matt Golombek, Jackie Gottlieb, Paul K. J. Han, Julian Hough, Ayanna Howard, Joseph Kable, Brian Odom, Stuart Russell, Robb Rutledge, Andrei Semenov, and Sam Sommers.

Several institutions have taken a chance on supporting my work. Special thanks are due to Peter Miller and the Bard Graduate School, where I was a Visiting Fellow; to Albert LeCoff and the Center for Art in Wood, where I was a Scholar-in-Residence; to Charles Harvey at the University of Central Arkansas, where I was an Honors College Scholar-in-Residence; and to Lance Strate of the Media Ecology Association, which honored my book *Distracted* with a Dorothy Lee Award. I also want to thank Glen Murphy, formerly of Google. I gratefully acknowledge that much of this book was written on the historic homelands of the Lenape and the Wampanoag nations.

Libraries are my second homes, and their remarkable stewards are integral to my research and writing. My gratitude goes to the staff of the New York Society Library, especially to Kirsten Carleton, Steve McGuirl, and Carolyn Waters, and to Sara Holliday, Patrick Rayner, Susan Chan, Linnea Savapoulas, Harriet Shapiro, Janet Howard, and Harry Abarca. They all make the library the inspiring place that it is. My sincere thanks go to the staff of the New York Public Library, especially the MaRLI program for scholars; the Columbia University libraries, especially Ann Thornton; Brown University's Rockefeller Library; Rhode Island School of Design's Fleet Library; and the Brownell Library in Little Compton.

I have been fortunate to work with stellar editors including Brian Bergstein at the *Boston Globe*, Eleanor Barkhorn and Rick Gladstone of the *New York Times*, Zan Boag at *New Philosopher*, and Danny Heitman of *Forum*. A segment of the introduction first appeared in the *Boston Globe* and part of the Ann Atwater story was published in *New Philosopher*. Jake Bonar has been all that a writer could wish for in an editor, and my gratitude also goes to Shana Capozza, Emily Jeffers, Jessie McCleary, Bruce Owens, the Art Department, and everyone else at Prometheus and Rowman & Littlefield for their enthusiastic embrace of the book. I am deeply grateful for the patience and ingenuity of the wonderful Richard Pine and Eliza Rothstein and indebted to all their colleagues at Inkwell. Thank you to Peter Guzzardi for his insight and for believing in the book at a crucial time. Thank you to Tom Neilssen and all at BrightSight. Sherry Turkle, Nicholas Carr, Alan Lightman, Bill McKibben, and Ellen Galinsky have been generous in their support.

Mike Posner, Phil Zelazo, Danny Heitman, and Mike Duffy read much or all of the work, and I am grateful for their suggestions. I thank Zan Boag, Karen Smul, Kristin Stolte, and Marilyn Wyatt for proofreading help. All errors are my own.

Many others inspired, assisted, and deepened this work, and I am appreciative. For help with the DNA discovery, I thank Alex Rich and Christof Koch; for help with chess research, Neil Charness and Vittorio Busato; in medicine, Wen T. Shen and Yvan Prkachin; for help with Alan Turing and the Enigma, Jack Copeland, Andrew Hodges, David Kenyon, Stephen Budiansky, and Mark Sprevak; for insight into Darwin, John van Wyhe and Carl Zimmer; in Los Angeles, Stephanie Vergara and Jennifer Kim; in Durham, the late Ed Stewart and C.P. Ellis's son and daughter; in political science and sociology, Paul Beck and David Broockman; in mountaineering studies, Julie Rak and Kathy Barker; in space exploration, Andrew Good, Jeff Johnson, Leon Golub, Dwight Steven-Boniecki, and John Uri, as well as astronauts Ed Gibson and John Herrington; in New Mexico, Rosa Wright, Starr Gibson, Maycee Mackey, Dorothy Fields, and Trip Jennings; in Minneapolis, teachers Laurie Ostertag and Nichol Siedow; in AI and robotics, Andrea Bajcsy, Jaime Fisac, Rich Pak, James Zou, Brian Christian, Scott Niekum, as well as Nikolay Malkin, Moksh Jain, and Emmanuel Bengio at Mila, and Losey Lab members Shahabedin Sagheb, Soheil Habibian, Shaunak Mehta, Ananth Jonnavittula, plus Ada Lovelace expert Adrian Rice; in psychology and neuroscience, Kevin Alschuler, Jennifer Sheehy-Skeffington, Mattias Horan, George Loewenstein; Charley Wu, Benjamin Storm, Ken Norman, Matt Wilson, the late Howard Eichenbaum, Clara Hill, Jay McClelland, Scott Barry Kaufman, Cindy Schupak, Steven Petersen, Matt Fisher, Jonathan Smallwood, Igor Grossmann, Kurt Hugenberg, Ming Ming Chiu, Mary Waller, Mo Khalil, Steve Fleming, Adam Kleinbaum, Howard Aldrich, Celeste Kidd, Ozlem Ayduk, Nicholas Carleton, and Gary Stasser for sharing his murder mystery. Special thanks as well to Bill Bishop, Jason Chin, Travis Heggie, Reed Hansuld, Jennifer L. Roberts, Robert Sobak, Helga Nowotny, Daniel Rhodes, John Dewey, and, for his forbearance and inspiration, Doug Peterson.

For bountiful support, I am grateful to: Gabriella Augustsson, Per Augustsson, Maureen Ahn, Ting Bao, Ard Berge, John Bessler, Marc Bohn, Arjen Bongard, Edith Borden, David Borden, Leslie Brody, Robert Burge, Dale Deletis, Clem Desjardins, Caroline Fenn, Mark Gallogy, Alyssa Gurskey, Meredith Hawkins, Alexandra Heerdt, Matt Heyd, Angela James, Bill James, Gene Kim, Amy Klobuchar, the late Irene Kunii, Alisa LaGamma, Marc LeGrez, Christian Lemaire, Harriet Linskey,

T. L. Linskey, Kumiko Makihara, Wallis Miller, Anne Moore, Cindy Murphy, Dan Murphy, Linda Nanni, Lars Nittve, Lynn Novick, Shideh Shaygan, Spencer Smul, Fred Sparling, Isa van Eeghen, Marianne Cabot Welch, Carol Weston, and Roger Winter. A big thank you to Lisa Brainerd; to Karen Smul for creative camaraderie; to the indomitable Michael Herchen; and to Lise Strickler, a wise and loving friend. Hats off to the Mermazons and the Sea Bears, especially to Stephen, Melinda, Lisa, Beth, Midori, Suellen, Diane, and David for all the spirit, splash, and joy. Thank you to the Jackson-Hitchcock-Bailey clan: Li, Jim, Ann Marie, Margot, Betty, Jimmy, Sally, David, Pam, Tom, Peter, Tanya, and the younger set. And never least, oceans of love to John, Emma, and Anna for their insight, patience, sagacity, humor, inspiration, and ginger cake. Life's surprises are all the better when shared with you.

INDEX

abstract thinking, xxvi, 32, 68–69, 88–89, 91, 94, 98
Acelero Learning, 186
acetylcholine, 39, 63
adaptability, xviii, xxv; and arousal, 37–38, 44–45; and experts, xvi, 19, 21; precarity and, 163–76
adaptive experts, 19–21
aleatory uncertainty, xiv–xv
al-Haytham, Ibn, 33
Allison, Kyle, 81–84, 103–4
AlphaGo, 203
alternate uses test, 97
ambiguity, tolerance of, xvi–xvii, xix–xxi, 22–23
amnesia: H.M. and, 60–62, 68; learning and, 59, 63, 73. *See also* forgetting
Amodei, Dario, 195–96
amygdala, 174–75
Anderson, Carol, xiv
Andreasen, Nancy, 88
antibiotics research, 81–84, 103–4
Antonelli, Paola, 176
approach mode, 44–47; Turing and, 53. *See also* arousal; stress
Approximate Man, 31, 36
Arendt, Hannah, 130
arguments. *See* disagreement, social
Aristotle, xviii, 133
arousal: adaptive, 44–45; focused, 38, 92; hypervigilance, 172; neuroscience of, 37–40, 92; versus rest, 63–64; reward focus and, 42–44. *See also* stress; surprise; uncertainty
artificial intelligence (AI), 191–208; alignment problem, 194–97, 201, 205; bias in, 195–96; risks of, 196–97; Sorcerer's Apprentice tale and, 198, 208; standard

theoretical basis of, 192, 194–95, 200–201; uncertainty and, 199–205, 293
artists: Da Vinci, 102; Gustin, 77–80; Hamilton, 57; Picasso, 24; sketchbooks of, 101–3. *See also* creativity
Asch, Solomon, 143
attention, xviii, 42–43; attentional priority, 37; focused arousal, 38, 92; priority map, 37
Atwater, Ann, 127–32
autonomy supportive caregiving, 187
axons. *See* neurons, structure of

Babbage, Charles, 207
Bajcsy, Andrea, 201, 293
Baldwin, James, xii
Baram, Tallie, 166
Barber, Samuel, *Adagio for Strings*, 199, 202
Barrett, Lisa Feldman, 34
Bartlett, Frederic, 65–69, 75, 80
Bassett, Danielle, 45
Bayes' theorem, 200. *See also* probability
Bengio, Yoshua, 204
Big Sort, 121, 265
Birch, Frank, 50
Bletchley Park, 27–30, 50–53
Blumenschein, Laura, 204
Bogener, Stephen, 279
Bomba/Bombe, 51–52, 238
Boorstin, Daniel, xxv
Borges, Jorge Luis, 69
Bostrom, Nick, 196
brain: accelerated maturation of, 174–75; neural development of, 173–74; neurons of, 61–62. *See also* myelination
Breuer, Josef, 85
Bromberg-Martin, Ethan, 40–42
Broockman, David, 119, 127

Dickinson, Emily, 4, 163

disagreement, social: collaboration and, 148–53; Mars Explorer Rover team and, 153–58; neuroscience of, 139–40; Skylab mission and, 133–34, 143–46; tolerance of uncertainty and, xix–xxi

dissent, 151, 152–53, 157

distraction, reward-driven, 42–43

diversity: and decision making, 137–38, 147–58; declining in workplaces, 136; friction in, 150–51; Kelley on, 149; of knowledge, 141–43. *See also* dissent

DNA structure, xxvi–xxix

Dolan, Ray, 64

Dönitz, Karl, 28

dopamine, 37, 40–42, 45, 194

dorsal medial subsystem, 88

doubt: Kahneman on, xviii, 213; and medicine, 3–6; and science, 153–58

Dragan, Anca, 199–201, 206

dreaming, 58–59, 67; Darwin and, 70; H.M. on life as, 61; meaning-making of, 69

drug development, 81–84, 103–4, 204

Duncker, Karl, 10

Dunne, John, 34

Durkheim, Émile, 138

economic issues, precarity and, 164–65

education, studies related to, 73–76, 163–65, 177–88. *See also* learning

Eichenbaum, Howard, 64

Einstein, Albert, 96

Einstellung effect, 9

elaboration memory technique, 64

Elgin Marbles, 13

Ellis, Bruce, 170

Ellis, C. P., 128–32

empathy, 116–19, 131. *See also* perspective taking

Enigma machine, 27–30, 50–53

Enlightenment, xxiv

epilepsy, 60

epistemic uncertainty, xv

Esterly, David, 21

European Union expansion, xvi–xvii

evolution, Darwin on, 70–73

executive brain networks, 94–95

executive function, 177–83

expectations, and perception, 33–34

experience, Lewis on, 27

expert, 21

expertise, 3–25; adaptive and routine types, 19–20; carryover mode and, 12; disillusionment with, 20–24; heuristic thinking of, 6–10, 15–18, 21, 32; inaccuracy and, 8–10; superior thinking of, 17–20, 21

fallow time, 57–80; Darwin and, 70–73; Gustin and, 77–80; Rhodes and, 78. *See also* pausing; rest; sleep

fear: and norepinephrine, 44; uncertainty and, xiv, xxv, xxix, 21–24, 44, 84, 104, 112, 122, 174–76, 184, 207. *See also* uncertainty, unsettling nature of

Fermi, Enrico, 24

Fermi-izing, 24

Fields, Dorothy, 184–86

Fleischer, Dave, 112–17, 119

fluency, xii, 6–12, 14, 210, 222

focused arousal, 38, 92. *See also* attention

forgetting, benefits of, 73–77. *See also* amnesia

Frankenhuis, Willem, 168–70, 175–76

Franklin, Rosalind, xxvii, xxviii, 217

Frenkel-Brunswik, Else, xviii–xxix. *See also* cat–dog experiments

frequency effect, 84

Freud, Sigmund, 85

frontal lobes, xvii

Frontiers of Innovation, 183

fusiform face areas, 110

future: of AI, 199, 205–7; daydreaming and, 87–96; marshmallow test and, 166–68, 171–72; precarity and, 171; predictive processing and, 32–34, 67; of uncertainty, 208

gadfly, uncertainty as, xvii–xviii. *See also* arousal; stress

Gardiner, Laura, 116

Gardner, Howard, 90

Gaylord-Harden, Noni, 172

Gee, Dylan, 175, 285

gender, and daydreaming, 85

Generative Flow Networks, 204

German, Tamsin, 11

Gibson, Ed, 134, 144, 146

Gibson, Starr, 184–85

ABOUT THE AUTHOR

Maggie Jackson is an award-winning author and journalist known for her pioneering writings on social trends, particularly technology's impact on humanity. Her acclaimed book *Distracted* (2nd ed., 2018) launched a global conversation on the steep costs of fragmenting our attention and won the 2020 Dorothy Lee Award for outstanding scholarship in the ecology of culture. A former contributing columnist for the *Boston Globe*, Jackson has written for the *New York Times*, *Wall Street Journal*, *New Philosopher*, *Le Monde's Courrier International*, and other publications worldwide. Her writings have been translated into multiple languages and featured in anthologies such as *Living with Robots*, *The State of the American Mind*, and *The Digital Divide*. Jackson has appeared in documentaries and in media around the globe, including the *Washington Post*, Wired.com, MSNBC, *Harvard Business Review*, *All Things Considered*, BBC, and Italy's top investigative news show *Presa Diretta*. She is the recipient of numerous grants, fellowships, and awards and has spoken at venues from Google to a CNN Town Hall. Born in Boston, Jackson holds degrees from Yale University and the London School of Economics. She lives in New York and Rhode Island.